Prayer Book Studies
Volume One

Initial Liturgical Efforts, Issues I-IV

Edited by
Derek A. Olsen

Seabury Books
A division of Church Publishing Incorporated

Copyright © 2026 The Domestic and Foreign Missionary Society of the Protestant Episcopal Church in the United States of America

The English text of the liturgies presented in this book is in the public domain and is freely available for quotation without restriction.

Unless otherwise noted, Scripture quotations are from The New Revised Standard Version Bible, copyright © 1989 National Council of the Churches of Christ in the United States of America. Used by permission. All rights reserved worldwide.

Seabury Books
19 East 34th Street
New York, NY 10016
www.churchpublishing.org

Seabury Books is an imprint of Church Publishing Incorporated.

Cover design by Newgen
Typeset by Integra Software Services Pvt. Ltd.

ISBN 978-1-64065-921-6 (paperback)
ISBN 978-1-64065-922-3 (hardback)
ISBN 978-1-64065-923-0 (eBook)

Library of Congress Control Number: 2025945257

CONTENTS

Introduction ix

Prayer Book Studies I: Baptism and Confirmation

Preface 3

The Need of Revision 6

History of the Rites of Christian Initiation 8

The Revision of the Baptismal Service 12

The Revision of the Confirmation Service 18

The Ministration of Holy Baptism 20
    The Preparation 21
    The Promises 22
    The Blessing of the Font 24
    The Baptism 24
    The Thanksgiving 25

The Order of Confirmation 26
    Introduction 26
        Psalm 27. Dominus illuminatio 26
    The Presentation of the Candidates 28
    The Renewal of the Vows of Baptism 28
    The Confirmation 29

Prayer Book Studies II: The Liturgical Lectionary

Preface 33

The Epistles and Gospels 36
    1. Importance of the Liturgical Lectionary 36
    2. Defects of the Liturgical Lectionary 36
    3. No New System Proposed 38
    4. The Western Tradition 40

The Seasons of the Christian Year 42

1. Advent 42
2. Christmas 46
3. Epiphany 54
4. Lent 56
5. Holy Week 59
6. Easter 62
7. Ascension and Whitsunday 65
8. Trinity-tide 69

The Fixed Holy Days 77

1. Adjustments of Length 77
2. Replacements 79

Occasional Services 81

Summary of Proposed Changes 82

1. The Question of Alternatives 85
2. Effect on the Correlation with the Western Tradition 86

The Text of the Liturgical Selections 88

Prayer Book Studies III: The Order for the Ministration to the Sick

Preface 93

The Need for Revision 95

Christian Healing 95

The Anglican Prayer Books 98

Principles of the Proposed Revision 102

Comments on the Service 104

The Order for the Ministration to the Sick 107

The Preparation 107
Order 1. The Great Physician 108
    The Lesson: St. Mark 1:29 109

Order 2. The Commission to Heal 109
    The Lesson: St. Matthew 10:1. 110
Order 3. Repentance 110
    The Lesson: St. Matthew 9:2 111
Order 4. Faith 112
    The Lesson: St. Matthew 9:27. 112
Order 5. The Holy Spirit 113
    The Lesson: St. Luke 11:34. 113
Order 6. The Holy Name 114
    The Lesson: Acts 3:1 114
Order 7. Holy Unction. 115
    The Lesson: St. James 5:14 115
The Litany of Healing 116
Prayers 118
The Laying on of Hands and Holy Unction 120
    The Consecration of the Oil. 120
    The Laying on of Hands and Anointing 121
    The Blessing 122

Prayer Book Studies IV: The Eucharistic Liturgy

Preface 125

Origins 128
1. Knowledge of Sources 128
2. The Last Supper 129
3. The Jewish Background 131
4. The Early Liturgy. 135

The Evolution of the Great Rites 136
1. The Domain of Antioch. 136
2. Alexandria 138
3. The Western Church 138

The English Rites 142
1. The First Prayer Book 142
2. The Second Prayer Book 166

The Elizabethan and Jacobean Prayer Books 179

The Scottish Liturgy of 1637 180

The Restoration Prayer Book of 1662 181
1. Influence of the Scottish 1637 181
2. New Features. 182

The Liturgies of the Non Jurors 184
1. The Schism 184
2. The 'Communion Office' of 1718 185
3. The Evolution of the Scottish Liturgy 186

The American Revisions 189
The First American Prayer Book 189
1. Scottish Contributions. 189
2. Influence of the 'Proposed Book' 191
3. Influence of Local Conditions 192

The Revision of 1892 194
1. Influence of the Scottish Draft of 1889 195
2. Other Changes 196

The Last Revision of 1928 197
1. Restorations of Pre-Reformation Features 198
2. Restorations of Features of the First Prayer Book 200
3. Contemporary English Contributions 202
4. Scottish Contributions. 205
5. Features Originating in the American Rite 205
6. Defeated Amendments. 206

Other Anglican Revisions 207
The Scottish Liturgy 207
Revision in the Church of England 209
1. Resistance to Change. 209
2. The Ritual Controversies 210
3. The Revision of 1928 212
Provincial Revisions 215
1. South Africa 217
2. India and Ceylon 219
Conclusions 222

Part Two: Proposals for the Revision of the Liturgy 223

General Considerations 223
1. The Need of Revision 223
2. The Title of the Service 228

3. Subtitles	232
4. The Order of Parts	234

The Ministry of the Word ... 244

1. The Introit	244
2. Preliminary Provisions	245
3. The Collect for Purity	247
4. The Law of Love	248
5. Kyrie Eleison	249
6. Gloria in Excelsis	251
7. The Collect, Epistle, and Gospel	252
8. The Creed	255
9. The Announcements and the Sermon	260

The Offertory ... 261

1. The Question of Order	261
2. The Offertory	264
3. The General Intercession	273
4. The Penitential Preparation	291

The Consecration ... 295

1. Name and Contents	295
2. The Preface	296
3. The *Sanctus* and the *Benedictus*	297
4. The Prayer of Consecration	303
5. The Lord's Prayer	322

The Holy Communion ... 326

1. The Breaking of the Bread	327
2. The 'Humble Access' and the *Agnus Dei*	328
3. The Administration of the Holy Communion	331
4. The Postcommunion	334

Appended Matter ... 337

1. The General Rubrics	337
2. The Exhortation	341
3. The Proper Prefaces	342

The Holy Liturgy ... 354

INTRODUCTION

The Series as a Whole

The *Prayer Book Studies* (PBS) series documents the 26-year process of study and conversation that led to the adoption of the American 1979 Book of Common Prayer. It falls broadly into two parts, distinguished by the use of Roman numerals and Arabic numerals. PBS I-XVII were published by the members of the Standing Liturgical Commission between 1950 and 1966 to communicate research and draft liturgies leading toward a revision process; PBS 18-29 were published by the various drafting committees between 1970 and 1976 once the revision process was formally begun and the earlier drafts were being transformed into new usable liturgies, leading up to the adoption of the new prayer book in 1979. Finally, PBS 30 and its commentary were added in 1989 to discuss inclusive and expansive language for God for further liturgical efforts.

Context of these Studies

The studies contained in this volume, PBS I-IV, should be seen within the broader context of PBS I-XIV. These fourteen studies that appeared in ten publications (four volumes contain two studies) systematically explore all of the liturgical materials within the 1928 Book of Common Prayer, incorporating scholarly research alongside input from clergy and congregations, concluding each study with a sample liturgy based on the study and reflection of the Commission.

Each of these fourteen studies begin with an identical preface laying out the guiding principles: to objectively and impartially inform the broader church on the principles and issues involved in the revision of each portion, not for the benefit of one theological party, but to the education of all.

The overwhelming impression of these documents is of a committee, anchored by Bayard Jones, Morton Stone, and Massey Shepherd Jr.—the professors of the leading Episcopal seminaries of the day—that accomplished its work in a careful and thorough fashion. A great deal of thought, discussion, and argument has gone into these materials. The results are careful and fairly conservative modifications, assuming a retention of the "traditional" Elizabethan/Jacobean idiom of the English Prayer Book and the King James Bible.

These Studies

PBS I and II

The initial study on Christian initiation specifically identifies baptism and confirmation as the two rites that have raised the largest numbers of suggestions and criticisms received by the commission. Not only were there complaints about the structure and intent of the baptismal liturgy, but even then, the purpose and ecumenical implications of confirmation were hotly debated.

This study provides the basic template that will be followed in many of the successive works: an historical survey incorporating the latest liturgical thought on the matter, a discussion of the principles of revision based on that historical and liturgical work, and a revised text of the rite for study and reflection–but not use. That last point is important; there was no mechanism for trial use at this time, so the liturgies could only be read and debated rather than fully experienced.

The second study focuses on the Eucharistic lectionary, considering the purposes of the seasons of the Church Year, then proposing a slightly amended version of the 1928 lectionary. At all points, keeping step with the contemporary Roman Catholic lectionary is kept in view. Of interest as well is a final section that advocates for largely retaining the historical text of the King James Bible, except for certain words where the sense is no longer the same. In these cases, substitutes from the Revised Version are being considered–but no changed texts are included here.

PBS III

This third study on the visitation of the sick recommends a complete shift away from the rites of earlier prayer books and radically revamps the tone, structure, and intent of the rite. This study gives a first glimpse into what "radical" revision might look like, the boundaries of what "radical" might encompass, and the attention to earlier rites and patterns even when proposing something "radical." It also represents a path not taken, as none of the forms here appear in the revised prayer book.

PBS IV

This fourth study on the Eucharist contains ten times more words than either PBS I or III. The first part, "The History of the Liturgy," rehearses the history of the Eucharistic rite from the New Testament to the present, incorporating the latest liturgical scholarship on the matter. A great deal of attention is given to the transition from the Latin Sarum Mass to the first Book of

Common Prayer, comparing the texts section by section. From that point, each English prayer book is discussed, including the Non Jurors and Scottish liturgies that would contribute to the American branch. Each American book is then discussed in turn. Finally, all Anglican revisions from 1928 to 1952 receive discussion.

The second part, "Proposals for the Revision of the Liturgy," begins with general considerations that are then implemented as every portion of the liturgy is discussed in detail, concluding with the proposed rite itself. The resulting rite is very similar—but not identical—to the current Prayer II of the Rite One Eucharist.

PRAYER BOOK STUDIES I: BAPTISM AND CONFIRMATION

The Standing Liturgical Commission
of the Protestant Episcopal Church in the
United States of America

1950

PREFACE

The last revision of our Prayer Book was brought to a rather abrupt conclusion in 1928. Consideration of it had preoccupied the time of General Convention ever since 1913. Everyone was weary of the long and ponderous legislative process, and desired to make the new Prayer Book available as soon as possible for the use of the Church.

But the work of revision, which sometimes has seemed difficult to start, in this case proved hard to stop. The years of debate had aroused widespread interest in the whole subject: and the mind of the Church was more receptive of suggestions for revision when the work was brought to an end than when it began. Moreover, the revision was actually closed to new action in 1925, in order that it might receive final adoption in 1928: so that it was not possible to give due consideration to a number of very desirable features in the English and Scottish revisions, which appeared simultaneously with our own. It was further realized that there were some rough edges in what had been done, as well as an unsatisfied demand for still further alterations.

The problem of defects in detail was met by continuing the Revision Commission, and giving it rather large 'editorial' powers (subject only to review by General Convention) to correct obvious errors in the text as adopted, in the publication of the new Prayer Book. Then, to deal with the constructive proposals for other changes which continued to be brought up in every General Convention, the Revision Commission was reconstituted as a Standing Liturgical Commission. To this body all matters concerning the Prayer Book were to be referred, for preservation in permanent files, and for continuing consideration, until such time as the accumulated matter was sufficient in amount and importance to justify proposing another Revision.

The number of such referrals by General Convention, of Memorials from Dioceses, and of suggestions made directly to the Commission from all regions and schools and parties in the Church, has now reached such a total that it is evident that there is a widespread and insistent demand for a general revision of the Prayer Book.

The Standing Liturgical Commission is not, however, proposing any immediate revision. On the contrary, we believe that there ought to be a period of study and discussion, to acquaint the Church at large with the principles and issues involved, in order that the eventual action may be taken intelligently, and if possible without consuming so much of the time of our supreme legislative synod.

Accordingly, the General Convention of 1949 signalized the Fourth Centennial Year of the First Book of Common Prayer in English by authorizing the Liturgical Commission to publish its findings, in the form of a series of *Prayer Book Studies*.

It must be emphasized that the liturgical forms presented in these *Studies* are not — and under our Constitution, cannot be — sanctioned for public use. They are submitted for free discussion. The Commission will be grateful for copies or articles, resolutions, and direct comment, for its consideration, that the mind of the Church may be fully known to the body charged with reporting it.

In this undertaking, we have endeavored to be objective and impartial. It is not possible to avoid every matter which may be thought by some to be controversial. Ideas which seem to be constructively valuable will be brought to the attention of the Church, without too much regard as to whether they may ultimately be judged to be expedient. We cannot undertake to eliminate every proposal to which anyone might conceivably object: to do so would be to admit that any constructive progress is impossible. What we can do is to be alert not to alter the present *balance* of expressed or implied doctrine of the Church. We can seek to counterbalance every proposal which might seem to favor some one party of opinion by some other change in the opposite direction. The goal we have constantly had in mind — however imperfectly we may have succeeded in attaining it — is the shaping of a future Prayer Book which *every* party might embrace with the well-founded conviction that therein its own position had been strengthened, its witness enhanced, and its devotions enriched.

The objective we have pursued is the same as that expressed by the Commission for the Revision of 1892: "*Resolved,* That this Committee, in all its suggestions and acts, be guided by those principles of liturgical construction and ritual use which have guided the compilation and amendments of the Book of Common Prayer, and have made it what it is."

☩ ☩ ☩

The Commission records its loss in the deaths of two of its members, whose final contributions to the Church they served are reflected in this first issue of the Prayer Book Studies.

The Reverend Henry McF. B. Ogilby, late Secretary of the Commission, contributed to the Study on "Baptism and Confirmation."

The Reverend Doctor Burton Scott Easton, late Associate Member, in his published work on the Epistles and Gospels of the Christian Year, furnished the foundation and inspiration for the Study on "The Liturgical Lectionary."

These papers are therefore dedicated to their memory.

THE STANDING LITURGICAL COMMISSION:

G. ASHTON OLDHAM, *Chairman*
GOODRICH R. FENNER
BAYARD H. JONES, *Vice Chairman*
MORTON C. STONE, *Secretary*
JOHN W. SUTER, *Custodian of the Book of Common Prayer*
MASSEY H. SHEPHERD, JR.
CHURCHILL J. GIBSON
WALTER WILLIAMS
WILLIAM J. BATTLE
SPENCER ERVIN

The two Studies presented in this issue were thoroughly discussed, and approved for publication, by the Liturgical Commission at its meetings in 1948 and 1949.

The Committee on the Orders of Baptism and Confirmation consisted of the Rev. Massey H. Shepherd, Jr., Ph.D., the Rev. Henry McF. B. Ogilby, and the Rev. Charles E. Hill. The Committee on the Liturgical Lectionary consisted of the Rev. Bayard H. Jones, D.D., the Rev. Cuthbert A. Simpson, Th.D., and the Rev. Edward Rochie Hardy, Jr., Ph.D.

BAYARD H. JONES, *Editor of Publications*
April 28, 1950.

The Need of Revision

During the past twenty years, the Standing Liturgical Commission has received a voluminous corpus of suggestions and criticisms in regard to the present Prayer Book rites of Baptism and Confirmation. Careful study and consideration have been given to all the proposals received. In the present report of its findings to the Church, the Commission offers for review and study its own collation of the material which has been received. Every effort has been made to take account of conflicting interests and prejudices, without sacrificing the basic principles of our liturgical inheritance.

The Commission is agreed that the most helpful and practical way of collating its findings is in the form of complete revised services, embodying such alterations as have seemed worthy of attention. Only in this way can proposed changes in detail be viewed and assessed in proper perspective and to the best advantage, whether they be matters of phraseology in the spoken forms, or of rubrical direction. An honest attempt has been made to answer the constant demand that the structure and meaning of the initiatory rites of Baptism and Confirmation be simplified and clarified, and, where necessary, be enriched in content. Such aims are essentially practical, the fruit of pastoral experience in the use of the Prayer Book offices. In no case has the Commission proposed any alteration of the current Prayer Book rites without thorough consideration of their conformity with liturgical tradition and the authoritative doctrine of the Church.

It has not been thought necessary to repeat in detail the history of the Christian initiatory rites. This has been treated with sufficient thoroughness in well-known, standard handbooks of liturgics. But the problems involved in any review of the rites of Baptism and Confirmation, whether they be liturgical, theological, or practical, are of a long-standing, historical inheritance. They are principally due to the separation by the Western Church into two distinct rites, of what was originally one. No little confusion has resulted in Western theology with regard to the significance and necessity of Confirmation; and there has been an ambiguity in interpretation of the distinctive operations of the Holy Spirit in the two rites. Difficulties have by no means been diminished by the development, in both East and West, of infant baptism rather than adult baptism as the normative usage of the Church. The most ancient formularies in our present rite of Baptism derive from a time when infant baptism was exceptional.

Another factor in the problem, somewhat peculiar to Anglicanism, though derived from the Church Orders of the Lutheran Reformers, has been the delay in administering Confirmation until children have come "to a competent age" after due catechetical instruction, when they are able to "ratify and confirm" on their own responsibility the promises made for them by their sponsors at Baptism. What was originally a pre-baptismal discipline has thus become a pre-Confirmation preparation. From this procedure has come inevitably a corollary discipline, inherited from the Church in England before the Reformation, and different from the practice of other Western Churches both before and since the Reformation — the refusal of admission to the Holy Communion, except in extraordinary cases, of baptized but unconfirmed Christians.

The divergence of opinion in Anglicanism regarding the exact meaning of Confirmation, particularly as it relates to Baptism, has been signally revealed in the discussions provoked by a report entitled *Confirmation Today*, published in 1944 by a commission of the Convocations of Canterbury and York. The report was concerned chiefly with practical problems, but it contained certain historical and theological statements that aroused considerable controversy, so much so that a new commission has been appointed to restudy the subject.

In the American Church, the differences of interpretation have not as yet been so openly and sharply evident. But the considerable bulk of criticisms of our initiatory rites which the Liturgical Commission has received is certainly symptomatic of widespread dissatisfaction with the provisions of the traditional services, if not of confusion as to the exact nature of the traditional teaching of them. Furthermore, the debates of recent years over proposals of organic union between our Church and other Christian bodies have revealed that there are serious disagreements within our Church respecting the significance of Confirmation. Such differences are not due to captious partisanship, but are the inevitable result of divergent approaches of long standing.

It is obviously not the province of the Liturgical Commission of the American Church to settle the many questions and issues which have arisen in recent discussion. Nor would it be proper for one branch of the Anglican Communion to make any radical alteration in its liturgy and practice of Christian initiation without benefit of counsel from its sister Churches. It may be noted in this connection that the Church of England in Canada has recently set forth a proposed revision of Holy Baptism. Its findings have been duly considered by our Commission. All that our Commission claims for the present study is that an attempt is made to take a forward step in clarifying certain fundamental principles of our liturgical inheritance, in terms consonant with the teaching of Holy Scripture and the ancient Fathers, in the light of the best historical scholarship of the present day, and in loyalty to the truth as our Church has received the same.

The section of this discussion immediately following is designed to give a brief sketch of the historical developments in the Church's administration of initiation. It is hoped that it will serve, despite its brevity, in furnishing the proper perspective in which the task of revision must be set. In the third and fourth sections one will find a detailed review of the specific alterations from our present rites, and the reasons for them.

History of the Rites of Christian Initiation

On the basis of the *Apostolic Tradition* of St. Hippolytus (early third century) and of scattered notices in the Fathers, it is now possible to reconstruct in considerable detail the initiatory ceremonies of the pre-Nicene Church. The evidence serves to illuminate the fragmentary and often elusive and debatable references in the New Testament, not only in the narratives of the Book of Acts, but also in the epistles of both the apostolic and sub-apostolic age, such as Rom. 6:4-6, 2 Cor. 1:21-22, Eph. 1:13-14, 4:30, 5:26-27, Heb. 6:2-5, and Titus 3:5. The initiation consisted of two distinct but inseparable stages:

1) the washing with water wherein the candidate received remission of sin, regeneration and adoption by God; and 2) the "sealing" with the Holy Spirit through the laying on of hands and anointing with chrism as an earnest of eternal redemption and inheritance. So far as the evidence goes there was never any restriction regarding the minister of baptism in water. But only an apostle — and later, after the establishment of monepiscopacy, only a Bishop — could confer the gift of the Spirit.

At this point it may be useful to outline briefly the initiatory rite as it is given by Hippolytus, inasmuch as it clearly underlies the later forms of the Western Church. The service took place towards dawn on Easter or Pentecost, after the lengthy night vigil of scripture readings and exposition. After the blessing of the water in the font the candidates, stripped of all clothes and ornaments, gave to the presbyter the triple renunciation of Satan, his service (pomps) and his works. When the candidate had descended into the water, a triple confession, in the form of a paraphrase of the Creed, was put to him. At each profession of belief, in the Father, the Son, and the Holy Spirit, the candidate was baptized in the font. Anointings with blessed oils were made upon each candidate before and after the baptism, but these were carefully distinguished from the chrism by the bishop which was to follow. After the baptized persons had put on their clothes they were brought at once to the bishop before the congregation. He laid his hand upon each one severally, praying for the gift of the Spirit; then he anointed and sealed each one on the forehead with the consecrated chrism and gave to each one the kiss of peace. The Holy Communion followed, beginning with the Offertory, and the newly initiated made their first communion.

Hippolytus gives no form for the Blessing of the Font. He does give the forms used by the bishop at the laying on of hands. The first is a prayer which is obviously the source of the Gelasian form still found in our Prayer Book service (page 297). It reads:

> O Lord God, who hast vouchsafed these (thy servants) to be deserving of the forgiveness of sins through the washing of regeneration, (make them worthy to be filled with) thy Holy Spirit, send upon them thy grace, that they may serve thee according to thy will, for to thee is the

glory, to the Father and to the Son with the Holy Spirit in the holy Church, both now and ever, world without end. Amen.

At the signing and sealing of the candidates with the chrism he says:

> I anoint thee with holy oil in God the Father Almighty and Christ Jesus and the Holy Spirit.

Not until the fourth century do we meet with specific forms for the Blessing of the Font. One of the earliest is to be found in the Syrian *Apostolic Constitutions* (VII. 43). After a lengthy exordium of thanksgiving to God for His work in creation and redemption, the blessing reaches its climax in these words:

> Look down from heaven, and sanctify this water, giving it grace and power, that he who is to be baptized according to the command of thy Christ, may be crucified with Him, and die with Him, and may be buried with Him, and rise with Him unto the adoption which is in Him, that he may be dead unto sin but alive unto righteousness.

Further illustration of the early Church's tradition of initiation need not here be elaborated. One can find it in the prayers of the Egyptian bishop Sarapion (*ca.* 350-56), or in the mystagogical lectures to catechumens of St. Cyril of Jerusalem (348) or of Theodore of Mopsuestia (*ca.* 400). A great wealth of patristic evidence has been collected in the authoritative work of Dr. A. J. Mason, *The Relation of Confirmation to Baptism as Taught in Holy Scripture and the Fathers* (Dutton, 1891). What is germane to our purpose is to note the gradual separation of the two elements in initiation, water-baptism and confirmation with the Spirit, which took place in the fourth century as a consequence of the rapid growth of the Church in numbers, especially in areas remote from the larger cities where a bishop resided. To meet the new need, presbyters and deacons were allowed the right of baptizing in water without the bishop's presence. The completion of the initiation, however, by the laying on of hands and sealing with chrism was reserved for such time as the bishop could conveniently perform it. Precedent for this development can be traced, of course, to pre-Nicene times, in the cases of clinical baptism of those *in extremis*, particularly in times of severe persecution; also in the decisions reached generally by the Church regarding admission to the Catholic Church of persons baptized in schismatical bodies: namely, to accept their baptism in water, but require the imposition of hands by a Catholic bishop.

Already by the end of the fourth century the confirmation by the bishop personally was disappearing altogether in the Eastern churches. The only relic of his ancient presidency over initiation was his reservation of the right to bless the chrism which the presbyter used in anointing the candidates after their baptism in water. This is still the custom in the Eastern Churches. But the West also was quick to take up the Eastern development. In North Africa, Spain and

Gaul the direct action of the bishop in confirmation gradually disappeared, as presbyters were given the right to baptize in local parishes and to anoint with chrism. Only in Italy did the older customs prevail, thanks to the conservatism of the Roman see.

In the famous letter of Pope Innocent I to Bishop Decentius of Gubbio (416) the indefatigable pontiff wrote:

> The sealing of the forehead of children is obviously a duty clearly reserved to the bishop.... Priests in baptizing, whether apart from the bishop or in his presence, can anoint the baptized with chrism, so long as it has been consecrated by the bishop; but he cannot anoint the forehead with this same oil. That is reserved solely to bishops, when they confer the Spirit, the Paraclete.

It should be remembered that it was easier to enforce the ancient custom in Italy than in other parts of the West, both because the dioceses in Italy were much smaller in size, and because political conditions there during the period of the barbarian migrations and settlements did not tempt the bishops to become so engrossed in matters of state and to absent themselves from their dioceses for long periods of time.

Another factor which hastened these developments was the shift from adult to infant baptism as the normative practice. This was not solely the result of the nominal Christianizing of peoples of the West and the passing of the old paganism. It was accelerated by the accent put upon the guilt and need of remission of original sin which arose as a result of the bitter controversies over the teachings of Pelagius. Indeed, the Pelagian heresy had actually come to the fore by its direct attack upon the traditional teaching of the Church that in infant baptism, no less than in adult baptism, there was given remission of sin, without which little infants, dying unbaptized, had no earnest of eternal salvation.

When the Roman rite was introduced by Charlemagne's efforts into the Gallican churches, with the consequence that Roman service books became the norm of liturgical usage throughout Western Christendom, episcopal confirmation was re-introduced almost as it were an innovation, and not without some confusion as to its meaning and necessity. At the same time no effort was made to restore the ancient discipline that admission to the Eucharist must come after confirmation. The indifference of medieval bishops in administering confirmation is notorious. Yet it reflects the uncertainties of medieval theologians about the importance and significance of the rite. Even so eminent a scholastic theologian as Alexander of Hales (*Summa* IV, q. 9, n. 1) could maintain that the rite was invented by the Church at a Council at Meaux in the year 845!

In general the teaching of Peter Lombard, expanded by Thomas Aquinas, tended to prevail. It was based on the excerpts of the teaching of the Fathers which happened to be preserved in the Decretals of the Canon Law, including the statement in the letter of Pope Innocent I quoted above. In brief the teaching of Lombard and Aquinas was that Confirmation is a sacrament distinct from Baptism, which confers "the gift of the Holy Spirit for strength." It is not necessary to salvation in the way that Baptism is, but is needed for the fulness of grace, for spiritual power, and the bringing of a man to a perfect spiritual age. Baptism gives a man power to achieve his own salvation; Confirmation gives power to witness for the Faith and to combat its enemies. The essential matter and form of Confirmation are the signing of the forehead with chrism (not laying on of hands) and its accompanying formulary: "I sign thee with the sign of the cross and confirm thee with the chrism of salvation, in the Name of the Father and of the Son and of the Holy Ghost, Amen." The normal minister is the bishop, but Confirmation may be delegated to priests provided they use chrism blessed by the bishop. This is the scholastic theory, in which the decrees of the Council of Trent made no essential change.

The history of Confirmation in the English Church has been exhaustively told by Canon Ollard, in the two-volume work, *Confirmation or the Laying on of Hands* (S.P.C.K., 1926-7). Cranmer made two important changes in the Prayer Book rite from the medieval practice. Children were not to be confirmed until they could say the catechism and were come to "years of discretion." In the administration of the rite the use of chrism was dropped. In the 1552 Book even the signing with the cross on the forehead was omitted, and the formula said by the bishop at the imposition of his hand was changed from "I sign thee," etc.,[1] to the familiar prayer "Defend, O Lord, this thy child,"[2] etc. Another alteration in the 1552 Book of far-reaching consequence was the revision of the prayer said by the bishop before the laying on of hands. In 1549 the old Gelasian wording was kept, and the prayer continued to be an invocation of the indwelling Spirit.[3] But in 1552 the central petition was changed from an invocation to an intercession for the strengthening graces of the Spirit.[4] This revision, probably more than any

---

1. Ed. note: *N.* I sign thee with the sign of the cross, and lay my hand upon thee: In the name of Father, and of the Son, and of the Holy Ghost. Amen.

2. Ed. note: Defend, O Lord, this thy Child with thy heavenly grace; that *he* may continue thine for ever; and daily increase in thy Holy Spirit more and more, until *he* come unto thy everlasting kingdom. Amen. (As the text implies, this prayer from 1552 is the one used in the 1928 prayer book as well.)

3. Ed. note: Almighty and everliving God, who has vouchsafed to regenerate these thy servants of water and the Holy Ghost: And hast given unto them forgiveness of all their sins: Send down from heaven, we beseech thee, O Lord, upon them thy Holy Ghost the Comforter, with the manifold gifts of grace, the spirit of wisdom and understanding; the spirit of counsel and ghostly strength; the spirit of knowledge and true godliness, and fulfil them, O Lord, with the spirit of thy holy fear.

4. Ed. note: Almighty and everliving God, who has vouchsafed to regenerate these thy servants **by** water and the Holy Ghost, and hast given unto them forgiveness of all their sins: **Strengthen them,** we beseech thee, O Lord, **with** the Holy Ghost the Comforter, **and daily increase in them thy** manifold gifts of grace: the spirit of wisdom and understanding; the spirit of counsel and ghostly strength, the spirit of knowledge and true godliness: and fulfil them, O Lord, with the spirit of thy holy fear. (Changes from the 1549 prayer are in bold.)

other, has contributed to the ambiguities in Anglican thought with respect to the meaning of Confirmation. It should be noted, too, that in the 1552 Book Cranmer dropped the anointing with chrism made by the priest after Baptism, with its reference to "the unction of His Holy Spirit." Theologically considered, Baptism and Confirmation remained very much the same in the English Church after the Reformation as they were before, except that in the Thirty-Nine Articles it was denied that Confirmation was a sacrament of the Gospel or generally (i.e., universally) necessary to salvation.

It remains to be said that the much-debated 'Confirmation Rubric' making admission to the Holy Communion dependent upon confirmation was no invention of Cranmer's, but was taken by him from the Sarum Manual, which in turn goes back to a decree of Archbishop John Peckham of Canterbury in 1281. That it remained largely a dead letter, not only in the later Middle Ages but after the Reformation, is a matter of history. Only within the past hundred years has the Anglican Communion as a whole revived its disciplines with regard to Confirmation and given to the rite its proper place in the Church's life.

The Revision of the Baptismal Service

The changes proposed in the following revision of Holy Baptism may be subsumed under three headings: the length of the service, the clarification of rubrics to meet modern needs and demands, and the simplification of the ritual text. In all three instances the Commission has tried to deal fairly with the wealth of criticism which it has received. Problems arising from varying local circumstances and prejudices derived from partisan bias have made the task of adjusting conflicting opinion extremely delicate. It must be remembered that every alteration in detail has to be viewed in the larger context of its effect upon the service as a whole. The Commission has always kept to the fore in its discussions the principle to make no change in the rite which would imply any change in essential doctrine.

One of the most common complaints about the Prayer Book rite of Baptism concerns its length. Parish worship is unduly prolonged when the present office is used with the Daily Offices on Sundays and Holy Days, as the rubrics direct, or (following ancient precedent) with the Holy Communion, where that is the principal service of corporate worship. Yet everyone seems agreed that the practice of private baptism, except in necessary cases, should be discouraged, and that Baptism be administered according to the Prayer Book direction in the context of the public worship of the parish. It has not been an easy matter, however, to excise material from the rite without jeopardizing significant content.

It is conceivable that even greater shortening of the service might be made, than the Commission here proposes, by the omission of the entire introduction of the Baptism rite, so that the office, when used in conjunction with the Daily

Offices or Holy Communion, would begin with the Promises. The Commission would welcome comment upon this proposal. Meanwhile it offers a rubric (the third at the beginning of the service) which allows the omission of one lesson and canticle at the Daily Office, rather than the excision of the introduction of the Baptism service itself.

We have omitted the first question in the present service ('Hath this Child been baptized, or no?'). The Minister, of course, knows the answer to that question before he asks it. In medieval times, when there was practically no pre-baptismal instruction, such a question was needed, since people often sought the grace of baptism for their children as frequently as possible. Such a superstition being no longer with us, the only practical effect of asking the question is to stun the people into not answering it at all, since they know the Minister has the answer. Nor is the question needed any longer to teach the unrepeatable character of Baptism. The general tenor of the whole service conveys that truth. To many persons the question has served only as an unexpected and unexplained stumbling-block at the very beginning.

The consolidation of the separate baptismal offices in the 1928 revision brought together the Gospel lesson from St. Mark for the Baptism of Infants and that from St. John for Adults.[5] The new provision of the 'great commission' from St. Matthew to serve for a Baptism of both infants and adults was added at the same time. In practice, it has been found that the selection from St. Matthew makes an admirable substitute for the long and not readily intelligible selection from St. John, at a baptism of adults alone. It is therefore proposed to drop the passage from St. John. Its basic teaching has already been covered in the opening address or bidding to the service. Another reason for its excision — as well as for other cuts which are proposed — is to make the service more readily followed by the laity. They will not need to be instructed to turn the page in order to keep up with the Minister.

The bidding and prayer on page 276 have been dropped, but their content has not been lost.[6] The bidding has been subsumed in the preface to the Promises,

---

5. Ed. note: The readings given in the 1928 book are Mark 10:13-16 ("Suffer the little children to come unto me...") used in both "The Ministration of Public Baptism of Infants, to be used in the Church" and "The Ministration of Private Baptism of Children, in Houses" from the 1892 book and also John 3:1-8 (Nicodemus is told he must be born again of the Spirit) used in "The Ministration of Baptism To Such as are of Riper Years, and able to answer for themselves" in the 1892 book.

6. Ed. note: (the Bidding) AND now, we being persuaded of the good will of our heavenly Father toward *this Child* (*this Person*) declared by his Son Jesus Christ; let us faithfully and devoutly give thanks unto him and say,[¶ Minister and People.] ALMIGHTY and everlasting God, heavenly Father, We give thee humble thanks, That thou hast vouchsafed to call us to the knowledge of thy grace, and faith in thee: Increase this knowledge, And confirm this faith, in us evermore. Give thy Holy Spirit to *this Child* (or *this* thy *Servant*), That *he* may be born again, And be made *an heir* of everlasting salvation; Through our Lord Jesus Christ, Who liveth and reigneth with thee and the Holy Spirit, Now and forever. Amen.

and phrases of the prayer have been taken up into the final thanksgiving. Further shortening has been achieved by putting together the Promises made by sponsors for infants and by adult candidates. The supplications on page 278 have been reduced to a single prayer,[7] and the lengthy introduction to the Lord's Prayer on page 280 has been excised to avoid redundancy.[8]

There have been a few slight additions, however. In some cases the purpose has been to increase congregational participation in the office, such as the addition of *Gloria tibi* and *Laus tibi Christe* before and after the Gospel, and the versicles and responses after the Promises. Many have objected that the present service does not include the Apostles' Creed, which actually originated in the baptismal service. It only makes allusion to it. On the other hand many complaints have been received that the form of the question as it now stands regarding the Creed is obscure and that it raises unnecessary scruples. After much debate and weighing of arguments the Commission has decided to adopt a further suggestion, frequently made, that the Creed be paraphrased in interrogatory form by presenting it, so to speak, by title. This is exactly the way it was done in the rite described by St. Hippolytus. Stylistically it seems more effective than the use of the entire Creed in interrogatory form, as it is found in Cranmer's rite.

One additional promise for sponsors has been inserted, which conforms to the new rubric concerning the Church status of Sponsors (the sixth at the beginning of the proposed service). Surely no justification is needed for such efforts to strengthen the Church's requirements for Sponsors. It will be noted, too, that the last promise for Sponsors has been reworded. The reason will be obvious. A sponsor may sincerely promise to do all in his or her power to lead a child to Confirmation. But Confirmation is the result of a person's own decision. No one can honestly promise to make that decision for another.

The new prayer, "O God, our heavenly Father," permitted to be used before the final Blessing, fills a long-felt need, as the Prayer Book has hitherto had no specific prayer for Sponsors. The use of a prayer here would seem preferable to any restoration of an Exhortation, such as the service had at this place until the 1928 revision.

---

7. Ed. note: O MERCIFUL God, grant that like as Christ died and rose again, so *this Child* (*this thy Servant*) may die to sin and rise to newness of life. *Amen.*

Grant that all sinful affections may die in *him*, and that all things belonging to the Spirit may live and grow in *him*. *Amen*

Grant that *he* may have power and strength to have victory, and to triumph, against the devil, the world, and the flesh. *Amen.*Grant that whosoever is here dedicated to thee by our office and ministry, may also be endued with heavenly virtues, and everlastingly rewarded, through thy mercy, O blessed Lord God, who dost live, and govern all things, world without end. *Amen.*

8. Ed. note: SEEING now, dearly beloved brethren, that *this Child* (or *this Person*) is regenerate, and grafted into the body of Christ's Church, let us give thanks unto Almighty God for these benefits; and with one accord make our prayers unto him, that *this Child* (or *this Person*) may lead the rest of *his* life according to this beginning.

The first three rubrics are designed to lay stress particularly upon the *public* character of Baptism as the normative use; and the reasons for this are given in the first rubric, the wording of which has been taken from the English Prayer Book. Inasmuch as many parishes now have the Holy Communion always at the principal service on Sundays, it has been thought advisable to suggest at what place in that service a ministration of Baptism would be most fittingly inserted, if the Baptism does not take place immediately before the service. On the analogy of the Daily Office this would seem to be after the lessons and before the Creed. Incidentally one of the reasons for not restoring the Creed in its full form to the Baptism office has been the assumption that Baptism, administered publicly, would come within the framework of a service which contained the full recitation of the Creed.

The purpose of the fourth rubric in the proposed service is to emphasize the importance of pre-baptismal instruction for parents and sponsors regarding their duties. In view of modern conditions of family and social life many clergy have become disturbed over what they call the 'indiscriminate baptizing of children.' Certainly all forethought and care should be exercised today to see that children have a chance to grow in the knowledge and love of God and of His Christ. With this in view, the Commission proposes in the sixth rubric a specific demand that Sponsors be baptized persons, and that where possible they be communicants of the Church. This rubric is to be understood as disciplinary, and in no way questioning the validity of a baptism in which the sponsors are not professing Christians. It would be wiser to have no sponsors at all than to allow persons who cannot honestly take the vows of the service to be admitted to this high dignity and responsibility. The office of Sponsor is not necessary in Baptism, even though it be highly desirable. It is the whole faith of the Church which bears up the little infant presented unto God, as St. Augustine said (*Epistles* 98.5):

> For it is proper to regard the infants as presented by all who take pleasure in their baptism, and through whose holy and perfectly-united love they are assisted in receiving the communion of the Holy Spirit.

The direction to fill the font with pure water has been transferred to a place immediately before the Blessing of the Font. This would seem to be the natural place for the ceremony, to mark off a new section in the rite. It should serve also to deter the common disobedience of our present rubric, in many places where the font is prepared some time before the minister and sponsors with those to be baptized have come to the font.

Textual changes made in the prayers have aimed at clarifying the meaning of Baptism with Water in such a way that the laity may more readily understand the office. Many alterations are purely verbal, to avoid archaic expressions or words whose connotation in modern usage is different from that originally intended. For example, in the opening bidding "goodness" has been substituted for "mercy";

in the Blessing of the Font, "Regard the supplications of thy congregation" has been simplified into "Hear the prayers of thy people"; and in the final thanksgiving, "We give thee thanks" takes the place of "We yield thee thanks." A few phrases have been dropped altogether, such as: "may enjoy the everlasting benediction of thy heavenly washing." The idea of the phrase is adequately taken care of elsewhere in the office. Its unnatural sound makes it obscure to the layman's ear. So likewise the words "regeneration" and "regenerate" have, whenever feasible, been translated into the vernacular as "spiritual birth" or "born anew." But even for the literal-minded, it should be superfluous to point out that this simplification of phrase does not imply any weakening whatsoever of the Church's adherence to the doctrine of Baptismal Regeneration.

The opening prayer of the service (page 274) has been much simplified, partly by reference to its Latin original in the Gregorian Sacramentary. The exordium of the prayer in the Latin has five descriptive phrases. Cranmer reduced these to four. The present revision has made them into two, but kept the essential elements of the original. The allusion to God as "the resurrection of the dead" has lost its primary relevance here, since the rite is no longer associated chiefly with the Easter season. Hence it has been dropped altogether. The invocation of the prayer was much altered by Cranmer. A literal translation of the Latin reads: "We invoke thee in behalf of this thy servant, N., who, seeking the gift of thy Baptism, desires to obtain thine eternal grace of spiritual regeneration." It will be seen at once that Cranmer interpolated the reference to "remission of sin." The Commission has considered it advisable to retain Cranmer's addition, but to restore something of the phrasing of the original — at least to make the gift of regeneration coordinate with that of forgiveness.

The Blessing of the Font has similarly been re-worked. The obscurity of the reference to the "water and blood" has been eliminated. There has been no agreement either among the early Fathers or among modern Biblical exegetes as to what the Fourth Evangelist had specifically in mind by this testimony. In place of it the new form brings out the symbolism of death, burial and resurrection with Christ which Baptism effects, and leads more logically to the recalling of the Great Commission of Christ to His disciples. The phrase, "may receive the fulness of thy grace" has been excised since it is not altogether clear in its meaning.

Indeed, phrases such as this last one mentioned raise the fundamental problem of what gifts of grace are bestowed respectively in Baptism and in Confirmation, particularly as regards the action of the Holy Spirit in the two rites. There has been no little ambiguity in Anglican theology on this question, the result as we have seen of a long-standing historical development. It may be pertinent at this point to quote a few paragraphs from a brief brochure by the Rev. Dr. Oscar Hardman entitled "*Bishoping*" (S.P.C.K., pp. 17-18):

> Some have answered that Baptism only cleanses, while Confirmation strengthens, and that the Holy Spirit acts from without in the former,

and does not make His actual abode with the baptized until the laying on of hands has taken place. They suggest that the term "baptism," in its popular use as equivalent to initiation, must be held to include both Baptism in its stricter sense and Confirmation also, and that a person who has received only the baptismal washing is not yet completely baptized.

Over against this is more generally held that Baptism that is to say, the washing alone — admits to Church membership and to fellowship with the Holy Spirit, while Confirmation adds to the gifts that the Spirit has hitherto bestowed, or, to put it in another way, brings the baptized into a still more intimate relationship with the already indwelling Holy Spirit.

Neither of these positions is really convincing. The former magnifies Confirmation at the expense of Baptism, while the latter may be pressed to mean that Confirmation is a rather superfluous supplement to Baptism; and both of them describe the relationship between the Holy Spirit and the individual Christian in terms which are symbolical, and therefore not to be accepted as anything more than picturesque generalizations in which the essential mystery and subtlety of the situation is missed.

It would certainly be an intolerable doctrine which denied that by Baptism in Water in the Name of all three Persons of the Holy Trinity the Holy Spirit was not given to the baptized, or that He acted upon the baptized purely in an external way. One cannot become a member of Christ or of His Church, which is His Body, and not be a partaker of His Spirit. And surely the Holy Spirit is capable of influencing the growth in grace of a child after Baptism. As Dr. Hardman says later in his work (pp. 21-22):

> We are bound to believe that the Holy Spirit is able to bring His personal influence to bear upon the child's development at least as soon as we ourselves are able to do the same. From the moment when the living soul is brought forth into the world there is no point in his progress at which it may be plausibly represented that the Spirit of God is powerless to influence him. The Church initiates the child into the Christian relationship with the Spirit at the earliest possible moment, and when the child has grown so as to reach at length the point where it can claim him as a third party consciously and responsibly active in association with the Holy Spirit and the Church, the process of initiation may be duly completed.

There is always the danger of theologians' attempting to over-refine in definitions what is a great mystery. All that the present revision claims for itself is that it has sought to avoid any phraseology which would foster an interpretation of

Baptism with Water in such a way that it usurps or makes superfluous the normative and necessary place of Confirmation in the perfecting of the Christian, or would reduce the meaning of Confirmation to a mere strengthening of what has been received in Baptism.

The interrelation of the two rites of Baptism and Confirmation can be set forth with striking effect when the two services are used together. Hence the last rubric of the proposed Baptism rite gives direction as to the way both services may be integrated into one continuous service, when those who are to be baptized are to be confirmed immediately by the Bishop without delay. This would apply, of course, only to adults who have been prepared for the reception of full Christian initiation, Baptism and Confirmation, at one and the same time.

The Revision of the Confirmation Service

The principal feature of the proposed revision of the Order of Confirmation is the short service of corporate worship, with propers suitable to the occasion, immediately prior to the presentation of the candidates. The justification for this permissive 'enrichment' will be obvious. The present rite when used alone has seemed to many to lack a sufficient devotional preparation of the congregation for the solemnity of the rite. It begins too abruptly, and it lacks certain elements of corporate worship to make it, so to speak, a complete service of common prayer. Often it is inexpedient to combine it with one of the regular offices of the Prayer Book, whether Morning or Evening Prayer or the Holy Communion. The purpose of the accompanying proposal is to afford an adequate substitute, whenever it may be so desired, which is liturgically apt and also sufficiently flexible in form so as to make it adaptable to varying needs and circumstances.

The structure of the proposed introductory service follows in general the pattern of the Daily Office — an opening sentence, a psalm, a lesson followed by a hymn (or canticle), the Creed and prayer. One of the familiar canticles might be used after the lesson in place of a hymn, if that is preferred. The lesson has been chosen from the Old Testament in view of the fact that the Confirmation rite proper has a New Testament lesson. The Collect chosen for the service, to be used after the Collect for the Day, will be recognized as the one on page 182 of the Prayer Book — for the first Communion on Whitsunday.

The Renewal of the Vows of Baptism has been rephrased to make it conform to the vows taken by the candidates or their sponsors at Baptism itself. The Bishop's declaration to the confirmands immediately prior to his questions is based upon the forms to be found in the Scottish and the English 1928 Prayer Books.

The most significant alteration in the prayers which follow are designed to restore the primitive view of Confirmation as the gift of the indwelling Spirit in all His fulness to the baptized, and not merely as an added, strengthening grace. Thus, "Send into their hearts thy Holy Spirit" is substituted for "Strengthen them with the Holy Ghost" as in the present form. This brings the prayer closer not only to the 1549 form, but also to the original Gelasian wording: *immitte in eos Spiritum sanctum*. Similarly, "Confirm" has replaced "Defend" in the prayer said by the Bishop at the imposition of his hand. This change makes it clear that Confirmation means primarily the action of God in confirming His children. In our present rite the word "confirming" is confusingly used only of the action of the candidate in renewing his vows. Moreover the word "confirm" includes all that is implied in "defend" and more!

One of the most difficult questions presented to the Commission has been the proposal to restore, permissively, the use of the ancient ceremony of the signing and sealing candidates with chrism, in conjunction with the Bishop's laying on of hands. In the 1549 Book, Cranmer kept the signing of the forehead with the cross, but eliminated the Sarum mention of chrism in favor of an apparently metaphorical "inward unction of the Holy Ghost." In 1552, all reference to 'signing and sealing' was excised. And this omission of any suggestion of the use of chrism has characterized all Anglican Prayer Books since that time, until the Scottish Book of 1929 restored the 1549 provisions.

At the present time, many of our bishops do actually use chrism in connection with the laying on of hands. They justify this additional ceremony on the ground that in the paucity of ceremonial directions in the Prayer Book some actions not expressly ordered by the present rubrics must necessarily be added, and other traditional actions are sometimes inserted without rebuke. The difficulty of this view of the question is that there is a distinction between the employment of a mere embellishment, such as the use of incense at the celebration of the Eucharist, which in no manner affects the essence of the Sacrament, and the importation of a ceremony which may set up a claim to be the actual 'Matter' of a Sacrament itself. And it cannot be gainsaid that Anglicanism has consistently viewed the 'Matter' or essential ceremony of Confirmation to be the laying on of hands, as against the scholastic theory that it was the anointing with chrism. In this regard, Anglicanism has always claimed that it had effected a return to the conceptions of the New Testament, and of the Primitive Church.

Modern students of New Testament documents would doubtless be less dogmatic than Cranmer and his associates about primitive evidence. It is true that the actual descriptions of 'Confirmation' in the Book of Acts — upon which our Anglican formularies are primarily based — make no mention of chrism, but only of the laying on of hands. But in the Epistles, there are numerous references to Christian initiation in terms of an 'anointing' or 'sealing.' Some scholars maintain that such references are purely metaphorical. Others believe that they refer to an actual use of chrism. Symbolic significance was given by the earliest Christians to the 'anointing,' with which the ancients accompanied any 'bath.' They considered that their initiation into Christ anointed them as kings and priests unto God.

Moreover, the very word *Christos* means 'anointed one.' It is instructive to analyze the play upon this idea in such a passage as 1 John 2:18-27.

It is true also that when we examine the liturgical evidence of the second century, we find that our two chief witnesses to the rite of Christian initiation, the *Didache* and Justin Martyr, make not the slightest reference to chrism — but then, they mention nothing comparable to Confirmation at all. However, by the turn of the third century, both chrism and the laying on of hands are fixed features of the rite, as may be seen in Hippolytus and Tertullian. Eventually, in both East and West, the chrism overshadowed the undoubted 'scriptural' ceremony of the laying on of hands: in the East, the sacramental rite is known only as 'The Holy Chrismation'; and in both the contact of the Bishop's hands with the candidate's head has been reduced to the touch of the tip of his thumb upon the forehead.

In view of the uncertainties of New Testament evidence about the use of chrism on the one hand, and also of the unbroken and undisputed Anglican emphasis upon the laying on of hands on the other, the Commission has considered it unwise to introduce into the proposed revision of the Confirmation Service any specific reference to 'signing and sealing.' This would leave the question of the added ceremony of the use of chrism on exactly the same basis that it is at present.

The Sarum Collect, "O Almighty Lord, and everlasting God," introduced before the Blessing in the 1662 Prayer Book, has been omitted. It adds little to the preceding prayer, and its American associations are rather with the Communion Service. It is anticlimactic.

The form of the Bishop's dismissal has been suggested by the English 1928 Book. This dismissal serves the same purpose as the excised Collect, in that it relates the liturgical action to the Christian's life in the world.

The Ministration of Holy Baptism

¶ *The Minister of every Parish shall often admonish the People, that they defer not the Baptism of their Children, and that it should be administered upon Sundays and other Holy Days, when the most number of people come together: as well for that the Congregation there present may testify the receiving of them that be newly baptized into the number of Christ's Church, as also because in the Baptism of infants every man present may be put in remembrance of his own profession made to God in his Baptism.*

¶ *If necessity so require, Baptism may be administered upon any other day; but except for urgent cause, Baptism shall always be administered in the Church.*

¶ *On Sundays and Holy Days, Baptism shall be administered immediately after the Second Lesson at Morning or Evening Prayer, or after the Gospel at the Holy*

Communion; but the Minister may in his discretion appoint such other time as he shall think fit. And NOTE, *That when Baptism is administered at Morning or Evening Prayer, the Minister may omit one Lesson and one Canticle of the Order of Morning or Evening Prayer.*

¶ When there are Children to be baptized, the Parents or Sponsors shall give timely notice to the Minister, that he may give them sufficient instruction in the duties and responsibilities of their promises.

¶ There shall be three Sponsors for every Child to be baptized, when they can be had: for a Boy, two Godfathers and one Godmother; and for a Girl, one Godfather and two Godmothers; and Parents may be admitted as Sponsors.

¶ Sponsors shall be baptized persons, and shall, if possible, be Communicants of the Church.

¶ When any Persons as are of riper years are to be baptized, the Minister shall take due care for their examination, whether they be sufficiently instructed in the Principles of the Christian Religion; and that they may be directed to prepare themselves, with Prayers and Fasting, for the receiving of this holy Sacrament.

¶ At the time of the Baptism of an Adult, there shall be present with him at the Font at least two Witnesses.

The Preparation

¶ Those to be baptized, with their Sponsors, shall meet the Minister at the Font, and he shall then say as followeth, the People all standing.

DEARLY beloved, forasmuch as our Saviour Christ saith, None can enter into the Kingdom of God, except he be regenerate and born anew of Water and of the Holy Ghost; I beseech you to call upon God the Father, through our Lord Jesus Christ, that of his bounteous goodness he will grant to *this Child* (*this* thy *Servant*) that which by nature *he* cannot have; that *he*, being baptized, may be received into Christ's holy Church, be made a living *member* of the same, and *an inheritor* of the kingdom of heaven.

¶ Then shall the Minister say,

Let us pray.

ALMIGHTY and immortal God, the helper and defender of all who call to thee in need, the life and peace of those who believe; We call upon thee for *this Child* (*this* thy *Servant*), that *he*, coming to thy holy Baptism, may receive remission of sin, and thine eternal grace of spiritual birth. Receive *him*, O Lord, as thou hast promised by thy well-beloved Son, saying, Ask, and ye shall have; seek, and ye shall find; knock, and it shall be opened unto you. So give now unto us who ask; let us who seek, find; open the gate unto us who knock; that *this Child* (*this* thy *Servant*), being born anew, may be received into the company of Christ's flock, and may come into *his* inheritance of the eternal kingdom of thy Son, Jesus Christ our Lord. *Amen.*

¶ *Then the Minister shall say as followeth.*

Hear the words of the Gospel according to Saint Mark.

¶ *The People shall answer,*

Glory be to thee, O Lord.

THEY brought young children to Christ, that he should touch them: and his disciples rebuked those that brought them. But when Jesus saw it, he was much displeased, and said unto them, Suffer the little children to come unto me, and forbid them not: for of such is the kingdom of God. Verily I say unto you, Whosoever shall not receive the kingdom of God as a little child, he shall not enter therein. And he took them up in his arms, put his hands upon them, and blessed them.

¶ *The People shall say,*

Praise be to thee, O Christ.

¶ *Or this.*

Hear the words of the Gospel according to Saint Matthew.

¶ *The People shall answer,*

Glory be to thee, O Lord.

JESUS came and spake unto them, saying, All power is given unto me in heaven and in earth. Go ye therefore, and make disciples of all nations, baptizing them in the name of the Father, and of the Son, and of the Holy Ghost: teaching them to observe all things whatsoever I have commanded you: and, lo, I am with you alway, even unto the end of the world.

¶ *The People shall say,*

Praise be to thee, O Christ.

The Promises

¶ *The Minister shall speak on this wise to the Sponsors, and to such Adults as are to be baptized.*

DEARLY beloved, we have prayed unto God our Father that he of his good will and favour, declared unto us in the Gospel of his Son Jesus Christ, would vouchsafe to forgive you all your sin, receive you into the body of Christ's Church, and give you the heritage of the kingdom of heaven.

Dost thou, therefore, renounce the devil and all his works, the vain glory of the world, and all evil desires, so that, by God's help, thou wilt not follow, nor be led by them?

> *Answer.* I renounce them all; and by God's help, will endeavour not to follow, nor be led by them.
>
> *Minister.* Dost thou believe in God the Father Almighty, Maker of heaven and earth; And in Jesus Christ his only Son our Lord; And in the Holy Ghost?
>
> *Answer.* I do.
>
> *Minister.* Wilt thou be baptized in this Faith?
>
> *Answer.* That is my desire.
>
> *Minister.* Wilt thou then obediently keep God's holy will and commandments, and serve him all the days of thy life?
>
> *Answer.* I will, by God's help.
>
> ¶ *When the Office is used for Children, the Minister shall ask of the Parents and Sponsors the following questions.*

HAVING now, in the name of this Child, made these promises, wilt thou also on thy part take heed that this Child shall be instructed in the Creed, the Lord's Prayer, and the Commandments of God, and encouraged to resist all evil, and to worship and serve his Saviour Jesus Christ in his holy Church?

> *Answer.* I will, by God's help.
>
> *Minister.* Wilt thou undertake to set *him* an example by the faithful exercise of the duties of a Christian?
>
> *Answer.* I will, God being my helper.
>
> *Minister.* Wilt thou endeavour to bring this Child, so soon as sufficiently instructed, to the Bishop to be confirmed by him?
>
> *Answer.* I will endeavour so to do.
>
> ¶ *Then shall be said,*
>
> *Minister.* O Lord, save thy servants;
> *People.* That put their trust in thee.
> *Minister.* Send unto them help from above;
> *People.* And evermore mightily defend them.
> *Minister.* Lord, hear our prayer;

People. And let our cry come unto thee.

Minister. Let us pray.

O MERCIFUL God, grant that *this Child* may have power and strength to have victory, and to triumph, against sin, the world, and the devil; and may so persevere in running the race that is set before *him*, that at length, with the whole company of thy faithful servants, *he* may attain unto thine eternal joy, through thy mercy, O blessed Lord God, who dost live, and govern all things, world without end. *Amen.*

The Blessing of the Font

¶ *Then the Minister shall pour pure Water into the Font, and after that shall say,*

The Lord be with you.

People. And with thy spirit.
Minister. Lift up your hearts.
People. We lift them up unto the Lord.
Minister. Let us give thanks unto our Lord God.
People. It is meet and right so to do.

¶ *Then shall the Minister say,*

IT is very meet, right, and our bounden duty, that we should give thanks unto thee, O Lord, Holy Father, Almighty, Everlasting God, for that thy dearly beloved Son Jesus Christ, for the forgiveness of our sins, did suffer death upon the Cross, and was buried, and did rise again the third day, that we might live unto thee in newness of life by the power of his Resurrection; and gave commandment to his disciples to go teach all nations, and baptize them In the Name of the Father, and of the Son, and of the Holy Ghost. Hear, we beseech thee, the prayers of thy people; Sanctify this Water by thy Spirit for the mystical washing away of sin; that *this Child* (*this* thy *Servant*), now to be baptized therein, may be numbered among thy faithful children, and may grow in thy grace and favour until he come unto thine everlasting kingdom; through the same Jesus Christ our Lord, to whom, with thee, in the unity of the same Holy Spirit, be all honour and glory, now and evermore. *Amen.*

The Baptism

¶ *Then shall the Minister take the Child into his arms, or take the Adult by the hand, and shall say unto the Sponsors or Witnesses,*

Baptism and Confirmation

Name this Child (Person).

¶ And then, naming the Child or Adult after them, he shall dip him in the Water discreetly, or shall pour Water upon him, saying,

N, I baptize thee In the Name of the Father, and of the Son, and of the Holy Ghost. Amen.

¶ Then shall the Minister say,

WE receive *this Child* (*Person*) into the congregation of Christ's flock, and do sign ✠ [Here the Minister shall make a Cross upon the Child's (or Person's) forehead.] *him* with the sign of the Cross, in token that hereafter *he* shall not be ashamed to confess the faith of Christ crucified, and manfully to fight under his banner, against sin, the world, and the devil; and to continue Christ's faithful soldier and servant unto his life's end. Amen.

The Thanksgiving

¶ Then shall the Minister say,

And now, as our Saviour Christ hath taught us, we are bold to say,

OUR Father, who art in heaven, Hallowed be thy Name. Thy kingdom come. Thy will be done, On earth as it is in heaven. Give us this day our daily bread. And forgive us our trespasses, As we forgive those who trespass against us. And lead us not into temptation, But deliver us from evil. For thine is the kingdom, and the power, and the glory, for ever and ever. *Amen.*

¶ Then shall the Minister say,

WE give thee hearty thanks, O heavenly Father, that thou hast vouchsafed to call thy people to the knowledge of thy grace, and faith in thee; Increase this knowledge, and confirm this faith in us evermore; and grant that *this Child* (*this* thy *Servant*), now born again by Baptism, and incorporated into thy holy Church, may so die unto sin and live unto righteousness, that finally *he* may come unto thine everlasting kingdom; through Jesus Christ our Lord. *Amen.*

¶ The Minister may add,

O GOD, our heavenly Father, who hast wonderfully made the earthly family after thy likeness, and hast blessed it with the joy and care of children; Assist with thy grace, we beseech thee, these thy servants, who have brought *this child* to thy holy Baptism, that they may bring *him* up in thy faith, fear, and love; that as *he grows* in years *he* may grow in grace, and in the knowledge of thee and of thy Son, Jesus Christ our Lord. Amen.

¶ Then shall the Minister say,

THE Almighty God, the Father of our Lord Jesus Christ, of whom the whole family in heaven and earth is named; Strengthen you with might by his Spirit in the inner man; that, Christ dwelling in your hearts by faith, ye may be filled with all the fulness of God. *Amen.*

¶ Every Adult, thus baptized, should be confirmed by the Bishop, so soon after his Baptism as conveniently may be; nor shall an Adult be baptized, except for weighty cause, unless he signify his desire to be confirmed without delay, and to be admitted to the Holy Communion.

¶ When Adults are to be confirmed immediately after their Baptism, the Minister shall conclude the service with the signing of the Candidate upon the forehead with the Cross; and the Bishop shall proceed at once with the Order of Confirmation, beginning at the Versicle, "Our help is in the Name of the Lord."

The Order of Confirmation

Or Laying on of Hands Upon Those That are Baptized, and Come to Years of Discretion.

¶ This Service may be used by itself, or after Morning or Evening Prayer, or at the Holy Communion.

¶ And NOTE, *this service may be shortened by beginning with the Presentation of the Candidates.*

Introduction

¶ The Minister appointed shall begin the service by reading the following Sentence.

YE shall receive power, after that the Holy Ghost is come upon you: and ye shall be witnesses unto me both in Jerusalem, and in all Judæa, and in Samaria, and unto the uttermost part of the earth.

¶ Then shall be read the following Psalm,

Psalm 27. *Dominus illuminatio.*

THE Lord is my light and my salvation; whom then shall I fear? * The Lord is the strength of my life; of whom then shall I be afraid?

One thing have I desired of the Lord, which I will require; * even that I may dwell in the house of the Lord all the days of my life, to behold the fair beauty of the Lord, and to visit his temple.

For in the time of trouble he shall hide me in his tabernacle; * yea, in the secret place of his dwelling shall he hide me, and set me up upon a rock of stone.

Therefore will I offer in his dwelling an oblation with great gladness: * I will sing and speak praises unto the Lord.

Hearken unto my voice, O Lord, when I cry unto thee; * have mercy upon me, and hear me.

My heart hath talked of thee, Seek ye my face: * Thy face, Lord, will I seek.

O hide not thou thy face from me, * nor cast thy servant away in displeasure.

Thou hast been my succour; * leave me not, neither forsake me, O God of my salvation.

Teach me thy way, O Lord, * and lead me in the right way, because of mine enemies.

I should utterly have fainted, * but that I believe verily to see the goodness of the Lord in the land of the living.

O tarry thou the Lord's leisure; * be strong, and he shall comfort thine heart; and put thou thy trust in the Lord.

Glory be to the Father, and to the Son, * and to the Holy Ghost;

As it was in the beginning, is now, and ever shall be, * world without end. Amen.

¶ *Then shall be read the following Lesson from the Book of the Prophet Ezekiel, in the thirty-sixth Chapter, at the twenty-fifth Verse.*

THEN will I sprinkle clean water upon you, and ye shall be clean. A new heart also will I give you, and a new spirit will I put within you: and I will take away the stony heart out of your flesh, and I will give you an heart of flesh. And I will put my Spirit within you, and cause you to walk in my statutes, and ye shall keep my judgments, and do them. And ye shall dwell in the land that I gave to your fathers; and ye shall be my people, and I will be your God.

¶ *Here may be sung a Hymn.*

¶ *Then shall follow the Apostles' Creed; and after that, the Minister shall say,*

The Lord be with you.

People. And with thy spirit.

Minister. Let us pray.

ALMIGHTY and most merciful God, grant, we beseech thee, that by the indwelling of thy Holy Spirit, we may be enlightened and strengthened for thy service, through Jesus Christ our Lord, who liveth and reigneth with thee in the unity of the same Spirit ever, one God, world without end. Amen.

The Presentation of the Candidates

¶ Here may be sung a Hymn.

¶ All that are to be confirmed shall be presented by the Minister to the Bishop, sitting in his chair near to the Holy Table or at the entrance to the Choir, the People all standing until the Lord's Prayer; and the Minister shall say,

REVEREND Father in God, I present unto you these persons to receive the Laying on of Hands.

¶ Then shall the Bishop say,

Have you examined them, and found them ready and desirous to be confirmed?

¶ And the Minister shall answer,

I have examined them, and believe them so to be.

¶ Then the Bishop, or some Minister appointed by him, shall say,

Hear the words of the Evangelist Saint Luke, in the eighth Chapter of the Acts of the Apostles.

WHEN the Apostles which were at Jerusalem heard that Samaria had received the word of God, they sent unto them Peter and John: who, when they were come down, prayed for them, that they might receive the Holy Ghost: for as yet he was fallen upon none of them: only they were baptized in the name of the Lord Jesus. Then laid they their hands on them, and they received the Holy Ghost.

The Renewal of the Vows of Baptism

¶ Then shall the Bishop say,

YE who are to be confirmed must now declare before this congregation your stedfast purpose, with the help of the Holy Spirit, to follow Christ our Master, and to fulfil the Christian duties to which your Baptism pledged you.

Do you believe in God the Father Almighty, Maker of heaven and earth; And in Jesus Christ his only Son our Lord; And in the Holy Spirit?

Answer. I do.

Bishop. Will you then obediently keep God's holy will and commandments, and serve him all the days of your life?

Answer. I will, by God's help.

The Confirmation

Bishop. Our help is in the Name of the Lord;

People. Who hath made heaven and earth.

Bishop. Blessed be the Name of the Lord;

People. Henceforth, world without end.

Bishop. Lord, hear our prayer.

People. And let our cry come unto thee.

Bishop. Let us pray.

ALMIGHTY and everliving God, who hast vouchsafed to regenerate these thy servants by Water and the Holy Spirit, and hast given unto them forgiveness of all their sins; Send into their hearts, we beseech thee, O Lord, thy Holy Spirit, and daily increase in them thy manifold gifts of grace: the spirit of wisdom and understanding, the spirit of counsel and strength, the spirit of knowledge and true godliness; and fill them, O Lord, with the spirit of thy holy fear, both now and for ever. *Amen.*

¶ *Then shall the Bishop lay his hand upon the head of every one severally, saying,*

CONFIRM, O Lord, this thy Child with thy heavenly grace; that *he* may continue thine for ever; and daily increase in thy Holy Spirit more and more, until *he* come unto thine everlasting kingdom. Amen.

¶ *Then shall the Bishop say,*

The Lord be with you.

Answer. And with thy spirit.

Bishop. Let us pray.

¶ *Then shall the Bishop say the Lord's Prayer, the People kneeling and repeating it with him.*

OUR Father, who art in heaven, Hallowed be thy Name. Thy kingdom come. Thy will be done, On earth as it is in heaven. Give us this day our daily bread. And forgive us our trespasses, As we forgive those who trespass against us. And lead us not into temptation, But deliver us from evil. For thine is the kingdom, and the power, and the glory, for ever and ever. Amen.

¶ *Then shall the Bishop say,*

ALMIGHTY and everliving God, who makest us both to will and to do those things which are good, and acceptable unto thy Divine Majesty; We make our humble supplications unto thee for these thy servants, upon whom, after the example of thy holy Apostles, we have now laid our hands, to certify them, by this sign, of thy favour and gracious goodness towards them. Let thy fatherly hand, we beseech thee, ever be over them; let thy Holy Spirit ever be with them; and so lead them in the knowledge and obedience of thy Word, that in the end they may obtain everlasting life; through our Lord Jesus Christ, who with thee and the same Holy Spirit liveth and reigneth ever, one God, world without end. *Amen.*

¶ *Then the Bishop shall bless the newly-confirmed, saying thus,*

GO forth in peace: be of good courage: hold fast that which is good, rejoicing in the power of the Holy Spirit; And the Blessing of God Almighty, the Father, the Son, and the Holy Ghost, be upon you, and remain with you for ever. *Amen.*

¶ *The Minister shall earnestly move the Persons confirmed to come, without delay, to the Lord's Supper.*

¶ *And there shall none be admitted to the Holy Communion, until such time as he be confirmed, or be ready and desirous to be confirmed.*

PRAYER BOOK STUDIES II: THE LITURGICAL LECTIONARY

The Standing Liturgical Commission
of the Protestant Episcopal Church in the
United States of America

1950

PREFACE

The last revision of our Prayer Book was brought to a rather abrupt conclusion in 1928. Consideration of it had preoccupied the time of General Convention ever since 1913. Everyone was weary of the long and ponderous legislative process, and desired to make the new Prayer Book available as soon as possible for the use of the Church.

But the work of revision, which sometimes has seemed difficult to start, in this case proved hard to stop. The years of debate had aroused widespread interest in the whole subject: and the mind of the Church was more receptive of suggestions for revision when the work was brought to an end than when it began. Moreover, the revision was actually closed to new action in 1925, in order that it might receive final adoption in 1928: so that it was not possible to give due consideration to a number of very desirable features in the English and Scottish revisions, which appeared simultaneously with our own. It was further realized that there were some rough edges in what had been done, as well as an unsatisfied demand for still further alterations.

The problem of defects in detail was met by continuing the Revision Commission, and giving it rather large 'editorial' powers (subject only to review by General Convention) to correct obvious errors in the text as adopted, in the publication of the new Prayer Book. Then, to deal with the constructive proposals for other changes which continued to be brought up in every General Convention, the Revision Commission was reconstituted as a Standing Liturgical Commission. To this body all matters concerning the Prayer Book were to be referred, for preservation in permanent files, and for continuing consideration, until such time as the accumulated matter was sufficient in amount and importance to justify proposing another Revision.

The number of such referrals by General Convention, of Memorials from Dioceses, and of suggestions made directly to the Commission from all regions and schools and parties in the Church, has now reached such a total that it is evident that there is a widespread and insistent demand for a general revision of the Prayer Book.

The Standing Liturgical Commission is not, however, proposing any immediate revision. On the contrary, we believe that there ought to be a period of study and discussion, to acquaint the Church at large with the principles and issues involved, in order that the eventual action may be taken intelligently, and if possible without consuming so much of the time of our supreme legislative synod.

Accordingly, the General Convention of 1949 signalized the Fourth Centennial Year of the First Book of Common Prayer in English by authorizing the Liturgical Commission to publish its findings, in the form of a series of *Prayer Book Studies*.

It must be emphasized that the liturgical forms presented in these *Studies* are not — and under our Constitution, cannot be — sanctioned for public use. They are submitted for free discussion. The Commission will be grateful for copies or articles, resolutions, and direct comment, for its consideration, that the mind of the Church may be fully known to the body charged with reporting it.

In this undertaking, we have endeavored to be objective and impartial. It is not possible to avoid every matter which may be thought by some to be controversial. Ideas which seem to be constructively valuable will be brought to the attention of the Church, without too much regard as to whether they may ultimately be judged to be expedient. We cannot undertake to eliminate every proposal to which anyone might conceivably object: to do so would be to admit that any constructive progress is impossible. What we can do is to be alert not to alter the present *balance* of expressed or implied doctrine of the Church. We can seek to counterbalance every proposal which might seem to favor some one party of opinion by some other change in the opposite direction. The goal we have constantly had in mind — however imperfectly we may have succeeded in attaining it — is the shaping of a future Prayer Book which *every* party might embrace with the well-founded conviction that therein its own position had been strengthened, its witness enhanced, and its devotions enriched.

The objective we have pursued is the same as that expressed by the Commission for the Revision of 1892: "*Resolved*, That this Committee, in all its suggestions and acts, be guided by those principles of liturgical construction and ritual use which have guided the compilation and amendments of the Book of Common Prayer, and have made it what it is."

☩ ☩ ☩

The Commission records its loss in the deaths of two of its members, whose final contributions to the Church they served are reflected in this first issue of the Prayer Book Studies.

The Reverend Henry McF. B. Ogilby, late Secretary of the Commission, contributed to the Study on "Baptism and Confirmation."

The Reverend Doctor Burton Scott Easton, late Associate Member, in his published work on the Epistles and Gospels of the Christian Year, furnished the foundation and inspiration for the Study on "The Liturgical Lectionary."

These papers are therefore dedicated to their memory.

THE STANDING LITURGICAL COMMISSION:

G. ASHTON OLDHAM, *Chairman*
GOODRICH R. FENNER
BAYARD H. JONES, *Vice Chairman*
MORTON C. STONE, *Secretary*
JOHN W. SUTER, *Custodian of the Book of Common Prayer*
MASSEY H. SHEPHERD, JR.
CHURCHILL J. GIBSON
WALTER WILLIAMS
WILLIAM J. BATTLE
SPENCER ERVIN

The two Studies presented in this issue were thoroughly discussed, and approved for publication, by the Liturgical Commission at its meetings in 1948 and 1949.

The Committee on the Orders of Baptism and Confirmation consisted of the Rev. Massey H. Shepherd, Jr., Ph.D., the Rev. Henry McF. B. Ogilby, and the Rev. Charles E. Hill. The Committee on the Liturgical Lectionary consisted of the Rev. Bayard H. Jones, D.D., the Rev. Cuthbert A. Simpson, Th.D., and the Rev. Edward Rochie Hardy, Jr., Ph.D.

BAYARD H. JONES, *Editor of Publications*
April 28, 1950.

The Epistles and Gospels

1. Importance of the Liturgical Lectionary

The Christian Year is one of the most valuable possessions of the Teaching Church. As is well known, during the first half of its cycle, from Advent to Trinity Sunday, its primary emphasis is upon the Christian Belief, taking up the great assertions of the Creed clause by clause, and even phrase by phrase, and dramatizing them in a series of Festivals. Then in the remaining half, from Trinity Sunday to Advent again, the moral implications of the Faith are carried into the living of the Christian life.

The content of this teaching is conveyed in the Liturgical Lectionary of the Epistles and Gospels read at the celebrations of the Holy Communion throughout the year. It is this basic Lectionary which gives the Christian Year its actual substance, and determines the quality of its varying seasons. Moreover, until very recent times it was the only Lectionary of any kind and of any branch of the Church which was so ordered, since the system of Lessons at the Daily Offices in every Church was an altogether subordinate scheme, based upon a somewhat mechanical method of reading the Bible in course: a plan which took very little account of the distinctive character of the particular seasons. In the Roman Church, even this has been reduced to the very slightest dimensions, being little more than a mere 'token' outline of a former comprehensive plan. In the Anglican Prayer Books, however, there has been an increasing awareness of the Christian Year, and a growing tendency to bring the lessons at the Offices into harmony with the Scriptures appointed for the centrally important Eucharist. The most recent American Lectionary, adopted by General Convention in 1943, carried out this objective completely and systematically.

2. Defects of the Liturgical Lectionary

This undertaking to correlate the Lessons at Morning and Evening Prayer with the Scriptures read at the Holy Communion throughout the Christian Year necessitated some extensive investigations of the origins and growth of the Church's Calendar, and of the Liturgical Lectionary used therewith.

One primary authority thus utilized was the book entitled *The Eternal Word in the Modern World*, by Burton Scott Easton and Howard Chandler Robbins (Scribners, New York, 1937). This admirable guide to expository preaching on the basis of the Epistles and Gospels of our Prayer Book contained critical notes by Dr. Easton on the sources of the Church Year and its lections, which, taken together, amounted to the first adequate historical estimate of the Liturgical Lectionary ever to appear. Dr. Easton's outspoken exceptions to some of the less adequate assignments have had a considerable influence on the minds of the clergy of our Church, and are to be recognized in many of the suggestions for revision which have come to the Liturgical Commission. Therefore the Committee on the Liturgical Lectionary used this book as the starting-point of their considerations, and checked every proposal against Dr. Easton's important findings. Frequent references to these will be made in the following discussion.

The result of this and other studies was to establish the fact that the Church's cycle of commemorations was not a system which was systematically planned and executed at any one time, but a collection which was gradually piled up through many centuries.

Easter and Whitsunday were primordial, and were attested from the beginning of the second century. Lent, Easter-tide, and the Ember Seasons date from the third century; Christmas from the fourth; Advent and Pre-Lent from the sixth. Thus far, other Sundays were merely 'common Sundays,' with no more thought of proper provisions for them than if they had been so many weekdays. Lists of lessons for them began to appear in the seventh century, at first in undifferentiated blocks, and were gradually assimilated into fixed patterns and sequences up to the eleventh century. Trinity Sunday, originating in the tenth century, was not adopted at Rome until the fourteenth. Even then, the development was not at an end: proper lessons were assigned for our Epiphany VI in 1662, and for our Christmas II in 1928!

This unplanned development resulted in an accumulation of scriptural provisions from many sources. Some were chosen specifically for their places with the highest intelligence, and to the utmost effect. Some perpetuate the protocol of the papal court, or local Roman circumstances, or the passing events of the times when they originated; others represent borrowings from the Orthodox East, or contributions from the eager Gallic spirit. And so down to the uninspired efforts of medieval systematizers of small information and ability to fill gaps and reconcile divergencies, which have left us with unsatisfactory assignments for such supremely important occasions as Christmas, Easter, and the season of Lent.

The eventual result is now justly venerated for its centuries of use. It is full of curious interest for the technical student of liturgical origins. It is even very fairly representative of the best passages available in Holy Scripture for its purposes: since the very variety of its sources have assured that it would not be a solo on a single string.

It would be out of the question to abandon this traditional pattern, and extremely unwise to change its emphases. But it is quite worth while to use the information now available (which is more than was in possession of any previous age), in order to search out any demonstrable defects in the details of its execution, and to consider what may reasonably be done to remedy them.

For example, consider the repetitions of the same essential themes, in identical but overlapping passages from the same book, or in doublets of the same incident from the accounts of different Evangelists, in the following duplications: the three 'Miraculous Feedings' on Lent IV, Trinity VII, and the Sunday before Advent; *The Signs of the End* on Epiphany VI and Advent II; St. Luke's *Great Supper* on Trinity II, and St. Matthew's *Marriage Feast* on Trinity XX; St. Matthew's *Healing of the Centurion's Servant* on Epiphany IV, and St. John's *Healing of the Nobleman's Son* on Trinity XXI; the very similar warnings against carnal sins in the Epistles for Lent II and III; St. Paul's joy in his converts, and hopes for their perseverance, in the 'salutation' passages of his Epistles to the Philippians and the Colossians, on Trinity XXII and XXIV; the repetition of the whole of the Epistle for Easter Monday on Whit-Monday; and the borrowing of part of the Epistle for Palm Sunday for the Feast of the Circumcision.

Lections whose intrinsic excellence does not justify a place in the plan are certainly two very rabbinical arguments from Galatians, on Lent IV and Trinity XIII. The appropriateness of the Gospels for Lent II and V has also been challenged in some quarters.

There are also some inadequate assignments: perfectly good as far as they go, but needing supplement of one sort and another. Such are the provisions for Easter Day, which stop with the negative fact of the Empty Tomb, without adding the positive evidence of the Appearances of the Risen Lord. Consider also the Gospel for the First Sunday after Easter, which stops with the events of the evening of Easter Day, without continuing the occurrences of one week later, which other historic Churches, Eastern and Western alike, have always regarded as proper to this date. With this may be ranked the Epistle and Gospel for the Sunday within the Octave of the Ascension, which make no reference whatever to that event, but are merely proleptic to Whitsunday.

Finally, there are otherwise unexceptionable passages which are widely felt to be out of their proper place in the pattern of the Christian Year. These are the Triumphal Entry before the Passion, on Advent Sunday; and the Flight into Egypt on Christmas II, where it occurs actually before the Epiphany.

These all deserve careful consideration: and at least some of them seem to demand action. Besides these major matters, there are also a few relatively minor considerations of the exact length of the assignments, questions of the translations of particular phrases, and the like, which will be discussed later. Nevertheless, the foregoing list represents approximately the total dimensions of the changes which we are disposed to consider advisable at this time.

3. No New System Proposed

We must emphasize at once that there is no purpose in the mind of anyone connected with the Standing Liturgical Commission to embark on a general revision of the traditional Liturgical Lectionary, so as to supplant it with an essentially different scheme, thus embodying his own ideas of what he would like to see taught in the Church.

No doubt it would be perfectly practicable to pick out some selections from the Epistles which would be more striking than some of those now employed. And certainly there are passages from the Gospels which would carry much more weight than some now in use.

Likewise, there might be a temptation to try to bring one's own ideas of order into the absolute chaos — there is no other word for it — of the Gospels in Trinity-tide. Twenty-three of the twenty-four are chosen from the Synoptics; but there is no arrangement of them whatever, whether sequential, biographical, chronological, or theological. Neither in the Roman collation of these Gospels with the series of Trinity-tide Epistles, nor in the Sarum (which is older), is there any actual relevance between the Epistle and the Gospel of any Sunday, save by way of sheer coincidence. And much the same is true of the Sundays in the seasons of Advent, Epiphany, Lent, and Easter: even when both lessons have been chosen 'topically' to fit the season, they very commonly exploit quite divergent themes. Only sporadically does one find the close coordination of subject which characterizes the great feasts commemorating specific events of our Lord's life.

It is a curious fact that no Lectionary of any Church ever made a systematic attempt to secure a definite 'liturgical harmony,' featuring a single common theme between all the portions read at each service, until the American Lectionary of 1943. This plan has the obvious advantage of integrating all the teaching of a given service upon a single emphasis. But the older method — or more often complete lack of method — has its points too, in providing two or even more subjects, which are available for exposition on the same occasion in different years. This sort of variety is attainable in the Office Lectionary by offering complete alternative sets of lessons. The Liturgy, however, should retain a single system of prescriptions; alternatives are quite out of place. And if it does, any attempt to correlate the subjects of the Epistles and Gospels would simply narrow the available coverage of teaching in the words of Holy Scripture.

Projects of this order, however attractive, must be rejected. The fact is that the temple of the Christian Year is a structure which we have inherited from our forefathers in the faith, not something which we own, and may treat at our own will. It would be folly to pull it all down, and erect in its place a modernistic edifice in the current fashion. Some few corners of it may need repairs, because its first builders or subsequent re-modelers, improvising according to the best of their ability at the time, did not in fact choose the most durable materials to be placed upon the securest foundations. Consequently, these elements no longer express the purpose of their makers, nor are they adequate for the uses for which they were intended. We are justified in touching the traditional edifice, hallowed by the devotion of many generations, only at those details which have broken down: and even then, we should be at pains to preserve the plan of the founders.

In other words, it is none of our concern to impose any individualistic idea of our own as to what the Christian Year is, much less to reform it to what we might like to make it. As a matter of fact, we know what the Christian Year is only by studying what it has been: and any emendations we may make should be limited to those which will actually enable it to say better what it is evidently trying to say.

4. The Western Tradition

Even under these conservative limitations, there will be those who will express a fear of diverging from 'the Great Liturgical Tradition of the West' — i.e., of getting out of step with the provisions of the Church of Rome. This fear is by no means confined to those who look to that communion as the sole fount of all things authentically Catholic. This fear is based upon an entire misapprehension.

The fact is, that though the Anglican and the Roman systems of Epistles and Gospels are both descended from the same seventh-century sources, they have pursued their own separate evolution ever since. They have remained in substantial and essential harmony with each other as to underlying plan, total coverage, and general effect. Yet since the seventh century, one or the other of them has adopted alterations in the length of the selections, in substitutions of other passages, or transfers to other occasions of the year, to such an extent that they now actually coincide at very few points indeed. It will probably astonish nearly every member of our Church to learn that it is only on six Sundays out of 55, and on six Holy Days out of 37, that we read precisely the same Epistle and Gospel as those in the Roman Missal. Eleven more Sundays, and ten more Holy Days, have substantially the same assignments, differing only the precise length of the Epistle or Gospel, or both: making altogether 17 Sundays and 16 Holy Days where differences are only *de minimis*. If we disregard not only these questions of length, but also the matching of the same Epistle with the same Gospel, practically the same Epistles are used on 23 Sundays and 20 Holy Days; the same Gospels on 17 Sundays and 30 Holy Days. Entirely different Epistles are used on six Sundays and 14 Holy Days; different Gospels on seven Sundays and five Holy Days. Equivalent selections are transferred to other occasions in the case of 26 Epistles and 31 Gospels for Sundays, and for four of each on Holy Days.

These divergencies arose first of all in the fact that the Reformers followed the Sarum list in the main, though they have been increased at each of four revisions since. The Sarum provisions were wholly derived from the seventh-century Roman assignments, which they actually preserved in much more nearly their original form than the present Roman does: so that the dislocations are to be charged chiefly to the not very intelligent method with which the Roman Missal has assimilated the ancient material. The modern Roman differs from Sarum in three Epistles and six Gospels on Sundays, and five Epistles and four Gospels on Holy Days; transfers the same assignment to a different day in the case of 31 Epistles and 32 Gospels for Sundays, and one Epistle on Holy Days; and coincides with Sarum only for 21 Epistles and 18 Gospels on Sundays, 33 Epistles and 35 Gospels on Holy Days.

The First Prayer Book of 1549, besides making seven alterations in material which was Sarum but not Roman, eliminated one set of propers from a Sunday, and two from Holy Days; substituted two Epistles and one Gospel on Sundays, 15 Epistles and one Gospel on Holy Days; and transferred two Sunday Epistles and Gospels, and two Holy Day Epistles and four Gospels. On the other hand, Cranmer preferred the Roman sequence for the first five Sundays after Epiphany to the Sarum, and similarly with the Roman length of the Epistle for Pentecost XXIII (Trinity XXIV), and the Roman selection of the Epistle for St. Barnabas' Day, which he adopted in part; though this last may have been thought up independently.

The Second Prayer Book in 1552 eliminated the alternative provisions for Christmas and Easter, and added the pre-Reformation Gospel for Whitsunday to the Gospel for the Vigil, which was all that was given for this day in 1549. The revision of 1662 made new assignments for Epiphany VI, and restored the old Epistle for the Purification, both of which had been lacking since 1549; and adjusted the length of six Gospels. The American Book of 1892 restored the alternative services for Christmas and Easter (dropped in 1552), and also the Feast of the Transfiguration (eliminated at the Reformation), with the Roman Epistle and an altered Gospel. Our last revision in 1928 made new provisions for an alternative celebration on Whitsunday, and for the new liturgical day of Christmas II (taking its Gospel from the Roman Vigil of the Epiphany); restored the pre-Reformation Gospel for Maundy Thursday as an alternative; transferred two Epistles on Sundays and two on Holy Days; made substitutions for two Epistles and three Gospels; and altered the length of three selections. At the same time, the English and Scottish revisions made still further changes, which will be noted below.

Thus it is evident that there is nothing either unprecedented or improper in now making some needed adaptations of the Liturgical Lectionary as it has come down to us. Indeed, at several important points our present Prayer Book is decidedly behind the development of the latest British books. If the changes now suggested are more numerous that at any time since Cranmer, that is because this is the first time that the whole subject has been systematically studied for its own sake. As for a fear of further divergence from Roman standards, that has been appreciably counterbalanced by the proposed adoption of a considerable number of the Roman provisions, wherever they show distinctive merit.

Thus we are not advocating anything like a new system: only a more effective form of essentially the same system as that which prevails throughout the West, and which is in living continuity with that which St. Augustine brought to England.

The Seasons of the Christian Year

1. Advent

In the First Prayer Book, Cranmer followed the Sarum arrangement of the Sundays in Advent, which had stood unaltered from the seventh-century Roman lists. Rome, however, has since found the ancient provisions unsatisfactory, and made a radical rearrangement. While the Roman changes in some respects have caused worse evils than they cured, there are grave reasons for thinking that some changes are advisable.

Advent is really a season of twofold meaning, reflecting both the First and the Second Comings of our Lord. Primarily, and properly, it is a preparation for Christmas. Rome always rejected the Gallican tendency to make Advent a penitential season — a second Lent — and originally called these Sundays merely those Before the Nativity. It is significant that Sarum always observed them in white, not violet. Then the theme of the Second Advent at the end of the world was added, to provide an august background and the cosmic setting for the annual commemoration of the First Advent of our Lord in the flesh. But these overtones of reflection upon the Last Things were strictly secondary, and have been still further subordinated by the later development of the season in both Anglican and Roman lectionaries.

In the seventh century, Rome began the season with Matt. 21:1-9, the Triumphal Entry, selected as the most stirring and significant narrative available to dramatize the theme of the Advent of our Lord to his redeeming work. As such, it has of course to be treated in a quasi-allegorical rather than a strictly historical way. When, however, in the ninth century, the Church of Rome adopted this same Gospel for the Palm Sunday liturgy, in its true historical setting in the chronology of our Lord's life, they found themselves unable to think of it in a merely typological way, but only as the specific Coming of Christ to Jerusalem, and to his Passion. So they removed this Gospel from Advent Sunday, set the whole Advent series back one week, and filled in Advent IV with Luke 3:1-6, a third Gospel of John the Baptist as the Forerunner, and a doublet of the other two. This last is anything but a satisfactory solution.

Sarum, however, clung to Matt. 21:1-9 to the end of its days. The Reformers in the first English Prayer Book eliminated the Palm Sunday liturgy, along with all other interesting anomalies which had formerly distinguished the various seasons; so they had no reason to fault the Triumphal Entry here as a duplication. They displayed, perhaps, a slight uncertainty as to the entire appropriateness of this lection in this season, by lengthening it to verses 1-13 to include the Cleansing of the Temple — thus making the added point that this incident was a typical Coming to Judgment. If this Gospel is to be retained, and used typologically, this must be regarded as a successful move.

The Liturgical Commission has frequently been petitioned to initiate steps toward authorizing the present Advent Sunday Gospel as an alternative on Palm

Sunday — a provision which has been made in the English and Scottish books. More requests have been made for this change than for any other in the entire liturgical lectionary. Yet if this were done, in precisely this form, it might well be predicted that our Church would have the same experience that Rome has had, and that the continued use of this passage on Advent Sunday would become a practical impossibility. The Committee on the Epistles and Gospels originally proposed to deal with this problem in advance, rather than see the Church forced to do so at a later date. But the suggestion of any substitute for the Gospel of the Triumphal Entry on Advent Sunday met with determined opposition by the rest of the Liturgical Commission, as well as of most others whom we consulted. Admitting the general undesirability of what amounts to an allegorical use of historical narratives, they still felt that the 'typical' value of this incident made it the best possible beginning of the Christian Year. If Sarum could preserve it, so could we; and we had best cleave to our native Anglican tradition.

Consequently, the Triumphal Entry on Palm Sunday is now proposed in the simpler and more factual form of Mark 11:1-11; and the Cleansing of the Temple, that pivotal turning-point which actually precipitated the great tragedy of the Crucifixion, in Matt. 21:10-17, upon the Monday in Holy Week upon which it originally occurred. Both of these selections for Holy Week are preferable on their merits for that place; and employing them would reduce an outright duplication to a 'concord.'

But there are other problems in the Advent Gospels which are not so easily met. Our Gospel for Advent II (for Advent Sunday in the Roman), is Luke 21:25-33, the Signs of the End, the one absolute apocalyptic passage in the season. But since 1662, we have had a direct doublet of this in the form of Matt. 24:23-31 on Epiphany VI. The Matthean version is distinctly the better of the two; and moreover, it is virtually indispensable for the last Sunday after the Epiphany, which, as one of the two 'Wandering Sundays,' has an interesting dual use in the Calendar. It is only with the last four dates of Easter that it occurs in its nominal place as a Sunday after the Epiphany, where this Gospel presents our Lord's Coming at the end of the world as the final and supreme 'Epiphany.' But with the first twelve dates of Easter — i.e. something more than three-fourths of the time that it actually appears in the scheme for the year — Epiphany VI is employed as a Second Sunday Before Advent. Hence it may occur either three weeks before Advent II, or ten weeks thereafter. Now certainly the use of doublet passages is to be avoided in the limited provisions for the Sundays of the Christian Year; and even if any such doublets as now occur should be retained, it is intolerable that they should appear at any such close intervals. In other words, either the Gospel for Epiphany VI or for Advent II ought to be replaced. Rome uses Matt. 13:31-35, the Parables of the Mustard Seed and the Leaven, for Epiphany VI: but this, though in a vaguely apocalyptic context, is much too slight in content to be at all desirable.

For Advent II, we propose the finest of all passages on the moral meanings of the Second Coming, Matt. 25:31-40: "When the Son of man shall come in his glory, and all the holy angels with him," with all the august pageantry of the Last Judgment, and the deeply significant application, "Inasmuch as ye have done it unto one of the least of these my brethren, ye have done it unto me." This is a saying that in sublimity and profundity is not matched anywhere else in the Gospel — a perfect synthesis of faith and conduct, translating the Christian's mystic yearning for personal contact with his Lord into the most potent of all motives for effectual beneficence of life. This magnificent passage was unaccountably missing from the liturgical lectionary until the American revision of 1928 adopted it for marginal use for the Common of Saints. It is undoubtedly the best possible expression of the apocalyptic element of the Advent season, suited alike to the temporal expectation of the Incarnation, and to the cosmic and eternal significance of that event as well. We originally proposed it for Advent Sunday itself; and have no doubts whatever about the advisability of substituting it for the doublet Gospel on Advent II.

Incidentally, even if the Gospel of the Second Sunday were not a doublet, its concluding words contain an expression which makes it anything but suitable for an occasion which has been distinguished as 'Bible Sunday' ever since the Reformation brought in a new Collect for this day. The expression is: "Verily I say unto you, this generation shall not pass away, till all be fulfilled. Heaven and earth shall pass away: but my words shall not pass away." It is one of the more serious problems of scriptural interpretation that the early Church's expectation of a speedy end of the world, so vividly set forth in this very lection, was not fulfilled. It is a distinct inconvenience to have to avoid that issue, which stares us in the face in the present assignment for this 'Bible Sunday.'

There is also a real question about the Gospel appointed for Advent IV. John 1:19-28 appears in the earliest Roman lists of the seventh century. As this is the only Sunday following an Ember Week which did not stand 'vacant' of any provisions whatever at this period, it is evident that this is a pre-Christmas rather than an Advent or an Ember selection, chosen probably for the rather dim reason of its mention by St. John Baptist of one "who coming after me is preferred before me."

There are two objections to it: one is that it is in the wrong order, since it belongs to a stage of the Gospel narratives much anteceding the other lection on St. John Baptist, Matt. 11:2-10, for Advent III. The latter, which is quite effective, must of course stay where it is, since its mention of "my messenger, which shall prepare thy way before thee," has been incorporated into the Reformation Collect for that Sunday. The other reason is that the Johannine passage, when it is not paralleling the Gospel of the Sunday before, is a doublet of Mark 1:1-11 which our last revision adopted for Epiphany II. This new Gospel of our Lord's Baptism was an excellent addition to the Epiphany sequence; but it does not seem to have been realized that its version of "the voice of one crying in the wilderness" in a better setting, deprived the Gospel for Advent IV of the one really distinctive contribution which it made to the picture of the Precursor.

The net result has been "too much of John the Baptist." It was all very well for the American Lectionary of 1892 to fill up three Sundays of Advent at Morning Prayer with lessons on St. John Baptist as preparation for Christmas: indeed, this feature, partly discarded in 1928, was restored in the Lectionary of 1943. But enough is enough. The new Epiphany-tide Gospel has so impaired the effectiveness of that for Advent IV as virtually to compel the selection of some better choice to conclude this significant season.

A real enrichment, and an important strengthening of the great theme of the Incarnation, would be effected by doing in this sequence of Advent Gospels exactly what we are now doing in the course of lessons at Morning Prayer, and incorporating the Gospel of the Annunciation, in the form of Luke 1:26b-38 (beginning, "The Angel Gabriel ").

This move would certainly be in accord with the natural trend of the Advent Sundays. In all lectionaries, the nearer we come to Christmas, the less stress there is upon the subordinate 'Second Advent' theme, and the stronger is the sense of an immediate expectation of the Incarnation. Hitherto, however, there has remained a distinct hiatus of thought between the *Vox clamantis* of Advent IV and the events of Christmas Day. Who has not felt this; especially when this Sunday actually falls upon Christmas Eve? (Rome evades this last, by the way, by permitting the mass of the Vigil of Christmas, containing the Annunciation to Joseph, to supplant that of Advent IV when Christmas occurs on Monday.)

True, the Annunciation occurs as a festival at its relative chronological place in the year. But as this is always in Lent, the rules for precedence prevent its ever being celebrated upon a Sunday. It seems a pity that this Gospel, in some ways the very strongest of all those bearing upon the Incarnation, should never be read "when the most number of the people come together": since under modern conditions attendance at any weekday service of however exalted a rank is unhappily (save for Christmas itself) a marginal matter.

What we are proposing is actually to take for Advent IV the Roman Gospel for the Advent Ember Wednesday, just as Rome has filled up this Sunday with the Gospel for the Ember Saturday. This Ember Wednesday indeed was the native Roman commemoration of the Annunciation, before the adoption of the feast on March 25 from the East. The 'Liturgical Movement' in the Roman Church makes much of what they call 'the Golden Mass' on this day, for pre-Christmas services for their young people. This Gospel also has other strong associations with the season in the Roman missal, being assigned to all votive Masses of the Blessed Virgin in Advent; the Franciscans and some Spanish churches use it for the festival of the *Exspectatio partûs* on December 18; and it occurs in part on the feast of the Immaculate Conception on December 8, which outranks Advent II in Roman use.

Disregarding any side-issues of 'Mariolatry,' which in any event have nothing to do with the position of our Church, the important fact remains that there are three figures which point the way to the Coming of our Lord: Isaiah, John the Baptist, and the Virgin Mary. Isaiah dominates the weekdays of Advent; the Precursor is featured on two of the Sundays; and it would seem very well to conclude the season with the mention of the mother of our Lord, and with that prophetic event without which Christmas itself would not bear its Christian meaning.

Therefore, despite the boldness of these measures, these reassignments of the Advent Gospels are recommended, in order to integrate the teaching of the season, and to present it in a consistent order. We consider that they would bring out the message which the seventh-century assignments were evidently trying to present, but with considerable indirection and obscurity, and which the distinctly inept Roman attempts to clarify resulted only in transforming into a confusion worse confounded.

For one further detail in this season: Dr. Easton comments on the Epistle for Advent III: "The opening verse is an admirable text for preaching on the ministry, though it is often egregiously misused as if it taught the dignity instead of the humility of the clergy. If used for an ordination sermon it should be taken in connection with 3:21-23 which it immediately follows."[1] Accordingly, a better balance of teaching would be obtained by lengthening this Epistle from 1 Cor. 4:1-5 to 3:21b-4:5 (beginning, "All things are yours ").

2. Christmas

The arrangement of the Gospels in Christmastide, which set forth the events connected with the Nativity, leaves a great deal to be desired. It is distinctly unfortunate that we should commemorate the Massacre of the Innocents before the Circumcision, and the Flight into Egypt and Return to Nazareth on Christmas II before the Epiphany; to say nothing of the incident of Christ in the Temple at the age of twelve on Epiphany I, before the Feast of the Purification on February 2.

a) Ancient Development of the Christmas Season

The observance of Christmas Day seems to have originated somewhere near the year 300 in Rome. The narrative lections were confined to the Gospel of St. Luke, which was itself of Roman provenance. Luke 2:1-14, the proclamation of the Nativity to the Shepherds, was read at the midnight Vigil service, and Luke 2:15-20, the Visit of the Shepherds to the Manger, on Christmas Day. Then the

---

1. B. S. Easton and H. C. Robbins, *The Eternal Word in the Modern World* (Scribners, 1937), 35.

Octave of the Nativity continued with Luke 2:21-32, the Circumcision and the Presentation in the Temple, to the end of the Song of Simeon. This plan was of course perfectly simple, and sufficiently comprehensive, so far as the Lucan account was concerned.

In the course of the fourth century, this native Roman observance on December 25 was brought into competition with the parallel and independent Eastern celebration of the Nativity on January 6. The Eastern Church in like manner based its commemoration on the Antiochene Gospel of St. Matthew, originally reading Matt. 2:1-12, the Visit of the Magi, on its Nativity Day, and Matt. 1, the Genealogy, Annunciation to Joseph, and the Birth and Naming, on the Sunday before.

This conflict was eventually resolved by each region's adopting the other's festival. The East accepted the date of December 25, and transferred the Visit of the Magi to it; continuing with St. Matthew's account of our Lord's Baptism on January 6. The West accepted the original Eastern Epistles of the Nativity, in Titus 2 and 3, which still remain on January 6 in the Eastern rite, for two of its masses on Christmas, and the Eastern Gospel of the Magi for the new feast of the Epiphany.

The Western reconciliation of these doublet festivals, and of the added Gospel narrative, was as acceptable as any could be. St. Matthew certainly intimates that the formal Naming of the Child took place before the Visit of the Wise Men — i.e., the Circumcision should come before the Epiphany. The only anachronism, so far, in the pattern, was the fact that the Gospel for the Octave of Christmas went on from the Circumcision to the Presentation in the Temple forty days after — an event which was certainly later than the Visit of the Magi. But the content of this matter was something which was desirable to read in the Nativity Season, and the chronological difficulty could hardly be said even to have appeared before the adoption of the Purification in the sixth century, and even then it was not felt until the Reformation.

The first real confusion was introduced by the new Feast of the Holy Innocents on the third day after Christmas, which came in from the Carthaginian Calendar in the fifth century. Its Gospel was originally Matt. 2:13-23, comprising not only the Massacre of the Innocents, but the Flight into Egypt and the Return to Nazareth. All this follows the story of the Magi in the text of St. Matthew, but was made to precede the Circumcision in the order of observances!

By the sixth century, a third mass was added to the provisions for Christmas Day. No more narrative matter being available for this purpose, the purely 'theological' passage of John 1:1-14 was adopted. That it was of later origin than the other Gospels for Christmas is shown by the fact that it was, and is, not this Gospel, but that for the second celebration on Christmas, Luke 2:15-20, which is employed in the Roman use for a vacant day within the Octave.

Though the Innocents' Day still had its extended lection, by this time the latter part of it, Matt. 2:19-23, the Flight into Egypt and the Return to Nazareth, had been appropriated also for the Vigil of the Epiphany, as something which was already there in the tract between Christmas and Epiphany, and certainly associated with the Visit of the Magi — though unfortunately as a result rather than a preparation for that event.

The Feast of the Purification on February 2 had also come in, reading Luke 2:22-32 from the Gospel of the Octave of Christmas. And a continuation of that passage, Luke 2:33-40, Simeon and Anna, concluding with the Return to Nazareth, had been imported to serve for the only Sunday without other provisions for a coinciding feast which could occur in the Roman Calendar between Christmas and Epiphany, thanks to their observance of St. Silvester on December 31 and the Vigil of the Epiphany on January 5. This final confusion of the chronology of the period was perpetrated in all innocence, and in fact made the situation which already existed no worse. The Presentation material was employed on the Octave of Christmas, and had been so used from the beginning, and found congruous with Christmastide. Its continuation was equally unobjectionable (even if not particularly valuable in itself), except for the final Return to Nazareth: and that really bad chronological contradiction had implanted itself on the Epiphany Vigil, and went back to the one primary and irremediable blunder of the North African Church in attaching the Day of the Holy Innocents to the Feast of the Nativity, instead of putting it after the Epiphany.

In the course of the next century or two, Matt. 1:18-21, the Annunciation to Joseph, was prefixed to Christmas Day as the Gospel for a Vigil in the new sense of a service the previous morning. The Gospel for Holy Innocents' was shortened to its present dimensions, to avoid duplicating the portion already appropriated for the Vigil of the Epiphany. And the Gospel for the Octave of Christmas, now first called the Circumcision, relinquished the long portion for the Purification, and was thus reduced to the unprecedented dimensions of the single verse Luke 2:21.

Such was the evolution of the provisions for the season of the Nativity as they appeared in the Sarum Missal, and remain to this day in the Roman. They do not represent a consistent plan, but a rather haphazard growth. The later occasions of the Epiphany Vigil and the feast of the Purification were supplied simply by a division of the extended lections formerly provided for the Holy Innocents and the Octave of Christmas; and the Christmas Vigil furnished with a logical supplementary passage, and the Sunday after Christmas with an illogical one. The successive changes were most conservatively made, in strict accordance with the provisions in effect at the time. It is neither necessary nor possible to blame anyone for making them. But this does not alter the fact that the final result is very unfortunate.

It would help immeasurably for the removing of chronological contradictions and the presenting of the whole 'harmonized' narrative in something like a consistent order, if the Calendar could be altered, and the Holy Innocents placed in the Octave of the Epiphany instead of the Octave of Christmas. That, of course, cannot now be done. We cannot interfere with that triad of feasts which follows Christmas, and which has been enshrined in the hearts of Christians for a millennium and a half. Of these feasts, it seems that St. Stephen and St. John were actually observed before Christmas was, since the Armenian Church, which has always clung to the earliest Eastern celebration of the Nativity on January 6, nevertheless keeps these two commemorations in December. The Innocents' Day, of course, was intentionally added to the Calendar on the nearest day to Christmas available. But this triad has now been assimilated into a unit of thought — as by the rather fanciful but devotionally useful classifying of St. John as a Martyr 'in will but not in deed,' of the Innocents as Martyrs 'in deed though not in will,' and St. Stephen as a Martyr 'both in will and deed' — so that it is not now possible to separate them. Certainly the children of our Church Schools would not thank us for removing the Innocents' Day from its proximity to Christmas, just to satisfy some fussy adults! And it does not seem there is much we can do, with both the Church of the Past and the Church of the Future against us.

b) Assignment of Gospels

At the Reformation, the Epistle and Gospel for the Sarum midnight mass was retained for the first celebration on Christmas Day, those for the third mass for the principal celebration; but the provisions for the mass at dawn were dropped, apparently because Cranmer wanted its Gospel, Luke 2:15-20, to supplement the single verse of Luke 2:21 which, as we have seen, was all that was left of the former Gospel on the Feast of the Circumcision after the transfer of nearly all its matter to the Purification.

The Prayer Book of 1552 dropped the early service also (leaving only the 'theological' Gospel of John 1:1-14 on Christmas Day): and the Church of England has never really got it back yet, save in the optional provision in the appendix of the Proposed Book of 1928; though the American Book of 1892 restored it for us, and the Scottish of 1929 did the same.

But a number of requests have been received for the restoration of the Epistle and Gospel for the dawn service in the Sarum Missal, namely Titus 3:4-7 and Luke 2:15-20. It would certainly seem valuable to have the Visit of the Shepherds read on Christmas Day, confirming and completing the prophecy of the Angels at the first celebration. It might be hoped that this move would do something to restore interest in the services of Christmas Day itself, now often thrown out of balance by the attention drawn to the midnight celebration in many parishes.

Incidentally, these three propers for Christmas, as well as the two provisions for Easter and Whitsunday, should be arranged in the Prayer Book in the order in which they will be used: not those for the principal service first, and the early celebration afterward — a backward scheme confusing in some degree to everyone, from the laity who try to follow them, to liturgical students who desire to refer to them.

For the Sunday within the Christmas Octave, Cranmer rightly rejected the Sarum Luke 2:33-40, Simeon and Anna and the Return to Nazareth, which, as we have noted, was inconsiderable in content, and chronologically out of place. Instead, however, he prescribed something of a liturgical monstrosity, namely all 25 verses of Matt. 1, including the formidable genealogy from Adam to Joseph! It was not until 1662 that this was shortened to Matt. 1:18-25. This represents the Sarum Gospel for the mass of the Christmas Vigil, containing the Annunciation to Joseph, lengthened to cover also the Birth and Naming of the Child. But even this is not altogether satisfactory. On this Sunday after Christmas, it is not quite in order to make a new start, harking back to events considerably before the Nativity,[2] especially in the quite independent account of another Evangelist from the one we have been following for the Christmas narratives; nor yet to anticipate the feast of the Circumcision with St. Matthew's record of the Naming. It would be better to reserve this passage to introduce the Epiphany, as we shall see presently; and for Christmas I simply to repeat the Gospel of Luke 2:15-20 which we have newly restored to the second celebration on Christmas Day. It will be remembered that this, as the original Western Gospel for the day of the Nativity, is the one which Rome still uses for any unappropriated weekdays in the Octave so that it may be assigned to this Sunday with equal justice.

It must not be forgotten that in Christmastide the customary priorities of the rest of the Christian Year are actually reversed: it is the Fixed Days which are primary in both origin and importance; the Sundays are entirely derivative and dependent. And the repetition of this Gospel from this one of the three Christmas services can hardly prove burdensome, since four of the seven days upon which it can fall are already occupied by festivals which will displace its reading upon this Sunday. Even where there is a daily celebration, it would not be used upon more than five weekdays: which surely does not seem too much for the rehearsing of this basic narrative.

The reader will have gathered that we do not propose to continue including this passage on the Feast of the Circumcision. Cranmer was perfectly right about one thing — a one-verse Gospel is not to be regarded as a liturgical possibility. But it does not seem a good idea to retain this narrative which precedes that one verse in St. Luke's account, which will be so much more significant on Christmas Day itself, and so much more useful on the Sunday within the Octave, than it

---

2. Cf. Easton and Robbins, *The Eternal Word*, 40.

ever has been on this Octave Day. It would be so much better to do precisely what the earliest Western lectionary did, and continue the one verse proper to the day with the material which follows it, reading Luke 2:21-32. This would restore completely the original scheme of the fourth century, whereby Luke 2:1-32, containing all the significant parts of the narrative of the Nativity by this Evangelist, was read in its entirety upon Christmas and its Octave Day.

The desirability of having this very lovely and very meaningful passage read within the Octave of the Nativity quite outweighs the minor difficulties of chronology. The restoration of this passage would indeed restore the duplication of its matter on the Feast of the Purification, which the eighth and ninth centuries conscientiously removed after the introduction of that festival in the sixth or seventh centuries. But that matter is of no great importance, since the Circumcision and the Purification fall upon different days of the week, and hence both cannot appear upon Sunday in the same year.

We have here in fact a conflict between two different systems of commemoration of the events of our Lord's life, which might be called anniversarial, and biographical. The one attempts to observe the incidents associated with the Nativity on their relative dates of the year: the Annunciation nine months, the Nativity of St. John Baptist six months, before Christmas, and the Circumcision eight days, the Epiphany twelve days, and the Purification forty days, thereafter. The other devotes itself to furnishing a condensed summary of the salient facts of Christ's redeeming work in the space from Christmas to the Ascension. Each system has it own peculiar effectiveness; because of their different bases, each is capable at times of seeming to jar with the other; yet this should not be allowed to preclude the best use of either. We have urged that the anniversarial date of the Annunciation should not inhibit the biographical employment of this matter for the immediate foreshadowing of the Nativity in the Advent season. On the other side, we find Dr. Easton complaining that the Purification, interjected into "the orderly sequence of Christ's manifestations" in the post-Epiphany season finds us "recalled suddenly to the Infancy," and stigmatizes it as "a blunder, which is particularly grave in those years when the Purification follows Septuagesima."[3] Yet obviously we can hardly obliterate this anniversary on such grounds. We may well, however, counterbalance this by duplicating this 'Infancy' passage on the Circumcision, where it will be most effective in rounding out the biographical summary. There is a particular appropriateness, which perhaps the early Western Church was in better position to appreciate than medieval times, in conjoining the two formal rites of the Circumcision and the ceremony of the Redemption of the Firstborn at the Presentation in the Temple.

We have observed that the Western use of the seventh century had no need for separate provisions for a Second Sunday after Christmas. At the time of

---

3. *The Eternal Word*, 258.

the Reformation, the Sarum Missal, like the present Roman, had only one day, December 30, on which even Christmas I would be regularly used, "sive Dominica sive non"; and none at all for Christmas II, as the dates January 2-4 were completely filled by the Octave Days of the Christmas triad of feasts, and January 5 of course was the Vigil of the Epiphany. The simplified Reformation Calendar, however, cleared January 2-5: but no provision was made for a Sunday in this period, other than the direction to use the Epistle and Gospel for the Circumcision until the Epiphany, on a Sunday or weekdays alike. The Prayer Book of 1662 made the entry of Christmas II in the Calendar of Lessons; and our revision of 1928 erected the Sunday into a full liturgical day. We have noted that the Gospel then adopted, Matt. 2:19-23, the Flight into Egypt and the Return to Nazareth, is painfully out of chronological course, containing matter which, if used at all, ought to come after the Visit of the Wise Men on the Epiphany, and not before it. We have also seen that there was perhaps some excuse for putting this lection on the Epiphany Vigil in the seventh century — it would be no worse having it there than on the Innocents' Day, from which it was taken; but it was much too trustful of our revisers to follow the lead of Rome by bringing back into the sequence a chronological contradiction of which we were well rid.

Accordingly, the English and Scottish books, not seeing any further narrative material which would fit into the pattern, have provided for Christmas II the short section of John 1:14-18, linking on some further teaching on the theological meaning of the Incarnation to that already given at the principal celebration on Christmas Day. But it is doubtful if more theology is needed in a season where the events themselves are so charged with their own significance.

Yet there is in fact a narrative selection which is perfectly suitable for the Sunday between the Circumcision and the Epiphany. This of course is Matt. 1:18-25, which we have been reserving for this place. Used here, it gives a brief and effective summing up of the preceding events of the Birth and Naming of the Child, and also furnishes the best of introductions to the supplementary story of the Visit of the Magi, which follows immediately upon it in the text of St. Matthew.

The result of the foregoing reassignments would be, not only that the primitive Western account of the Nativity according to St. Luke would be read in its right order on the Western festival of Christmas and its Octave, but that the original Eastern account according to St. Matthew would be concentrated upon the Eastern festival of the Epiphany, and the Sunday immediately before it. The two narratives would be completely disentangled from each other, and their inversions entirely straightened out — with the single exception of the day of the Holy Innocents, which must perforce be left 'out of course.'

c) Assignment of Epistles

There are only two of the Epistles in this tract which seem to need any attention. On Christmas II, our revisers in 1928, who adopted the Sarum Gospel for the

Epiphany Vigil, found nothing there to serve as an Epistle, since Sarum simply repeated the Epistle for Christmas I. Apparently they derived no inspiration from the incident of the Flight into Egypt: which really (with all respect) might have given them some pause as to the value of that lection in this place. Be that as it may, they wound up by making a new selection of their own, Isa. 61:1-3, designed simply to give an arresting keynote to the first Sunday of the civil year.

Having restored a really significant Nativity Gospel to Christmas II, we now propose as its Epistle the wonderful passage in 1 Pet. 2:1-10, not now used at the Liturgy, as an effective interpretation of the moral meanings of the Divine Infancy and the importance of the Incarnation as the Corner Stone of Holy Church; and in both senses a strong selection suitable to this 'New Year's Sunday.'

This would release Isa. 63:1-3 for the Feast of the Circumcision, which is likewise New Year's Day. The Church of Rome in the seventh century took distinct account of the fact that the Octave of the Nativity fell upon the first day of the civil year, by providing a special *Missa ad probibendum ab idolis*, in protest against the license of the pagan orgies ushering in the New Year — a license which we must regretfully admit is still with us thirteen centuries later.

We have seen that the original observance of this day was as a generalized Octave of the Nativity, with two incidents of the Infancy, which we now propose to restore entire. It has been only since about the ninth century that the Purification has been allowed to impoverish this day in the Western use of all but the single verse recounting the Circumcision 'on the eighth day,' which has resulted in a considerable emphasis upon a not very edifying fact.

The Sarum and Roman Epistle for this occasion was for the Nativity Octave only, repeating that for the Dawn Mass of Christmas Day. Cranmer, with the laudable idea of securing both variety and coverage of Scripture, substituted Rom. 4:8-14; a selection which has been justly criticized as an essay on the practice of circumcision, quite unsuited to the Feast of the Circumcision of our Lord.

The English and Scottish books in their last revisions propose instead Eph. 2:11-18. This, no doubt, is the most elevated and spiritualized of all the various Pauline rationalizations of this Jewish custom, and a very weighty passage, with, if anything, almost too many important new ideas suggested. We may note Dr. Easton's comment on this day: "In the Pauline theology the fact that Christ was born under the Law is utilized for certain incidental arguments but is no vital part of the Apostle's thinking. Reformation hyper-Paulinism endeavoured to go further and make Christ's circumcision essential to soteriology; an attempt not to be commended."[4] It is questionable whether just this kind of hyper-Paulinism would not be given a new lease of life by such phrases in the British selection as "But now in Christ Jesus ye who sometimes were afar off are made

---

4. *The Eternal Word*, 253.

nigh by the blood of Christ . . . having abolished in his flesh the enmity, even the law of commandments contained in ordinances," and so forth.

Whether or not our revisers in 1928 knew of this British substitute, the fact is that they decided to reject altogether any attempt to stress the 'circumcision' theme in the Epistle, and instead selected Phil. 2:9-11, whose import is entirely upon the 'Holy Name' of Jesus. This idea was excellent in itself; but the passage is not suitable. In the first place, it is used in a highly 'accommodated' sense, which in fact relies upon a very widespread but very fundamental misconception. As Dr. Easton says, "Traditional miscomprehension has created the only real difficulty by taking 'the name of Jesus' to mean 'the name which is Jesus' instead of 'the name which Jesus received' at His exaltation. This name is 'Lord'; it is in recognition of his Lordship that every knee bows."[5] Besides, this selection is only a snippet or fragment of an august argument of St. Paul's, which is much more adequately represented in the Epistle for Palm Sunday, from which this mere excerpt was somewhat injudiciously torn. Borrowing from one Epistle to make another Epistle is in general as little laudable as the 'scissors-and-paste' manufacture of a Collect out of phrases from other Collects: certainly it should be avoided when possible.

But though there are some magnificent *phrases* in the New Testament about the Name of Jesus, there does not appear to be any other *passage* which is suitable for an Epistle here. Some who have objected to so abusing the passage from Philippians have suggested Acts 4:8-12, which is the Roman Epistle for the Feast of the Holy Name. But though this selection culminates in the incomparable verse, "There is none other name under heaven given among men, whereby we must be saved," nevertheless it is a part of a narrative which neither in this form nor in the full text of the Acts is completely told, so as to appear both abrupt and irrelevant. The sudden appearance of the vigorous personalities of St. Peter and the Jewish Rulers, and the (unexplained) figure of the Impotent Man, would certainly be felt to be an intrusion upon the Feast of the Circumcision of our Lord.

Hence it seems best to abandon the idea of 1928 of making the Circumcision a sort of Anglican Festival of the Holy Name; and, as before suggested, simply to transfer Isa. 61:1-13 from the New Year's Sunday to this New Year's Day.

3. Epiphany

The Gospels for the Sundays after the Epiphany present an intelligent plan, as they all set forth significant 'Epiphanies' or Manifestations of the Incarnate Life. The only one at all questionable is that for Epiphany III, the Miracle of Cana, which can hardly be taken as factual by any modern mind; but it has so embedded itself in

---

5. *The Eternal Word*, 124.

the popular idea of the season, and in what might be called the poetry of religion, that any proposal to touch it would meet with an impossible amount of protest.

As for the Epistles, ever since the seventh century there has been a short course from Romans 12 on Epiphany I to III; to which Cranmer added Rom. 13:1-7 on Epiphany IV to express that Royal Supremacy on which he relied so heavily, and in the end, so tragically for himself. The purpose of this course is very obscure — indeed, it may be said that its basic appropriateness to the season is hardly understood at all in the Church: and there has been a certain amount of pressure to alter it, from two different points of view.

Dr. Easton has criticized the division of Romans 12 into verses 1-5, 6-16a, and 16b-21, which has remained unaltered since the seventh century, as not corresponding to the units of thought, and indicated a preference for the paragraphing of the Revised Version, which consists of verses 1-2, 3-8, and 9-21.[6]

But this would cause the Epistles to be of very uneven length; and though this alteration has been carefully considered, the Committee reached the opinion that for any purpose except perhaps for exhaustive exposition as wholes, the passages are in actually better balance as they are. In other words, it is quite possible that the man who made the liturgical assignments knew his own business quite as well as the paragrapher of the Revised Version, if not better.

Others have expressed some discontent with this 'mere course-reading' of essentially 'moralistic' matter, and advanced the suggestion that these four Epistles be supplanted in whole or in part by selections from the two preceding chapters of Romans, which afford some very fine passages on Christian Missions, which might carry out the idea of the Day of the Epiphany, in our sub-title of the Feast, "The Manifestation of Christ to the Gentiles." This idea looks very attractive: and indeed Rom. 10:1-12, Rom. 10:13-18, and Rom. 11:25-27, 33-36 would furnish Epistles admirably suited to this end.

Nevertheless, this would be doing precisely what we have said before that in principle we ought not to do: it would be remoulding the Christian Year to what we might think it ought to be, instead of confining ourselves to a better interpretation of what it is. And understood or not, there is in fact a reason for the ancient provisions. These Epistles were not, as might be thought, a mere lazy relapse into 'course-reading' for a tract of 'common Sundays' which did not matter: they were vitally integrated to the idea of a passage which was the original Epistle for the Day of the Epiphany, and which we still have, at the head of the lections on the Incarnation.

That passage is Titus 2:11-15, which now appears at our first celebration on Christmas Day. To this day it is the Epistle for the Epiphany in the Eastern Church, where it originated. As early as the fourth century, it was so used in the West, being transferred to the first mass of Christmas after the 'doublet'

---

6. *The Eternal Word*, 50, 55, 60.

festivals of Christmas and Epiphany were discriminated. Indeed, it was this Epistle which is probably responsible for the adoption of the term 'Epiphany' in the West (the East calls it the 'Theophany'): note the first word, ἐπεφάνη, and the word ἐπιφάνειαν in verse 13.

Now the key-note of this Epistle is an extremely practical application of faith to morals: "The grace of God that bringeth salvation hath appeared to all men, teaching us that, denying ungodliness and worldly lusts, we should live soberly, righteously, and godly in this present world." It is these *moral consequences* of the Manifestation of our Lord in human life which are so well expanded and applied in the little series from Romans, radiating from the comparable point of departure in its exordium in Rom. 12:2: "And be ye not conformed to this world: but be ye transformed by the renewing of your minds."

While all this ancient history is not commonly known in the Church, nevertheless it may be said with some confidence that the appropriateness of the underlying idea has always been felt instinctively: that the religion of the Incarnation must be applied in practice, or it is no religion; that the new divine forces manifested in the human life of Christ must be manifested in our lives also. Without this effective series of passages on applied religion, this tract of the year would stand in some real danger of being merely theological: so we should resist the specious temptation to change them. The themes contained in these four Epistles are some of the most incisive, and most practical, anywhere in Scripture outside the Sermon on the Mount. They certainly cannot be spared from the plan for the Christian Year: and as certainly they should not be removed from this portion of it, where they give so adequate and so needed an application of the great event of the Incarnation to the circumstances of our daily lives.

As to the Gentiles' theme, that has been adequately taken care of by 'seeding' a number of the best lessons for missionary purposes in the provisions for Morning and Evening Prayer on the Sundays after Epiphany. In the Lectionary, that can be done by way of enriching the meaning of the season, without changing its traditional character; but an alteration of the plan of the Epistles would be a definite impoverishment.

4. Lent

Some concern has been expressed about the fact that the Epistles for Lent II and III are both closely concerned with carnal sins — so closely indeed that these Epistles almost appear as doublets of each other, saying much the same thing in slightly different terms.

There is really something in this criticism. No one can doubt the advisability of warning even the most proper and most cultured people of the 'deceits of the flesh' in the bluntest and frankest terms — particularly in the season of Lent. But it is a serious question whether the same theme is profitable for reiterated treatment on two successive Sundays.

Of the two, the Epistle for Lent III is on the whole decidedly preferable; especially as in that for Lent II, certain gloomy speculations on the part of the commentators have attached detrimental and not well authenticated meanings to such words as 'matter,' and 'vessel,' which may color the mind of the expositor, even when he rejects them.

It would be a real enrichment if, instead of this reiterated emphasis on carnal sins, we replaced the Epistle for Lent II with one of the 'missionary' passages from Romans which we were reluctantly unable to accept for Epiphany-tide. This message is present, but obscurely, in the present Gospel for this Sunday. If that Gospel is to be retained (which we will discuss in a moment), it would need exactly this sort of support. If it is to be supplanted, this theme is nevertheless in place on an 'Ember Sunday'; and in any case, it would seem most desirable to present it in the season of Lent, with its full congregations. To go with the present Gospel, perhaps Rom. 10:12-21 would be the best selection.

But a suggestion has been made to us that we might displace the Gospel, Matt. 15:21-28, the incident of the Woman of Canaan, which comes down to us from the Sarum list, in favor of the Roman choice for this Sunday, which is Matt. 17:1-9, the account of the Transfiguration. It is true that the present Gospel is rather unsatisfactory: it has the least content of any in Lent; and many have been unable to escape a feeling of acute discomfort at the open affront with which our Lord saw fit to try the woman's faith. It was an awkward moment! And it is likewise true that this is the only Gospel in Lent which is out of its proper chronological sequence in the events of our Lord's life. All the rest throughout the season are chosen in strict biographical order. But the Gospel for Lent II on this pattern ought to come between those for Lent IV and V. The reason for this irregularity in the time-scheme, as well as for the inadequate character of the Gospel, is that it was never designed to be a Sunday Gospel at all. Sarum probably derived it from a former weekday service (Rome still places it on the preceding Thursday) to fill up what originally had been an actually 'vacant' Sunday, with no liturgical provisions of its own, which was the case in early Western use for all of the Sundays following the Ember Weeks, except that in Advent.

But in these respects, the Transfiguration is not one whit better. It also belongs in the chronological interval between Lent IV and V. It also was a filling of the vacant Sunday with weekday matter — in this case merely repeating the Gospel for the Ember Saturday the day before. There is of course not the slightest objection to helping ourselves to a Roman assignment, when it is a good one. But apart from the concluding mention of the coming event of the Resurrection (which, by the time the Transfiguration actually occurred in our Lord's life, was very near), there is nothing proper to Lent in this incident. Thus the source of this lection was just as accidental in the Roman scheme as in the English; its place in the continuous synopsis of the life of Christ is precisely as dislocated; its contribution to the teaching of the season just as remote. It may be predicted that an attempt to introduce into Lent matter which we have always regarded as purely festal would be felt to be a violent and gratuitous intrusion.

If one desires to fill this original *lacuna* with something which exactly fits the time-pattern of the rest of the Lenten Sundays, and which has some appropriateness to the general tenor of the season, about the only suitable choice would seem to be Matt. 7:24-29, the telling conclusion of the three chapters of the Sermon on the Mount with the parable of 'the House on the Rock and the House on the Sand.' This, in our judgment, would be a very considerable strengthening of the Lenten teaching. This parable is one of the strongest of the Gospel lections which the unplanned evolution of the Christian Year has allowed to be omitted from the Liturgical Lectionary. It might best be placed in this location; though it could go on Trinity XXI, where there is a case of supplanting a doublet lection. If it is to go here, then the best 'missionary' Epistle to accompany it would perhaps be Rom. 11:25-27, 33-36.

On Lent IV, the Epistle is the notorious 'Hagar-Sinai' passage, which has provoked a maximum amount of objection from the clergy of the Church. It was originally chosen at Rome for the occasion of the papal 'Station' or official Bishop's Visitation to the local parish church which bore the name of *Santa Croce in Gerusalemme*: the purpose being to pay it a discerning compliment in the form of the beautiful verse, "But Jerusalem which is above is free, which is the mother of us all." Unfortunately, this verse is dearly bought at the expense of the contentious and intensely rabbinical argument in which it is embedded, and which most clergy and all laity find simply bewildering.

The English and Scottish books offer the alternative of Heb. 12:22-24. This preserves the allusion to the 'heavenly Jerusalem'; but it concludes with the note of 'the blood of sprinkling,' which would be much more appropriate to Passion Sunday than to this traditional 'Refreshment Sunday' on Mid-Lent.

Why should an Anglican Church be at pains to preserve that early local Roman note at all? Its value, after all, is only archeological, and its interest the monopoly of the historical liturgiologist. What is really needed for this Sunday is a passage for the Epistle which strikes the 'Refreshment' note; which contributes a genuine thought of its own to the teaching of the Lenten season, without overdoing it by anticipating Passion-tide; and which will make a good introduction to the Gospel of the Sunday, which is the Feeding of the Five Thousand, and which, as we shall observe later, the Church originally intended to be a picture and an allegory on the largest scale of the Eucharistic Feast. All of these *desiderata* will be found in Isa. 55:1-7: one of the supreme prophetic passages, one which has always been one of the chief glories of the Lenten lessons at the Offices, and one which most thoroughly deserves inclusion in the Liturgical Lectionary.

On Passion Sunday, a good many people seem to be distinctly uncomfortable about the Gospel. It must be admitted that its setting is most unfortunate, being a violent quarrel between Jesus and the Jews, exacerbated by the employment of unrestrained abuse on both sides. These characteristics would have been fatal to the use of a passage of lesser weight. But the very heat of the argument is made to distill that supreme assertion, "Before Abraham was, I AM": setting forth our Lord's claim to share in the eternal being of God. The sublimity of that statement is unmatched in the New Testament. Its value for Christology cannot be exaggerated. From it we properly infer the infinite and eternal significance of the Passion. Yet that is only an inference, and not an immediate one by any means. If we examine carefully the text of this Gospel, it will be found to contain very little that is directly appropriate to Passion Sunday. In that respect, perhaps its most significant statement is "If a man keep my saying, he shall never see death," which conveys — though again indirectly — the idea of the redemptive power of the Passion.

A passage lacking these grave defects, and much better adapted to express the real meaning of this day would be John 12:23-32, containing not one but many such sayings of the greatest cogency: "The hour is come, that the Son of man should be glorified; . . . Except a grain of wheat fall into the ground and die; . . . For this cause came I unto this hour; . . . I, if I be lifted up from the earth, will draw all men unto me." However much one may regret the awe-inspiring climax of the present Gospel, there would seem little doubt that the one proposed would be found of much greater spiritual profit.

5. Holy Week

The provisions for Palm Sunday and Holy Week present some problems. We have preserved most of the main outlines of the ancient plan, but with some modifications which have not proved altogether successful in practice.

The most important matter, in both the Sarum and the Roman Missals, was to secure the reading of the narratives of the Passion entire, according to each of the four evangelists. This was done by assigning all (or nearly all) of two chapters to each day: St. Matthew to Palm Sunday, St. Mark to Tuesday, St. Luke to Wednesday, and St. John to Good Friday. Palm Sunday was further distinguished by prefacing the Mass of the Passion by the liturgy for the Blessing of the Palms, containing another Epistle and Gospel, of which the latter was the Triumphal Entry according to St. Matthew. Monday in Holy Week had most of John 12: the incident of Mary of Bethany anointing Jesus 'against the day of his burying,' the Triumphal Entry again, etc. Maundy Thursday (which, like all other Thursdays of the year, had no service of its own before the eighth century — Thursday was 'Jupiter's Day' in classical use, and the early Christians avoided that day completely) was filled in with John 13:1-15, Jesus' washing his disciples' feet at the Last Supper. Easter Even had a long vigil service, ending with the first mass of Easter: originally held at midnight, though now anticipated to Saturday morning.

At the Reformation, Cranmer, in the name of simplicity, swept away all the special ceremonies and features of these services, and reduced them to the same uniform pattern as the rest of the year. Thus all mention of the Triumphal Entry vanished from what Cranmer called simply the Sixth Sunday in Lent — though the popular name survived, until it was restored in our Prayer Book of 1928. The Passion according to St. Mark was divided between Monday and Tuesday, that according to St. Luke between Wednesday and Thursday; and on Easter Even Cranmer invented an entirely new commemoration of the Burial of Christ, which was a chronologically correct commemoration of the day in the Tomb, and had useful connections of thought with the Easter Eve Baptisms; but its Scriptures had no precedent except for a like individuality in the Mozarabic Rite in Spain.

In 1662, the two-chapter Gospels which Cranmer left on Palm Sunday and Good Friday were lightened by transferring the first chapter of each to Morning Prayer. The early Church may have been conditioned to stand for a four-hour service; but everyone seems agreed that twenty minutes is too much to demand of our degenerate age to stand for the reading of a liturgical Gospel. The Church of Rome takes care of that by appointing all but a very few verses to be read simply as a Lection, during which the people may be seated, exactly as they may during a Gospel lection at the Offices. Only the last of each Holy Week Gospel is proclaimed with the accustomed liturgical ceremonies.

But although we have preserved Cranmer's plan, as modified in 1662, on paper, it has been rather seriously broken into in practice. Cranmer removed the Blessing of the Palms from Palm Sunday, with the result that there was no mention of the Triumphal Entry on that day in any Anglican Prayer Book until our American book of 1892 restored the Johannine version of it at Evensong. 1928, however, put the Marcan account of it at Morning Prayer, thus depriving the Sunday of the first half of the complete Passion according to St. Matthew. Matt. 26 has been restored to the 1943 Lectionary, but, necessarily, as one of the plural options provided for every Sunday. It is very dubious as to how many churches use it. Most of the interest seems in the other direction: witness the repeated requests for permission to use the Advent Sunday Gospel, containing the Triumphal Entry, as an alternative at the Eucharist.

Cranmer's division of the complete Passion according to St. Mark between Monday and Tuesday remains, untouched and unthreatened — but, of course, with smaller attendance than any other days of Holy Week. The first half of St. Luke's narrative also survives on Wednesday; but 1928 introduced the Sarum Gospel, John 13:1-15, as an alternative to the second half on Maundy Thursday, with the result that nearly everyone avails himself of the shorter provision, and the really important part of the witness of St. Luke goes unread. The pattern of 1662, dividing St. John's Passion between Morning Prayer and the Eucharist, is undisturbed on Good Friday: but here the Prayer Book provisions have been unthinkingly, and unwisely, passed over by very many churches, in favor of the entirely unliturgical Commemoration of the Three Hours.

All of this represents a somewhat serious breakdown of ancient customs, whose value surely no one could deny. It is very evident that rather radical methods will have to be adopted to clear up the accumulated confusions of both plan and practice. The primary necessity is to restore the reading of the Passion in the Four Gospels complete, according to the original purpose, and for the greatest effect upon the minds of the people. And the obvious and perfectly feasible method to do that is to put a special rubric under the days in question, allowing the reading of the great bulk of the narratives as a special Lesson, interposed between the Epistle and such portion of them as is to be read with the honors of a Liturgical Gospel.

This method is recommended for Palm Sunday, Tuesday, Wednesday, and Good Friday. Maundy Thursday may be left with what is now its alternative Gospel in possession of the field. Since 1928, it has approved itself in use. As for Monday, Rome has cut the Sarum use of 36 verses of John 12 to the first nine verses, the Anointing at Bethany. But this incident is recounted in the Passion narratives both of Matthew and Mark, and the repetition serves no useful purpose. It would seem far better to take Mark 11:11-12a, 15b-19 (reading "And on the morrow, when they were come from Bethany, Jesus went into the temple," etc.) We have here an obviously careful chronology, ignored by the other Evangelists in their interest in other phases of the story, which fixes the Cleansing of the Temple as the major event of this Monday. Since, as before remarked, it is also absolutely pivotal to the whole story, it seems strongly to be recommended that it be placed here.

The only remaining question is what part of the long passages of the Passions shall be set apart for a formal Liturgical Gospel. Rome in every case uses the narrative of the Burial, which Anglican use appropriates to Easter Even, and omits from the Passion entirely. The most satisfactory alternative seems to be to adopt the very beautiful conclusions of the story, after the moment of our Lord's death, in the form of Matt. 27:51-54, Mark 15:38-41, Luke 23:47-49, and John 19:31-37.

The use of a Lesson of the Passion narrative is allowed by rubric of the English book of 1928 for Palm Sunday and Good Friday, but with the Roman division of the special Liturgical Gospel: a half-measure not to be commended.

Another feature of both the English and the Scottish revisions is the permission to use the Advent Sunday Gospel of the Triumphal Entry, Matt. 21:1-13, as an alternative on Palm Sunday when there is more than one celebration on that day, *provided* the Gospel of the Passion is used at one service. This seems to be a very good idea. The Passion certainly should be read entire upon this last Sunday in Lent, as well as on Good Friday. It should not be supplanted by the attractive pageantry of the Triumphal Entry, which, however significant in its setting, is certainly no substitute for the tremendous drama of Calvary.

Subject to that important qualification, there seems nothing to be lost and much to be gained by providing an alternative Epistle and Gospel on Palm Sunday. The Roman Epistle, Exodus 15:27-16:7a, was apparently chosen for the incidental mention of the seventy palm-trees at the oasis of Elim, and goes on to the gift of manna. There is not much use in that. Zech. 9:9-12, which is actually echoed in the Gospel, and which is already familiar to us by use in the Lectionary, would be a much better selection. We have also used in the Lectionary since 1928 the version of the Triumphal Entry according to Mark 11:1-11. This has a superior simplicity and convincing directness, over the Matthæan parallel. This therefore, rather than the Advent Sunday Gospel, is now proposed for use in this place.

6. Easter

Perhaps the most crucial of all the defects of the present Liturgical Lectionary lies in the provisions for Easter Day. Both of the Gospels now provided convey nothing beyond the purely negative message of the Empty Tomb. Dr. Easton comments:

> During Easter Week services were held every day, in the course of which the accounts of the resurrection were read through. Hence the Gospels for Easter Day itself contain only the preliminary sections, describing the discovery of the empty tomb but not the appearances of the risen Christ. Thus both the present Easter Gospels end on a note of sheer perplexity, something that is most unfortunate. In any future revision of the Prayer Book this defect is entitled to primary attention.[7]

In the early days of the Church of Rome, Easter was celebrated with a Midnight Mass; as is still the case with the conservative Eastern Orthodox Church. The Gospel at this service was Matt. 28:1-7, which is perhaps the most striking and dramatic of all the accounts of the Resurrection, the narrative which best expresses the glory, wonder, and power of that great event, and the one which probably most moderns would agree with the ancients should be employed upon the principal service of the feast.

About the year 400, however, this midnight service, together with the very lengthy preparations for and solemnization of the Easter Baptisms, was anticipated to Saturday morning. This was the first of the Roman 'Vigils,' afterward prefixed to other important festivals; all now celebrated on the morning of the day before, although, as the name indicates, reminiscent of a time when they were 'watch-services' during the night hours of the Eve, culminating in a Midnight Mass. Christmas, for example, has a Vigil Mass the morning before in the Roman

---

7. *The Eternal Word*, 127.

rite; although this day has also alone preserved the old custom of an actual celebration at midnight.

The anticipation of the original Easter celebration to 'Holy Saturday' actually left Easter Day itself 'vacant': which vacuum was hastily, and not very judiciously, filled by coopting Mark 16:1-7 from one of the Easter Week services. To this day this remains the only Gospel of the great feast in the Roman use.

At the Reformation, Cranmer kept the Marcan lesson for the principal celebration, though he added verse 8, thereby much accentuating that "note of sheer perplexity" of which Dr. Easton so justly complains, with its disheartening final "for they were afraid." But Cranmer also added for an early celebration John 20: 1-10, which tells precisely the same story of the Empty Tomb. In the Roman rite this is the Gospel for Saturday in Easter Week, and it is used on Easter Day in the Mozarabic; but it is doubtful if Cranmer knew about that. With this Gospel, Cranmer assigned as Epistle Col. 3:1-7 again an unwise lengthening of Col. 3:1-4, which was the Sarum and Roman Epistle for 'Holy Saturday,' and hence, as we have seen, of the primordial Roman Easter Mass.

The Second Prayer Book of 1552 dropped the provisions for Cranmer's principal service, retaining only the very ancient Epistle and the very modern Gospel which he had allotted to the early celebration. Our Prayer Book of 1928 quite wisely shortened that Epistle to its original length; and restored Cranmer's principal service for use at an early celebration — attracted, no doubt, by the very appropriate note of verse 2, "And very early in the morning the first day of the week, they came unto the sepulchre at the rising of the sun."

If one were to proceed on a purely Anglican basis, in the light of the provisions to which we are accustomed, it might look very logical to drop the Marcan Gospel, as the least impressive of those at hand; to put the present Johannine passage on the Empty Tomb at the early service; and for the chief service to supply John 20:11-18, which records the first definite Appearance to Mary Magdalene, and effectively continues the narrative up to the Appearance to the Disciples, which is the Gospel for the Easter Octave Day of Low Sunday.

But if this were done, we would be parting company again with the Roman Church: since in 1892 we restored for the early service the passage which is the only Roman Gospel on Easter Day. We may cordially admit that this might be the barest possible Gospel for a principal service, and that the Romans of the fifth century who adopted it as their *only* Gospel for the day made a disastrous blunder, which, after all this time, is probably irretrievable for them. But for a first service, as we use it, this earliest account of the earliest events of the day is very nearly ideal. All that it needs to be perfect for its purpose is to remove that last verse which Cranmer injudiciously included.

Likewise, the Appearance to Mary, unique as it is and lovely as it is, in itself is little more than a kind of 'Easter idyll.' It simply does not adequately express 'the power of his Resurrection.' Rome felt this, by making it the last of the Gospels to be assigned to Easter Week (on Thursday).[8] Definitely, it belongs upon a weekday in the Easter Octave, and as such we recommend it to the Committee on the Calendar which is minded to propose optional proper services for those weekdays. But it is not sufficient for the chief celebration on Easter Day.

The history of the Easter observances which we have reviewed to explain the poverty and ineptitude of the present Roman provisions, and in nearly equal measure, of our own, perhaps holds the key to the best attainable solution of the problem. The primordial Gospel of the earliest Western Church for the feast of Easter was on the whole very much the most adequate for the purpose. It is open to us to redress the regrettable mistake of the fifth century, which banished the great Gospel lection from St. Matthew from Easter Day: continuing the pericope, however, to comprise Matt. 28:1-10, with the Appearance to the two Marys, to meet the objection that Easter now mentions *only* the Empty Tomb.

A possible further defect of the provisions for Easter Day lies in the inadequate character of the Epistles. The ancient assignment of Col. 3:1-4, which Rome has on the Vigil, and we at the principal celebration of the Day, is extremely fine, though it is, and must remain, extremely brief. (We have noted that the well-meaning Reformation attempt to provide it with a more adequate 'liturgical length' was definitely a blunder, which we in America have redressed.) Its greatest value is that it stresses the very important fact that the meaning of the Resurrection is not only doctrinal but moral, in an application of religion to practical living.

But the Epistle for the early service (the Roman for the Day) is little more than a portion of the familiar Anthem 'Christ our Passover,' which replaces the *Venite* on Easter at Morning Prayer. We have been urged to replace this with 1 Cor. 15:1-11, the Epistle for Trinity XI, as the first written account of the Resurrection Appearances. But it is questionable whether this is just the sort of thing we want on Easter Day. The Roman instinct was to choose *minima* for Epistles both on the Vigil and the Day, leaving the principal scriptural emphasis to be carried by the Gospel narratives. Especially an early service, where there would normally be no sermon, would be a somewhat futile place for such an Epistle, which indeed is rather too homiletical in itself to belong there. The plan of the old lectionary was to put it in the neutral ground of Trinity-tide, where one might review as thoroughly as he liked the whole historical evidence of the Resurrection Appearances. Easter Day certainly has neither the time nor the mood to go into all that.

Perhaps the best balance could be obtained by replacing 1 Cor. 5:6b-8 at the early service with Col. 3:1-4 from the late one; and for the principal celebration, adopting a still stronger passage, Phil. 3:7-14 (in the Revised Version, for the sake of a minor detail of taste, and one question of clarity). This selection is certainly the strongest possible Epistle to express 'the power of his resurrection,' as well as

---

8. *Cf.* what has been said on p. 59 as to the liturgical use of Thursdays in the early Church.

the most effective of all interpretations of its meaning as applied to the Christian life; and should prove a fruitful point of departure for Easter sermons.

On Easter Tuesday, Acts 13:26-41 does not have a proper *incipit*; it is overlong; the accumulation of Jewish proof-texts does not help the argument to the modern mind; and its conclusion is unpleasant. The Sarum and Roman version of this Epistle was Acts 13:16a, 26-33a, concluding with "in that he hath raised up Jesus again." The passage could, of course, be continued through verses 34, 37, or 39, though there is little to be gained by doing so: but in any case it seems to us that this Epistle should be provided with the Sarum *incipit*, and should stop short of verses 40-41.

On the other hand, the Gospel for Low Sunday should certainly be extended from its present John 20:19-23 to at least verse 29, to include the Appearance to the Disciples *with Thomas, on the eighth day*. What we have now recounts only the events of the evening of Easter Day. The Sarum and Roman since the seventh century continued the Gospel through verse 31: and although the last two verses are not relevant to the occasion, the other matter certainly is. The Reformers seem to have been self-conscious about verses 24-29 (31), as already having occurred on the feast of St. Thomas. But we need not be: not only is that feast at some distance in the year, but it is another Holy Day which can never be celebrated on a Sunday. Dr. Easton comments: "Verses 26-29, in fact, are so obviously appropriate to this day" — i.e., Low Sunday "that their use seems to be almost universal outside of Anglicanism; this is one of the very few instances where the Eastern and Western Churches agree in their selections."[9]

Dr. Easton comments adversely on the Epistle for Easter IV: "This is a poorly selected passage, containing the end (verses 17-18) of one section and the beginning (verses 19-21) of another, which is only vaguely connected with the first"; and goes on to intimate that the units of thought are really James 1:12-18 and 19-27.[10] Likewise in his exposition of the Epistle for Easter V, he is compelled to go back to matter read the Sunday before.[11] Properly to utilize this valuable matter from the Epistles-General, the assignments for these two Sundays should be adjusted to the logical divisions as Dr. Easton has given them.

7. Ascension and Whitsunday

Rightly to evaluate the provisions for this short but important period, we shall have to bear in mind the developments which gave it birth, and which have affected its character.

---

9. *The Eternal Word*, 132.
10. *The Eternal Word*, 148.
11. *The Eternal Word*, 152.

It happened that the early Church did not speak of Eastertide (*Tempus Paschale*), but of *The Pentecost*: meaning thereby not the original *Fiftieth Day*, but the entire *fifty days* from Easter to Whitsunday. This continuous festal season between these two termini goes back to the most primitive stratum of the Christian Year, as early as we have any information about it. It was not until the fourth century that the festival of the Ascension was interposed, marking off a definite Easter Season comprising the Forty Days of the Risen Life; and it was not until the twelfth century that the Ascension was dignified with an Octave of its own.

This rather laggard development of the present pattern accounts for the very extensive anticipations of the ideas of the Ascension, and of the Coming of the Spirit, during the Sundays between Easter and Whitsunday. The season was influenced by both poles: it first looked backward to Easter, then forward to Pentecost. The events connected with the Resurrection were thoroughly exploited during the Easter Octave only. Easter II was devoted to a characteristic 'pictorial' summing up of the Redemption by presenting the figure of The Good Shepherd, "which," as Dr. Easton says, "captured the imagination of the early church and dominated its iconography, as in the catacombs at Rome, where representation of the crucifixion does not appear for several centuries."[12] But from Easter III through Ascension I, all is anticipation of Pentecost. During these four Sundays, John 15:26-16:33 is read virtually complete, in the order 3 2 4 1.

This rearrangement of the scriptural order is very skillful, in the interests of a logical development of thought. Easter III looks forward to the Ascension: "A little while, and ye shall not see me: and again, a little while, and ye shall see me, because I go to the Father.... Ye now therefore have sorrow: but I will see you again, and your heart shall rejoice." Easter IV further unfolds the teaching of the necessity of the Ascension as integral to the plan of the Redemption itself: the termination of Christ's local presence with his Disciples under conditions of the flesh was indispensable to secure his universal presence with his own at all times and places through the Spirit: "Nevertheless, I tell you the truth; It is expedient for you that I go away: for if I go not away, the Comforter will not come unto you; but if I depart, I will send him unto you. . . . He shall receive of mine, and show it unto you." Easter V concludes this Ascension theme by making it the final proof of the Lordship of Christ: "I leave the world, and go to the Father. His disciples said unto him, . . . by this we believe that thou camest forth from God." Then Ascension I picks up again the notes of "the Comforter, even the Spirit of truth," already adumbrated on Easter IV, in immediate preparation for Whitsunday.

If therefore Ascension I has nothing really suitable to the Sunday within the Octave of the Ascension, but is a mere 'Expectation Sunday' looking to the coming

---

12. *The Eternal Word*, 137.

Pentecost, the historical reason for this undesirable situation is plain: it was never designed for the Sunday within the Octave, since that Octave was a feature added some eight centuries after the pattern of the Gospels was fixed. Perhaps also, they may have felt that this did not so much matter, as the theological significance of the Ascension had been quite fully set forth on the three Sundays preceding.

This does not alter the fact that it would be highly desirable to have some final word on this subject on this Sunday: especially since under modern conditions few churchmen, however devout, are able to attend the service of this great feast upon the weekday on which it is solemnized.

Postponing the solution of that problem for the moment, let us look at the provisions for Whitsunday. Since the seventh century, the Latin lectionary has divided the passage John 14:15-31 between the Vigil and the Feast, with verses 15-21 on the former, 23-31 on the latter. As a matter of fact, in the last-named, verses 23-26 are all that are really germane to Whitsunday: the remaining verses of the chapter being apparently appended to secure a more suitable 'liturgical length' for so important a festival.

The first English Prayer Book of 1549 took only the Sarum Gospel for the Vigil for Whitsunday itself; 1552 combined the two: a result that has continued ever since. Dr. Easton objects: "The Reformation lengthening of this Gospel was a mistake, since it is now too long for orderly exposition."[13] Perhaps this statement is a little too sweeping. If we should now limit this Gospel to John 14:15-26 — which contains all the matter that is actually apropos to the occasion — it will be found that such a Gospel is not too long for a major feast; and further, that Cranmer's combining the passages for the Vigil and the Feast is really most fortunate, in bringing together the salient texts which unite to make the great point that the Holy Spirit has been sent not to be the Vicar of Christ's absence, but the effectual means of his presence to the end of the world: "I will not leave you orphans: I will come to you. . . . I will love him, and will manifest myself to him. . . . My father will love him, and we will come unto him, and make our abode with him": together with the final summary verse about "the Comforter, which is the Holy Ghost," whose mission is to "teach you all things, and bring all things to your remembrance, whatsoever I have said unto you."

Once this desirable shortening has been carried out, then the *rest* of the chapter, John 14:27-31a, which we shall have removed from this place as something which never really contributed anything on Whitsunday save as filling and ballast for a former Sarum selection which was really too short, will be found to be very well adapted to supply a Gospel for Ascension I which will be much better than the mere anticipation of Whitsunday which now occupies it: "My peace I give unto you. . . . Ye have heard how I said unto you, I go away, and come again unto you. If ye loved me, ye would rejoice!"

---

13. *The Eternal Word*, 162.

The Epistle also for Ascension I is purely pre-Pentecostal though barely and rather inferentially even that, since it is not a particularly strong passage. Its exordium, "The end of all things is at hand," strikes a note which does not seem at all at home in this festal season. A selection much better adapted to the Sunday within the Octave of the Ascension would be Eph. 1:15-23: which is not only a worthy expression of the Heavenly Session, but in verses 17-18 retains also the old message of the 'Expectation Sunday' idea much better than any of the present assignments.

While the foregoing constitute perhaps the major problems of this tract of the Calendar of the year, there are four more points which really stand in need of a better treatment.

One is Ascension Day itself. This is one of the few occasions, so striking when they occur, where the Epistle actually outweighs the Gospel, and is the primary carrier of the scriptural narrative of the event. Until 1928 the Gospel was Mark 16:14-20 — the entirely unauthentic synoptic paraphrase of matters in other Gospels which was got together at some very early date to replace the 'lost ending' of St. Mark. At the last revisions, England (optionally) and America (absolutely) replaced this with Luke 24:49-53. But this has not proved very satisfactory. It is not useful to have the story told twice over, and by the same author at that, in the Gospel and the Acts. A number of the best qualified students of the New Testament have united in suggesting to the Commission that a better choice would be Matt. 28:16-20, which happens to avoid recounting the actual occurrence of the Ascension, but unmistakably identifies itself with that incident, and provides the dynamic interpretation of the meaning of our Lord's farewell to his Disciples, in the form of the Great Commission.

The new assignment to the early celebration on Whitsunday is not satisfactory. Certainly it was a blunder to appoint Luke 11:5-13 to the Rogation Days, and Luke 11:9-13 to this service on Whitsunday, both of which appeared in 1928. Perhaps this action originated in different committees, and passed unremarked because the portions were far apart in the text of the Prayer Book; but the duplicate Gospels are actually read within less than two weeks of each other. This passage does well enough on a Rogation Day; but it is quite inadequate for any service on Whitsunday. Its only connection with Pentecost is the concluding "how much more shall your heavenly Father give the Holy Spirit to them that ask him?" The appositeness of this phrase is very tenuous, and almost purely verbal — this mention of the "Holy Spirit" is the Lucan variant of the more germane "good things" of St. Matthew's version. And the fact that it rests on a confused textual tradition, and is not in the Vulgate at all, makes it no better. We should much prefer to substitute the strongest of the unappropriated passages on the Spirit, "God is a Spirit: and they that worship him must worship him in spirit and in truth," in John 4:19-24, in this place.

The provisions for the two days following Whitsunday also need some attention. We have noted (p. 37 above) that the Epistle for Easter Monday, Acts 10:34-43, is repeated entire as part of that for Whit-Monday, Acts 10:34-48. The

Sarum and Roman assignments for these two days attempted to avoid that, by apportioning Acts 10:34a, 37-43 to the former, and 10:34a, 42-48a to the latter. This provides the same needed *incipit* to both, which is very well; but on Whit-Monday it leaves verse 42 without any antecedents to its pronouns: the two *he's* referring respectively to God and to Christ. But in fact St. Peter's summary of the life, death, and resurrection of our Lord is really indispensable to motivate that acceptance of the Lord by these Gentiles which made possible the outpouring of the Spirit upon them.

This Easter selection therefore must be a part of the Whitsuntide lection. In fact, St. Peter's little discourse here is actually a very effective condensed précis of his great sermon on the Day of Pentecost. It can hardly be further abbreviated, without giving a fatally mutilated form of his argument: which is exactly what the Sarum-Roman version of this Epistle is. The best that can be done would seem to do something which it was hardly worth while to suggest for Easter Monday, and to follow Sarum in removing the rather irrelevant exordium of St. Peter's remarks, reading for the Whit-Monday Epistle Acts 10:34a, 36-48a (ending with the words, "to be baptized in the name of the Lord.")

Then Dr. Easton comments on the Gospel for Whit-Monday (John 3:16-21): "This Gospel has nothing to do with Whitsunday. On this day the Station was at St. Peter-ad-Vincula, the Prefecture church; hence the 'judgment' theme."[14] However, it might seem desirable to have the 'Little Gospel' of John 3:16 on the liturgical list; and the missing theme of the Spirit could be very readily supplied by adding to the present assignment the verses 31-36a from the same chapter: "God giveth not the Spirit by measure unto him."

The Gospel for Whit-Tuesday is now John 10:1-10, Christ as the Door of the Sheep: a passage which appears as a Lesson on Easter II, sidelighting the 'Good Shepherd' Gospel for that Sunday. But it has no note of the Spirit, and the best Dr. Easton can make of it is to suggest that it *may* have been in tended to convey some sort of reference to the newly baptized.[15] But since Whitsuntide baptisms are now only a reminiscence of the remote past, why retain it? Especially since we should have available the Gospel due to be displaced from Ascension I, John 15:26-16:4a, with its definite mention of "the Comforter, the Spirit of truth."

8. Trinity-tide

a) Adjustments of Length

In this long season, there are six questions about the exact length of the pericopes: five quite small readjustments of Epistles, and one more extensive possible alteration of a Gospel.

---

14. *The Eternal Word*, 309.
15. *The Eternal Word*, 310.

On Trinity II, Dr. Easton criticizes the Reformation lengthening of the Epistle from 1 John 3:13-18 to 13-24 as making it "rather cumbersome, but at least public reading is secured for the important verses 19-22."[16] Perhaps it is not the actual length of the passage which is at fault, so much as the author's method of repeating the conclusion of each sentence as the basis for a fresh assertion, which is reiterated in its turn. And the termination of Cranmer's passage attempts to finish off this kind of 'chain-stitch' with a rather clumsy knot, in which the word 'commandment' is repeated four times over, giving an undue emphasis to that particular idea, and leaving us with a somewhat blurred notion of the real message of the lection. This could he obviated, and a satisfactory conclusion obtained, by stopping with the words "love one another," in verse 23.

On Trinity VII, Dr. Easton remarks of the Epistle, Rom. 6:19-23, "This section unfortunately begins in the middle of a sentence, and the expositor will have to go back to verse 15 to gain clarity."[17] As a matter of fact, verse 16 makes a better liturgical beginning; and Rom. 16:16-23 is recommended.

The first verse of the Epistle for Trinity XV, Gal. 6:11-18, is really quite irrelevant: and its use would become practically impossible if the text should be corrected to the more accurate translation of the Revised Version.[18] There would be no loss in eliminating verse 11.

On Trinity XVI, Dr. Easton comments on the Epistle, Eph. 3:13-21, "The inclusion of verse 13 was unfortunate, and gives an entirely wrong force to 'for this cause' in verse 14."[19] It would make a better *incipit* anyhow to begin at verse 14.

On Trinity XXI, the Sarum Epistle was Eph. 6:10-17, which Cranmer lengthened through verse 20. Dr. Easton says: "The expositor should close with verse 18 and its impressive final exhortation to intercessory prayer. The pre-Reformation section ended too abruptly, but the Reformers went to the opposite extreme."[20] We therefore recommend Eph. 6:10-18.

The Gospel in question is that for Trinity IX, where the last revision of our Prayer Book substituted Luke 15:11-32, the Parable of the Prodigal Son, for the former Luke 16:1-9, the perplexing Parable of the Unjust Steward. No one thinks it anything but great gain to have secured this, one of the most magnificent and affecting of the Parables, for the Liturgical Lectionary. And yet a good many clergy have expressed the feeling that this passage, which is completely satisfactory as a Lesson on Ash Wednesday, is quite unaccountably something of an infliction as a Gospel on Trinity IX.

---

16. *The Eternal Word*, 173.
17. *The Eternal Word*, 186.
18. *The Eternal Word*, 209.
19. *The Eternal Word*, 211.
20. *The Eternal Word*, 225.

One reason for this feeling is no doubt its length of 22 verses, which makes it much the longest of the Sunday Gospels, with the exception of the 54 verses of the Passion according to St. Matthew on Palm Sunday. Whitsunday has 17 verses, Septuagesima 16, and Lent III 15. The average length of the Sunday Gospels, including Palm Sunday and Trinity IX, is a little over 10½ verses; excluding them, a little over 9½. And it may be noted that for intrinsic reasons we have proposed to shorten the Gospel for Whitsunday, and to convert most of the Passion narratives to an intermediate Lesson, so that their actual rendering as liturgical *Gospels*, to a standing congregation, would be brought to a very brief compass.

Another reason may be that the Prodigal Son is virtually a sermon in itself, with a definite homiletical 'application' in the concluding instance of the Elder Brother. It seems actually to be too complete for its own good, in the company of numerous other parables which occur as Gospel lections, brief and pungent, inviting and indeed expecting expansion at the hands of the expositor, instead of providing their own sermon.

If it should develop that this expressed opinion of a few clergy, that this Gospel as it stands is somewhat overloaded, represents the general sentiment of the Church, and is not merely the reaction of some individuals who may be hypersensitive, it is of course true that this Gospel could be brought into much more compact form by reducing it to Luke 15:11-24a (... and is found.), stopping at the actual Return of the Prodigal, and leaving the appended contrast and application of the case of the Elder Brother to be treated, or not, by the preacher. However, it may be observed that the Greek Church, which uses this passage on our Septuagesima Sunday, and the Roman, which has it on Lent II Saturday, both give it entire as we have it now. One scholar whom we consulted observed: "As you say, it is a short sermon in itself; and it seems to me that having invited our Lord to preach to us, we should hear him to the end. As a matter of fact, I do not think the Prodigal Son story seems long when read, owing to its dramatic character; its appearance on the page merely suggests to the anxious clergyman that it would." That is sound reasoning; but not quite so final as to prevent our presenting this question to the judgment of the Church.

b) *Replacements*

Trinity-tide also contains two Epistles and four Gospels for which outright substitutions have been suggested.

1) Epistles: On Trinity XIII we have Gal. 3:16-22: a passage on Abraham and his 'seeds,' the Law and the Covenant, what is a Mediator? etc. This is another very rabbinical passage of St. Paul's, which has been viewed by our clergy with almost as much distaste as the other passage from Galatians on Lent IV. The English and

Scottish books register this objection by providing an alternative. But the selection which they offer, Heb. 13:1-6, appears to be most ill-advised.

In the first place, it is a flagrant breach of the ancient pattern, surviving from the seventh century to the present day, of a course-reading from the Pauline Epistles in their scriptural order on the eighteen Sundays from Trinity VI to XVII, and XIX to XXIV, which is broken only on Trinity XVIII (which was originally the Sunday attached to the September Ember Days, and which has another Pauline passage, though out of sequence.) To be sure, there is nothing absolutely sacrosanct about this particular method, which is discontinuous enough to be a list rather than a true series. It represents a somewhat random choice from the seventh-century list of 42 selections and not by any means the best of them. It has been altered from time to time: for example, our present assignments contain three which were not even in the parent list of 42. Yet all the alterations managed to preserve the pattern of Pauline Epistles in the same order in which they appear in the Bible: which would seem to show that the medieval revisers were aware of that pattern, and recognized its value enough to respect and retain it; and it would appear that our British cousins did neither.

Moreover, it is very difficult to detect what merit they thought they found in that particular bit of the final miscellany of practical advice in the Epistle to the Hebrews. Perhaps someone thought — and very rightly — that there ought to be some place in the list which might not only invite but virtually compel a sermon on Holy Matrimony, in our troubled times, and chose this section for the verse "Marriage is honourable in all, and the bed undefiled: but whoremongers and adulterers God shall judge." Really, we can do better than that, from any point of view!

For a substitute on Trinity XIII, let us do what the British revisers failed to do, and take a look at the unexhausted resources of the seventh-century list; remembering that some of the very finest gems still remain in that mine. And of the three pericopes in that list intervening between its #10, which we have on Trinity XII, and #14, which is our Trinity XIV, it may be said that #12, consisting of 2 Cor. 5:1-10, is one of the finest in the whole ancient *Epistolarium*: mentioning "an house not made with hands ... Not that we would be unclothed, but clothed upon, that mortality might be swallowed up of life ... the earnest of the Spirit ... Whilst we are at home in the body, we are absent from the Lord ... We must all appear before the judgment seat of Christ; that everyone may receive the things done in his body." That all this has nothing to do with the Gospel of the Day, the Parable of the Good Samaritan, is of no importance: neither has the present Epistle; nor in fact any other in Trinity-tide, save by sheer coincidence.

The remaining substitution of an Epistle is by no means as necessary as that on Trinity XIII; yet there is much to recommend it. It happens that on Trinity XXII we have the exordium of St. Paul's Epistle to the Philippians, and on Trinity XXIV similarly the beginning of his Epistle to the Colossians; and further, that the Apostle had very much the same things to say on the two occasions. In spite of the lack of notable coincidences of phrase, so that a man might preach from particular texts on the two Sundays without any great sense of the repetitions of thought, these passages must be ranked as virtual doublets, in that it would be impossible to treat them homiletically as wholes without realizing the essential duplications.

Of the two, that for Trinity XXII is perhaps preferable; besides, our seventh-century list offers a great number of choices for Trinity XXIV. Of these, the best in this place seems to be 2 Thess. 2:15-3:5: "Stand fast, and hold the traditions which ye have been taught . . . Now our Lord Jesus Christ himself . . . stablish you in every good word and work . . . that the word of the Lord may have free course, and be glorified . . . And the Lord direct your hearts into the love of God, and into the patient waiting for Christ." This final note seems particularly in place on a Sunday so very near the end of the official Christian Year, and the consequent approach of Advent.

2) Gospels: The proposed substitutions of Trinity-tide Gospels are all designed to remove needless repetition of doublet passages, the telling over again of what is recognized to be the same incident in the 'concordant' version of another Evangelist.

On Trinity VII, Mark 8:1-9, the Feeding of the Four Thousand, and on the Sunday Next Before Advent, John 6:5-14, the Feeding of the Five Thousand, comprise a doublet, and an outright reiteration, respectively, of the use of John 6:1-14 on Lent IV.

While to the modern mind it seems perfectly extraordinary that these narratives of the so-called 'Miraculous Feedings' should be allowed to preoccupy no less than three of the limited number of the Sundays of the Christian Year, the historical cause of this peculiarity happens to be something which serves to explain another outstanding anomaly of the Liturgical Lectionary: namely that the historic Churches, which center all their worship in the Holy Eucharist, apparently make not the slightest reference to that rite in the Scriptures provided for any Sunday. The fact that simultaneously solves both these striking riddles is that where the present age would look for a definitive narrative, like that in 1 Cor. 11, or a direct theological exposition, like the long latter part of St. John 6, as a scriptural background for the Church's teaching on the Eucharist, the primitive Church preferred to bring before the people a sort of living picture and parable. For this purpose the early Church coopted not only these three stories of the great Cultus Meals (as we now recognize them to have been), but also still another pair of essential doublets, St. Luke's 'Great Supper' on Trinity II, and St. Matthew's 'Marriage Feast' on Trinity XX. Thus at the time of the framing of the Liturgical Lectionary, the Church was so far from ignoring the heart of its worship in the Sacrament of Holy Communion, that it considered that it was devoting no less than five Sundays — a tithe of the year — to setting the stage for expounding and enforcing its teaching on this subject.

It has seemed well to leave one example of the great Cultus Meal on Mid-Lent Sunday, where it has always been thrown into the highest emphasis, and become thoroughly familiar to the maximum number of lay people, whose attendance at Church is about at its height in that season. Removing it from that place, even in favor of a version of the same ultimate theme which might seem more direct and profitable to our modern habits of mind, would not be desirable: certainly the passage would be sadly missed by many there. But there can be no excuse for keeping it also in the other two places in Trinity-tide. If now we desire to carry out the intent of the primitive Church to provide Gospels for Trinity VII and Advent -I which shall present the Christian Eucharist for consideration, the available material is as follows:

1) The Synoptics give the bare narrative of the Institution, in its Passion-tide setting, without comment or explanation of any sort. As this narrative is incorporated in the Consecration Prayer, there is nothing left to be added as a liturgical Gospel.

2) The Fourth Gospel, which found it otiose to repeat the Institution Narrative, as contained in the Synoptics, and already in constant use in the Liturgy, does give some very extended passages on the meaning of the Sacrament: a) in the sixth chapter, a long *haggadah* or homiletical exposition on the significance of the rite, based on the incident of the Feeding of the Five Thousand; and b) five whole chapters, 13-17, containing our Lord's discourses to his Disciples during, and after, the last *Agapé*.

Of these five chapters, in the 13th, our Lord's washing the Disciples' feet before the Supper has been appropriated to Maundy Thursday, and the balance of it is concerned with the Betrayal. The 14th and 16th chapters contain the forecasts of the Ascension and the coming of the Spirit, and, as we have seen, are used up almost completely between Easter III and Whitsunday. The 17th is the 'High-Priestly Prayer' of intercession for the Church: and though a grand example of 'giving thanks for all men,' it is too closely knit to be divided, and much too long for liturgical use as a whole; it can be used for a Lesson, but is really not available as a Gospel.

This leaves chapter 15, which falls into three divisions: 1) The Vine and the Branches; 2) The Commandment, That ye love one another; and 3) The servant is not greater than his Lord. These are all employed in our Prayer Book, as they were in the Sarum Missal, for the festivals of SS. Mark, Barnabas, and Simon and Jude — not in the light of any particular appropriateness, but essentially as 'commons'; any of them might be used on the feast of any Saint. Rome in fact uses other 'commons' for the first two, coinciding with the Sarum assignment for the third. The Gospel for any one of these Saints' Days could be used on either of the

Sundays in question, if not at too close an interval, or another assignment made for the Saint's Day.

In none of these three passages is the bearing upon the Last Supper direct and commanding. But the first of them, which is the most individual and striking, happens to have two very strong ties of an indirect character with the Eucharist. The little allegory of 'the Vine and the Branches' is entirely unique to the Fourth Gospel. It has every indication of being an expansion of the idea of 'the Vine of David' from the prayer in the *Didaché*, just as this in turn was a Messianic version of the thanksgiving for 'the fruit of the vine' at every Jewish table. Moreover, the moral application to the purpose of the Holy Communion is complete, in the thought of the life of the Branches depending on their union with the Vine. In the light of these considerations, we recommend using John 15:1-8 as the Gospel for Trinity VII.

Much more room for choice exists in the long argument in John 6. The cumulative reasoning there seems confusing to some, giving an impression of going around in circles. Actually, it is not: it is going up in spirals! We would hardly choose to fill up both the 'Eucharistic' Sundays in question from this passage, as the resulting Gospels would give most people the impression of being entirely equivalent, even though they had really been taken from different levels. For a single Gospel, we should be well advised to select the topmost loop, and the final summary of the whole argument, in the form of John 6:47-58, for the Sunday Next Before Advent. In that place, it goes very well with the Epistle, and has the advantage of tying in to the season with the eschatological note, "I will raise him up at the last day."

With regard to the doublet of the 'Great Supper' on Trinity II and the 'Marriage Feast' on Trinity XX, there is no absolute necessity to do anything about that for their own sake. They are five months apart in the year; and besides, their emphasis in detail is sufficiently different that few clergy have been conscious of constraint even when preaching on both Gospels the same year. The chief complaint about Trinity XX seems to be that the structure of the parable as St. Matthew tells it is not well put together, and that there would be a palpable absurdity in rebuking a man just haled in off the street for not having on a 'wedding garment.' As Dr. Easton says, St. Matthew's addition "voices early post-apostolic experience. The Apostles went out into the highways and hedges and compelled them to come in — but the result was sometimes unfortunate. The allegory is not skillful; how could a man pressed into the palace under such conditions be expected to appear in proper clothing? ... But ... this does not trouble the Evangelist; every one knows that converts are expected to amend their lives, and this man did not try to do so."[21]

This objection, which seems particularly to trouble one logical type of mind, could of course be met by shortening the Gospel to Matt. 22:1-10. But if this were

---

21. *The Eternal Word*, 221.

done, one of the most valuable lessons of the passage, and one of the chief reasons why some might like to retain this later version of St. Luke's account, would be lost.

We have, however, mentioned that there is a deep and widespread feeling in the Church that there ought to be some Sunday on which the dominant theme is directly that of Holy Matrimony. Of course, any clergyman can preach on that subject at any time. But at present, the best the Liturgical Lectionary offers him by way of a scriptural point of departure therefor would seem to be to take a very sharply tangential line on Epiphany III, with its Marriage at Cana, or here on Trinity XX, with the Marriage Feast.

Trinity XX, however, presents its own invitation to improve upon that. It is almost with a touch of awe that we note that the Epistle for a Nuptial Eucharist, Eph. 5:20-33, actually slightly overlaps the Eph. 5:15-21 which has come down to us from the seventh century for this Sunday, and realize that it would not interfere in the slightest with the overall pattern of the Epistles if we substituted Eph. 5:18b-33 (beginning, "Be filled with the Spirit").

It may be that this, read together with the Gospel of the Marriage Feast, would be enough. But all those whom we have consulted thought not. They felt so profoundly the need of our times for the strongest and directest teaching on Christian Marriage, that they voted for a suggestion which had been made to substitute for this Gospel something of the order of Matt. 19:4-6, 13-15. This is the present Gospel at a Marriage, together with the further sayings about the 'little children,' which round out the Christian family. The parallel passage in Mark 10:6-9, 13-16 is still more appealing, and is therefore recommended. The Marcan passage could, of course, be read without omission of verses. But this does not seem desirable in a Sunday Gospel. In the first place, it is better to present the positive side of the matter alone, as is done at the Nuptial Eucharist. And also, it is the opinion of some recent scholars of considerable weight, that St. Mark's version of the divorce question is less authentic than the independent tradition recorded by St. Matthew: verse 12, for instance, which reflects the actually higher marital ethic of Roman society, is plainly incompatible with a Jewish setting.

The final doublet to be considered is the Gospel for Trinity XXI, John 4:46b-54, the Healing of the Nobleman's Son, which is on the whole an inferior and less authentic version of St. Matthew's story of the Healing of the Centurion's Servant, which is the Gospel for Epiphany IV.[22] The Johannine rendering has, of course, its distinctive merits in detail: and it is a fact that this is the least obvious, and hence least objectionable, of all the 'concords' of parallel Gospels which have found their way into the Liturgical Lectionary. But it is a question whether it is best to retain this passage, which on any reckoning is of rather secondary importance, when there are so many first-line selections from the Gospels which are now excluded from the list.

---

22. See Dr. Easton's comments in *The Eternal Word*, 233.

Place has been found for a good many of these passages on previous occasions of the year. Certainly, however, if Matt. 7:24-29, the House on the Rock, is not to be substituted for the Gospel on Lent II, it would undoubtedly outrank the Nobleman's Son in value and interest here. If it is put on Lent II, then perhaps the best choice for this place, beside the very stirring Epistle on the Armour of God, would be Luke 17:5-10, where 'the faith that moves mountains' would form a desirable connection of thought with the note "above all, the shield of faith," in the Epistle.

The Fixed Holy Days

The Epistles and Gospels for the Fixed Holy Days received no attention whatsoever in the Anglican Prayer Books between 1549 and 1928, except that in 1662 the Purification was provided with an Epistle, which it had previously lacked entirely, and its Gospel was (injudiciously) lengthened. The last American revision furnished new Epistles for St. Thomas, SS. Simon and Jude, and the Circumcision, and omitted the 'Twelve Tribes of Israel' from the middle of the All Saints' Epistle, with a compensating addition at the end.

The assignments in the First Prayer Book were based upon the Use of Sarum, and comprised nine Epistles and 20 Gospels which are identical in both the Sarum and the Roman Missals, one Epistle and three Gospels which are Sarum but not Roman, and one Epistle which is Roman and not Sarum. But there were eleven Epistles which were new in 1549; and two Epistles and seven Gospels were lengthened at the Reformation.

1. Adjustments of Length

Some of these lengthenings were slight, others proportionately considerable, and one (St. John Baptist) really formidable. A collation with the original pericopes shows that in a majority of instances the Sarum-Roman form was actually better. The following readjustments are therefore recommended:

Holy Day	Epistle	Instead of:	Gospel	Instead of:
Andrew	Rom. 10:9-18	Rom. 10:9-21	[No change]	
John Evangelist	[No change]		John 21:19-24	John 21:19-25
Purification	Mal. 3:1-4	Mal. 3:1-5	[No change]	
Barnabas	Acts 11:21b-26 and 13:1-3	Acts 11:22-30	[No change]	
John Baptist	[No change]		Luke 1:57-68	Luke 1:57-80
Luke	2 Tim. 4:5-13	2 Tim. 4:5-15	[No change]	

The Reformation lengthening of the Epistle for St. Andrew, comprising three verses to the end of the chapter, does nothing but provide an unpleasant conclusion. For St. John Evangelist, the addition, again to the end of the chapter, is only one verse; but it is irrelevant to the occasion. Both remarks — irrelevance, and a rather dispiriting ending — apply to Bishop Wren's lengthening by one verse of the old Epistle for the Purification, which he very properly insisted on restoring: from 1549 to 1662, this feast had no Epistle of its own, but was directed to use that for the preceding Sunday!

At the Reformation, the Sarum Gospel for the Purification, Luke 2:22-32, was curtailed to end with verse 27a. Bishop Wren in 1662 lengthened it to verse 40, which concludes St. Luke's account of the Infancy, and brings us up to the incident of our Lord's boyhood which we read on Epiphany I. This Gospel is fairly long, and it might be some temptation to shorten it, as far as the interests of this particular commemoration are concerned. But the Reformation dropped from the Sarum provisions for Christmas I the reading of Luke 2:33-40, which recounted the Return to Nazareth before the day of the Circumcision; we now propose to do the same with the parallel from St. Matthew, which presented the same event before the Epiphany. The conclusion of St. Luke's narrative of the Infancy certainly ought to appear somewhere, and the Return to Nazareth ought not to be omitted completely, even though it is a dislocating factor in the actual Nativity Season. Unquestionably this is the place for it.

But the 24 verses of the Gospel for the Nativity of St. John Baptist are something of a liturgical monstrosity. Most clergy moreover have felt that the reading of the canticle *Benedictus* entire conveys a minimum of spiritual profit, especially in view of the conflict of its 'King James' text in the Prayer Book Gospel with the more familiar 'Great Bible' version in which it is sung at Morning Prayer. Therefore the Sarum-Roman device of introducing it only by title, as it were, and concluding the Gospel with the first verse of that canticle, seems altogether to be recommended.

The Epistle for St. Luke's Day was new at the Reformation. Dr. Easton comments: "It is a pity that the Reformers did not end the selection with verse II a, for what follows has no expository value."[23] But perhaps to conclude with "Only Luke is with me" would be too abrupt. Hence we recommend that we continue with the personal notes, which are not without their interest, through verse 13; but in any event to omit the ominous figure of Alexander the Coppersmith!

The suggested provision for St. Barnabas' Day adopts the Roman form of the Epistle exactly, where Cranmer deserted the Sarum norm to follow it only diffidently and in part. Dr. Easton says of the latter: "The inclusion of verses 27-30 was a mistake, since the mention of Barnabas at the end of verse 30 does not associate him with the contents of the paragraph."[24] Rome realized this, it

---

23. *The Eternal Word*, 293.
24. *The Eternal Word*, 275.

seems, if Cranmer did not; and furthermore here, as elsewhere, was not to be intimidated by a 'discontinuous' passage, but boldly leaped from chapter 11 to the beginning of chapter 13, which had something really significant to add about Barnabas — namely his solemn commission, with St. Paul himself, to commission others as ministers in the churches they were being sent forth to found. These three verses, perhaps the most significant in the New Testament on the basic principle of the Apostolic Succession (and incidentally a passage most unjustly and unaccountably ignored or even belittled by Anglican apologists) are not in our Liturgical Lectionary anywhere: and surely it will hardly be disputed that they ought to be.

It may also be remarked that there is another reason for omitting Acts 11:27-30 from the Epistle for St. Barnabas, and that is that these four verses are repeated on the feast of St. James, a little over six weeks later. As the rest of St. James' Epistle (Acts 11:27-12:3a) has also been read on St. Peter's Day, less than four weeks before, the present assignment leaves nothing whatever actually proper to St. James' Day. Now Acts 12:2 records his martyrdom — he being the only Apostle whose death is recorded in the New Testament. The Reformers therefore did well in appointing this Epistle, instead of the generalities of the older Commons of Apostles in the Sarum and Roman rites; even though it is true that the first verses of Acts 12 form a necessary introduction to the narrative of St. Peter's imprisonment on his festival. Dr. Easton, however, criticizes the inclusion of Acts 11:27-30 on St. James' Day, saying, "Unfortunately, to gain better liturgical length they prefixed the last four verses of Acts 11, which are wholly irrelevant to the theme of the day."[25] Yet it can be maintained that this stricture is not altogether true. Acts 12 begins, "Now about that time Herod the king stretched forth his hands to vex certain of the church." Now the expression, "about that time," would have no meaning without the previous verses which define it as the time that Paul and Barnabas brought the charitable offerings of the Gentiles to Jerusalem. While this, of course, has no ideological connection with the martyrdom of St. James, it does date it, and it does supply a realistic background in its picture of the living society of the Church in those times. It may be said that these four verses, which do not happen to mention St. James, are actually needed for his festival, not for mere mechanical reasons of 'liturgical length,' but in order to contribute a sense of the historical reality of the story; but while they do mention St. Barnabas, they are quite aimless and superfluous on his day.

2. Replacements

Besides these adjustments of length, there are five substitutions which seem advisable in the Propers for the Holy Days.

---

25. *The Eternal Word*, 282.

The Gospel for the Conversion of St. Paul is of the nature of a mere Common of Apostles. It not only contains nothing particularly appropriate to St. Paul, it is, as Dr. Easton pointed out,[26] actively inappropriate to him, since the allusion to the "twelve thrones," while perfectly applicable to the twelve Disciples to whom these words were originally addressed, would *ipso facto* exclude St. Paul, and may even have been deliberately added to the Antiochene Gospel of St. Matthew to do so — this note being lacking in the parallel passage in St. Luke, which is the Gospel on St. Bartholomew's Day. The Prayer Book rightly lists St. Paul as one of *fourteen* Apostles whom we commemorate; but certainly he was never one of the Twelve.

The Roman Missal for its observance of the Martyrdom of St. Paul on June 30 very appropriately uses our Lord's prophecy of the persecutions of the Apostles, which is part of his Charge to them, immediately after the formal Call of the Twelve in Matt. 10. It would therefore be entirely in order to follow this lead in the case of the Conversion of the great Apostle to the Gentiles, by taking for the Gospel the continuation of this Charge, in the injunctions to the Apostles to preach the word, in Matt. 10:24-32: "It is enough for the disciple that he be as his master, and the servant as his Lord. . . . What I tell you in darkness, that speak ye in light: and what ye hear in the ear, that preach ye upon the housetops. . . . Whosoever therefore shall confess me before men, him will I confess also before my Father which is in heaven."

On St. Mark's Day, we have noted that there is nothing whatever proper to this Evangelist in the present Gospel, John 15:1-11, 'The Vine and the Branches,' which we have inherited from the Sarum Rite. We need this passage for Trinity VII. The Roman is no better, being Luke 10:1-11, the Sending of the Seventy, which we have on the feast of St. Luke. It would seem that a selection from his own Gospel, Mark 13:9-13, would be eminently suitable to this man who fulfilled in his own life all that is there set forth in the words of our Lord as to the qualification of the preachers of the Word, as an exile and a Martyr, a witness and an Evangelist, speaking with the assistance of the Holy Ghost. This substitution would avoid the repetition of the same Gospel on Trinity VII, which would be eleven to thirteen weeks away, on the occasions when St. Mark's Day falls on a Sunday.

The Feast of the Transfiguration was dropped at the Reformation, but restored in the American Book of 1892: an action followed by the latest English and Scottish provisions. The Scottish Book has the Sarum and Roman propers, 2 Pet. 1:16-18 and Matt. 17:1-9. Our Prayer Book has the same Epistle, but has substituted Luke 9:28-36 for the Gospel. Dr. Easton observes, "The Markan section would have been preferable to either."[27] That is perfectly true: the earlier and

---

26. *The Eternal Word*, 256.
27. *The Eternal Word*, 262.

simpler narrative actually has a greater verisimilitude; the version in St. Luke, and still more, that in St. Matthew, carrying certain 'literary' embellishments which inevitably impart a slightly mythological tone to the incident. Evidently the English revisers felt as much also, for they put Mark 9:2b-7 for the Gospel. But Mark 9:2b-9 would be more complete.

The English book also rightly rejected the passage from 2 Peter for the Epistle. We may thoroughly understand that a bygone age had quite different standards of literary integrity from our own: that in perpetrating something which modern critics would call by the abhorrent name of a forgery, they had no more intent to deceive or corrupt than did W. S. Landor in his *Imaginary Conversations*, or Andrew Lang in his *Letters to Dead Authors*; that the author of this Epistle wrote with all simplicity and sincerity what he believed St. Peter would have said about this event, or perhaps even what he may have felt that the Apostle from heaven was desiring him to say on his behalf! Yet no modern man can read out to the people with a quiet conscience a passage which he knows to be a fiction, however pious: "For we have not followed cunningly devised fables, when we made known unto you the power and the coming of our Lord Jesus Christ, but were eyewitnesses of his majesty.... And this voice which came from heaven we heard, when we were with him in the holy mount."

The English substitute for this is 1 John 3:1-3, which is the beginning of the Epistle on Epiphany VI. While quite appropriate to this occasion, it is fragmentary, with an abrupt ending. A far better choice would be 2 Cor. 3:12-18, not otherwise used in the Liturgical Lectionary.

For St. Bartholomew's Day, Acts 5:12-16 was adopted at the Reformation in lieu of the Sarum Eph. 2:19-22, 'the foundation of the Apostles and Prophets.' This Sarum selection was only a 'Common of Apostles,' and our 1928 book adopted it for SS. Simon and Jude, to match the collect of that day. But the passage from Acts is just another such 'Common,' on the apostolic gifts of healing: St. Peter is the only one mentioned by name — St. Bartholomew, if present at all, is hidden behind him. It would seem much better to take another ancient Common which the Roman Missal assigns to this day: 1 Cor. 12:27-31a ('first Apostles,' etc.).

Occasional Services

Following the assignments for All Saints' Day, the Prayer Book presents a sort of appendix, with provisions for celebrations on some special occasions not belonging to the cycle of common worship throughout the Christian Year. This collection is somewhat miscellaneous, and falls into three classes: 1) Optional services, which may be added at discretion to the Church Year, comprising a Common of Saints, the Dedication of a Church, and single provisions for the Ember and Rogation Days — these falling into the category of services which the English Prayer Book describes as "permitted, but not enjoined"; 2) two National Days, Independence and Thanksgiving, which are not Holy Days, but patriotic occasions recognized by the Church; and 3) Propers for Eucharists at a Marriage and a Burial.

The two last might profitably be transferred to immediate connection with the Marriage and Burial Offices, as the Communion of the Sick accompanies the Office of Visitation. The other classes should be maintained where they are, and considerably extended. A single Epistle and Gospel does not make an adequate provision for any and every kind of Saint's Day: Commons for various classes of Saints, such as Martyrs, Confessors, etc., are needed. The Committee on the revision of the Calendar has such suggestions in hand. That Committee also has proposals for proper Epistles and Gospels for a considerable list of marginal commemorations for both Movable and Immovable days: the more outstanding Saints of the history of the Church, and Octaves, weekdays in Lent, the twelve Ember and the three Rogation Days, and the like. Such material, as 'permitted, not enjoined,' might well appear in this part of the Prayer Book. It is designed, however, that the Epistles and Gospels in question should simply be indicated in the same manner as the Lessons in the Lectionary tables, not printed out in full.

Hence this Committee will offer no comment on the assignments for a Saint's Day, which are due to be replaced by more flexible provisions; in the light of which, our proposal to use its Gospel for Advent Sunday does not matter.

But it is doubtful if the lections for the Eucharist at a Marriage are the best obtainable. We are proposing that its Epistle and Gospel be used in a somewhat different form on Trinity XX. They will really do much better as addressed to the instruction of a general congregation, than upon the occasion of a wedding. The Church of England has made a distinctly better choice for the latter purpose, in the form of Eph. 3:14-21 (borrowed from Trinity XVI), and John 15:9-11.

The Gospel for Thanksgiving Day would be improved by dropping the last verse. The text should be completely conformed to the Revised Version in this passage, as on Trinity XV, instead of the partial and compromise corrections which now appear on Thanksgiving.

Summary of Proposed Changes

In the following Table, the selections are distinguished by these conventions:

New Matter, not in the present Epistles and Gospels, is *italicized*.
(Omitted Matter) of lections to be eliminated, by (parentheses).
Omitted) (Verses, of lections to be shortened, by half) (parentheses.
$^{1\text{-}14}$ Transferred matter, by exponential figures before the citations.

The Liturgical Lectionary 83

Day	Proposed Epistle	Present Epistle	Proposed Gospel	Present Gospel
Advent 2			[1]Matt. 25:31-40	(Luke 21:25-33)
Advent 3	1 Cor. *3:21*-4:5	1 Cor. 4:1-5		
Advent 4			[2]Luke 1:26b-38	(John 1:19-28)
Xmas B	*Titus 3:4-7*		[3]Luke 2:15-20	
John Evangelist			John 21:19b-24	John 21:19b-(25
Xmas 1			[2]Luke 2:15-20	[4]Matt. 1:18-25
Circumc.	[5]Isa. 61:1-3	(Phil. 2:9-11)	[6]Luke 2:21-32	[3]Luke 2:15-)25
Xmas 2	*1 Pet. 2:1-10*	[5]Isa. 61:1-3	[4]Matt. 1:18-25	(Matt. 2:19-23)
Lent 2	*Rom. 11:25-27, 33-36*	(1 Thess. 4:1-8)	*Matt. 7:24-29*	(Matt. 15:21-28)
Lent 4	*Isa. 55:1-7*	(Gal. 4:21-31)		
Lent 5			*John 12:23-32*	(John 8:46-59)
6A	*Zech. 9:9-12*		*Mark 11:1-11*	
Lent 6B		[Lection: Matt.*26:1*-27:50]	Matt. 27:51-54	Matt. 27:1-54
... Mon.			*Mark 11:11-12a,15b-19*	[7]Mark 14
... Tue.		[Lection:[7] Mark 14:1-15:37]	Mark 15:38-*41*	Mark 15:1-39
... Wed.		[Lection: Luke 22:1-[8]23:46]	[8]Luke 23:47-49	Luke 22
... Thu.			John 13:1-15	[8]Luke 23:1-49
... Fri.		[Lection: John *18:1*-19:30]	John 19:31-37	John 19:1-37
Easter A	[9]Col. 3:1-4	(1 Cor. 5:6b-8)	Mark 16:1-7	Mark 16:1-(8

Day	Proposed Epistle	Present Epistle	Proposed Gospel	Present Gospel
B	*Phil. 3:7-14* RV	[9]Col.3:1-4	*Matt. 28:1-10*	(John 20:1-10)
... Tue.	Acts 13:*16a*, 26-33a	Acts 13:26-(41		
Easter 1			John 20:19-*29*	John 20:19-23
4	James 1:*12*-18	James 1:17-[10]21		
5	James 1:[10]19-27	James 1:22-27		
Ascension			*Matt. 28:16-20*	(Luke 24:49-53)
Asc. 1	*Eph. 1:15-23*	(1 Pet. 4:7-11)	[11]John 14:27-31a	[12]John 15:26-16:4a
Whitsunday A			*John 4:19-24*	(Luke 11:9-13)
B			John 14:15-26	John 14:15-[11]31a
... Mon.	Acts 10:34a, 36-48a	Acts 10:34()-(48	John 3:16-21, *31-36a*	John 3:16-21
... Tue.			[12]John 15:26-16:4a	(John 10:1-10)
Trinity 2	1 John 3:13-23a	1 John 3:13-(24		
Trinity 7	Rom. 6:*16*-23	Rom. 6:19-23	[13]John 15:1-8	(Mark 8:1-9)
Trinity 13	*2 Cor. 5:1-10*	(Gal. 3:16-22)		
Trinity 15	Gal. 6:12-18	Gal. 6:11)-18		
Trinity 16	Eph. 3:14-21	Eph. 3:13)-21		
Trinity 20	Eph. 5:18b-[14]33	Eph. 5:15)-21	*Mark 10:6-9, 13-16*	(Matt. 22:1-14)
Trinity 21	Eph. 6:10-18	Eph. 6:10-(20	*Luke 17:5-10*	(John 5:46b-54)
Trinity 24	*2 Thess. 2:13-3:5*	(Col. 1:3-12)		

The Liturgical Lectionary 85

Day	Proposed Epistle	Present Epistle	Proposed Gospel	Present Gospel
Before Advent			*John 6:47-58*	(John 6:5-14)
Andrew	Rom. 10:9-18	Rom. 10:9-(21		
Paul			*Matt. 10:24-32*	(Matt. 19:27-30)
Purification	Mal. 3:1-4	Mal. 3:1-(5		[6]Luke 2:22-40
Annunciation				[2]Luke 1:26b-38
Mark			*Mark 13:9-13*	[13]John 15:1-11
Barnabas	Acts 11:*21b*-26 and *13:1-3*	Acts 11:22-(30		
John Baptist			Luke 1:57-68	Luke 1:57-(80
Transfiguration	*2 Cor. 3:12-18*	(2 Pet. 1:13-18)	*Mark 9:2b-9*	(Luke 9:28-36)
Bartholomew	*1 Cor. 12:27-31a*	(Acts 5:12-16)		
Luke	2 Tim. 4:5-13	2 Tim. 4:5-(15		
Marriage	Eph. 5:14-21	[22]Eph.5:20-(33	[13]John 15:9-11	(Matt. 19:4-6)
Thanksgiving			Matt. 6:25-33	Matt. 6:25-(34
A Saint's Day				[1]Matt. 25:31-40

1. The Question of Alternatives

It will be noted that in the foregoing Table, as in the previous discussions, it has been recommended that any alterations determined upon shall be made outright, without retaining the present assignments as alternatives to the new ones.

It seems altogether desirable that such perfectly clean-cut action be taken when general agreement has been reached, and a majority approval obtained, rather than that an attempt be made to conciliate conservative inertia by allowing those wedded to the old selections to continue to use them. This, after all, would be only a sort of crab-like and sidling effort at progress by compromise. Changes in the Liturgical Lectionary were made absolutely in all Revisions before 1928, in accordance with the sound old practical motto, "Be sure you are right — then go ahead!"

But the latest attempt to revise the Prayer Book of the Church of England was faced with divided counsels — which indeed proved insuperable to its adoption. In an endeavor to put all the evidence fairly before the Church (which was most laudable), and also to satisfy everybody (which is forever impossible), the revisers produced what was really a dual Prayer Book, presenting the old and the new material side by side and in the case of the new liturgical lections, retaining the old even for employment in the new rituals. As a book for study, such a work is valuable; as a manual for the people's use, it is all but intolerable.

At the same time the Scottish Church, which hitherto had always known its own mind, and had been bold enough in making what it considered desirable changes, in this matter followed the English lead in retaining for alternative use lections surely marked for ultimate deletion, such as the Unjust Steward Gospel and the Hagar-Sinai Epistle, from a dutiful desire not to get out of step with English standards.

This fear of being smitten for the sin of Uzzah affected even the American revisers in one place, where a new Gospel for Maundy Thursday was offered as an alternative rather than a substitute. In this case they were doubtless moved by the fact that they did not at all know what to do with the Passion according to St. Luke in that particular place, and passed the responsibility to the users. We now know how that experiment came out, and are prepared to recommend the very bold measures which seem indispensable to deal with the resulting situation.

Now obviously the adjustments of the length of the lessons, and the transfers of material from one occasion of the year to another, as shall have been agreed upon, will have to be made absolutely and at one stroke. It would certainly be preferable to carry out substitutions likewise at the same time and in the same way. To leave supplanted lections as alternatives merely clutters up the Prayer Book in a very cumbersome way, to the confusion rather than the edification of the laity. It would be better to get the whole matter thoroughly discussed until the mind of the Church is unmistakably evident, and then to adopt a single straightforward course of Epistles and Gospels without alternatives.

2. Effect on the Correlation with the Western Tradition

We may be allowed to repeat that the whole aim of the present proposals has been not to innovate with a new scheme of our own invention, but at every point to enable the existing plan for the Christian Year to say more effectively what it is evidently trying to tell us. This, we trust, has been evident enough in the foregoing detailed discussions. But the sight of the accumulated result in the preceding Table may again arouse some qualms, as to just what the total effect would be in causing us to diverge further, perhaps, from the traditional standards of the Western Church, especially as somewhat roughly but sufficiently represented in the current Roman Missal.

In the first place, thirteen of the proposed alterations would have no effect whatever one way or the other, since they are changes in matter adopted at or after the Reformation, or in provisions where Rome and Sarum had already gone their separate ways before that time. For instance, we can do anything we like with the Epistle for Christmas II, and the Epistle and Gospel for the early service on Whitsunday, without altering the relative situation, since Rome has nothing to correspond with these novel assignments which we adopted in 1928. Substitutes for the Sarum Gospels for Lent II, the Sunday Next Before Advent, or the feast of St. Mark, or for Epistles for Trinity XV and St. Luke's Day and Gospels for Christmas I and the Monday before Easter, adopted in 1549, or for the Epistle on the Circumcision and the Gospel on the Ascension, which date from 1928, again would not matter, since Rome has different assignments to begin with. Changing the present Gospel of the Transfiguration from St. Luke's version to St. Mark's, where Rome has St. Matthew's, would leave correspondences just where they are.

In the rest of the list, to put the matter at once at its worst: seven Epistles and eight Gospels contained in the Roman scheme for both the Christian Year and the Fixed Holy Days as a whole have been marked for deletion, as against only two Roman Epistles and three Gospels which we propose to restore. However, only five of the seven Epistles and three of the eight Gospels now occur on the same day in the American and the Roman patterns. Therefore, on a point-to-point collation of the provisions for the same occasions, the net 'adverse balance' would be only three lections.

Moreover, the effect of these shifts is distinctly mitigated by the results of the proposed alterations in the length of the selections. Some of these, as in the case of the Epistles for St. Barnabas and Trinity XX, and the Gospels for the week before Easter, on Low Sunday, and St. John Baptist's Day, are so considerable as to be about as important, one way or the other, as outright substitutions. And of these, seven Epistles and eight Gospels have been brought nearer to the Roman assignments, as against six Epistles and two Gospels which have been altered in the opposite direction.

Therefore, counting both kinds of changes together, we find that out of services which both Churches now hold on the same day, seven Epistles and ten Gospels have been brought into closer correspondence, as against seven Epistles and five Gospels which are in greater divergence. In the entire scheme, taking corresponding lections wherever found, nine Epistles and eleven Gospels are closer, thirteen Epistles and ten Gospels are more remote. This again presents a total 'adverse balance' of three lections. However it is reckoned, it cannot be said that any of these figures, out of the total number of 190 lections involved in the pattern, could be considered as a serious assault against the 'great liturgical tradition of the West.'

The Text of the Liturgical Selections

Consideration also must be given to the text of the Scriptures printed in the Prayer Book for the liturgical Epistles and Gospels.

The original text of the Bible used in the Book of Common Prayer was that first officially 'authorized' version known as the 'Great Bible' of 1539. This version still remains the underlying Prayer Book standard for the Psalter, the Decalogue, Offertory Sentences, Comfortable Words, Burial Anthems, etc. But in 1662, the new Authorized Version of 1611 was adopted for the Epistles and Gospels.

The American Prayer Book of 1928 made a number of changes in scripture texts in various parts of the book, incorporating readings from the Revised Version. Much the most striking of these was a very thorough overall recension of the Psalter, whereby a very large number of the more precise renderings of the R. V. were incorporated directly into the rich and poetical text of the Psalms in the 'Great Bible,' without destroying its matchless rhythm and rhetoric.

The Epistles and Gospels were touched much more sparingly; but some of their more glaring inaccuracies and infelicities were remedied. For instance, the textually spurious 'Three Witnesses' verse was eliminated from the Epistle for Low Sunday. The Hebraic allusion to 'bowels,' where we would say 'heart' — disconcerting to modern taste, however correct as a matter of physiological psychology — was altered in two of the Epistles where it occurred, those for Epiphany V and Trinity XXII; though not in two others, for Trinity II and Monday in Holy Week. The Gospel for Trinity XV, 'Anxiety for the Morrow,' was adopted in the Revised Version throughout; though, as we have noted, substantially the same passage on Thanksgiving Day was corrected only in part.

The English and Scottish Prayer Books of the same year carried out minor emendations of phrase within the general framework of the Authorized Version in a considerable number of places which were not altered in our revision.

It would appear that the present undertaking to review the whole Prayer Book systematically now affords us a unique opportunity to do this sort of thing comprehensively, instead of casually and sporadically, as in previous revisions. Hitherto Prayer Book revision has been a patchwork process, directed to glaring faults: as the popular expression goes, "It's the squeaky wheel that gets the grease!" While we are about it, we ought to seek to amend every expression in the Epistles and Gospels which is obscure or erroneous, not merely those which affront our taste.

In the existing assignments, there are a rather surprising number of cases where the English words have shifted their meaning, so that a quite wrong understanding is conveyed by them when they are read. For example:

Word	Sense	Word	Sense
armour	weapons	meat	food
blaspheme	revile	at meat	at table
charity	love	notable	notorious
coast	region	offend	cause to sin
corn	grain	patience	endurance, steadfastness
conscience	consciousness	power	authority
convenient	befitting	prevent	precede
conversation	conduct	prove	test, try
creature	creation	purge	purify
doctrine	teaching	quick	living
evil speaking	slander	scrip	bag
fasting	lack of food	tempt	try, prove
fowls	birds	temptations	trials
glass	mirror	testament	covenant
his, her	its	wanted	lacked
honest	honourable	watchings	sleeplessness
lively	living	worship	kneel before, reverence, honour

The fact that these and other apparently perfectly simple words, used in archaic and obscure senses in Scripture, are perfectly intelligible to a highly literate body of clergy in the Church, does not justify their being read in this form to the people, to whom they no longer convey their original meaning, or even convey a wrong meaning entirely. Certainly our Church places the greatest possible weight on the importance of its teaching through the public reading of the Holy Scriptures; and of all such teaching, the solemn proclamation of the Word of God in the liturgical Epistles and Gospels occupies the highest ritual rank, and carries with it the maximum effect upon the minds of the hearers. Can we, in conscience, continue to offer them chaff along with the wheat? Must conservative inertia bind us to the archaisms of time past, which now serve only to obscure what the Prayer Book calls the 'clearness and excellency of God's holy Word'?

For this purpose, we should proceed along the lines of what has been done before in the previous revisions which have been mentioned, and as carefully and comprehensively as possible correct the particular readings in the interests of the greatest attainable clarity and force.

The new revision of the New Testament known as the 'Revised Standard' is a great help in this. Its renderings take advantage of much new knowledge of the vernacular used in the time of the New Testament which was not previously available; moreover, it measurably attains its announced goal of the literary tone and quality of the King James' Bible, a standard which former Revised Versions sometimes culpably neglected in favor of crabbed pedantries of expression.

Our last General Convention added the Revised Standard to the versions authorized by the Church for reading the Lessons at Morning and Evening Prayer. But it cannot be adopted outright for the text of the Epistles and Gospels. Its modernization of its language, which eliminates the *thee's* and *thou's*, simplifies sentence-structure, and sometimes flattens language lifted by emotion to poetic levels down to a prosaic quality, would make Epistles and Gospels in this idiom suffer drastically by comparison with the prayers of the Liturgy wherein they are set, which prayers carry on the glories of former versions. In this hieratic background, the lections at the Eucharist should proclaim their message in the most stately and most exalted terms. A slightly archaic style only bestows on them a certain elevation and distinction. The only point is that this style must not obscure their meaning.

Dr. W. K. Lowther Clarke, commenting on the changes of readings proposed in England in 1928, sums up the whole matter by saying that "the ideal is a Corrected Authorized version, that is to say, the traditional Bible of the English-speaking race with such changes only as are needed to remove serious misconceptions."[28]

The project therefore of reviewing the present text of the 'Authorized Version' of the Epistles and Gospels to be printed in the Prayer Book, and of making judicious modifications of obscure or misleading phrases in the present translation, has been and is being prosecuted in conference with able scholars in the text and meaning of Holy Scripture, as well as with working parish clergy with a fine sense of phrase, and a love of our great classical version of the Bible as it is.

Since this matter is voluminous, detailed, and necessarily technical, it does not seem desirable to publish the present stage of this investigation at this point. Of course it must be submitted at the time that any actual process of Prayer Book Revision is in hand, just as the 1928 version of the Prayer Book Psalter was printed in a separate Report of its own.

The only objective here is exactly the same as that governing other phases of the review of the Liturgical Lectionary, as has been several times noted before: to enable the Scriptures assigned to be read at the Holy Communion to present more clearly and forcefully what the Church is trying to convey by them.

In this spirit the foregoing examination of the history and content of the Liturgical Lectionary is submitted to the consideration of the Church: in the hope that it may yield the fruit of better understanding of the Church's teaching in the present, and perhaps may pave the way to the attainment of still more valuable provisions in the future.

---

28. *Liturgy and Worship* (N.Y.: Macmillan, 1932), 301.

PRAYER BOOK STUDIES III: THE ORDER FOR THE MINISTRATION TO THE SICK

The Standing Liturgical Commission
of the Protestant Episcopal Church in the
United States of America

1951

PREFACE

The last revision of our Prayer Book was brought to a rather abrupt conclusion in 1928. Consideration of it had preoccupied the time of General Convention ever since 1913. Everyone was weary of the long and ponderous legislative process, and desired to make the new Prayer Book available as soon as possible for the use of the Church.

But the work of revision, which sometimes has seemed difficult to start, in this case proved hard to stop. The years of debate had aroused widespread interest in the whole subject: and the mind of the Church was more receptive of suggestions for revision when the work was brought to an end than when it began. Moreover, the revision was actually closed to new action in 1925, in order that it might receive final adoption in 1928: so that it was not possible to give due consideration to a number of very desirable features in the English and Scottish revisions, which appeared simultaneously with our own. It was further realized that there were some rough edges in what had been done, as well as an unsatisfied demand for still further alterations.

The problem of defects in detail was met by continuing the Revision Commission, and giving it rather large 'editorial' powers (subject only to review by General Convention) to correct obvious errors in the text as adopted, in the publication of the new Prayer Book. Then, to deal with the constructive proposals for other changes which continued to be brought up in every General Convention, the Revision Commission was reconstituted as a Standing Liturgical Commission. To this body all matters concerning the Prayer Book were to be referred, for preservation in permanent files, and for continuing consideration, until such time as the accumulated matter was sufficient in amount and importance to justify proposing another Revision.

The number of such referrals by General Convention, of Memorials from Dioceses, and of suggestions made directly to the Commission from all regions and schools and parties in the Church, has now reached such a total that it is evident that there is a widespread and insistent demand for a general revision of the Prayer Book.

The Standing Liturgical Commission is not, however, proposing any immediate revision. On the contrary, we believe that there ought to be a period of study and discussion, to acquaint the Church at large with the principles and issues involved, in order that the eventual action may be taken intelligently, and if possible without consuming so much of the time of our supreme legislative synod.

Accordingly, the General Convention of 1949 signalized the Fourth Centennial Year of the First Book of Common Prayer in English by authorizing the Liturgical Commission to publish its findings, in the form of a series of *Prayer Book Studies*.

It must be emphasized that the liturgical forms presented in these *Studies* are not — and under our Constitution, cannot be — sanctioned for public use. They are submitted for free discussion. The Commission will be grateful for copies or articles, resolutions, and direct comment, for its consideration, that the mind of the Church may be fully known to the body charged with reporting it.

In this undertaking, we have endeavored to be objective and impartial. It is not possible to avoid every matter which may be thought by some to be controversial. Ideas which seem to be constructively valuable will be brought to the attention of the Church, without too much regard as to whether they may ultimately be judged to be expedient. We cannot undertake to eliminate every proposal to which anyone might conceivably object: to do so would be to admit that any constructive progress is impossible. What we can do is to be alert not to alter the present *balance* of expressed or implied doctrine of the Church. We can seek to counterbalance every proposal which might seem to favor some one party of opinion by some other change in the opposite direction. The goal we have constantly had in mind — however imperfectly we may have succeeded in attaining it — is the shaping of a future Prayer Book which *every* party might embrace with the well-founded conviction that therein its own position had been strengthened, its witness enhanced, and its devotions enriched.

The objective we have pursued is the same as that expressed by the Commission for the Revision of 1892: "*Resolved*, That this Committee, in all its suggestions and acts, be guided by those principles of liturgical construction and ritual use which have guided the compilation and amendments of the Book of Common Prayer, and have made it what it is."

THE STANDING LITURGICAL COMMISSION:

G. ASHTON OLDHAM, *Chairman*
GOODRICH R. FENNER
BAYARD H. JONES, *Vice Chairman*
MORTON C. STONE, *Secretary*
JOHN W. SUTER, *Custodian of the Book of Common Prayer*
MASSEY H. SHEPHERD, JR.
CHURCHILL J. GIBSON
WALTER WILLIAMS
WILLIAM J. BATTLE
SPENCER ERVIN

The Need for Revision

The very able article of Dr. Charles Harris on the 'Visitation of the Sick' in *Liturgy and Worship* (1934) does not devote itself, as most of the contributions to that valuable volume do, to a justification of the alterations proposed by the English Revision of the Prayer Book in 1928, but boldly calls for a far more radical revision of this Office. Dr. Harris begins by saying:

> By common consent, and by the admission of the Lambeth Conferences in 1908, 1920, and 1930, the existing Offices for the Sick (1661) do not adequately represent, and indeed to some extent even misrepresent, the present mind of the Church toward disease. Accordingly, they need, not merely enrichment and improvement in detail, but thorough reconsideration, recasting, and great enlargement, in the light of the Church's fresh orientation of attitude towards ministration to the sick (p. 472).

That precisely this situation is equally true of the Church in America, is immediately evident from the complete disuse of the Visitation Office as a whole, and the very scanty usefulness of any of its constituent elements. Some of the reasons for this state of affairs will appear in the following review of the history of the Church's ministration to the sick; and the discussion will conclude with a presentation of the new office which the Liturgical Commission proposes to meet the challenge of the actual conditions, as forthrightly expressed by Dr. Harris.

Christian Healing

A great part of our Lord's ministry was devoted to healing the sick. We do not know how many people he healed, but the number must have been very large. There are forty-one instances related in the Gospels. But these were the more striking cases, and undoubtedly there were many others not recorded. Some of the instances which are mentioned involved large groups of people, as when 'all the city was gathered at the door, and he healed many' (Mark 1:33-34).

The methods which our Lord used were various. Sometimes he used material media, as when he anointed the eyes of the blind man with clay (John 9:6). Often he used the laying on of hands, as in the case of the woman with the infirmity (Luke 13:13). But generally the spoken word was sufficient, especially in mental cases (Mark 1:23). About half of the accounts mention our Lord's word of command, sometimes together with his touching the patient with his hand. There is no record of his using oil. But the Apostles did, and as it was a common Jewish practice, he may have done so.

The evangelists evidently thought that the ministry of healing was tremendously important, both as a sign of our Lord's divine power, and as an integral part of his work of redemption.

For St. Matthew it was not just that Christ bore our sins, but 'himself took our infirmities and bare our sicknesses' (Matthew 8:17). Salvation — which to many people today means safety in another life beyond the grave — in the New Testament referred to wholeness and health of body and soul in this life as well. There is no evidence that Christ thought of any sickness as incurable, or limited his ministrations to what we call 'functional disorders.' He healed the blind, the leper, the paralysed, the crippled, and the mentally diseased. The only condition was the response of faith and repentance.

Our Lord did indeed recognize that sickness is sometimes caused by sin, as in the healing of the paralytic (Mark 2:5), and of the blind man (John 5:14), in which case the soul must be purified before the body can be healed. But the whole trend and weight of his teaching and practice was to contradict the Jewish view — a view revived in the West in the middle ages, and still prevalent — that sickness is sent by God as a punishment for sin, or as a trial of patience. When the Apostles asked 'who did sin, this man or his parents, that he was born blind?' our Lord replied 'Neither hath this man sinned, nor his parents: but that the works of God should be made manifest in him' (John 9:2-3).

The Apostles continued our Lord's work of healing as a normal part of their ministry, for 'Jesus sent them to preach the kingdom of God, and to heal the sick' (Luke 9:2), and 'he gave them power against unclean spirits, to cast them out, and to heal all manner of sickness and all manner of disease' (Matthew 10:1). We find thirty-two instances of healing by the Apostles in the New Testament, and some of these too were of large groups of people.

What may be considered as our Lord's 'Words of Institution' of the healing ministry are given by St. Matthew, 'Heal the sick, cleanse the lepers, raise the dead, cast out devils: freely ye have received, freely give' (Matthew 10:8) ; and St. Mark adds that they went forth and 'anointed with oil many that were sick, and healed them' (Mark 6:13).

This is the only record of the Apostles using oil for healing. Like our Lord they used various methods, chief among which was the spoken word and the laying on of hands, as in the case of the lame man at the Beautiful Gate of the temple (Acts 3:6-7). But by the time the Epistle of St. James was written, apparently the usual practice was Holy Unction, probably joined with the laying on of hands, as was customary in later use, for he says:

> Is any sick among you? Let him call for the presbyters of the Church; and let them pray over him, anointing him with oil in the Name of the Lord: and the prayer of faith shall save the sick, and the Lord shall raise him up. And if he have committed sins, absolution shall be given him. Confess therefore your sins one to another, and pray one for another, that ye may be healed (James 5:14-16).

This, of course, is the classic scriptural basis for the use of Holy Unction. The translation used here is more accurate than the more familiar one in the King James version. The word 'presbyter' — transliterated from the Greek — is used rather than 'elder' because St. James is quite definitely referring to the official ministry of the Church and not to old men. Likewise, 'absolution shall be given him' is to be preferred to 'they shall be forgiven him' as a translation of *aphethēsetai autō*, because most independent scholars join with the majority of the ancient Fathers[1] in recognizing that the plain force of the Greek idiom in its context, as well as the natural interpretation of the account in its scriptural setting, agree in indicating that St. James was speaking of confession and absolution preceding the anointing, rather than of the conception of the Roman teaching of medieval times, that the primary purpose of the anointing was a particularly solemn and effectual absolution of sin. It may doubtless be true that a remission of sin may be a *secondary* effect of the anointing, exactly as it may be of the Holy Eucharist, and of many other acts of religion. It may even be, as some of the more penetrating theologians have maintained, that there is sometimes evidence that in healing the soul *in order* that the body may be cured, the very *root* of sin may be destroyed by the holy anointing. But this is by no means the same thing as Absolution.

Throughout the period of the undivided Church healing was taken for granted as a function of the ministry. Churches were considered 'temples of healing,' and people resorted to them as we now go to hospitals. If a person was too sick to go to Church, the Bishop or Priest, accompanied by laymen of the congregation, visited him, and administered Holy Unction together with the Laying on of Hands; the oil being blessed either in the Church or in the presence of the patient by the minister, whether Bishop or Priest.

Moreover, the ministration was not confined, as in modern Roman practice, to those in danger of death. Anyone, slightly or seriously ill, might be anointed, not only once but many times. Frequently patients were anointed every day for a week, or longer, if necessary. And if the minister could not come every day, laymen were authorized to administer the oil blessed by the clergy.

All of these characteristics of the ministration have been preserved to this day in the use of the Eastern Churches, orthodox and schismatic alike. In the West they remained unaltered in the Sacramentary which Pope Hadrian sent to Charlemagne at the end of the eighth century; and they are still found in the Roman Pontifical.

But the ninth century, which ushered in that 'Deformation Period' which distorted so many other elements of Christian worship, began a radical shift of the belief and practice of the Western Church in the use of Anointing. Instead of being regarded as a 'Sacrament of Healing,' to be administered to all the sick,

---

1. Cf. *Liturgy and Worship*, p. 509.

and repeated as often as necessary, it was now formally named a 'Sacrament of the Dying,' bestowed only upon those for whose recovery little hope could be entertained, and restricted to be received only once in the course of a given illness. It became '*Extreme* Unction' — and though some tried to maintain that this meant only the *last* of the Church's anointings which began with Confirmation, in fact it was the anointing of those *in extremis*. And a misinterpretation of the incidental words of St. James, inaccurately translated in the Vulgate, fixed the conception of its grace as a final solemn Absolution in the hour of death, not a restoration to physical and spiritual wholeness. Its form, as found in the Roman *Rituale*, became an unction of seven parts of the body, with specific prayers for remission of the sins committed through the several organs of sense.

The Anglican Prayer Books

Such was the resulting state of the Office as it lay before Cranmer in the Sarum 'Manual.' He followed the structure and contents of that office with only slight condensations in the first Prayer Book. The 'Visitation of the Sick' was laid out in five parts or movements, as follows:

1. First, there was a short liturgical service by way of introduction. This consisted of the salutation, 'Peace be to this house,' followed by one of the Seven Penitential Psalms (143), formerly said on the way to the house, concluding with an Antiphon, 'Remember not, Lord, our offences,' as in the Litany; then the Kyries, Lord's Prayer, suffrages, and two out of the nine Sarum Collects, praying for relief and for healing.
2. The second division was a pastoral preparation of the sick person for the Sacraments of Penance, Unction, and Communion which were to follow. It began with a long set exhortation upon the moral values of sickness, expanding the medieval ideas of resignation to the 'Chastisement of the Lord' in the Sarum original, and omitting the note of hope of recovery. This exhortation concluded with an examination of the sick person's faith, in terms of the Apostles' Creed. The remainder of the Sarum exhortation was represented by a series of rubrics directing the priest to assure that the patient had set his spiritual and temporal affairs in order, by reconciliation to his neighbors, and by disposing of his goods by will.
3. Then followed the Sacrament of Penance, of necessary:

    Here shall the sicke person make a speciall confession, yf he fele his conscience troubled with any weightie matter. After whiche confession, the priest shall absolue him after this forme: and thesame forme of absolucion shall be vsed in all pryuate confessions.

Our Lorde Iesus Christe, who hath lefte power to his Churche to absolue all sinners, which truely repent & beleue in him: of his great mercy forgeue thee thine offences: and by his autoritie committed to me, I absolue thee from all thy synnes, in the name of the father, and of the sonne, and of the holy gost. Amen.

This Absolution was a strengthened version of the Sarum form, and is in fact the most emphatic known example of a declaratory Absolution. And it is further reenforced by the prayer 'O most merciful God' (as on p. 313 of the present American Prayer Book).[2] In the Gelasian Sacramentary of the seventh century, in the days before 'indicative' or even 'imperative' formulas were preferred for the administration of the Sacraments, this 'precatory' form was provided for the solemn Absolution of a dying penitent.

4. The office of Unction began with the recitation of Psalm 71 with its Antiphon, 'O Saueour of the worlde' (now on p. 313).[3] Then followed the powerful confirming words, 'The almighty Lord, whiche is a moste strong tower,' etc. (p. 314).[4] In our present service this has something the effect of a concluding Benediction. In the original text it was a trumpet-peal to summon up triumphant faith in the effectualness of the following ministration.

The Unction was a single anointing, 'vpon the forehead or breast onely,' praying for an inward anointing of the soul with the Holy Ghost, 'who is the spirite of all strength, coumfort, reliefe, and gladnes.' The prayer went on to salvage from other parts of the Sarum office some surviving vestiges of the primitive conceptions of a Sacrament of Healing:

---

2. Ed. note: O MOST merciful God, who, according to the multitude of thy mercies, dost so put away the sins of those who truly repent, that thou rememberest them no more; Open thine eye of mercy upon this thy servant, who most earnestly desireth pardon and forgiveness. Renew in *him*, most loving Father, whatsoever hath been decayed by the fraud and malice of the devil, or by *his* own carnal will and frailness; preserve and continue this sick member in the unity of the Church; consider *his* contrition, accept *his* tears, assuage *his* pain, as shall seem to thee most expedient for *him*. And forasmuch as *he* putteth *his* full trust only in thy mercy, impute not unto *him his* former sins, but strengthen *him* with thy blessed Spirit; and, when thou art pleased to take *him* hence, take *him* unto thy favour; through the merits of thy most dearly beloved Son, Jesus Christ our Lord. Amen.

3. Ed. note: O SAVIOUR of the world, who by thy Cross and precious Blood hast redeemed us; Save us, and help us, we humbly beseech thee, O Lord.

4. Ed. note: THE Almighty Lord, who is a most strong tower to all those who put their trust in him, to whom all things in heaven, in earth, and under the earth, do bow and obey; Be now and evermore thy defence; and make thee know and feel, that there is none other Name under heaven given to man, in whom, and through whom, thou mayest receive health and salvation, but only the Name of our Lord Jesus Christ. Amen.

> And vouchsafe for hys great mercie (if it be his blessed will) to restore vnto thee thy bodely health, and strength, to serue hym: and sende thee release of all thy paynes, troubles and diseases, both in bodye and mynd.

But it also, unhappily, incorporated the medieval notion of a solemn remission of the sins of the body:

> to pardone thee all thy synnes, and offences, committed by all thy bodely sences, passions, and carnall affeccions:

and it ends upon a note of impending death.

Psalm 13, 'How long wilt thou forget me, O Lord,' was said after the Anointing, with no other conclusion: the assumption being that the priest would go on at once to the fifth and final ingredient of the ministration,

5. the Communion of the Sick.

As the Prayer Book from Cranmer's day to ours has presented this as a separate Office, it will make for simplicity if we defer examining its content and history to a later place.

It is very clear from the foregoing analysis that the Visitation Office of the First Prayer Book was thoroughly medieval in its conceptions. Its whole tone was not of encouragement, but of resignation. It did not exclude hope of recovery; but it was constructed throughout with the purpose of making systematic preparation for imminent death. It is because that idea was fundamental to its plan, and integral to its contents, that with the advancing achievements of medical science the Visitation Office has grown less and less useful; and that the modifications of the Office in the succeeding Prayer Books have been powerless to ameliorate its fundamental defects.

In the Second Prayer Book of 1552, Cranmer dropped the Anointing, in accordance with the criticisms of Bucer on the retention of 'Extreme Unction.' But this move only intensified the difficulties of the service, instead of removing them. Until that time, the Holy Anointing had been the integrating *terminus ad quem* of the whole action, whose purpose was to lead up to that climax of the ministration. As long as that objective and goal was in mind, there were constructive and animating values in the preceding spiritual exercises. The exhortation to patience, designed to eliminate futile resentments and terrors at the illness itself; the examination of faith and conscience, and the setting in order of the patient's affairs, spiritual and temporal; and the conclusive Confession and convincing Absolution: these were all positive and encouraging, so long as they were explicitly preparations for the final supreme Sacrament of healing soul and body. Without it, they collapsed of their own weight, and became negative and depressant, since the only goal to which they led was simply death.

The Prayer Book of 1662 finished off the Visitation office with the Aaronic Benediction: thus sundering the service from its former final hopeful act of the receiving of the Holy Communion. While of course this could be added, it was no longer in mind as an integral part of the normal ministration.

The first American Prayer Book of 1789 banished the third Sacrament from the Office, by removing all mention of Confession and Absolution. (The ancient Gelasian prayer for remission was, as it were, inadvertently retained, not being recognized as a precatory form of Absolution: but, deprived of its context, it was also deprived of affirmative force: its net effect is a cry of that sort of contrition which is inspired by sickness.)

Meanwhile, during the time that the Visitation Office was actually deteriorating in its content and quality, the whole setting of the sick-bed has been altered. The great advances of medical knowledge have made an increasing number of ailments curable, which only a few years ago were inevitably fatal. No longer is it the chief task of the physician to make the patient as comfortable as possible until death overtakes him, or until the indomitable urge of all life towards health has wrought its own cure. He is engaged in a confident battle with sickness and death, with inflexible hope of victory. He will welcome the ministrations of the Church if they are constructive, removing troubles of the mind and soul which impede concentration upon the task of recovery — but not if they give up the fight by merely instilling resignation to the approach of death. It is very significant that the most modern views of both therapeutics and theology join in affirming the procedures which are perfectly expressed in the most ancient of our Scriptures on this subject, in that passage from the book of Ecclesiasticus which the Church reads upon the feast of St. Luke the Physician:

> My son, in thy sickness be not negligent: but pray unto the Lord, and he shall make thee whole. Leave off from sin, and order thy hands aright, and cleanse thy heart from all wickedness. . . . Then give place unto the physician, for the Lord hath created him. . . . There is a time when in their hands there is good success (*Ecclus.* 38:9-10, 12-13).

But the more that emphasis is placed upon the value of the elements of hope and comfort in the ministrations of the Church, the less has been the value of the Visitation Office, and the rarer its employment.

From time to time, attempts have been made to supplement the manifest deficiencies of the Visitation Office. The English revision of 1662 added a number of prayers for special contingencies of a sickness; and the American books from the first brought in still more prayers. Our last revision in 1928 supplanted the old set exhortation with a cycle of five short Psalms, each preceded by an Antiphon and followed by a brief Collect. It also restored provisions for a special Confession of the sick person: but faltered at bringing back the powerful and convincing Absolution of the English books, contenting itself with a direction that 'the Minister shall assure him of God's mercy and forgiveness.' The Rubric about the making of wills, which through the ages had been productive of such abuses that the civil law now restricts its operation, by declaring invalid any charitable bequests made less than thirty days before death, was firmly removed to the end of the whole section of the Prayer Book, in this form:

> The Minister is ordered, from time to time, to advise the People, *whilst they are in health*, to make Wills arranging for the disposal of their temporal goods, and, when of ability, to leave Bequests for religious and charitable purposes.

And this revision also pioneered in restoring the 'Unction of the Sick' — thus anticipating the action of the Lambeth Conference of 1930, which, after much study and discussion of the matter, advised the reinstatement of the rite of Holy Unction, or at least the Laying on of Hands, not as a preparation for death, but as a means of healing. But the American form consisted only of a prayer and a declaratory formula, to be joined, at the Minister's discretion, to 'such portions of the foregoing Office as he shall think fit': it did not provide as the Scottish Prayer Book of 1929 did, a self-complete action of its own. Moreover, it placed the 'Unction of the Sick' after the 'Litany for the Dying,' thereby suggesting, unintentionally no doubt, the medieval and Roman view of it as a 'last rite.'

Principles of the Proposed Revision

In the light of all this, the Liturgical Commission has come to the conclusion that what is needed is not further patching and piecing of the existing Visitation Office, with supplementations of what is little better than a disorganized miscellany in its accumulated provisions, but a general reconstruction of a new 'Order for the Ministration to the Sick' upon a consistent plan.

We believe we are on firm ground in basing our reconstruction on the following considerations:

1. The experience of the early Church, which employed a sevenfold Order for ministrations upon successive days, thus achieving a continuous and cumulative effect, instead of the medieval attempt to do everything for the purification and preparation of the soul in one single Office of inordinate length and weight.
2. The experience of many parishes during the last forty years, in the employment of public services of healing in the Church, with corporate intercessions for the sick, whether present or absent, and specific acts of benediction of those present. For this purpose, the ancient sevenfold cycle of devotions, varied and cumulative as they are, is ideally suited.

3. The tentative move of our revision of 1928, which gave five groups of Antiphon, Psalm, and Collect. This was a step in the right direction, but rather indeterminate in its purpose, and inadequate in its content. But it needed only a better selection and alignment of themes, and the addition of a strong affirmative Lesson from Holy Scripture, to furnish a sufficient nucleus of a form for a single ministration, public or private.
4. The experience of the Christian ages, that spiritual help, and *therefore* also physical betterment, is to be expected of the scriptural ministration of the Holy Anointing, or the Laying on of Hands. Roman commentators have often noted with a certain sort of wonder that *Extreme* Unction, though administered as a Sacrament of the Dying, when all hope has been abandoned, is *usually* followed by at least partial and temporary physical improvement. We propose to revive this 'lost Pleiad of the Anglican Sacraments'[5] as a normal ministration to the sick; to make it familiar again to the people by public use in Church; and to present it as the conclusion and objective of the Office.

In these days of psychosomatic medicine, it ought to be clear that spiritual ministration in sickness is of great importance, and that the point of view of the New Testament and the undivided Church is perfectly sound scientifically as well as theologically. At any rate, throughout the Anglican Communion there is a large and growing movement to obey our Lord's command, and to restore the healing ministry, not as a substitute for the work of the medical profession, but in cooperation with it, especially in dealing with the spiritual causes of sickness.

The results of this revived ministry are most encouraging, sometimes as amazing as the accounts in the New Testament. Of course there are some failures, but these are to be expected. Medicine does not always cure either, but we do not give it up for that reason. However, we do need a more adequate service in the Prayer Book, both as a liturgical tool for the clergy, and as a means of cultivating that confident faith in our Lord's continuing power to heal, and that real repentance for hindering sins, which are necessary prerequisites for healing.

Whether the proposed service is adequate can only be determined by actual use over a sufficient period of time. But it is based on the New Testament record, and makes use of ancient liturgical material uncontaminated by the later medieval point of view.

For further study of the whole question, the reader is referred to the following books: *Christian Healing*, by Evelyn Frost, the best work on the view of the early Church; the article on the Visitation of the Sick in *Liturgy and Worship*,

---

5. Ed. note: A "pleiad" is one of a group of seven items or objects. (Think of the Pleiads, a constellation of seven stars.) The quoted passage here (not footnoted in the original) is from Alexander Penrose Forbes, *Exposition of the XXXIX Articles*, vol. II, p. 463.

edited by Clarke, an adequate but somewhat involved account of the whole history of the matter; the similar article in *The American Prayer Book*, by Parsons and Jones, an excellent short summary; *Body and Soul*, by Percy Dearmer, an older but still valuable account, giving all the Biblical references; and *Stretching Forth Thine Hand to Heal*, by Richard Spread, an account of modern practice.

Comments on the Service

As indicated by the first two rubrics, this service is intended for public as well as private use. The title, therefore, has been changed to 'The Order for the Ministration to the Sick' because 'Visitation' implies merely private use in the sick room, and also there is a flavor of the medieval idea that in sickness God 'visits' us for our sins.

A large number of parishes throughout the Anglican Communion, following the practice of the early Church, now have weekly services for the sick who can come to Church. Until people generally become accustomed to the public ministry, and see the Laying on of Hands and Holy Unction performed as a normal and regular part of the Church's work, there will be little demand for private ministration. People take for granted the ministry of the medical profession. Regular public services help to create a similar confidence in the value of spiritual ministration, and eliminate the idea that Holy Unction is intended only as a blessing on the dying.

The first rubric allows the minister to use as much or as little of the office as is advisable, at his discretion. At a private ministration in serious illness only the bare essentials of the rite would be used. But at a public service, where only slightly sick persons are present, the whole order may easily be used. Normally this would be the Preparation, one of the seven Orders — varying each week for seven weeks — the Litany, which may be substituted for one of the Orders, or the Special Prayers, followed by the Consecration of the Oil and the Laying on of Hands and Anointing. Even when there is a short instruction, this service takes less than half an hour, and, without the address, only about fifteen or twenty minutes.

The second rubric restores the practice of the early Church in inviting sick people to come to Church for the ministration if they are able, and if unable, to notify the priest, and not leave it to chance that he may hear about it. Incidentally, if notified, the priest will know that the patient wants the ministration, and therefore has some confidence in its value.

The third rubric provides for the attendance of lay persons at private ministrations. In the early Church the private ministration was a corporate act of the Church, and members of the congregation accompanied the minister. Sometimes the patient is not able to join audibly in the service, and such lay persons may take the responses. Thus the usually merely social visits of friends may become more effectual and encouraging to the patient.

The fourth rubric provides for private confession before the service if desired. The present Prayer Book rubric says 'Then shall the sick person be *moved* to make a special confession of his sins.' The new rubric requires only that the priest *ask* if he desires to do so, largely depending on whether the patient is accustomed to making such confession. When a person is sick, it is hardly the time to argue about the value of auricular confession.

The fifth rubric, with all similar rubrics concerning posture throughout the service, of course applies only to a public ministration, not to private use.

The Preparation begins the service with versicles containing the giving of the Peace. Then comes the Confession in the revised form proposed for the Holy Communion and the Penitential Office.[6] If the patient at a private ministration has already made a special confession, the confession in the service is omitted.

The rubric after the Absolution provides for a Hymn. Needless to say such hymns should be encouraging and inspire confidence, not the gloomy hymns which used to be listed in the Hymnal under 'Visitation,' many of which are directly contrary to the teaching of Christ. Care should be taken to avoid any which teach that God *sends* sickness, or that sickness is a 'bearing of the cross.' Patiently enduring persecution or misunderstanding is "bearing the cross," not sickness. Sickness, like sin, is an evil which we should fight against as our Lord did.

If there is to be an instruction of sermon, it would normally follow the Lesson in the Order used. Such instruction has been found extremely valuable in the public service, as an opportunity to present the New Testament view of healing, and its place in the ministrations of the Church.

The seven Orders which follow — only *one* of which is used at any one service — provide variety at the public ministration. Each one centers in a theme related to healing as given in the Lesson taken from the New Testament. They may also be used, when advisable, in the sick room, at successive visits. And the patient may use them for private devotion on days when the priest cannot come. All of them are compiled with a view to inspiring confidence, and to cultivating proper dispositions of faith and repentance. The collects, which are new, were composed to summarize this teaching.

The Litany of Healing, which follows the seven Orders, may be used in addition to one of the Orders, or in place of it, or even as a separate service of intercession for the sick and for those who minister to them. The Litany repeats the teaching of the seven Orders, and in such phrases as 'Son of David, have mercy upon us' and 'Jesus of Nazareth, have mercy upon us' uses the appeal of the sick to our Lord as given in the Gospels.

---

6. Ed. note: This comment is a reminder that the first several volumes of this series should be seen as part of a coherent group of materials produced at this first stage of work and not as a set of disjointed pamphlets.

The special Prayers which follow the Litany may be used according to need, at the discretion of the minister. Some of them are taken from the present Prayer Book office, the rest are derived from a booklet for the sick issued by the Forward Movement.

While 'The Laying on of Hands and Holy Unction' has a separate title, indicating that it may be used by itself, at a public service especially it is intended to be the *climax* toward which the preceding devotions lead. Attention is called to the second rubric in this section which provides that those who have only minor ailments may receive the ministration, and that it is not confined to those seriously ill, nor is Holy Unction limited to *one* administration in a sickness. The third rubric permits the use of the Laying on of Hands without Holy Unction when desirable.

According to Hippolytus, the oil for the sick ordinarily was consecrated on the altar with a prayer similar to the Eucharistic prayer. 'The Consecration of the Oil' in this office is taken in part from the ancient Roman Pontifical, which was not influenced by later medieval thought, as is the case with the *Rituale*. But the now rather meaningless references to the anointing of prophets, priests, and kings has been omitted, and the emphasis is upon our Lord's commission to heal. This prayer would be used at the altar at a public service, or at the bedside of the patient at a private ministration. The consecration of the oil in the presence of the patient makes a deep impression. Of course, where weekly services are held, the priest may 'reserve' the oil for use at sick calls during the week. And the prayer may be used also by the Bishop on Maundy Thursday where it is customary for him to follow the later practice of consecrating the oil for the diocese, such oil being 'reserved' for use during the year.

The words of administration are the result of long study and practice, and have been carefully thought out to convey exactly the meaning intended, and at the same time to be short and easily memorized. 'By the authority committed unto me' implies that this is really a necessary part of the work of the Ministry. 'That all evil may depart from thee' refers to both the mental and physical causes of sickness, and may be thought of as a modern equivalent to the ancient exorcism. 'In the name of Jesus Christ of Nazareth' reflects the use of the Apostles who healed 'in His Name,' and the doxology makes it also an invocation of the Blessed Trinity, customary in such forms.

As at Baptism, Confirmation, and Holy Matrimony, the Lord's Prayer follows, both as a prayer concerning the ministration, and as a thanksgiving for it. The service concludes with St. Paul's beautiful benediction of soul and body, from 1 Thess. 5:23.

MORTON C. STONE
For the Commission

The Order for the Ministration to the Sick

¶ *The following Service, or any part thereof, may be used both publicly in Church, and privately in the sick room, at the discretion of the Minister.*

¶ *Sick persons should come to Church for the Ministration, but if unable, notice shall be given thereof to the Priest, who shall minister to the patient privately.*

¶ *At a private Ministration it is desirable that one or more lay persons be present, both to join in the responses, and to encourage the patient by the supporting prayers of the Church.*

¶ *Before a private Ministration the Priest shall inquire whether the patient desires to make a special Confession, and if so, the Confession and Absolution in the Service shall be omitted.*

The Preparation

¶ *All standing, the Minister shall begin by saying the following Versicles with the People.*

GRACE be unto you, and peace, from God our Father, and from the Lord Jesus Christ;

And with thy spirit.

O God, make speed to save us;
O Lord, make haste to help us.
Glory be to the Father, and to the Son, and to the Holy Ghost;
As it was in the beginning, is now, and ever shall be, world without end. Amen.

¶ *All kneeling, Minister and People shall say together the Confession, the Minister first saying,*

Let us humbly confess our sins unto Almighty God.

The Confession

ALMIGHTY God, Father of our Lord Jesus Christ, Maker of all things, Judge of all men; We acknowledge and confess our manifold sins which we have committed, By thought, word, and deed, Against thy Divine Majesty. We do earnestly repent, And are heartily sorry for these our misdoings. Have mercy upon us, most merciful Father; For thy Son our Lord Jesus Christ's sake, Forgive us all that is past; And grant that we may ever hereafter, Serve and please thee in newness of Life, To the honour and glory of thy name; Through the same Jesus Christ our Lord. *Amen.*

The Absolution

¶ The Priest alone standing and turning to the People shall say,

ALMIGHTY God, our heavenly Father, who of his great mercy hath promised forgiveness of sins to all those who with hearty repentance and true faith turn unto him; Have mercy upon you; pardon and deliver you from all your sins; confirm and strengthen you in all goodness; and bring you to everlasting life; through Jesus Christ our Lord. *Amen.*

¶ Here a Hymn may be sung. Then one of the following seven Orders shall be used, the Minister first announcing the number, the People sitting until the Collect, when they shall kneel. And if there be an Instruction or Sermon, it shall follow the Lesson of the Order used.

Order I. The Great Physician

Antiphon. He that believeth on me, the works that I do shall he do also; * and greater works than these shall he do, because I go unto my Father. *St. John 14:12.*

From Psalm 118. Confitemini Domino.

O GIVE thanks unto the Lord, for he is gracious;
Because his mercy endureth for ever.
The Lord is my strength and my song;
And is become my salvation.
The voice of joy and health is in the dwellings of the righteous;
The right hand of the Lord bringeth mighty things to pass.
The right hand of the Lord hath the preeminence;
The right hand of the Lord bringeth mighty things to pass.

I shall not die, but live:
And declare the works of the Lord.
I will thank thee, for thou hast heard me;
And art become my salvation.
Glory be to the Father, and to the Son, and to the Holy Ghost;
As it was in the beginning, is now, and ever shall be, world without end. Amen.

The Lesson. St. Mark 1:29.

FORTHWITH, when they were come out of the synagogue, they entered into the house of Simon and Andrew, with James and John. But Simon's wife's mother lay sick of a fever, and immediately they told him of her. And he came and took her by the hand, and lifted her up, and the fever left her, and she ministered unto them. And at even, when the sun did set, they brought unto him all who were sick or possessed with evil spirits. And all the city was gathered about the door. And he healed many who were sick of divers diseases, and cast out many evil spirits.

Heal me, O Lord, and I shall be healed;
Save me, and I shall be saved.

Let us pray.

ALMIGHTY Father, whose blessed Son healed many who were sick both in body and in soul; Grant us so to believe in him, that the works which he did we may do also: that those to whom we minister may be restored to health; through the same Jesus Christ our Lord. *Amen.*

Order 2. The Commission to Heal

Antiphon. Jesus sent them to preach the kingdom of God, * and to heal the sick. St. Luke 9:2.

From Psalm 91. Qui habitat.

WHOSO dwelleth under the defence of the Most High,
Shall abide under the shadow of the Almighty.
I will say unto the Lord, Thou art my hope and my stronghold;
My God, in him will I trust.
For he shall deliver thee from the snare of the hunter,
And from the noisome pestilence.
He shall defend thee under his wings, and thou shalt be safe under his feathers;

His faithfulness and truth shall be thy shield and buckler.
Thou shalt not be afraid for any terror by night,
Nor for the arrow that flieth by day;
For the pestilence that walketh in darkness,
Nor for the sickness that destroyeth in the noon day.
There shall no evil happen unto thee,
Neither shall any plague come nigh thy dwelling;
For he shall give his angels charge over thee,
To keep thee in all thy ways.
Glory be to the Father, and to the Son, and to the Holy Ghost;
As it was in the beginning, is now, and ever shall be, world without end. Amen.

The Lesson. St. Matthew 10:1.

WHEN Jesus had called unto him his twelve disciples, he gave them power over unclean spirits, to cast them out, and to heal all manner of sickness and all manner of infirmity. These twelve Jesus sent forth, and commanded them, saying, Heal the sick, cleanse the lepers, raise the dead, cast out evil spirits; freely ye have received, freely give.

Let thy priests be clothed with righteousness;
And let thy saints sing with joyfulness.

Let us pray.

O GOD, who by thy blessed Son sent forth the Apostles to preach the Gospel and to heal the sick; Grant that the ministers of thy Church may ever fulfil this thy command of mercy; that as they have freely received thy healing grace, so they may freely give to those who come to thee; through Jesus Christ our Lord. *Amen.*

Order 3. Repentance

Antiphon. If we confess our sins, God is faithful and just to forgive us our sins, * and to cleanse us from all unrighteousness. *1 St. John 1:9.*

From Psalm 103. Benedic, anima mea.

PRAISE the Lord, O my soul:
And all that is within me, praise his holy Name.
Praise the Lord, O my soul,

And forget not all his benefits:
Who forgiveth all thy sin,
And healeth all thine infirmities;
Who saveth thy life from destruction,
And crowneth thee with mercy and loving-kindness;
Who satisfieth thy mouth with good things,
Making thee young and lusty as an eagle.
The Lord is full of compassion and mercy,
Longsuffering and of great goodness.
He hath not dealt with us after our sins,
Nor rewarded us according to our wickedness.
For look how high the heaven is in comparision of the earth;
So great is his mercy also toward them that fear him.
Look how wide also the east is from the west:
So far hath he set our sins from us.
Yea, like as a father pitieth his own children;

Glory be to the Father, and to the Son, and to the Holy Ghost;
As it was in the beginning, is now, and ever shall be, world without end. Amen.

The Lesson. St. Matthew 9:2.

BEHOLD, they brought unto him a man who was paralysed, lying on a bed: and Jesus, seeing their faith, said unto the paralysed man, Son, be of good cheer; thy sins are forgiven thee, And behold, certain of the scribes said within themselves, This man blasphemeth. And Jesus knowing their thoughts said, Wherefore think ye evil in your hearts? For which is easier, to say, Thy sins are forgiven thee; or to say, Arise, and walk? But that ye may know that the Son of man hath power on earth to forgive sins (then saith he to the paralysed man) arise, take up thy bed, and go unto thine house. And he arose, and departed to his house. But when the multitude saw it, they were filled with awe, and glorified God, who had given such power unto men.

Lord, be merciful unto me;
Heal my soul, for I have sinned against thee.

Let us pray.

O MERCIFUL God, who hast given to thy Church power on earth both to forgive the penitent and to heal the sick; Absolve thy people from their offences; that their souls being freed from sin, their bodies may be restored to health; through Jesus Christ our Lord. Amen.

Order 4. Faith

Antiphon. Without faith it is impossible to please him: for he that cometh to God must believe that he is, * and that he is a rewarder of them that diligently seek him. *Hebrews 11:6.*

From Psalm 27. Dominus illuminatio.

THE Lord is my light and my salvation; whom then shall I fear?
  The Lord is the strength of my life; of whom then shall I be afraid?
  For in the time of trouble he shall hide me in his tabernacle;
  Yea, in the secret place of his dwelling shall he hide me, and set me up upon a rock of stone.
  My heart hath talked of thee, Seek ye my face;
  Thy face, Lord, will I seek.
  I should utterly have fainted,
  But that I believe verily to see the goodness of the Lord in the land of the living.
  O tarry thou the Lord's leisure;
  Be strong, and he shall comfort thine heart; and put thou thy trust in the Lord.
  Glory be to the Father, and to the Son, and to the Holy Ghost;
  As it was in the beginning, is now, and ever shall be, world without end. Amen.

The Lesson. St. Matthew 9:27.

WHEN Jesus departed thence, two blind men followed him, crying and saying, Thou son of David, have mercy upon us. And when he was come into the house, the blind men came to him: And Jesus said unto them, Believe ye that I am able to do this? They said unto him, Yea, Lord. Then touched he their eyes, saying, According to your faith be it unto you. And their eyes were opened.

  Lord, I believe:
  Help thou mine unbelief.

Let us pray.

O LORD, increase our faith; that trusting in thy power to heal, the prayer of faith shall save the sick, and thou wilt raise him up; through Jesus Christ our Lord. Amen.

Order 5. The Holy Spirit

Antiphon. God hath not given us the spirit of fear; * but of power, and of love, and of a sound mind. *2 Timothy 1:7.*

From Psalm 107. Confitemini Domino.

O GIVE thanks unto the Lord, for he is gracious,
And his mercy endureth for ever.
Let them give thanks whom the Lord hath redeemed,
And delivered from the hand of the enemy.
Such as sit in darkness, and in the shadow of death,
Being fast bound in misery and iron;
When they cried unto the Lord in their trouble,
He delivered them out of their distress.
For he brought them out of darkness, and out of the shadow of death,
And brake their bonds asunder.
He sent his word, and healed them;
And they were saved from their destruction.
O that men would therefore praise the Lord for his goodness;
And declare the wonders that he doeth for the children of men.
Glory be to the Father, and to the Son, and to the Holy Ghost;
As it was in the beginning, is now, and ever shall be, world without end. Amen.

The Lesson. St. Luke 11:34.

THE light of the body is the eye; therefore when thine eye is single, thy whole body also is full of light; but when thine eye is feeble, thy body also is full of darkness. Take heed therefore that the light which is in thee be not darkness. If thy whole body therefore be full of light, having no part dark, the whole shall be full of light, as when the bright shining of a candle doth give thee light.

O give me the comfort of thy help again;
And stablish me with thy free Spirit.

Let us pray.

DRIVE out from us, Lord, we beseech thee, all evil thoughts which possess us, and stir up thy Spirit within us; that our minds being no longer divided, we may serve thee in singleness of heart; through Jesus Christ our Lord. Amen.

Order 6. The Holy Name

Antiphon. There is none other Name under heaven given among men, * whereby we must be saved. *Acts 4:12.*

From Psalm 20. Exaudiat te Domine.

THE Lord hear thee in the day of trouble;
The Name of the God of Jacob defend thee;
Send the help from the sanctuary,
And strengthen thee out of Sion:
Remember all thy offerings,
And accept thy burnt sacrifices:
Grant thee thy heart's desire,
And fulfil all thy mind.
We will rejoice in thy salvation, and triumph in the Name of the Lord our God;
The Lord perform all thy petitions.
Now know I that the Lord helpeth his anointed, and will hear him from his holy heaven,
Even with the wholesome strength of his right hand.
Save, Lord, and hear us, O king of heaven,
When we call upon thee.
Glory be to the Father, and to the Son, and to the Holy Ghost;
As it was in the beginning, is now, and ever shall be, world without end. Amen.

The Lesson. Acts 3:1.

NOW Peter and John went up together into the temple at the hour of prayer, being the ninth hour. And a certain man, lame from his mother's womb, was being carried, whom they laid daily at the gate of the temple which is called Beautiful, to ask alms of those who entered into the temple; who seeing Peter and John about to go into the temple asked an alms. And Peter, fastening his eyes upon him, with John, said, Look on us. And he paid attention to them, expecting to receive something of them. Then Peter said, Silver and gold have I none; but such as I have give I thee; In the Name of Jesus Christ of Nazareth rise up and walk. And he took him by the right hand, and lifted him up, and immediately his feet and ankles received strength. And he leaping up stood, and walked, and entered with them into the temple, walking and leaping, and praising God.

I will praise the Name of God with a song;
And magnify it with thanksgiving.

Let us pray.

O GOD, who didst give to the Apostles power to heal in the Name of thy Son Jesus Christ; Be present with all thy sick servants, and give them such faith in this holy Name that it may be to them a medicine of health and a pledge of eternal salvation; through the same Jesus Christ our Lord. *Amen.*

Order 7. Holy Unction

Antiphon. The Apostles anointed with oil many that were sick, * and healed them. *St. Mark 6:13.*

Psalm 23. Dominus regit me.

THE Lord is my shepherd;
Therefore can I lack nothing.
He shall feed me in a green pasture;
And lead me forth beside the waters of comfort.
He shall convert my soul,
And bring me forth in the paths of righteousness for his Name's sake.
Yea, though I walk through the valley of the shadow of death, I will fear no evil;
For thou art with me; thy rod and thy staff comfort me.
Thou shalt prepare a table before me in the presence of them that trouble me;
Thou hast anointed my head with oil, and my cup shall be full.
Surely thy loving-kindness and mercy shall follow me all the days of my life;
And I will dwell in the house of the Lord forever.
Glory be to the Father, and to the Son, and to the Holy Ghost;
As it was in the beginning, is now, and ever shall be, world without end. Amen.

The Lesson. St. James 5:14.

IS any sick among you? Let him call for the presbyters of the Church; and let them pray over him, anointing him with oil in the Name of the Lord: and the prayer of faith shall save the sick, and the Lord shall raise him up. And if he have committed sins, absolution shall be given him. Confess therefore your sins one to another, and pray one for another, that ye may be healed.

Haste thee to help me, O Lord God of my salvation;
For I am anointed with fresh oil.

Let us pray.

O GOD of life and health, who by thy holy Apostle Saint James hast commanded thy Church to pray over the sick and anoint them with oil in the Name of the Lord; Grant that those who in faith receive this holy unction may be healed both in body and in soul; through Jesus Christ our Lord. *Amen.*

The Litany of Healing

¶ For use after one of the seven Orders, or instead of it, or separately at any time of intercession for the sick, all kneeling.

O GOD the Father, who willest for all men health and salvation;
Have mercy upon us.

O God the Son, who came that we might have life, and might have it more abundantly;
Have mercy upon us.

O God the Holy Ghost, who makest our bodies the temple of thy presence;
Have mercy upon us.

O Holy Trinity, in whom we live, and move, and have our being;
Have mercy upon us.

O SON of David, who went about doing good, and healed all who came to thee in faith and repentance;
Have mercy upon us.

O Son of David, who sent forth thy disciples both to preach the Gospel and to heal the sick;
Have mercy upon us.

O Son of David, who pardoneth all our sins, and healeth all our infirmities;
Have mercy upon us.

O Son of David, who art a rewarder of those who put their trust in thee;
Have mercy upon us.

O Son of David, who dost renew our minds by thy Spirit who dwelleth in us;
Have mercy upon us.

O Son of David, whose holy Name is a medicine of healing, and a pledge of eternal salvation:
Have mercy upon us.

O Son of David, who by thy Apostle has commanded us to anoint the sick with oil, that they may be healed;

Have mercy upon us.

WE beseech thee to hear us, O Lord; and that thou wilt grant thy grace to all who are sick, that they may be made whole;

We beseech thee to hear us.

That thou wilt grant to all who are disabled by injury or sickness, patience, courage, and sure faith in thee;

We beseech thee to hear us.

That thou wilt give to all sick children relief from pain, speedy healing, and fearless confidence in thee;

We beseech thee to hear us.

That thou wilt grant to all about to undergo an operation thy strength, that they be not afraid;

We beseech thee to hear us.

That thou wilt grant to all sufferers the refreshment of quiet sleep, that they may rest in thee;

We beseech thee to hear us.

That thou wilt grant to all who are lonely or despondent, having no one to comfort them, the sense of thy presence;

We beseech thee to hear us.

That thou wilt restore all who are in mental darkness to soundness of mind and cheerfulness of spirit;

We beseech thee to hear us.

That thou wilt give to all doctors and nurses thy wisdom, that with knowledge, skill, and patience they may minister to the sick;

We beseech thee to hear us.

That thou wilt grant to all who search for the causes of sickness and disease the guidance of thy Holy Spirit;

We beseech thee to hear us.

That thou wilt grant to the Ministers of thy Church such grace, that what is done by their ministry may be perfected by thy power;

We beseech thee to hear us.

Jesus of Nazareth;

Have mercy upon us.

Jesus of Nazareth;

Have mercy upon us.
Jesus of Nazareth;
Grant us thy peace.

Thou art the God that doest wonders:
And hast declared thy power among the people.
For with thee is the well of life;
And in thy light shall we see light.
Turn us again, O Lord God of hosts;
Show the light of thy countenance, and we shall be whole.
We wait for thy loving-kindness, O God;
In the midst of thy temple.
The Lord be with you;
And with thy spirit.

Let us pray.

ALMIGHTY God, the giver of life and health, who didst send thine only-begotten Son into the world, that all thy children might be made whole; Send thy blessing on all who are sick, and upon those who minister to them of thy healing gifts; that being restored to health of body and of mind, they may give thanks unto thee in thy holy Church; through the same Jesus Christ our Lord. *Amen.*

Prayers

¶ Any one of the following prayers may be used after the Litany, or instead of it.

For Healing

O GOD of heavenly powers, who, by the might of thy command, drivest away from men's bodies all sickness and all infirmity; Be present in thy goodness with *this* thy *servant*, that *his* weaknesss may be banished and *his* strength recalled; that *his* health being thereupon restored, *he* may bless thy holy Name; through Jesus Christ our Lord. *Amen.*

For Those for Whom Prayer is Desired

O HEAVENLY Father, who knowest the needs of all men; Be present with thy *servants, (NN.),* for whom our prayers are desired; bless the means made use of for *their* cure, and grant that *they* may be restored to health, with a grateful sense of thy mercy; through Jesus Christ our Lord. *Amen.*

For One about to Undergo an Operation

O LORD, holy Father, by whose loving-kindness our souls and bodies are renewed; Mercifully look upon thy servant, *(N.)*, about to undergo an operation; that *he* be not afraid, but may put *his* trust in thee; that every cause of sickness being removed, *he* may be restored to health; through Jesus Christ our Lord. *Amen.*

For the Sleepless

O LORD God, who alone makest us to dwell in safety; Refresh with quiet sleep those who are wearied with pain and sickness; that lying down in peace to take their rest, they may fear no evil, but may give themselves into thy holy keeping; through Jesus Christ our Lord. *Amen.*

For the Despondent

COMFORT, we beseech thee, most gracious God, thy *servant, (N.)*, cast down and faint of heart amidst the sorrows and difficulties of the world; and grant that, by the power of thy Holy Spirit, *he* may be enabled to go upon his way rejoicing, and give thee continual thanks for thy sustaining providence; through Jesus Christ our Lord. *Amen.*

For those in Mental Darkness

O GOD, whose Son our Saviour Jesus Christ, didst cast out unclean spirits, and healed those whose minds were possessed by evil and deluding thoughts; Have mercy upon all thy children who are living in mental darkness, and restore them to strength of mind and cheerfulness of spirit; that knowing again thy saving grace, they may ever abide in thy peace; through the same Jesus Christ our Lord. *Amen.*

For Physicians and Nurses

ALMIGHTY God, who didst send thy blessed Son to be the Great Physician of our souls and bodies; Give thy blessing and the guidance of thy Holy Spirit to all Doctors and Nurses; that ministering to the sick they may share thy healing work; through the same Jesus Christ our Lord. *Amen.*

For Hospitals

O GOD, whost blessed Son went about doing good, and healed all manner of sickness and all manner of disease among the people; We beseech thee to continue in our hospitals his gracious work, and bless all those who serve therein; that doing all that they do for love of thee, they may with wisdom and sympathy minister to the sick; through the same Jesus Christ our Lord. *Amen.*

Thanksgiving for Recovery

ALMIGHTY God, the giver of health and salvation; We bless thy holy Name because thou hast healed *this* thy *servant*, (who now *desires* to give thanks unto thee in thy holy Church;) make *him* ever mindful of thy love, and strong to do thy will; that serving thee with constancy upon earth, *he* may attain thy heavenly kingdom; through Jesus Christ our Lord. *Amen.*

The Laying on of Hands and Holy Unction

¶ For use after any of the foregoing devotions, or separately.

¶ Anyone who is sick in body or mind, slightly or seriously, may receive the Laying on of Hands and Holy Unction, and both may be administered as many times as is desired in the same illness.

¶ The Laying on of Hands may be used without Unction, the words concerning anointing in the sentence of administration being omitted.

The Consecration of the Oil

¶ The Bishop or Priest shall place the vessel of Oil upon the altar, or at a private Ministration upon a suitable table, and shall bless it as follows, first turning to the People, and saying,

The Lord be with you.
And with thy spirit.
Lift up your hearts.
We lift them up unto the Lord.
Let us give thanks unto our Lord God.
It is meet and right so to do.

¶ Then turning to the altar he shall continue,

IT is very meet, right, and our bounden duty, that we should at all times, and in all places, give thanks unto thee, O Lord, Holy Father, the giver of health and salvation; whose only-begotten Son came into the world that we might have life, and might have it more abundantly; who in his love for men, ministered to their bodily infirmities, and gave both power and commandment to his disciples likewise to heal the sick; Send down from heaven, we beseech thee, the Holy Ghost, and sanctify this oil, brought forth from the fruit of the olive tree for the refreshment of our souls and bodies; that as thy holy Apostles anointed with oil many that were sick and healed them, so those who in faith and repentance receive this holy unction may be made whole; through Jesus Christ our Lord, by whom, and with whom, in the unity of the Holy Ghost, all honour and glory be unto thee, O Father Almighty, world without end. *Amen.*

The Laying on of Hands and Anointing

¶ Then turning to the People the Priest shall say,

THE Almighty Lord, who is a strong tower to all those who put their trust in him, to whom all things in heaven, in earth, and under the earth, do bow and obey; Be now and evermore thy defence; and make thee know and feel, that there is none other Name under heaven given to man, in whom, and through whom, thou mayest receive health and salvation, but only the Name of our Lord Jesus Christ. *Amen.*

¶ The sick persons shall come forward and kneel at the altar rail, or if unable to do so, the Priest shall go to them. Then dipping his right thumb in the Holy Oil, the Priest shall first lay his hands on the head of each one, and then anoint them on the forehead with the sign of the cross, saying,

BY the authority committed unto me, I lay my hands upon thee, and anoint thee with oil; that all evil may depart from thee; and that thou mayest be healed; In the Name of Jesus Christ of Nazareth, to whom with the Father and the Holy Ghost, be all honour and glory, world without end. *Amen.*

¶ Then the Priest shall wipe the forehead of the person anointed with a piece of cotton (which cotton shall afterwards be burned), and when all have returned to their places, he shall recite the Lord's Prayer with the People, first saying,

As our Saviour Christ hath taught us, we have confidence to say,

OUR Father, who art in heaven, Hallowed be thy Name. Thy kingdom come. Thy will be done, On earth as it is in heaven. Give us this day our daily bread. And forgive us our trespasses, As we forgive those who trespass against us.

And lead us not into temptation, but deliver us from evil. For thine is the kingdom, and the power, and the glory, for ever and ever. Amen.

¶ The Priest shall conclude the Office with this prayer, then turning to the People, shall give the Blessing.

ALMIGHTY God, who for the need of the sick didst send thy blessed Son into the world to show forth thy healing power, and by his presence didst cause every pain and sickness to flee away; Mercifully regard this thy servant, that what this day is done by our ministry may be perfected by thy power; through the same Jesus Christ our Lord. *Amen.*

The Blessing

THE God of peace himself sanctify you wholly; and may your spirit and soul and body be preserved blameless unto the coming of our Lord Jesus Christ; to whom, with the Father and the Holy Ghost, be all honour and glory, world without end. *Amen.*

PRAYER BOOK STUDIES IV: THE EUCHARISTIC LITURGY

The Standing Liturgical Commission
of the Protestant Episcopal Church in the
United States of America

1953

PREFACE

The last revision of our Prayer Book was brought to a rather abrupt conclusion in 1928. Consideration of it had preoccupied the time of General Convention ever since 1913. Everyone was weary of the long and ponderous legislative process, and desired to make the new Prayer Book available as soon as possible for the use of the Church.

But the work of revision, which sometimes has seemed difficult to start, in this case proved hard to stop. The years of debate had aroused widespread interest in the whole subject: and the mind of the Church was more receptive of suggestions for revision when the work was brought to an end than when it began. Moreover, the revision was actually closed to new action in 1925, in order that it might receive final adoption in 1928: so that it was not possible to give due consideration to a number of very desirable features in the English and Scottish revisions, which appeared simultaneously with our own. It was further realized that there were some rough edges in what had been done, as well as an unsatisfied demand for still further alterations.

The problem of defects in detail was met by continuing the Revision Commission, and giving it rather large 'editorial' powers (subject only to review by General Convention) to correct obvious errors in the text as adopted, in the publication of the new Prayer Book. Then, to deal with the constructive proposals for other changes which continued to be brought up in every General Convention, the Revision Commission was reconstituted as a Standing Liturgical Commission. To this body all matters concerning the Prayer Book were to be referred, for preservation in permanent files, and for continuing consideration, until such time as the accumulated matter was sufficient in amount and importance to justify proposing another Revision.

The number of such referrals by General Convention, of Memorials from Dioceses, and of suggestions made directly to the Commission from all regions and schools and parties in the Church, has now reached such a total that it is evident that there is a widespread and insistent demand for a general revision of the Prayer Book.

The Standing Liturgical Commission is not, however, proposing any immediate revision. On the contrary, we believe that there ought to be a period of study and discussion, to acquaint the Church at large with the principles and issues involved, in order that the eventual action may be taken intelligently, and if possible without consuming so much of the time of our supreme legislative synod.

Accordingly, the General Convention of 1949 signalized the Fourth Centennial Year of the First Book of Common Prayer in English by authorizing the Liturgical Commission to publish its findings, in the form of a series of *Prayer Book Studies*.

It must be emphasized that the liturgical forms presented in these *Studies* are not — and under our Constitution, cannot be — sanctioned for public use. They are submitted for free discussion. The Commission will be grateful for copies or articles, resolutions, and direct comment, for its consideration, that the mind of the Church may be fully known to the body charged with reporting it.

In this undertaking, we have endeavored to be objective and impartial. It is not possible to avoid every matter which may be thought by some to be controversial. Ideas which seem to be constructively valuable will be brought to the attention of the Church, without too much regard as to whether they may ultimately be judged to be expedient. We cannot undertake to eliminate every proposal to which anyone might conceivably object: to do so would be to admit that any constructive progress is impossible. What we can do is to be alert not to alter the present *balance* of expressed or implied doctrine of the Church. We can seek to counterbalance every proposal which might seem to favor some one party of opinion by some other change in the opposite direction. The goal we have constantly had in mind — however imperfectly we may have succeeded in attaining it — is the shaping of a future Prayer Book which *every* party might embrace with the well-founded conviction that therein its own position had been strengthened, its witness enhanced, and its devotions enriched.

The objective we have pursued is the same as that expressed by the Commission for the Revision of 1892: "*Resolved*, That this Committee, in all its suggestions and acts, be guided by those principles of liturgical construction and ritual use which have guided the compilation and amendments of the Book of Common Prayer, and have made it what it is."

THE STANDING LITURGICAL COMMISSION:

GOODRICH R. FENNER, *Chairman*
ARTHUR C. LICHTENBERGER
BAYARD H. JONES, *Vice Chairman*
MORTON C. STONE, *Secretary*
JOHN W. SUTER, *Custodian of the Book of Common Prayer*
CHURCHILL J. GIBSON
MASSEY H. SHEPHERD, JR.
WALTER WILLIAMS
SPENCER ERVIN
JOHN W. ASHTON

The revision of the Eucharistic Liturgy has received the intensive consideration of the Liturgical Commission for the last nine years. Beside the very numerous suggestions made to us from every side in the Church, careful attention has been given to contemporary revisions in other branches of the Church. Reference is made especially to the Alcuin Club's *Anglican Liturgies* (Oxford University Press, 1939); and, for earlier texts to F. E. Brightman, *The English Rite* (Rivingtons, 1915).

BAYARD H. JONES

Origins

1. Knowledge of Sources

The Canon of our Church which sets up the Standing Liturgical Commission lays upon this body the task of evaluating the many proposals for the alteration or improvement of the constituent parts of the Prayer Book. This duty, which is being discharged in the current series of Prayer Book Studies, is always primarily dependent upon an understanding of the past history of the offices in question, of their sources and original intent, of the vicissitudes of their development, and of the principles underlying their use throughout the long life of the Church, which have made them what they are today, and which furnish most necessary standards of reference to judge what may be considered desirable or undesirable in any changes in them which are being advocated now. And in no other office of the Prayer Book is such an understanding so important as in the case of the centrally important Eucharistic Liturgy.

For some periods of its history, the available information on the Liturgy is greater than on any other office. Lifetimes have been spent in assembling the extraordinarily voluminous data of the multiform liturgical texts, the innumerable patristic allusions, and all the learned analyses. And especially in the last three centuries, the scholars of all communions have labored to integrate this complex information by comparative study a process by no means complete.

But there are other periods — which unfortunately include the first origins of our liturgical forms, and their nascent differentiation into regional types — for which explicit contemporary evidence is all but completely lacking. No over-all understanding of the subject is possible without some kind of tentative filling in of these vital lacunae in the record. Such reconstructions are necessarily speculative, since they are extrapolations of the provable evidence: and they certainly present pitfalls to anyone who is under the sway of the preconceptions inherent in the polemical position of his particular Church. For instance, Roman Catholics and their sympathizers are unconsciously more or less hostile to the distinctive witness of the ancient Greek liturgies, and put up a partisan resistance to any suggestion that the standards of Antioch are in any way older or better than those of Rome. Likewise, until recently, all Christians, Catholics and Protestants alike, have not taken into account the important bearing of Jewish beliefs and practice upon the Christian rite at its first institution.

Nevertheless, though much fruitful work remains to be accomplished in detailed demonstration, the discoveries and contributions of this present century have brought the general picture to light with much greater clarity and completeness than in any previous age. An integration of this general shape of the evidence, as we understand it, is here presented with some fulness, that the Church may see the background which has furnished the organizing principles underlying the recommendations which we are making for the revision of the Liturgy.

2. The Last Supper

In looking at the original Institution of the Christian Eucharist at the Last Supper, we should note that there are two points to which little consideration has been paid. Although the historic liturgies carefully preserved all that was of distinctive Christian significance in the rite of the Last Supper, they did not retain either the entire ceremonies of that observance, nor the words which expressed them. At the same time, the Liturgy is in vital dependence upon certain underlying religious concepts which were fundamental to this, as to every other, Sacred Meal among the Jews.

Since the Jewish family meal was always a religious occasion, it embodied a fixed ritual, always observed when friends and neighbors met at such a *Chabūrah* or 'Meal of Fellowship' (from *chabēr*, 'neighbor') as was the Last Supper. Like a formal modern 'company meal,' there was first a preliminary cup of wine, with appetizers, in the living-room. The so-called 'longer text' of the Narrative of the Institution in St. Luke's Gospel, which has caused some perplexity by mentioning two Cups, one before as well as one after the Blessing of the Bread, proves to be as accurate as it certainly is textually authentic by describing precisely this order of events at the Last Supper. And this is confirmed by the 'Lord's Supper' ritual of the very early, and recently recovered, *Didaché* or 'Teaching of the Twelve Apostles.'

Then, at table, the meal was blessed by the initial Blessing and Breaking of the Bread. The Supper followed, as St. Paul and St. Luke make clear — the first two Evangelists have so condensed their accounts as to obscure this point. The Fourth Gospel, which, as usual, does not reiterate matter sufficiently set forth in the Synoptics, gives no description of the ritual of the Supper: but in the 13th and 14th chapters it does give at length the conversation at table, in a manner which conforms entirely to the requirements stressed by Jewish writers, and cherished by Jews to the present day, that such conversation must always be serious, and preferably religious.

After the Supper, the meal concluded with the blessing and partaking of a final Cup of wine, which bore the distinctive Jewish name of 'The Cup of Blessing,' which St. Paul applies to it in 1 Corinthians 10:16.

The Christian rite was still being celebrated as a 'Lord's Supper,' in connection with a common meal, when St. Paul wrote so vigorously about it to the Corinthians. But at some very early date the Eucharist as such was separated from the Meal of Fellowship. St. Augustine surmises that this action may have been taken by St. Paul himself, in fulfilment of his promise that 'the rest will I set in order when I come' (1 Cor. 11:34).

The 'Meal of Fellowship,' translated by the Greek word *Agapé* ('Love Feast,' as in Jude 12), continued separately in Christian circles until at least the fifth century — indeed, it survives in the guise of Parish Suppers and Communion Breakfasts to the present day. But the Eucharist dropped all connection with the Common Meal, including the preliminary Cup: and the historic liturgies concern themselves only with the consecration of the eucharistic Bread and Cup by a single Prayer of Thanksgiving.

Fifty years ago, this would have been all that needed to be said about that subject. The Christian Prayer of Consecration would have been attributed to some kind of apostolic origin, without further inquiry. But now, it is recognized that the origin of this liturgical Prayer is not quite so axiomatic as that, in the light of a considerable body of evidence for the use at the primitive Eucharist of an entirely different form.

The *Didaché* sets forth prayers for consecrating what it explicitly calls 'The Eucharist.' These prayers are simply Messianic modifications of the accustomed Jewish Table-Blessings which we find in the *Mishna*. Beyond question, they preserve for us something very close to the words which Holy Scripture does not record, and the historic liturgies do not rehearse, which our Lord himself used when he blessed 'the Bread, and gave thanks' for the Cup.

In spite of the Messianic overtones, the prayers of the *Didaché* are strictly Jewish in character. They are not what we would call 'blessings' at all: they are 'thanksgivings.' Like every Jewish grace at table, they do not say, as we do, 'O God, bless this food,' but instead, 'Blessed be God, who hath given us this food.' They do not call upon God to do any particular thing in any particular way; they do not explain themselves at all by expressing for the users of them what they are supposed to effect. Their content lacks every significant expression of the Consecration Prayer of the historic liturgies. They include no Thanksgiving for Creation or Redemption, no mention of the Institution, no Commemoration of the Passion, no Oblation, no Invocation.

Because of the obvious difficulty of explaining how such general and unexplicit prayers as those of the *Didaché* could ever have been transformed into the very explicit and beautifully articulated structure of the Consecration Prayer of the Liturgy, it has been urged that perhaps the forms of the *Didaché* may have been used only for the *Agapé*, and never for the Liturgy at all. If this evidence stood alone, that might indeed be the most convenient hypothesis. But it also happens that we likewise have texts from the Gnostic *Acts*, dating from as late as the third century, which furnish express and undeniable forms of eucharistic Consecration that are just such modified Table-Blessings as those of the *Didaché*. Though from a heretical source, they can only reflect the 'orthodox' forms which it was their intent to rival. And the combined testimony of the *Didaché* and the Gnostic texts is too much to explain away. Therefore if we are not to argue against the evidence (which is never a candid, and seldom a safe thing to do), we are driven to the conclusion that a 'Lord's Supper' type of service for the Eucharist was in use at the beginning in Jewish-Christian circles, and that it actually persisted for some time in the 'back country' regions of Syria.

The fact is that it does not make any particular difference what conclusion we come to as to the precise use and meaning of the forms in the *Didaché*: we still have to face the problem which it was the contribution of the study of the *Didaché* to raise. If it could be demonstrated that the *Didaché* prayers were never used for the consecration of the Eucharist, it would remain true that it was prayers of this type, and conceivably in almost these very words, which were employed on the occasion of the Last Supper. The question is, How was the transition ever made from such a 'Lord's Supper' kind of service, so vague to our minds, so lacking in the definitive expressions we should consider essential to the significant 'Form' of the Sacrament, to the precise and explicit order of thought of the Consecration Prayer of the historic liturgies unanimously adopted in every region of the expanding Church throughout all its history?

3. The Jewish Background

But indeed the explanation of this remarkable transformation of the 'Lord's Supper' to the Liturgy is very simple. The fact is that the elaborated structure of the liturgical Consecration Prayer only made explicit what was already implicit in Jewish belief about the meaning of every Sacred Meal.

First and foremost, every meal was actually a sacrifice. It must not be understood by this that the Jew had any notion whatever that a Sacrifice was to be defined as consisting in 'the suffering of a victim, or the destruction of an offering,' which was the unhistorical rationalization of the term invented in medieval times. As in all other primitive religions, the Jew did not conceive that a Sacrifice was based upon the idea of pain or loss to man, but of Thanksgiving to God; and its purpose was not a propitiation of God, but a direct benefit to man. It was not of the essence of Sacrifice that any living thing should suffer or die: it was of its essence that the material thing offered to God must be *edible*.[1] In other words, primitive man made a symbolic Thankoffering to God of what to him was his most precious possession, the food by which his life was sustained. The actual Offering of the fruits of the earth was always, in the nature of things, only a dramatic gesture: the real outcome of the action was the giving back of the food to the offerer from the hand of God, raised to new spiritual significances by God's blessing.

While it is true that these ideas became obscured and formalized in the rites of public worship in the Temple Sacrifices, it is of the greatest importance to the first origins of our distinctive Christian worship that they remained uncontaminated in their primordial sense among the Jews in the oldest of all priesthoods and the most universal of all Sacrifices, the common Meal, presided over by the father of the family: for it was at just such a Meal that the Eucharist was instituted.

---

1. The actual slaying of an animal sacrifice was not a sacrificial act, but only an unavoidable preliminary. The animal had to be killed because it could not be used for food as long as it was alive. The slaying was performed by the offerer outside the temple; and it was only after that when the meat was brought to the priest in the temple for the proper sacrificial action. Cf. Heb. 13:1i ff.

Moreover, the Jew believed that the effect of his prayer of Thanksgiving was actually a blessing 'and a consecration.'[2] This essential Jewish concept finds perfect expression in 1 Tim. 4:4–5 (RSV): 'For everything created by God is good, and nothing is to be rejected if it is received with *thanksgiving*: for then it is *consecrated* by the word of God and prayer.' Hence the Jew conceived that man's part in the sacred action was limited to his Giving of Thanks: the effective 'blessing' or 'consecration' was the act of God. Yet the divine response was a necessary consequence of man's Thanksgiving: therefore there was no need to tell God what to do about it. The Jew saw no necessity to dramatize the essentially sacrificial action by enacting a formal Oblation; he did not beseech God to accept it; he did not invoke the power of God to make it something other than it was in its natural substance; he did not perform any objective and sacerdotal 'benediction' upon it. All these factors were understood, implied, and taken for granted — not formally expressed.

Yet the Jew believed that the result of the divine acceptance was definitely a Consecration, a sublimation of material means to spiritual purposes. The homely needs of food for the maintenance of the life of the body were filled with essentially *sacramental* power for the renewal of the life of the soul. The 'life' received was understood to be absolutely the life of God. Repeatedly, the Old Testament commands, 'Ye shall not eat the blood, which is the life thereof.' That is, when partaking of animal food, one does not *want* to receive the life of the animal — that must be given back to God who gave it — but to feed upon nothing less than the very life of God, imparted to sustain the human life of which also he is the only author and giver.

It may be said that it is not possible to understand the Christian Eucharist as anything but raw magic, except upon these foundations of these beliefs which already existed in the minds of the Disciples when the Sacrament was instituted. They already thoroughly understood, and unquestioningly accepted, these underlying Jewish conceptions of a Sacred Meal as providing nothing less than a Real Sacrifice, a Real Presence, and a Real Communion. The eucharistic faith of the historic Church is therefore not solely dependent upon the four words, 'This is my Body' — words which in themselves might be quite honestly taken in a purely metaphorical sense: as indeed most Protestants do take them.

But since the Disciples already held fast the belief that any Sacred Meal brought them into participation with the life of God, it was perfectly simple for them to accept the small element of *added* belief in the new observance which our Lord enjoined upon them: that the Christian Sacrament was to bring them in precisely the same way into union with the life of *Christ*. This must have been especially unmistakable in his words about the Cup: '*Drink ye all of it!*' As Jews, they had had constantly dinned into their ears, that they must *not* 'drink of the

---

2. *Cf.* the convertible use of the words 'blessed' and 'gave thanks' in the narratives of the Institution.

blood, which is the life' of the sacrificial animal. But the Christian, on the contrary, is not only made 'one body' with his Lord — he is privileged to be made partaker of his very life. The mental shock at the breaking of the immemorial tabu must have rammed the point home in the minds of the Disciples.

In the light of these considerations, it will now be clear why our Lord's prayers when he 'gave thanks' at the Last Supper (which everyone agrees must have been just such slightly modified Jewish Table-Blessings as we find in the *Didaché*) were accepted on that occasion not only as a sufficient Consecration, but as the Institution of an eternal Sacrifice of the New Covenant. And accordingly, during the short time that the membership in the Christian Church was confined to those who had been brought up in Judaism, it did not seem necessary to anyone to give any explicit expression to all these points of implicit faith. There is no reason why a 'Lord's Supper' type of observance, such as we find in the *Didaché* and the Gnostic *Acts*, should not have been used by Jewish Christians at the beginning, or why it should not have survived for some little time in the Semitic homelands of Syria.

There was a parallel situation in the case of Baptism. A Jewish convert needed only to confess his faith in Christ: and the Acts and Epistles mention nothing but Baptism in the Name of Jesus. It was only when Christianity began to take in Gentiles, who might believe in many gods, or none, that it became essential to require explicit profession of belief in the one God the Father as well, and to add from vital Christian experience confession also of the Holy Spirit. And it is significant that we first find the Trinitarian formula for Baptism in the Gospel according to St. Matthew, and in the *Didaché* — both of which documents seem to have originated in the Gentile region of Antioch.

Though of course no written evidence has come down to us from those very early days, the whole shape of the situation points with almost conclusive force to the hypothesis that it was for the understanding of the Gentile converts that the great Eucharistic Prayer of the Liturgy took form, putting in explicit terms all that had been taken for granted in Jewish use, and at the same time filling in with equal definiteness the new Christian contributions. For the former purpose, the Bread and Wine were formally offered in a consciously sacrificial action, with a prayer for their acceptance, and for their consecration by the divine power for the benefit of those who should partake of them. For the latter, the Thanksgiving was made to include the Redemption through Christ; the 'Charter Narrative' of the Institution was recited before God and man as the divine warrant for the action; and the Prayer of Oblation was especially linked with a Commemoration of the Passion.

It should be further realized that such an expanding and unfolding of latent meanings into explicit expressions would not have involved any actual innovation of method in Jewish practice. True, on the constant occasions of the daily meals, the explanations were almost necessarily omitted. But there were other occasions when the same basic observance of a Sacred Meal was utilized for a solemn

Commemoration of certain great events in the life of the nation, as outstanding climaxes of the ritual pattern of the year. Those times were recognized to have great teaching value for the youth of the people, and as carriers of the living traditions of their religion. Thus on the supreme Feast of the Passover, the underlying meanings of the progressive dramatic action were set forth in definite statements. A 'Charter Narrative' was recited; the Institution of the Divine Command was pleaded; and prayer was offered that the observance might be fruitful to the spiritual profit of the participants. The analogies to the plan of the Christian Prayer of Consecration are numerous and direct.

Now it is generally agreed that the Last Supper was not the Last Passover: the Church never considered that it was, before that idea acquired some popularity in the West during the Middle Ages — leaving us incidentally the legacy of the use of the Unleavened Bread of the Passover observance: the Eastern Church to this day employs only the Leavened Bread of ordinary meals. Nor was the ritual of the Liturgy derived from that of the Passover — both were parallel evolutions from the general form of every Sacred Meal. Nevertheless, it seems very probable that it was the precedent of the Passover Thanksgiving, which put basic teaching into explicit terms for the instruction of the children, which suggested to the early Jewish Christians a like technique in the Thanksgiving of the Liturgy for the instruction of the Gentiles, who were likewise new-born in the Christian Faith.

The conclusion must be that while 'the Lord's Supper' and 'the Liturgy' would seem to us to be sharply contrasting forms, with no words in common except the mention of 'Bread' and 'Wine,' yet they are related to one another as the simple seed to the fully developed plant. The latter pair also would appear to have nothing in common save their internal chemistry. Yet the towering tree, in all its majesty and beauty, is a true growth from the amorphous seed, an unfolding of latent living forces instinct in its humble origin. And in like manner, the almost completely indefinite phrases of the 'Lord's Supper' ritual gave birth to the significant expressions and the elaborate dramatic structure of the Liturgy by putting into words what the Jews implicitly believed about the meaning of the action of every Sacred Meal.

It is not without significance that all the Semitic languages use exactly the same verb to express what to us are the distinctly divergent ideas of 'to confess' and 'to give thanks.' Hence the Jews felt that every 'Thanksgiving' to God was also a 'Confession' of the faith of man. It bore a conscious element of affirmation, and hence implicitly of instruction. At the daily meals, it was sufficient to sum up all the implied meanings in the fundamental profession, 'Blessed be God.' At such times as the Passover, one might elaborate the why and how of the observance. And the Christian Liturgy made its teaching fully explicit.

Therefore there was no accident in the remarkable circumstance that the 'Thanksgiving' of the Liturgy took exactly the structure of the Creed, in a great

Affirmation of faith in God the Holy Trinity. Indeed, the liturgical Thanksgiving is much older than the formulation of the Creed as a separate feature, and may very probably have shown the way for its elaboration from the original simple Baptismal Profession. In any case, it is fortunate that the working out of the principle of giving adequate expression to fundamental beliefs, for the better understanding of the neophytes, resulted in embedding the basic faith of the Teaching Church in its central service. The Church's greatest act of public worship became the bearer and teacher of the Church's total faith.

4. The Early Liturgy

The result of this process of giving explicit expression to implicit beliefs was the formulation of a definite order of thought for the Eucharistic Prayer. This comprised a Thanksgiving for the Redemption, the recital of the Institution, a Commemoration-Oblation, and a concluding supplication for the Benefits of the Communion. This outline is basic to all historic liturgies, no matter how expanded or reduced, how elaborated or obscured, in all parts of the world. And it is found crystal-clear in the earliest written text of the service, the Apostolic Tradition of Hippolytus, which is now thought to have appeared as early as the year 198.[3]

Moreover, scholars are now in general agreement that Hippolytus' Prayer of Consecration is essentially the same as that described by Justin Martyr in his so-called *First Apology*, written about the year 150. Justin expressly mentions the Thanksgiving, cites the Institution Narrative in condensed summary, and alludes to the Benefits of the Sacrament. In several places in his other works, he enlarges upon the idea of a Sacrificial Commemoration. It is not surprising that in the *Apology*, which is in the form of a carefully non-technical and non-controversial 'Open Letter' to the pagan Emperor, he does not happen to mention the Invocation. Yet there would seem to be little doubt that this feature is necessarily implied in what he does say, namely that the celebrant 'gives glory and praise to the Father of all through the Name of the Son, and of the Holy Spirit.' For it has been convincingly maintained that this compendious expression is more rationally interpreted as indicating such a basic 'Trinitarian' structure of the Consecration Prayer as all later liturgies display, consisting of a Thanksgiving to the Father for the Redemption wrought through the Son, and concluding with a supplication for the effectual working of the Holy Spirit, rather than as being a somewhat gratuitous allusion to a mere appended Doxology at the end.

---

3. Cyril Richardson, 'The Date and Setting of the Apostolic Tradition of Hippolytus,' in *Anglican Theological Review*, Jan. 1948, XXX. 1.38–41.

Furthermore, certainly some, and conceivably all, of the constituents of this Consecration Prayer which we find in the first text of Hippolytus and the first description of Justin, can be traced still farther back: for they seem to have left decipherable traces upon the New Testament itself. St. Paul speaks of a 'Thanksgiving,' which appears to have been enough of a stated feature to have given a cue for the following congregational 'Amen' (1 Cor. 14:16). He sets forth a formula for the recitation of the Institution Narrative as a definite 'tradition,' received and handed on (1 Cor. 11:23–25). Together with his companion St. Luke, he stresses the Commemoration of the Passion (1 Cor. 11:24, 25, 26; Luke 22:19–20). The idea of a sacrificial Oblation certainly underlies such passages in the New Testament as 1 Cor. 5:7 f., Eph. 5:2, Heb. 13:15, and 1 Pet. 2:5.

It can even be argued with some cogency that even the controverted 'Invocation of the Holy Ghost' appears by indirection in Rom. 15:16 — a very unusual verse which has every air of echoing accustomed liturgical language, and applying it paraphrastically to a quite different situation, in which St. Paul nevertheless brings to light a somewhat startling analogy. He speaks of his offering of the fruits of his missionary work among the Gentiles in what appears to be deliberately sacerdotal terms, incorporating in this one verse no less than five phrases, all of which were subsequently applied with exclusive reference to the Eucharist: 'That I should be the liturgist of Christ Jesus to the Gentiles, performing the hierurgy of the Gospel of God, that the Oblation of the Gentiles might be acceptable, being consecrated by the Holy Ghost.' This is really very curious language to employ, if St. Paul were not in the habit of including an Invocation of the Holy Ghost in his liturgy: but as natural as it would be meaningful, if he were.

The cumulative trend of this evidence certainly suggests even though in any single instance it should be held to fall short of demonstrating — that the argument is entirely correct which maintains from the universal pattern of the Consecration Prayer in all the diverse historic liturgies, that the Prayer must go back to a very early date, and in fact to some sort of Apostolic institution. Its origin must be placed in the first century, and very probably at the Gentile center of Antioch. Of course it does not follow that the great Apostle to the Gentiles was necessarily its 'author.' No doubt, as he himself intimates, his service contained elements which he had 'received' as well as 'delivered' to his converts. Yet it would seem that he must have had a good deal to do with its dissemination and its unanimous acceptance throughout the world.

The Evolution of the Great Rites

1. The Domain of Antioch

We have noted that the earliest substantial attestations of the structure of the historic Liturgy which we have were first, a description by Justin Martyr in the middle of the second century, and then about fifty years later, a model text from the hand of Hippolytus. Now both of these were promulgated in the city of Rome. Yet neither of them is at all representative of the distinctive 'Western' type of the Liturgy. The present Roman Mass has less in common with the text of Hippolytus than any other liturgy has.

Justin, in fact, was a Greek-speaking Syrian, born at Shechem in Samaria, and a visitor in Rome. Hippolytus likewise wrote in Greek; and he was a pupil of Irenæus of Lyons, whose connections with the Eastern cradle-lands of the Christian faith and worship were most immediate. We have seen that both Justin and Hippolytus bear witness to essentially the same rite. And everything they have to say about this rite points in the direction of its being a formative stage of the service in the great Eastern center of Antioch.

The definite identification of Hippolytus' *Apostolic Tradition* was an achievement of the present century. In the natural enthusiasm at the recovery of an actual written text so much earlier than any other that has come down to us, it may be that its influence upon the fixation of the Great Rites has been exaggerated. For instance, the whole grandiose structure of the very lengthy and elaborate Liturgy of the Apostolic Constitutions in the fourth century has been explained as a greatly magnified projection of Hippolytus' brief and simple draft. It is true that these two forms correspond point by point in their order of thought; moreover, the critically important Oblation-Invocation passage of the Apostolic Tradition is incorporated word for word in the text of the Apostolic Constitutions. But in view of the fact that the voluminous writings of St. Chrysostom afford most extensive and minute substantiation of the Liturgy of the A.C., down to what we would think to be improbable details, as being actually in use both at Antioch and Constantinople in his time, there is a serious question as to whether it might not be truer to consider that Hippolytus was reproducing the formative state of the Liturgy of Antioch in his day, rather than that this great and really primitive Church should have elected to formulate and elaborate its liturgy from Hippolytus' outline some 150 years after he wrote it.

And if so, the fact that all other liturgies seem to display varying identities with Hippolytus' scheme may really bear testimony to the probability that it was at Antioch that the Liturgy received its first definitive formulation: and that it was from this primordial Christian center — the first of all the Patriarchates, the spiritual and temporal capital of all the East before Constantinople was built — that the various regions of the growing Church accepted guidance for the settlement of their orders of worship.

Certainly the Great Rite of Antioch dominated the whole East. All the liturgies of the Syrian group are descended from some such a form as is presented in the Apostolic Constitutions. At Jerusalem, St. Cyril in the middle of the fourth century attests a fine literary recension, considerably shortened, under an eponymous attribution to 'St. James,' which may possibly go back to the time of Bishop Macarius and the Council of Nicæa. Another shortening was the work of St. Basil of Caesarea, who died in the year 379. We have noted that there is evidence for the use of the full form of the parent Liturgy of Antioch at Constantinople as late as the time of St. Chrysostom (†407). But there are indications that by the year 431, the Anaphora (Consecration Prayer) of St. Basil was used in Constantinople, inserted in the existing Antiochene order of the service, and employed alternatively with a still briefer Anaphora under the name of 'St. Chrysostom,' which must indeed date from his time, but does not seem to be likely to be by his hand. These two have survived to the present day as the standard use of the Orthodox Eastern Church. And yet another generation of derivatives is found in the schismatic Churches, the Armenian and the Nestorian derived in different ways from the Byzantine texts, and the West-Syrian from the Liturgy of Jerusalem. And the influence of this whole Syrian group upon the liturgies of all other regions of the Church was profound, as the very numerous verbal borrowings demonstrate.

2. Alexandria

Simultaneously, another type of Greek Liturgy was growing up in the South. We have most interesting examples of the formative stages of the Egyptian Rite in the fourth century, in the fragmentary Papyrus from Dair Balyzeh, and the 'Sacramentary' of Serapion. These display verbal and structural peculiarities which are found afterward in the developed 'Liturgy of St. Mark' at Alexandria, and its descendants to this day in the Coptic and Ethiopic Churches. The most important of these individualities to us, because it affected the Roman, and through that, the English rites, was the fact that besides a normal Invocation in the usual Eastern place after the Oblation, there was also a kind of 'preliminary Invocation' before the Narrative of the Institution.

The Alexandrian Rite acted as a sort of bridge between East and West. In many details, where Rome differs from Antioch, Alexandria will be found to occupy a mediating position. This is natural, since Egypt was 'the granary of Rome,' and forty grain-ships a day sailed in either direction between their ports. Contacts were therefore continuous.

3. The Western Church

All the rest of the Christian world — namely North Africa in the vicinity of Carthage, and all Europe outside of Greece — was the domain of the Latin language. Except for some direct Eastern connections with Gaul in the early days, Western Christianity radiated primarily from Rome. With no thought of dominance on the part of the Church in Rome, and with a conspicuous lack of uniformity in detail, nevertheless the various Western 'Uses' were just as much one type of liturgy as those in the sphere of influence of Antioch.

The most striking difference between the Greek and the Latin rites lay in the different ways in which they reconciled the inextinguishable urge for liturgical creation, the contributions of individual devotion to the public worship of the Church, with the practical necessity that this worship in any region must have an agreed and familiar form and order.

The Eastern Churches provided for this by exploiting the system first invented at Constantinople, whereby different Anaphoras or Consecration Prayers, invariable in themselves, were inserted on different occasions within the fixed framework of a 'Common Order' of the service. Thus the Byzantine Rite employs two such alternative Anaphoras, the Nestorian three, the Coptic five, the Armenian ten, the Ethiopic fifteen, and the West-Syrian a number variously computed from 64 to 89!

On the other hand, throughout the Latin Churches the original plan seems to have been to treat the whole service as an Order, rather than a Text. The Order was quite definite: each item of the service had its own subject, and made its own contribution; yet each such constituent might vary indefinitely in its expression, from day to day and from church to church. In a typical book of the so-called 'Gallican' Use, one is confronted with as many different liturgies as one finds complete masses for the various occasions.

Until rather recently, it was the fashion to set off the 'Gallican' Rite, with its infinite variability in detail, in contrast to the Roman, with its fixed 'Canon' for the central prayers. But it has come to be generally recognized that this 'Gallican' type, evidence for which hails not only from France, but from England, Ireland, Germany, Switzerland, Spain, and even parts of Italy, and with which the lost Liturgy of North Africa is probably also to be classified, really represents the old Latin Use once common to all the West, Rome included. In the Roman Mass, the variable framework of the Common Order remains, but the central prayers have been 'frozen' in an invariable form, by the simple process of making a selection at each point from among the numerous alternative formula which were current at the time the Canon was framed. Consequently, in spite of its fixity, in which it resembles a Greek Anaphora, the Canon is not a single Prayer of Consecration, but a chain of collect-like short prayers, like its 'Gallican' sources. Four of these quasi-collects actually terminate with *'per Christum Dominum nostrum. Amen.'*

It does indeed seem reasonable to suppose that the variety and liberty of the old plan of the service in the West would be something which would not be likely to be challenged by anyone who had spent most of his life in the ministry of the Church — yet it would hardly be approved by an administrative mind, coming fresh to the task. Ambrose had been a civil executive of the Empire before he was so unexpectedly called to the Episcopate: and may well have been the man who brought order out of ritual chaos by giving the prayers at the heart of the service the same invariable form as the Eastern Anaphoras — exactly as Charlemagne four centuries later extinguished the protean diversity of the Gallican Rite throughout his domain in favor of the fixity of the Roman.

The first evidence for this sort of Canon is found in the catechetical lectures bearing the title *De Sacramentis*, attributed to St. Ambrose of Milan late in the fourth century. The authenticity of the Ambrosian authorship of this work, long maintained by the learned Benedictines, has now become the majority opinion. And with this has grown an increasing conviction of the probability that it was St. Ambrose himself who actually originated the nucleus of the Canon at Milan, and that the large but decidedly vague liturgical reputation of his friend St. Damasus may have been due to the entirely possible circumstance that Damasus may have adopted Ambrose's innovation at Rome.

If so, it might seem probable that it was Ambrose's lack of background and of long experience in the worship of a Church which he actually entered as a bishop, which can account for the fact that the choice of the material which makes up the Canon often seems to be unintelligent, in comparison with the clean-cut order of thought and lucidity of expression in the Eastern Liturgies.

In any case, it is no great wonder that whoever it may have been who put the Canon together in the days of Ambrose and Damasus did not do the best possible job. The constituent building-blocks that went into it were not, like those of the Eastern Rites, forms which had been thoroughly tested and progressively perfected by constant use: each was chosen from a host of variants upon the same theme, all of them doubtless familiar, but none of more than occasional employment in the ever-varying course of the services. Moreover, this infinite mutability of form brought an inevitable confusion of thought as to just what the essential pattern was. Comparison with the corresponding passages in all the Eastern Anaphoras shows that some of the 'Gallican' prayers which found their way into the Canon are distinctly aberrant from their original plan and purpose.

For instance, in the pure Gallican Rite the Institution Narrative, which in Western use began with the words '*Qui pridie*,' was followed by a prayer known as the *Post-pridie* which matches the Eastern passages covering the Commemoration, Oblation, Invocation, and Benefits of Communion. Some of the Gallican specimens treat all four of these themes: on the other hand, they may deal with any three, two, or even one of them. Now the Roman Canon at this point supplies three prayers (*Unde et memores*, *Supra quæ*, and *Supplices te rogamus*), any of which might have served on occasion as a Gallican *Post-pridie*. In fact, we find versions of the first two of them, to be identified by their unmistakable turns of phrase, in the strictly Gallican books.[4] And yet all three together fall short of expressing the full original cycle of ideas. They provide a complete, indeed a distinguished, Commemoration. The theme of Oblation is very strikingly set forth three times over. The Benefits are briefly alluded to in 'be filled with every heavenly benediction and grace.' But they contain no Invocation of the Holy Ghost. The very idea of an operative Consecration is only remotely and allegorically approached by a prayer that

---

4. *Cf.* W. H. Frere, *The Anaphora* (London: S.P.C.K., 1928), 149f.

the Oblations may be presented 'by the hands of thy holy Angel' upon the Heavenly Altar, in order that we, who by the partaking of this Altar on earth shall receive Christ's Body and Blood, may obtain the intended benefits! It is only in the last century that Roman scholars have recognized that this transferred and transformed Offertory Prayer was intended to fulfil the organic function of an Invocation.

Even in the matter of language, the time of the fixation of the Canon was unfortunate. In a period when Jerusalem, Cæsarea, and Constantinople, using already elaborated rituals, were perfecting liturgies of unequaled grace and splendor, the West was fitting together its rude vernacular form from the terials near at hand. The contrast is as vivid as between a building of polished marble and one of fieldstone. In the Western edifice there is indeed great strength, but little refinement. The language is terse, crude — at times, definitely ungrammatical. There is one whole paragraph in the Mass, the *Communicantes*, which begins with a 'dangling participle,' and never gets around to putting in a principal verb!

The Roman Canon now stands before us as one of the oldest and least changed of all liturgies. By the time of Innocent I (402–417) it appears that the original nucleus of the Canon as we find it in St. Ambrose had reached very much its present form by conflating into it the Intercessions, and other Offertory material. And it has not been altered by a word since it left the hands of Gregory the Great at the end of the sixth century. Because it is the direct parent of the English Rite, we naturally view it with the greatest interest, and with the respect which is due to its antiquity and its wide currency.

It is important for our present task that the Roman Mass should be justly assessed. Perhaps we are in better position to do so than in any previous age. The Latin Mass was virulently attacked and unfairly maligned at the Reformation, and accused of 'detestable enormities' which in fact it never contained. The pendulum has swung too far in the other direction now, in some quarters: there are those who have transferred the former zeal without knowledge which once spoke of 'our incomparable liturgy' to an equally uncritical adulation of the Roman Mass, and judge all things Anglican by the sole measuring-rod of 'The Western Rite.' Neither extreme position would be helpful in the task of the revision of our service. There is no argument for either accepting or rejecting any feature merely because it is Roman.

Around the central core of the unaltered Canon, the other parts of the Mass received progressive elaboration until the time of the Council of Trent. There was never any attempt on the part of the Roman authorities to impose their own standards upon regions using a different rite: yet the Roman Mass won its way over nearly all the other local Western Uses largely, it would appear, because of its vigor and its pregnant brevity. The Ambrosian Rite, which we have noted as the putative parent of the Roman, survives in the Province of Milan. But nothing is left of the 'Gallican' type once prevalent throughout Europe, except its Spanish variant, 'the Mozarabic,' in the primatial Cathedral at Toledo, and a very few parish churches.

The Roman Mass supplanted the original Gallican Rite of the ancient British Church at the Council of Whitby in 664. Thereafter, the 'Uses' of the various English dioceses were simply provincial forms of the Roman Mass. They were purely Roman as to the Canon, though a number of 'Gallican' details continued to decorate the rest of the service until the Reformation, just as they did at Paris until the eighteenth century, and at Lyons until the present day.

The famous 'Use of Sarum' was the local standard of the Diocese of Salisbury, which was brought to perfection of text and rubric by Bishop Richard le Poer in the thirteenth century, and became dominant in the Province of Canterbury. But there were others: notably York, very simple in its rubrication; Hereford, almost purely Roman in its Calendar and the private prayers of the celebrant; Lincoln, distinguished for its music; the monastic Use of Westminster.

It was the Use of Sarum which Cranmer employed chiefly, though not quite exclusively, in the First English Prayer Book. It was the Use of Sarum alone which was revived for all England under Queen Mary. And 'Sarum' furnishes a convenient term of reference, sufficiently accurate for most purposes, for the native Latin Rite of the Church of England before the Reformation.

The English Rites

I. The First Prayer Book

1. The Structure of the Liturgy

The Communion Service of Archbishop Cranmer's First Prayer Book in 1549 was basically an English version of the Sarum Mass, not a new composition. The whole order and structure of the familiar public service was preserved. The outstanding choral features were retained: not only the fixed *Kyries*, *Gloria*, Creed, *Sanctus*, *Benedictus*, and *Agnus Dei*, but the variable Introit, Offertory, and Communion Anthems in simplified form; and Merbecke immediately supplied the English words with plainsong settings. Only the Gradual Anthem disappeared: presumably because Cranmer could devise no ready simplification for the seasonal complexities of Gradual, Tract, Alleluia, and Sequence at this point.

The chain of eleven short prayers of the Latin Canon, comprising supplications of a General Intercession interpolated into and curiously entwined with the central prayers of the eucharistic action, were consolidated by Cranmer and sorted out into two consistent and continuous passages: first, an Intercession for both the Living and the Departed (themes which the Latin Rite divides, before and after the Consecration), and second, a complete Consecration Prayer after the model of the Eastern liturgies. All this matter was rewritten with a free hand, just as St. Luke rewrote the basic Gospel of St. Mark. Dr. Brightman aptly characterized the English text as 'a liberal translation,' and again as 'an eloquent paraphrase' of the Latin. Yet where Luther wiped the Canon out of existence in his service, Cranmer retained it in full equivalence, and in very much its former size and shape. The only omissions of the slightest consequence were the name of the Pope, and two mutually supplementary lists of Saints, which were vestiges of the old Diptychs.

On the other hand, all the private prayers of the celebrant which accompanied the ritual actions of the Vesting, the Preparation, the Censing, the Gospel, the Offertory, the Fraction and Commixture, the *Pax*, the Priest's Communion, the Ablutions, and the conclusion of the service, were very recent additions to the Mass in late medieval times, and displayed considerable variation among the current English Uses. All that the First Prayer Book retained out of all this matter was the celebrant's Lord's Prayer and Collect for Purity at the beginning.

Thus the external appearance of the rite remained the same, with no substantial deviation in any visible or audible particular: especially since certain General Rubrics retained the ancient Vestments, and somewhat grudgingly permitted the customary interpretative ritual gestures.

2. *The Text of the Canon*

All this careful preservation of the outward form of the service, in all its original proportions, organization, and movement, was obviously most judicious in commending the new vernacular version to a nation which had previously known only the semblance of the great action, performed in an ancient hieratic tongue. But from the beginning, the question has been raised whether this seeming correspondence of the new form with the old is actually authentic whether it fully and fairly represents the meaning of the Latin Liturgy, or whether on the other hand it was deliberately sophisticated so as to drain its essential teaching from it. It was the latter opinion which was the underlying reason why Leo XIII disallowed the validity of Anglican Orders in 1896. And such attacks upon the integrity of the Anglican Liturgy still continue.

Yet the aim of Cranmer's Reformation of Worship was not directed against the text of the Mass, but at theological distortions of its meaning. What that meaning was, he read in the light of the Eastern Liturgies: and from the standpoint of the principles he found there, he proceeded to reorganize and rearrange the Canon so as to integrate the abrupt and confused tenor of the Latin text into a more effective and intelligible order. But in the process, all the significant expressions were most meticulously preserved. Therefore our claim would be, not only that our service contains an adequate and honest equivalent of the content of the Latin Canon, but that it actually presents far more luminously and cogently what the fourth-century Latin is somewhat ineptly trying to say.

The only way in which one can judge between such conflicting points of view, and the only way in which one can assess what Cranmer was attempting to do, and how successful or unsuccessful he was in his manner of doing it, is by a side by side and point by point comparison of the Sarum original, and the resultant text of the First Prayer Book. Even the members of the Liturgical Commission found some of their discussions between themselves hard to follow without the texts before their eyes. The best thing to do seemed to present them here in parallel form, and in numbered lines to indicate transfers of matter to other parts of the service, and to facilitate identifications of passages referred to in the following analyses.

In the rendering of the Latin, 'the former translations' have been 'diligently compared and revised,' to insure as far as possible a just and adequate presentation of the sense, without tendentiousness, and without the classroom crudities of the vernacular renditions we find in the hands of the Roman laity — yet with no attempt to gloss over the native abruptness and roughness of the style.

In the English, Cranmer's original spelling and punctuation has been followed, just as in other citations from later Anglican Prayer Books the same conformity with the orthography of those Books will be observed in this discussion: partly because of its own quaint interest, but especially because this sort of contact with the contemporary standards of the documents of different bygone ages endues them with a kind of 'atmospheric perspective' which is not without its value in maintaining a feeling of their historical relationshps.

Phrases identical in the two texts are indicated by italics. When two such identical phrases occur in different contexts, a cross-reference is given from the one printed in one column to the line in which it is found in the other.

	SARUM	1549	
	Te Igitur Therefore, *most merciful Father,* *we humbly pray* and	Almightye and euerlyuyng God, whiche by thy holy Apostle haste taught vs to make *prayers* and supplications, and	
5	*beseech thee* through Jesus Christ thy Son our Lord *to receive* and bless *these* † *gifts*, these † offerings, these † 4	to geue thankes for all menne: *We humbly beseche thee most mercyfully to receyue* 142 *these* our *prayers:*	5

The Eucharistic Liturgy 145

	SARUM	1549	
10	holy undefiled sacrifices, *which we offer unto thee*, first of all for thy holy *catholic Church*, which do thou vouchsafe to keep *in peace, to de-*	*whiche we offre vnto thy* diuine Maiestie, besechyng thee to inspire continually the *vniuersall churche*, with the spirite of truethe,	10
15	*fend, unite,* and *govern* throughout all the world: together with *thy servant* our Pope N., and our *Bishop N.,*	*vnitie* and *concorde:* And graunt that all they that doe confesse thy holye name, maye agree in the trueth of thy holye worde, and lyue in *vnitie* and	15
20	14 17 and *our King N.,*	godly loue. Speciallye wee beseche thee to saue and *defende thy seruaunte, Edwarde our Kynge,* that vnder him we maye be Godly and quietely	20
25	15	gouerned. And graunte vnto his whole counsaile, and to all that bee put in authoritie vnder hym, that they maye truely and indifferently minister iustice,	25
30	4,18	to the punishment of wickednesse and vice, & to the maintenaunce of Goddes true religion & vertue. Geue grace (O heauenly *father*) to all *Bish-*	30
35		*oppes*, Pastors, and Curates, that they maye both by their life and doctrine, set furthe thy true and liuely worde, and rightely and duely admin-	35
40	*and all*	ister thy holye Sacramentes. *And to all* thy people geue thy heauenly grace, that with meke hearte and due reuerence, they maye heare and re-	40
45	orthodox believers, and maintainers of the Catholic and Apostolic faith. MEMENTO	ceyue thy holy worde, truely seruynge thee in holynes and righteousnes, all the dayes of their lyfe. And wee moste	45

	SARUM	1549	
50	Remember, O *Lord*, thy servants and handmaids N. and N., and *all*	humbly beseche thee of thy goodnes (O *Lorde*) to coumforte and succoure *all* them, whiche in this transytory lyfe bee in trouble, sorowe,	50
55	*here* present, whose faith is perceived, whose devotion is	nede, sycknes, or any other aduersitie. And especially we commend vnto thy merciful goodnes, thys congregation whiche is *here* assembled in	55
60	known unto thee: for whom we offer, or who themselves offer unto thee *this sacrifice of praise* for themselves and all who belong to them, for the	thy name, to celebrate the commemoration of the most glorious deathe of thy sonne: 208	60
65	hope of their salvation and safety, and who pay their vows unto thee, the eternal, true, and living God.		65
70	87 COMMUNICANTES In communion with, and	And here wee doe geue vnto thee moste high prayse, & heartie thankes, for the wonderfull grace and vertue, declared in *all thy sainctes*, from the begynninge of the worlde:	70
75	venerating the memory of, *first of all, the glorious ever-virgin Mary, mother of our God and Lord Iesu Christ, and* also thy *Apostles and Martyrs,* Peter	and *chiefly* in *the glorious* and most blessed *virgin Mary,* mother *of* thy sonne *Iesu Christ* our Lord and God, & in the holy Patriarches, Proph-	75
80	and Paul, Andrew, James, John, Thomas, James, Philip, Bartholomew, Matthew, Simon and Thaddeus; Linus, Cletus, Clement, Xystus, Cornelius,	etes, *Apostles and Martyrs,*	80

The Eucharistic Liturgy 147

	SARUM	1549	
85	Cyprian, Lawrence, Chrysogonus, John and Paul, Cosmas and Damian: and of *all thy saints:* by *whose* merits and prayers *grant* that we may	73 *whose examples (O Lorde)*	85
90	in all things be defended by help of thy protection. Through the same Christ our *Lord.* Amen. [MEMENTO ETIAM	and stedfastnes in thy faythe, and keping thy holye commaundementes, *graunte* vs to folowe.	90
95	Remember also, *O Lord, thy servants* and handmaids N. and N., *who have gone* before *us with the sign of faith, and rest in the sleep of peace.* Grant	We commende vnto thy mercie *(O Lorde)* all other thy seruauntes, whiche are departed hence from *vs, with the signe of fayth,* and nowe do	95
100	unto them, we beseech thee, O Lord, 106 *and* to *all* that have fallen	reste in the slepe of peace: Graunte vnto them, we besech thee, thy mercy, *and* euerlasting *peace,* and that at the daye of the generall resurrec-	100
105	asleep in Christ, a place of refreshment, light, *and peace.*	cion, we *and all* they whiche bee of the misticall body of thy sonne, maye altogether bee set on his right hand, and heare that his most ioyful	105
110		voice: Come vnto me, O ye that be blessed of my father, and possesse the kingdome, whiche is prepared for you, from the begynning of the	110
115	Through the same *Christ* our Lord. Amen.]	worlde: Graunte this, O father, for Iesus *Christes* sake, our only mediatour and aduocate. O God heauenly father, whiche of thy tender mercie,	115

	SARUM	1549	
120	Hanc Igitur Oblationem *We beseech thee*, therefore, O Lord, graciously *to accept this oblation*	diddeste geue thine only sonne Iesu Christ, to suffer deathe upon the crosse for our redempcion, who made there (by his one *oblacion* once of-	120
125	*of our service,* and *of* thy *whole* family, and to order our days in thy peace,	248 fered) a full, perfect, and sufficiente sacrifice, oblacion, and satisfaction, for the sinnes of the *whole* worlde, and did in-	125
130	and *command* that we be delivered from eternal damntion, and be numbered in the flock of thine elect. Through Christ our Lord. Amen.	stitute, and in his holy Ghospell *commaunde* vs to celebrate a perpetuall memorye of that his precious deathe, vntyll his comming again:	130
135	Quam Oblationem Which oblation do thou, O God, *we beseech thee, vouch-* *safe to* make altogether	Heare vs (*o mercifull father*) *we besech thee:* and with thy holy spirite and worde *vouchsafe to bl†esse*	135
140	bles†sed, ap†proved, rati†fied, *reasonable*, and acceptable, *that* 7 *it may be* made *unto us the* Bo†dy and Bl†ood of thy most	and sanc†tifie 222 *these* thy *gyftes*, and creatures of bread and wyne, *that they maye be vnto vs the bodye*	140
145	*dearly beloved Son* our Lord *Jesus Christ.* Qui Pridie *Who, the* day before *he* suffered, *took bread* into his holy	*and bloud of thy moste derely beloued sonne Jesus Christe.* *Who* in *the* same nyghte that *he* was betrayed: *tooke breade,*	145
150	and venerable hands, and lifting up his eyes toward heaven unto thee, O God his Father almighty, *giving thanks* unto thee, *he* bles†sed, brake, and	and when *he* had *blessed,* and geuen thankes: he brake it, and	150

The Eucharistic Liturgy 149

	SARUM	1549	
155	*gave it to his disciples, saying:* Take *and* eat *ye all of this,* For *this is my Body.*	*gaue it to his disciples, sayinge:* Take, eate, this is my bodye whiche is geuen for you; do this in remembraunce of me.	155
	Likewise after supper, taking	*Likewyse after supper he*	
160	also this glorious *Cup* into his holy and venerable hands, again *giving thanks* unto thee, he bles†sed, and *gave it to* his disciples, *saying:* Take and	*toke* the *cuppe,* and when he had *geuen thankes, he gaue it to* them, *saying:* drinke ye	160
165	*drink ye all of this. For this is* the Cup of *my Blood of the new* and eternal *Testament,* a Mystery of the faith, *which* shall be *shed for you and for*	all of this, for this is my bloude of the newe Testament, whiche is shed for you and for many, for remission of	165
170	*many for remission of sins. As often as ye shall do these* things, ye shall *do* them *in remembrance of me.*	sinnes: do this as oft as ye shall drink it, *in remembraunce of me* Wherefore, O Lorde and	170
175	UNDE ET MEMORES *Wherefore* also, O Lord, *we* thy servants, together with thy holy people,	heauenly father, accordyng to the Institucion of thy derely beloued sonne, *our* sauioure Iesu Christe, *we thy* humble *seruauntes* doe celebrate, and	175
180	189 *having in remembrance* both the *blessed Passion* of the same	make here *before thy* diuine *Maiestie,* with these *thy* holy *giftes,* the memoriall whiche thy sonne hath willed vs to make: *hauing in remembraunce*	180
185	*Christ* thy Son *our* Lord God, and his *Resurrection* from the dead, *and* also his *glorious Ascension* into heaven, *do* offer *to thine* excellent *Majesty*	*his blessed passion,* *mightie resurreccion, and glorious ascencion,* 180	185
190	of thine own gifts and bounties a pure † oblation, a holy † oblation, a spotless † oblation, the holy † Bread of eternal life, and the Cup † of everlasting	*renderynge vnto thee moste heartye thankes,* for the innumerable benefites	190

	SARUM	1549	
195	salvation. SUPRA QUÆ Upon which do thou vouchsafe to look with a favorable and gracious countenance, and	procured vnto vs by thesame, entyerely desyringe thy fatherly goodnes, mercifully *to accepte*	195
200	*to* hold them *accepted*, as thou didst vouchsafe to hold accepted the offerings of thy righteous servant Abel, and the sacrifice of our forefather		200
205	Abraham, and that which thy High Priest Melchizedech offered unto thee, a holy *sacrifice*, a spotless oblation. 62	*thys* our *Sacrifice of prayse* and thankes geuinge:	205
210	SUPPLICES TE ROGAMUS We *humbly beseech thee,* Almighty God:	moste *humblye besechinge thee* to graunte, that by the merites and deathe of thy sonne Iesus Christ, and through faith in	210
215	command these things	his bloud, wee and all thy whole church, may obteigne remission of our sinnes, and all other benefites of his passion. And here wee offre and present	215
220	 125	vnto the (O Lord) oure self, oure soules, and bodyes, to be a *reasonable*, holy and liuely sacrifice vnto thee: humbly besechyng thee,	220
225	*to be brought up by the* hands *of thy holy Angel to thine* Altar on high *before the sight of thy divine Majesty: that as many of us as shall,* by	260 that whosoever shalbee par–	225

The Eucharistic Liturgy 151

	SARUM	1549	
230	*this* altar-*partaking, receive the sacred Bo†dy and Bl†ood of thy Son, may be filled with* every *heavenly bene†diction and grace.*	*takers of this* holy Communion *maye* woorthely *receive the* most precious *body and bloude of thy sonne Iesu Christ; and bee* fulfilled *with*	230
235	Through the same *Christ* our Lord. Amen.	*thy grace and heauenly benediction,* and made one bodye with thy sonne Iesu *Christ*, that he maye dwell in them, and they in hym.	235
240	MEMENTO ETIAM: 94–117 above. NOBIS QUOQUE *And* to *us sinners* also, thy servants	*And* although *we* be vnworthy (through our many-	240
245	123 125 who trust in the multitude of	fold *synnes*) to offre vnto thee any Sacrifice: Yet we beseche thee to accepte this our bounden duetie and seruice,	245
250	thy mercies, vouchsafe to grant some part and fellowship with thy holy Apostles and Martyrs: with John, Stephen, Matthias, Barnabas, Ignatius, Alexander,		250
255	Marcellinus, Peter, Felicity, Perpetua, Agatha, Lucy, Agnes, Cecilia, Anastasia, and all thy Saints: into whose company admit us, we beseech		255
260	219 225	and *commaunde these* our prayers and supplicacions, *by the* ministerye *of thy holy Angels, to be brought vp into thy* holy Tabernacle *before the*	260

	SARUM	1549	
265	thee, *not* as a *weigher of merits, but* as a bestower of *pardon.* Through *Christ our Lord,* Through *whom*, O Lord,	*syght of thy diuine maiestie: not waying* our *merites, but pardoning* our offences, through *Christe our Lord,*	265
270	thou dost ever create, sanc†tify, quic†ken, bl†ess, and bestow upon us all these good things. By † him, *and with* † him,		270
275	and in † him, *in the unity of the Holy* † *Ghost, all honour and glory is unto thee,* O God the *Father* † *Almighty, world without end.* Amen.	*by whom, and with whom, in the vnitie of the holy Ghost, all honoure and glorye,* be *unto thee, O father almightie, world without ende. Amen.*	275

3. The Eucharistic Sacrifice

Now let us examine the charge that Cranmer's rendering of the Latin original was designed to vitiate the essential meaning of the old service on the principle of the Eucharistic Sacrifice.

It is true that Cranmer was utterly opposed to the medieval conception of the Mass as a ritual immolation of Christ in a factual repetition of Calvary, a Sacrifice 'truly *propitiatory* for the living and the dead,' as the Council of Trent afterwards asserted. Hence the vigor of the language in which he set forth the Death upon the Cross as 'his one oblacion once offered.' There is no question that he would not have hesitated to obliterate from the text any phrases which could be considered to express, to imply, or even to permit, any such idea as an 'Offering of Christ.' But there are no such cancellations in Cranmer's version. He rightly maintained that the conception of a Propitiatory Mactation (as the Romans do not scruple to call it to the present day) was not inherent in the ancient Western Liturgy: it was a rationalization that had been *read into* it, but was in no wise to be found in what it actually said.

The theme of the Oblation of the Eucharistic Sacrifice is dominant in the Latin Canon, being expressed in no less than eight of its constituent parts. But what is the 'actual matter' which is offered in sacrifice in all those passages? Here they are, in Latin and English:

hæc dona, hæc munera, hæc sancta sacrificia illibata	7	these gifts, these offerings, these holy undefiled sacrifices
hoc sacrificium laudis	62	this sacrifice of praise

hanc . . . oblationem servitutis nostræ	124	this oblation of our service
offerimus . . . de tuuis donis, ac datis, hostiam puram, hostiam sanctam, hostiam immaculatam, Panem sanctum vitæ æternæ, et Calicem salutis perpetuæ.	189	we offer . . . of thine own gifts and bounties, a pure oblation, a holy oblation, a spotless oblation, the holy Bread of eternal life, and the Cup of everlasting salvation.
accepta habere, sicuti accepta habere dignatus es munera pueri tui justi Abel, et sacrificium Patri arch nostri Abrahæ, et quod tibi obtulit summus sacerdos tuus Melchisedech, sanctum sacrificium, immaculatam hostiam.	200	to hold them accepted, as thou didst vouchsafe to hold accepted the offerings of thy righteous servant Abel, and the sacrifice of our forefather Abraham, and that which thy High Priest Melchizedek offered unto thee, a holy sacrifice, a spotless oblation.
hæc	219	these things
hæc omnia bona	272	all these good things

Now it is perfectly evident that although the expressions used are diversified into every available synonym, for the sake of variety, nevertheless all the terms employed to indicate the matter of the Sacrifice are identical in their referent: *dona, data, munera, sacrificium, oblatio, hostia*, all unequivocally denote the material elements of Bread and Wine which are offered up in a sacrificial action.

This point needs a little insisting upon. For though Roman liturgical authorities have always recognized the absolute equivalence of these expressions,[5] yet the translations of the Mass which the Roman Church puts in the hands of its people usually render the word *hostia* as 'Victim.'[6]

It is true that in classical Latin the word always refers to a living animal to be killed in the pagan sacrifices: but in the liturgical language of the Christian Church this meaning had to be completely laid aside, as irrelevant to a Sacrifice which did not employ animal food. Therefore its significance in the text and the rubrics of the Mass, and in the scores of variable Offertory Collects known as the *Secretæ*, is solely and simply the *res oblata* of the Elements: sometimes, as in the original usage of the text of the liturgy, both; but from early medieval times,

---

5. See Eisenhofer, *Handbuch der katholischen Liturgik* (Freiburg: Herder, 1934) II. 130: esp. the citation from Amalarius of Metz, 'nomen hostia: vel muneris, donive vel sacrificium seu oblationis.'

6. Gasquet and Bishop, in *Edward VI and the Book of Common Prayer* (London: Hodges, 1890) 208, venture to insert this tendentious translation in a professedly high-level discussion, for its occurrence in the *Unde et memores* passage; though the context forces them to a more candid rendering in the following *Supra quæ* paragraph.

in the rubrics and in common language, specifically the species of Bread, to form a convenient distinction from the Chalice. In that form the word has entered the English language. When one speaks of 'people's hosts,' for instance, there is no suggestion whatever of an allusion to 'the people's Victims!' And there is no question about the meaning of *hostia* in its contexts in the Latin Liturgy. The *hostia Pura, sancta, immaculata* is offered *de tuis donis ac datis*, 'from out of thine own gifts bestowed upon us,' in the *Unde et memores* (190); and aligned with and put upon the same level with the Patriarchal Sacrifices in the *Supra quae* (200). 'Victim' is just simply not an honest translation.

From one end of the Canon to the other, the things that are repeatedly offered in sacrifice, and upon which God's acceptance and benediction is again and again invoked, are clearly nothing else than the oblations of Bread and Wine. They are the people's symbolic gifts' to God, from the material bounties which he has given them. Nowhere is there any offering up of Christ, as 'the Lamb as it had been slain.' There is no trace of the idea of a piacular rite, to reconcile God to man.

This is not to assert that the primitive Roman Rite ever considered that the Christian Sacrifice consisted of a mere oblation of the material elements. Definitely as they are designated, they are always spoken of with the numinous reverence which belongs to their divinely ordained function as effectual tokens and channels of spiritual realities — they are 'pure, holy, undefiled, spotless.' The only place where the two Species are specifically named, they are called 'the holy Bread of eternal life, and the Cup of everlasting salvation' (193). And the offering of them is the expression of all our worship: 'this sacrifice of praise' (62), and 'this oblation of our service' (124).

It is obvious that Cranmer did not object to any of these sacrificial expressions in the Mass as such, since he was at considerable pains to preserve almost every detail of them somewhere in his Consecration Prayer. He did drop the comparison of the Eucharist with the Patriarchal Sacrifices (197–207); and also the mention of the 'good things' in the peroration of the Canon (269–273). This latter has survived from a blessing of oil, grain, grapes, cheese, and so forth, which took place at this very peculiar point of the service in the days of the Canons of Hippolytus and the Leonine Sacramentary on some special occasions. A Bishop's blessing of the Holy Oils on Maundy Thursday is still interpolated here, before the final Doxology, to the present day. The only possible interpretation of this anomalous state of affairs would seem to be that the early Roman Church had such a strong sense of the oblation of the Bread and Wine as a Sacrifice of the Fruits of the Earth, that it seemed to them quite in order to append to it lesser benedictions of other comestibles used not as Sacraments, but 'sacramentals.' This might have been perfectly reasonable, if it had been carried out say at the time of the Offertory: occurring here, after the Consecration, it showed no sense of form or appropriateness; and the vestigial phrases about all these good things[7] surviving in the Mass are only a stumbling-block to present understanding. As Fortescue says, 'It is a strange way of referring to the Blessed Sacrament.'[8] Cranmer was on sound ground in dismissing both the Patriarchal Sacrifices and the 'good things' passage as irrelevant, and perhaps as below his own views of the Sacrament.

But though Cranmer considered that the sacrificial language, properly understood in its own self-evident meaning, was perfectly innocent, and though it was authenticated innumerable times in the Fathers, the fact remained that it was not properly understood at the time of the Reformation, since the Middle Ages had forced upon it interpretations which he regarded as intolerable. In order to preserve its undoubted primitive witness, and at the same time to rid it of misinterpretations, he devised the method of shifting the expressions to new contexts, where he hoped they would be safe from the kind of eisegesis to which they had been subjected.

Accordingly, he removed every mention of any kind of oblation on the part of man until after the Consecration. It must be said at once that this is not a natural order for the development of the action. It has received some correction in later Prayer Books, and needs some further attention in any future revision. For the moment, it may suffice to say that it would appear that Cranmer's idea was that if the English order had been allowed to follow the Latin in offering gifts 'and sacrifices' in connection with the Intercession, and on behalf of the special objects there mentioned, there might be a continuing danger of interpreting the Sacrifice as in some sense *propitiatory*.

So, in his Prayer for the Church, he substituted 'these our prayers' (9) for the 'gifts, offerings, and sacrifices' of the *Te igitur*. The 'sacrifice of praise' of the *Memento* for the Living (62) is transferred to 208, where it coalesces with the 'sacrifice' of the *Supra quæ* to become 'thys our Sacrifice of prayse and thankes geuinge.' In the *Hanc igitur* (124), part of the idea of 'the oblation of our service' is retained *in loco*, and boldly transformed from *our* offering to that of our Lord, being expanded into 'who made there (by his one oblacion once offered) a full, perfect, and sufficiente sacrifice, oblacion, and satisfaction, for the sinnes of the whole worlde'— and then the whole expression of 122–125 is moved to the peroration of the Consecration Prayer in the reinforced paraphrase of 'we beseche thee to accepte this our bounden duetie and seruice' (246).

There is also one rather extraordinary *double* amplification of a single idea in the original, as a result of two divergent explanations of the same short Latin word which were current in Cranmer's time.

---

7. The sense of the phrases '*ut placatus accipias*' (123), and '*propitio ac sereno vultu respicere digneris*' (197), is that God would be so propitious as to accept them — not that he would be propitiated by having accepted them.

8. *The Mass* (London: Longmans, 1914), 357.

The prayer *Supplices* (210), which is the Roman Invocation, asks God to 'command *these things* to be brought up by the hands of thy holy Angel to thine Altar on high before the sight of thy divine Majesty: that as many of us as shall, by this altar-partaking, receive the sacred Body and Blood of thy Son, may be filled with every heavenly benediction and grace.'

This curious conceit seems to have originated as a Prayer of Incense: 'We offer incense before thy holy glory, O God: receive it upon thy holy and heavenly and spiritual altar, and send down upon us in its stead the grace of thy holy Spirit.'[9] This language, which must have seemed most natural and all but literal to those who watched the ascending incense-smoke, the symbol of 'the prayers of the saints' in the Apocalypse, was later appropriated to the idea of a purely metaphysical and mystical sublimating of the offered Gifts to the Heavenly Altar.[10]

Such a flight of fancy, which the grandiloquent Greeks took in their stride, proved to be an insoluble enigma to the literal-minded Latins of the Middle Ages. What, exactly, were the mysterious *hæc* 'these things' — which were to be rapt by angelic ministry to the Altar in Heaven? Obviously not the Elements, in any literal sense — and the Western mind never suspected the original mystical sense. But if not, what was?

Speculation settled on two different solutions. One was the somewhat timid hypothesis that it might be the Church's prayers which might be considered as presented at the Throne of Grace. The other was far bolder, and seized upon the soaring postulates of St. Augustine for the idea that the reality of the Christian Sacrifice was the Oblation of Christ's Mystical Body, so that here the Church was offering Itself at the Altar of the Heavenly Intercession.

No more than anyone else of his age did Cranmer know that neither one of these popular explanations had any bearing on the original purpose of this enigmatic passage in the rite. But he did consider that both were worth preserving for their own sake.

First, the effect of the existing pictorial expressions was to lift the mind of the worshiper to the heavenly places, and thus to align the Eucharist not with a past Calvary, but with the eternal Heavenly Intercession. So he brought in the whole passage in a full and nearly literal form as a kind of spectacular final climax to the whole Canon: 'Commaunde these our prayers and supplications, by the ministerye of thy holy Angels, to be brought vp into thy holy Tabernacle before the syght of thy diuine maiestie' (260–265). (We may note that though Cranmer freely used the word 'altar' in his rubrics, he excluded it from the text of the service, perhaps as raising overtones of propitiation. The allusion here is probably to the greater and more perfect tabernacle' of Hebrews 9:11.)

---

9. Brightman, *Liturgies Eastern and Western*: Byzantine, 359.34; Alexandrian, 118.26.

10. Brightman, *Liturgies Eastern and Western*: Syrian, 47b.30–38; Byzantine, 360.34; Alexandrian, 129.20.

However, the interpolation of the passage into the peroration of the Canon, just before the final Deprecation, 'not waying our merites,' proved none too successful, giving an effect of irrelevance in that place: and after being dropped in 1552, it has not been restored in any form or place in any subsequent Anglican rite, until the Indian of 1952.

But in addition to this version of the idea, at the exact point in the order of thought occupied by the original cryptic phrase, and specially cleared for the purpose by the above transfer elsewhere of the Heavenly Altar passage, Cranmer put in the Augustinian conception, in the unimpeachable form of a quotation of Romans 12:1: 'And here wee offre and present vnto the (O Lord) oure self, oure soules, and bodyes, to be a reasonable, holy and liuely sacrifice vnto thee' (219–223).

So put, this is perhaps the most distinctive feature of the Anglican Consecration Prayer. It has the great merit that it furnishes a direct and an adequate answer to the underlying question, What is the substance and reality of the Christian Sacrifice which is offered in the Liturgy? What is man's part in the *divina commercia* of the great Eucharistic Action?

Something more, surely, than a token oblation of Fruits of the Earth. So the Latin Mass indicated by indirect ways, by context, and by the use of language touched with emotion. It did not offer 'Christ,' and it did identify the 'basic matter' of the Oblation with the elements of Bread and Wine. But it offered them on the warrant of the divine Institution, in commemoration of the saving Passion, as an expression of our worship, and as a means of a divine Communion.

Yet these implications need to be clearly stated, if we are to get beyond the idea of a 'mere' Sacrifice of Bread and Wine. It has been noted that we do not offer *wheat* and *grapes* — the fruits of the earth as they come from the hand of God — but that man's own life and work go into the making of the Bread and Wine. Therefore, simple as they are, the eucharistic Elements are vital symbols of the fact that man is offering *himself* with the Holy Gifts. It is an outstanding merit of our Liturgy that this salient expression in the words of St. Paul makes all these inferences explicit and unmistakable, setting forth in the highest and most moving terms the offering of all that we are and have, that we may be 'accepted in the Beloved.'

In sum, then, the result of all Cranmer's realigning of the sacrificial language of the Canon was to remove every expression of direct verbal Oblation of the Elements, lest there should remain any idea of any ritual action of man which might be interpreted as a propitiation of God. Primary emphasis was thrown upon the atoning work of our Lord, in 'his one oblacion once offered,' as being the only actual substantive Sacrifice in the history of the world. From this Sacrifice, not even the idea of Propitiation was excluded, as the use of the added unscriptural word 'satisfaccion' shows. Yet man's action is not propitiatory, but eucharistic: he offers his 'Sacrifice of prayse and thankes geuinge' for the benefits of the Passion, his life as 'a reasonable, holy, and liuely sacrifice' to God, his prayers in union with the Heavenly Intercession.

4. Other Contemporary Sources

a) Lutheran: Although, as we have said, Cranmer's service was fundamentally an equivalent paraphrase of the Sarum Mass — indeed, a precise and intelligent translation of the Latin at all essential points — he nevertheless incorporated quite a bit of material from other sources, Eastern and Western, ancient and modern, Catholic and Protestant.

The most considerable in bulk of these borrowings were from Lutheran sources. In Cranmer's three years' stay abroad 'on the King's business,' he acquired first-hand familiarity with the liturgical experiments of the German Reformers. He helped himself freely to anything in this material which suited his purpose. However, what he omitted is considerably more significant than what he adopted. Thanks to his own profound acquaintance with the historic liturgies, he showed an undeviating instinct in rejecting every item of Reformation origin which was inconsistent with the theology, the principles, and the spirit of the inherited Catholic worship. Therefore, though the 'Lutheran' contributions to the English Rite loom fairly large in amount, it is simply the fact that there is not a particle of distinctive 'Lutheranism' in it.

The features of the Liturgy of the First Prayer Book which were derived from Lutheran rituals were these:

1. The announcement of the 'Chapter' of the Epistle and Gospel.
2. The placing of the Sermon after the Creed, instead of after the Gospel.
3. The following phrases in the Exhortation: 'Derely beloued in the Lord . . . must considre what S. Paule . . . diligently to trie and examine them selues . . . an earnest and lyuely faith in Christ our sauior . . . those holy misteries . . . for the redempcion of the worlde . . . both God and man . . . the excedyng loue of oure maister, and onely sauior . . . thus dying for vs, and the innumerable benefites, whiche (by his precious bloudshedyng) he hath obteigned to vs . . . a pledge . . . comfort and consolacion.'
4. Rubrics directing the people to bring up their offerings, and for the intending communicants to assemble in the choir.
5. The punctuation of the beginning of the Preface, 'O Lorde, holy father, almightie euerlasting God,' where the Latin has *'Domine sancte, Pater omnipotens, Æterne Deus.'*
6. The following italicized words in the Intercession: '*Almightye* and *euerlyuyng* God, *whiche* by thy holy *Apostle haste* taught vs . . . Bishoppes, *Pastors, and Curates . . . seruynge* thee in *holynesse and righteousnesse, all . . . coumforte . . . trouble*, sorowe, *nede, syckness,* or any *other* aduersitie . . . whiche is here *assembled*'.

7. In the Consecration Prayer: 'oure self, oure soules, and bodyes' (220).
8. In the General Confession: 'Almightie GOD, father of oure Lorde Iesus Christ, maker of all things, iudge of all menne, we knowledge & bewaile . . . most greuously haue committed . . . agaynste thy diuine maiestie . . . we . . . be hartely sory . . . haue mercie vpon vs, moste mercifull father, for thy sonne our Lorde Iesus Christes sake, forgeue vs all . . . serue and please thee in newnes of life, to the honour and glory of thy name: Through Iesus Christe our Lorde.'
9. In the Absolution: 'forgeuenesse of synnes . . . with heartye repentaunce and true fayth.'
10. The Comfortable Words.
11. At the Administration of the Holy Communion: 'whiche was geuen for thee,' 'whiche was shed for thee.'

In all this, there is not one word which is in conflict with the historic faith, nor even with any of the exaggerated interpretations of the Mass held at the time in the Roman Church — nothing indeed which does not blend in harmoniously and indistinguishably with the Roman contexts into which Cranmer inserted it.

b) Catholic: But while there is thus not a thing which is distinctively 'Protestant' in all the Lutheran contributions, there is one passage in the Consecration Prayer which is commonly taken to be a concentration of Protestant emphasis, which turns out not to be of Protestant origin at all. This is the initial Thanksgiving for the Redemption, with its powerful stress upon the sole sufficiency of Christ's Sacrifice upon the Cross.

Most of the 'Lutheran' passages cited above were derived from the *Consultation* of Archbishop Hermann von Wied of Cologne, who had espoused Lutheran views, and was shortly thereafter deprived of his see for that reason. But this Thanksgiving for the Redemption was drawn from the *Antididagma*, which was the counterblast to Hermann's pronouncements, issued by his learned and inflexibly Catholic cathedral chapter. It was this Catholic document which contributed to our service the following: '(by his one oblacion *once offered*) a full, perfect, and *sufficiente sacrifice*, oblation, and satisfaccion, *for the sinnes of the* whole *worlde . . . commaunde . . . memorye . . . of that his . .*'

Incidentally, the *Antididagma* gives direct support for the distinctive translations of the phrases 'Sacrifice of prayse and thankes geuing' (208), and 'our prayers and supplicacions' (260), already noted as prominent in Cranmer's thought.

c) Mozarabic?: Gasquet and Bishop, in their learned but controversial book, *Edward VI and the Book of Common Prayer*, argued that the vital Narrative of the Institution in the First Prayer Book follows the Lutheran form of the region of Brandenburg-Nurnberg, which was incorporated in the Catechism of Justus Jonas, which in turn Cranmer translated into English in his *Catechismus*.

The fact is that there is wide variation in the text of the Institution Narrative as rehearsed in all the historic liturgies. They all display a conflation of the four scriptural accounts in the Synoptic Gospels and in 1 Corinthians, with the apparent aim of including every possible detail of each of them. However, since this liturgical narrative was embedded in the great Consecration Prayer, it was inevitably colored by the devout emotion of its context: and all rites since the fourth century have interpolated rhetorical phrases into the account. These insertions, in the Latin version, comprise the following: 'took bread *into his holy and venerable hands, and lifting up his eyes toward heaven unto thee, O God his Father Almighty*, . . . this *glorious* Cup *into his holy and venerable hands* . . . *this is the Cup of* my Blood of the new *and eternal* Testament, *a Mystery of the faith*' (149–168).

But with the dawn of modern studies of the Holy Scriptures, and of a modern sense of literary integrity, there arose in more than one quarter a desire to conflate even more closely the content of the scriptural accounts, and to remove the non-scriptural additions. Exactly this was done in the Mozarabic Rite in Spain; this is what the German texts do; and there is some evidence that Cranmer went over the ground independently for himself. There is of course no doubt that it was the German texts which called the matter to his attention; though it is probable that the existence of this kind of treatment in the Mozarabic confirmed his purpose. Dr. Brightman points out that Cranmer's version can be completely accounted for by the hypothesis of a conflation of the Roman and the Mozarabic forms.[11] Nothing is found in the English rendering which does not appear in one or the other of these two Latin sources. But on the other hand, the version of 1549 has the expression 'and when he has *blessed, and* geuen thankes' (153), which is common to the Roman and the Mozarabic, but is missing from the Brandenburg Order and from Justus Jonas.

The insinuation of a 'Lutheran' origin of our Institution Narrative is entirely without weight, even as the taunt of a controversialist. Of course, feeble as it is, it is his only possible retort to the fact that our possession of what is both the *fullest* and the *purest* possible scriptural form of the 'Charter Narrative' is the most effective criticism of the legitimacy of the Roman interpolations. It is likewise in conflict with the Roman idea of a quasi-magical Formula as the essential instrument for a valid consecration of the Sacrament. (Incidentally, the Rubrics of the Missal indicate that their minimum indispensable formula for the Cup includes some of the above non-scriptural additions: '*Calix,*' '*æterni,*' and '*mysterium fidei.*') The Spanish Church, to be sure, politely evades making this kind of aspersion on the Roman Rite by substituting the Roman Narrative of the Institution at the actual performance of the Mass, instead of their own ancient form — which however

---

11. *The English Rite* (London: Rivingtons, 1915), I. cviii.

continues to be printed in the Mozarabic Missal, with the note that it is recorded only '*ne antiquitas ignoretur.*'

5. Influence of the Greek Liturgies

Much less impressive in extent than the above contemporary contributions, but far more important for the meaning of the rite, are the effects upon the text of the service which stem from Cranmer's reading of the Greek liturgies.

First, it was doubtless due to the influence of the Greek Rites that Cranmer gathered up the disjointed and displaced Offertory Prayers in the Latin Canon, and consolidated and reformed them into a single comprehensive General Intercession; and similarly with his transformation of the poorly connected chain of collects, remade into an unbroken Consecration Prayer, after the model of the 'Thanksgiving' of the Greek Anaphoras. Likewise, he reverted to Eastern standards by making the Thanksgiving after Communion into a substantial fixed supplication, in lieu of the fragmentary Postcommunion 'collects,' varying with the day, in the Western Rites.

But in addition to these structural influences, he conflated into his text some salient expressions from the Greek liturgies. In the *Communicantes* collect, he had recourse to the Liturgy of St. Basil for mention of the great classes of the Saints, instead of the Roman list of specific names: 'and *chiefly* in the glorious *and most blessed* virgin Mary, . . . and in the *holy Patriarches, Prophetes,* Apostles and Martyrs' (75–80).

We have noted that the collect *Quam oblationem* corresponded to the peculiar 'preliminary Invocation' of the Alexandrian rites. In medieval times it was conceived to be *the* Invocation of the power of God to consecrate the Sacrament which Western Christians considered was something which was carried into effect by the recital of the Words of Institution, which followed immediately. (Naturally no one in those days had the faintest idea that the prayer *Supplices te rogamus* was the original organic Invocation of the Roman Rite.)

Cranmer therefore adhered without question to the accepted order and rationale. But he considered the Latin 'which oblation do thou, O God, we beseech thee, vouchsafe to make altogether blessed, approved, ratified, reasonable, and acceptable' (136) to suffer severely in comparison with the direct and operative language of the Greek Invocations, and rewrote it, embodying expressions taken from the true Invocation after the Institution in the Liturgy of St. Basil: 'Heare vs (o mercifull father) we besech thee: and with *thy holy spirite* and worde vouchsafe *to blesse and sanctifie these* thy *gyftes*, and creatures of *bread* and *wine*,' etc.

Still another conflation from St. Basil, which Cranmer appended to his translation of the prayer *Supplices*, provides a really transforming heightening of the whole meaning of the rite: 'maye *woorthely* receiue the most precious body and bloude of thy sonne Jesus Christe: and bee fulfilled with thy grace and heauenly benediction, and *made one bodye with thy* sonne Iesu *Christ*, that he maye *dwell in* them, and they in hym' (231–239).

This passage has had really momentous consequences in developing the Anglican conception of the experience of receiving the Holy Communion. Thanks to certain paradoxes in the Roman theory of Transubstantiation, it is the teaching of that Church that the reception of the Sacrament is a very transient affair. The supposed miraculous conversion of the substance of the Bread and Wine into that of the Body and Blood of Christ is not permanent, but endures only so long as the Elements remain recognizably Bread and Wine. The instant they even begin to be assimilated, they are no longer the Body and Blood, but mere natural materials, to go the homely way of all digestion. Consequently, the Divine Presence is with the communicant only momentarily: then it is gone again. As against this mere meeting and greeting, this contribution from the Rite of St. Basil has enriched the Anglican Liturgy with a sacramental belief which is on an altogether higher plane: which embraces a 'Real Presence' upon a spiritual, not merely a material, level — and finds it tenfold more 'real' for that very reason — which is permanent, not fleeting, a union rather than a contact, an organic abiding and indwelling, whose effect is nothing less than an incorporation of the communicant into the very life of Christ.

Cranmer thought so much of the potency of this idea, that he underscored it by saying it over twice more in his Liturgy. In the Exhortation, the First Prayer Book said, 'then we *dwell in* Christ and Christ in vs, wee bee *made one with Christ*, & Christ with vs.' So also in the Prayer of Humble Access, where he expanded the theme of the Latin *Domine, non sum dignus* with still other phrases from St. Basil: '*We doe not presume to come to* this *thy table* (o mercifull lorde) trusting *in oure owne righteousnes*, but in *thy manifold* and great *mercies*:' concluding with this paraphrase of the matter already in the Consecration Prayer: 'Graunte vs therefore (gracious lorde) so to eate the fleshe of thy dere sonne Iesus Christe, and to drinke his blonde, in these holy Misteries, that wee may continually dwell in him, and he in vs, that oure sinful bodies may be made cleane by his body, and our souls washed through his most precious bloud.'

Few and brief as were the phrases which Cranmer drafted in from the Liturgy of St. Basil to clarify and enrich the text of his service, they have a force which it is impossible to exaggerate in enhancing the significance of our rite, and exalting it to a level above anything expressed in the Roman Mass.

6. *The Real Presence*

The foregoing analyses of sources, to see just what material was incorporated in Cranmer's work, and how he used and phrased it in such a way as not merely to preserve all the meaning that was in the Latin Mass, but to sublimate it to yet higher values and potencies, are essential in meeting some recent heavy assaults upon the integrity of the Anglican liturgies.

Granting that strong Calvinistic pressures resulted in 'Receptionist' expressions about the Sacrament in the Second Prayer Book, it has always been supposed that at least the First Prayer Book was perfectly orthodox in setting forth the Catholic doctrine of the Real Presence. But now the current critics have been maintaining that Cranmer's 'Zwinglian' views on the Sacrament were held by him throughout all the period of his life in which he was concerned with the Liturgy, and therefore were those which he attempted formally to express in the First Prayer Book.

Recent studies do in fact substantiate the fact that Cranmer was indeed in agreement with Zwingli's beliefs on the Eucharist. However, this does not mean that either of them considered that its significance lay only in that purely *mental* exercise of a grateful recollection of the Passion, which is all that is left nowadays out of Zwingli's actually far richer teaching. There is no doubt that both of them would have vigorously repudiated any such limitations. The point that both were trying to make was the paramount importance of man's response and cooperation with what both acknowledged to be the work of God, in recognizing and appropriating the personal presence of Christ within the soul. Without such inner and subjective appropriation, both considered that no degree of merely external and objective 'Presence' could amount to anything but sheer magic. The essential defect of their position lay in their consequently discarding the conception of an Objective Real Presence as useless — whereas actually it is indispensable: there can be nothing factual in talk about 'receiving' anything which has no substantive independent existence of its own.

But regardless of the question as to whether Cranmer's personal opinions were touched with such inadequacies, the plain fact is that the liturgy which he framed certainly was not. The reason for this easily verifiable fact is that Cranmer's 'Zwinglian' ideas about the Eucharist were not any *new objectives* which he was bent upon introducing into the service — they were only his rationalization of what it was that was accomplished by the historic liturgies. They were an explanation which he applied just as freely to the Latin Mass, or to the Greek liturgies which he so valued, as he did to his own version of the same service.

Thus the question of the Real Presence in Cranmer's service is quite different from the matter of the Eucharistic Sacrifice. We have seen that he was acutely aware of the distortions wrought by medieval ideas of a 'Propitiatory Sacrifice,' and used all his acumen to rearranging the sacrificial expressions in the Canon so that they would no longer be susceptible to such interpretations. But he had no such apprehension as to anything said or implied in the Mass as to the nature of the Consecration or the method of the Eucharistic Presence: his only concern was that whatever was accomplished in the Consecration and the Communion should be vitally realized in the soul. Consequently, instead of radically altering the expressions in the service at those supreme points, he retained and greatly re-enforced them, as we have seen.

Certainly one does not solemnly invoke the power of Almighty God in such terms as 'with thy holy spirite and worde vouchsafe to bl✝esse and sancttifie these thy gyftes, and creatures of bread and wyne, that they maye be vnto the bodye and bloud of thy moste derely beloued sonne Iesus Christe' (138), merely in order to assist a mere process of mental recollection of the Passion, or indeed with any less objective in mind than to give ministerial effect to a direct operation of God.

Furthermore, it has been pointed out that although Cranmer was a sort of 'Nominalist' in his doctrine of the Eucharist, he was a thoroughgoing Catholic 'Realist' on the basic subject of the Incarnation.[12] He believed that the process of human redemption was nothing less than a conformation to, by means of an actual incorporation in, the divinely perfected humanity of our Lord. When he states the effect of a worthy communion to be that the receivers are 'made one bodye with thy sonne Iesus Christe, that he maye dwell in them, and they in hym' (236), and then repeats this same conception in the Prayer of Humble Access, and yet a third time in the Long Exhortation, he has raised the religious philosophy of the Sacrament to such a power, that the question of his opinions upon the method of its operation is a mere detail of psychological rationalization, which might be capable of being right or wrong without in the least affecting the majesty and the verity of that great central fact.

The passages which have been thought to symbolize Zwinglian doctrine in the First Prayer Book are these:

> and did institute, and in his holy Ghospell commaunde vs to celebrate a perpetuall memorye of that his precious deathe, vntyll his coming again: (129)

> Wherefore, . . . according to the Institucion of thy derely beloued sonne, our sauioure Iesu Christe, we thy humble seruauntes doe celebrate, and make here before thy diuine Maiestie, with these thy holy giftes, the memoriall whiche thy sonne hath willed vs to make: (174)

> to graunte, that by the merites and deathe of thy sonne Iesus Christ, and through faith in his bloud, wee and all thy whole Church, may obteigne remission of our sinnes, and other benefites of his passion. (212).

The first and second of these, immediately preceding and following the Narrative of the Institution, are exactly coincident with the order of thought of the corresponding passages in the Liturgy of the *Apostolic Constitutions*. That rite also makes a dual mention of both the 'Memorial' and the 'Institution,' and alludes to the Death, and the Second Coming all of which, except the 'Memorial,' are missing from the Latin Mass. Although the *Apostolic Constitutions* were not actually printed until 1563, after Cranmer's death, it is perfectly possible that he may have been acquainted with a manuscript of it. The coincidences of thought

---

12. Cyril C. Richardson, *Zwingli and Cranmer on the Eucharist* (Seabury-Western Theological Seminary, 1949), 36 ff.

and structure are so striking as virtually to compel the conclusion that Cranmer made a conflation here from that ancient source. In any case, since the Liturgy of the *Apostolic Constitutions*, whatever its other peculiarities, has not hitherto been found to be tainted with Zwinglianism, Cranmer's treatment must be pronounced to be perfectly orthodox in intent and in fact.

In the third passage, the only strain of 'Zwinglian' tendentiousness to be found would be the focussing of attention upon 'the merites and deathe of thy sonne Iesus Christ,' and 'faith in his bloud' as the *immediate* source of the remission of our sinnes, and all other benefits of his passion,' which the Eastern Liturgies include in a longer and more detailed list of the Benefits of Communion. Yet it is something which is almost too obvious to state, that the Passion was the *ultimate* fount of such benefits. And such is certainly the sense in which our Church has always said these words in the liturgy.

Further light is thrown upon these texts by the so-called 'Long Exhortation,' which is still retained in curtailed form on p. 85 of our Prayer Book.[13] This small Homily was used to begin 'The Order of Communion' in 1548, where it was inserted after the Priest's Communion of the Latin Mass; in 1549 it occurred immediately after the Sermon. Cranmer intended it as a full presentation to the people of his estimate of the meaning of the Eucharist. No exposition of this subject has ever been made which expresses a more numinous awe in the presence of a great spiritual Verity, or which insists more poignantly upon the need of an utter purification of soul in approaching it. The infinite significance of Christ's Death and Passion is most searchingly set forth. Then follows this telling explanation of what Cranmer meant by a 'memorial':

> And to thend that wee shoulde alwaye remembre the excedyng loue of oure maister, and onely sauior Iesu Christe, thus dying for vs, and the innumerable benefites, whiche (by his precious bloudshedyng) he hath

---

13. Ed. note: DEARLY beloved in the Lord, ye who mind to come to the holy Communion of the Body and Blood of our Saviour Christ, must consider how Saint Paul exhorteth all persons diligently to try and examine themselves, before they presume to eat of that Bread, and drink of that Cup. For as the benefit is great, if with a true penitent heart and lively faith we receive that holy Sacrament; so is the danger great, if we receive the same unworthily. Judge therefore yourselves, brethren, that ye be not judged of the Lord; repent you truly for your sins past; have a lively and steadfast faith in Christ our Saviour; amend your lives, and be in perfect charity with all men; so shall ye be meet partakers of those holy mysteries. And above all things ye must give most humble and hearty thanks to God, the Father, the Son, and the Holy Ghost, for the redemption of the world by the death and passion of our Saviour Christ, both God and man; who did humble himself, even to the death upon the Cross, for us, miserable sinners, who lay in darkness and the shadow of death; that he might make us the children of God, and exalt us to everlasting life. And to the end that we should always remember the exceeding great love of our Master, and only Saviour, Jesus Christ, thus dying for us, and the innumerable benefits which by his precious blood-shedding he hath obtained for us; he hath instituted and ordained holy mysteries, as pledges of his love, and for a continual remembrance of his death, to our great and endless comfort. To him therefore, with the Father and the Holy Ghost, let us give (as we are most bounden) continual thanks; submitting ourselves wholly to his holy will and pleasure, and studying to serve him in true holiness and righteousness all the days of our life. Amen.

obteigned to vs, he hath lefte in those holy Misteries, as a pledge of his loue, & a continuall remembrance of thesame his owne blessed body, & precious bloud, for vs to fede vpon spiritually, to our endles comfort and consolacion.

Very clearly, Cranmer's conception was not in the least that the Bread and Wine were mere token 'reminders' of Christ's Body and Blood, acted metaphors of something not actually there, which may be all that is meant nowadays by 'Zwinglian' views of the Sacrament: it is the very Body and Blood, as great present spiritual realities, which bring to remembrance all that Christ suffered for us in his one atoning Sacrifice.

Nothing here, or anywhere else in Cranmer's service, degrades the meaning of the English Liturgy to the level of a mere psychological reaction, or to do anything else except what he not only intended but accomplished, namely to exalt and intensify human response and participation in this great act of God for the reconciliation of man. The First Prayer Book includes in this same Exhortation a passage which has since unfortunately disappeared from the American books as elsewhere twice expressed in the service, but which evidences the extraordinary weight which Cranmer put upon this concept, of which this is a *third* underscoring: 'For then we spiritually eate the fleshe of Christe, and drinke his bloude, then we dwell in Christ and Christ in vs, wee bee made one with Christ, & Christ with vs.' Has any liturgy ever been able to say more?

The plain fact of the matter is that we may search in vain in the primitive and confused language of the Latin Mass for any clear statement of the Real Presence. Indeed, one reason for the excessive ceremonial with which late medieval times cumbered the Mass, was a feeling for the necessity of putting into actions what was not expressed in the words of the service. Nor, as we have seen, have the illations and eisegeses of Roman theologians succeeded in elaborating an *adequate* conception of the Eucharistic Reality. While no human mind can ever exhaust the meaning of what Cranmer quite rightly, following Greek usage, repeatedly calls a 'Mystery,' it is evident that, so far from vitiating the idea of the Real Presence in the Liturgy, it was reserved for Cranmer to give the best expression which has yet appeared to what the Latin Mass was most unskilfully trying to say.

II. The Second Prayer Book

1. *Pressures for Change*

No sooner was the First Prayer Book in use, than Cranmer found himself under heavy pressure from Bucer, Peter Martyr, and other Continental Reformers who had taken refuge in England, for a radical further revision in the direction of the Calvinistic standards to which they were committed.

We have noted that Cranmer's original wise and temperate plan was to preserve as much of the outward plan and pattern of the traditional rite familiar to the people, complete with its ceremonies and music, with the same care as he gave to its inner content of thought and meaning, for the purpose of giving a manifest assurance of the unbroken continuity of the life, faith, and worship of the Church. But the intruding Calvinists cared nothing for continuity, and talked of 'abolishing' the Mass, not reforming it. They clamored for an outright breach with the old service. They assailed the rite of the First Prayer Book because its order, and its retention of innocent decorative detail, kept a visible likeness of the Mass; because its actual structure seemed to them to foster the idea of a 'Real Presence'; because it preserved an explicit Intercession for the Departed; and because they considered it deficient in penitential emphasis.

Cranmer seems to have been completely taken aback by such an attitude. His words, in the 'Act of Uniformity' prefixed to the Second Prayer Book, claim that the First Book was 'a verye Godlye ordre,' and intimates that the objections to it arose 'rather by the curiosities of the minister and mistakers, than of any other worthy cause.' Perhaps he might have resisted the pressure of his troublesome foreign supporters in their demand for change for the sake of change, if he had not found the ground cut from beneath his feet by the attitude of his conservative opponents. The latter group had, with whatever reluctance, acquiesced in the service of the First Prayer Book as a sufficient liturgy: and they were now proceeding to quote it against him as support for doctrines of Transubstantiation, and even of Sacrifice, of which he thought he had rid it.

But though Cranmer yielded to the Protestant pressures, and made some very extensive alterations which transformed the whole outward appearance of the rite, it has never been properly appreciated just how intensely conservative he was of its substance, how stubbornly tenacious of nearly every element of its thought and meaning. The only constituent of any theological importance which he eliminated outright was the Intercession for the Departed. Every other significant idea was included *somewhere*. His method of dealing with passages then under Protestant attack was precisely that which he had employed in 1549 in the case of the sacrificial expressions: he transferred to another context any portion which had proved vulnerable to misinterpretation where it stood.

2. Changes of Appearance

To meet the complaint that the English service was being so performed by some as to convey all the misleading associations which had become attached to the Latin Mass, Cranmer stripped the rite of a good deal of its decorative detail. He now eliminated the rubrics prescribing the Eucharistic Vestments, the offering of the Elements, and the Manual Acts at the Institution, and the General Rubrics permitting devotional 'gestures.'

He dealt in the same way with the musical features of the Introit and Communion Anthems, the *Benedictus qui venit* and the *Agnus Dei* — as well as with any mention of the singing of the Creed, or indeed of any other part except the *Gloria in Excelsis*. And with these were swept away even such tiny but significant articulations of the services as the *Gloria tibi*, the recurring Salutation of 'The Lord be with you' at the turning-points of the rite, the Prologue to the Lord's Prayer, and the *Pax Domini* after it — all of which had been chanted aloud in the Latin Mass.

Some slight vestiges of former customs were, however, left behind in this rubric of Morning Prayer: 'And (to thende the people may the better heare) in suche places where they do sing, there shall the lessons be song in a plain tune, after the maner of distincte reading: and likewyse the Epistle and Gospell'; and at the Ordination of Priests, 'then shall the Congregacyon syng the Crede.'

In general, it may be said that the rubrics of the Communion Service seem to have in mind throughout, the standard and pattern of the former 'Low Mass,' performed by the Priest alone. For instance, the Epistle and Gospel were directed to be read by the Priest, instead of mentioning other ministers appointed to do so, as in 1549.

This was a somewhat important shift of emphasis from the First Prayer Book, which was still in the tradition of all the ancient liturgies, which were drawn up on the assumption that their norm was the 'solemn' form, with assistant ministers, choir, and full ceremonial. To this day, it is considered impossible to perform any Eastern liturgy without a minimum of three officiants — the Celebrant, a Deacon, and one man to take the part of the Choir. With the rather simpler structure of the Latin Rite, it is quite possible for the Celebrant to read everything assigned to choir or assistants, as well as his own parts; yet this was unknown as a normal public service until the ninth century: and some of the ceremonial of 'Low Mass,' such as the reading of the Epistle from one corner of the altar and the Gospel from the other, still bears witness to the former presence of a Deacon and Subdeacon who are not there.

The 'plain service' adopted in 1552 for the gratification of the foreign Reformers has left many Anglicans with the erroneous impression that the simplest form must have been the most primitive, and that 'choral' or 'solemn' versions of it must needs have been gratuitous medieval elaborations. On the contrary, the fact is that the most ancient liturgical texts are the most elaborate, in the number of officiants called into action, and in the extent of their participation. This was an inevitable reflection of the primitive conception of the service as the corporate act of the whole congregation, not the function of a single hierophant: and as many of them were called into its performance as could be so employed.

3. *Changes of Order*

a) Causes: Of all the alterations of the Liturgy in 1552, by far the most revolutionary in their character, paradoxical in their form, and lasting in their effects upon the subsequent development of the rite, were the changes in basic structure and order.

But unlike the changes of appearance which we have noted, which were made in order to make the service seem different, and to veil its essential identity with the old Mass, the transpositions of parts which were now effected were not made arbitrarily, but under the impulsion of a new organizing conception.

The animating cause of all but one of the transfers of matter was the strong exception which the Calvinists took to the long series of devotions which intervened between the Consecration and the Communion in the rite of 1549. These comprised:

1. the prayers of Oblation,
2. the Lord's Prayer,
3. the *Pax*,
4. the proclamation 'Christ our Pascal lambe,'
5. the penitential approach of the Invitation, Confession, Absolution, Comfortable Words, and Prayer of Humble Access.

The forerunners of the Puritan position objected that such a delay before the actual Administration tended to foster the conception of an objective effect upon the Elements by the Prayer of Consecration — whose only purpose, to their minds, was to arouse the faith of the communicants. Since Cranmer agreed with them in believing in a real Communion, but denying an objective Presence in the Elements, he had no compunction about complying with this demand, and sweeping all this matter out of the way. Therefore in the Second Prayer Book, the Administration was made to follow the Narrative of the Institution immediately, without any intervening preparation whatever.

In disposing of this material, Cranmer eliminated outright the *Pax* and the 'Paschal Lamb,' as more decorative detail. But all the rest was sedulously preserved in the rite. The 'Oblation' and the Lord's Prayer were transferred to the Postcommunion section; and all the other constituents were fitted in to various places before the Institution. Yet this was not done at random: there were definite structural and liturgical reasons for every one of the sometimes startling shifts.

b) Transfers to the Postcommunion: The Lord's Prayer had always been said in more or less close sequence to the Canon, ever since it was first employed in the Liturgy early in the second century. Cranmer's removal of it to head the 'Postcommunion' portion of the service was based upon the analogy of its function in introducing the concluding prayers in Morning and Evening Prayer and in some of the Occasional Offices.

With the important exception of the *Anamnesis*, of which another disposition entirely was made, as we shall see in a moment, and some incidental pruning of phrases alluding to a coming Communion, the whole of the Consecration Prayer after the Institution was removed to the end of the service, where it was set as an alternative to the Postcommunion Thanksgiving. Since Cranmer in the

First Prayer Book had removed all sacrificial expressions until after the Consecration, it may have seemed to him a matter of indifference just how long after they were placed. The tenor of the Latin Mass itself may well have implanted such an idea in his mind: for the Mass keeps on offering, and offering, and offering the Christian Sacrifice through nearly every constituent Collect of the Canon: and even after the entire action has been completed with the Communion and the Ablutions, the Sacrifice is offered yet once more retrospectively, in the perfect tense, in the final Collect *Placeat tibi sancta Trinitas*. It seems probable that the precedent of the prayer *Placeat* furnished the suggestion and warrant for this move in the Second Prayer Book.

But the dislocation in 1552 was a little more serious than that. The service preserved the three outstanding expressions of the Sacrifice of Praise, of Ourselves, and of our Bounden Duty. But it brought them all in as after-reflections, as if they were a separate and subsequent spiritual exercise. They could not in fact be that, since their whole meaning depended on the previous Action of which they were the interpretation. Yet they were definitely in the wrong order of thought, to bear their part to the meaning of the Action as it unfolded.

The omission of a direct verbal Oblation of the Gifts at the Offertory is of no particular importance, since the very placing of the Elements upon the altar is inescapably an Act of Oblation. But the dislocation of 1552 broke all formal connection of the meaning of the Sacrifice with its matter, by omitting the mention of 'these thy holy giftes' (181) at the Great Oblation after the Institution, which all liturgies, including the Roman, have always regarded as essential.

The service of the Church of England has retained the arrangement of 1552 into the present century. But the Scottish, and all later revisions, have been at pains to restore the Great Oblation to its proper place and function. And our present comparative studies of the development of our rites have increasingly impressed upon us the necessity of considering the best place for the salient sacrificial expressions in the whole sequence of thought, straightening out the duplications which were inherent in the Latin original, and which were made yet more repetitious by the transfers which resulted from Cranmer's not very well founded fears.

c) The Anamnesis: But the Commemoration of the Passion, which had formed an important element of the 1549 Prayer of Oblation, was not removed to the Postcommunion with the rest of the prayer, and neither was it eliminated. With an ingenuity which seems to have completely escaped the commentators, its substance was incorporated into the Invocation, which in the English Rite precedes the Narrative of the Institution. This conflation was effected as follows:

The Eucharistic Liturgy 171

1549	1552	1549
Invocation	COMMEMORATION-INVOCATION	Commemoration

	Graunte that wee, recey- uyng	
with thy holy spirite and worde vouchsafe to bl†esse and sanc†tifie these thy gyftes, and creatures of bread and wyne, that they	these thy creatures of bread and wine,	
	according to thy sonne our sauior Iesus Christes holy *institucion, in remembraunce* of *his* death and *passion,*	*according to the Institucion of thy* dearly beloued *sonne, our sauioure Iesus Christe,* ... hauing *in remembraunce his blessed passion,* mighty resurreccion, *and* glorious ascencion, ...
may be vnto vs the bodye and bloud of thy most derely beloued sonne Iesus Christ.	may be partakers of his most *blessed* body and bloud.	

It should be realized that the primary purpose of the alteration here was to salvage the liturgical *Anamnesis,* displaced by the transfer of the 'Prayer of Oblation.' As a result of its adroit incorporation here, the English Rite since 1552 has enjoyed the anomaly of possessing not only a 'Preliminary *Epiclesis,*' but a 'Preliminary *Anamnesis*' as well.

The fusion of the two passages from 1549 was accomplished without overloading the resultant form by the rather regrettable elimination of the potent words ' with thy holy spirite .. vouchsafe to bl†esse and sanc†tifie these thy giftes,' which Cranmer had inserted in 1549 from St. Basil's Liturgy, so that they were lost to the English Rite: though the Scottish family, followed by our own and the English 1928, recovered them.

It is further possible that there may have been direct Calvinistic influence to give a 'receptionist' turn to the passage. There is such an emphasis to the language: though in the underlying thought, there is not a penny to choose between the entirely equivalent phrases, 'that wee, receyuyng them . . . may be partakers of,' and 'that they may be *vnto vs.*' The latter, indeed, is a direct translation of the Latin 'ut *nobis* . . . fiat.' To be sure, Cranmer in 1549 rendered 'fiat' as 'may be' rather than 'may be made,' which the Latin intended, but perhaps with no more consciousness of weakening the sense than the English Bible had of translating the Vulgate 'Fiat lux' of Gen. 1:3 as 'Let there be light.' In either version, the fact remains that the 'nobis' in the Latin Mass makes that expression inescapably as 'receptionist' a formula as is to be found in any liturgy.

d) The Prayer of Humble Access: The disposition which Cranmer made of the Commemoration, interpolating it in the Invocation, provides us with the key to Cranmer's organizing method in arranging the remaining matter which the Calvinists had insisted should be removed between the Institution and the Communion. Cranmer was willing to do this — but only upon the condition that certain passages which he considered to be indispensable to the interpretation of the eucharistic action should be brought in as closely as possible *before* the Institution. These vital passages, in the order of their importance, he rated as:

1. the Commemoration,
2. the Humble Access, and
3. the penitential preparation for the Communion.

As we have seen, he succeeded in incorporating the first of these within the Consecration Prayer. He did so, however, in such a way as to eliminate from it the Invocation of the Holy Spirit, and to concentrate attention upon the human response, to an extent which was entirely in harmony with Calvinistic views of the Sacrament, which linked its spiritual reality with the act of its reception, and even with Zwinglian ideas which stressed the importance of an inward appropriation of it through realizing acts of recollection.

But if so, response to *what*? While any Christian must admit that the response of man is absolutely essential to obtain the personal benefits of the Sacrament, Cranmer knew as well as we do that no mere act of man can accomplish what can only be the act of God. Helpful as the theories of Calvin or even of Zwingli might be to some minds as rationalizations and applications of the actual experience of Communion, in themselves they did not account for the estimation in which the Eucharist has always been held, and in which Cranmer held it himself. To Cranmer, the ultimate and causative reality lay in the power of the Incarnation, whose operation in the Eucharist was to effect an actual *incorporation* of the believer into Christ.

Therefore he was willing to reduce the Consecration Prayer to the slight content of that form in the rite of 1552 only if it were immediately prefaced by an expression of that transforming and abiding indwelling of the Body of Christ which was the climax of his Christology, and the salvation of his eucharistic doctrine. In his original draft of the Liturgy in 1549, he had embodied this great idea three times over, in terms derived from St. Basil: in the Exhortation after the Sermon, in the peroration of the Consecration Prayer, and in the Prayer of Humble Access immediately before Communion. The first of these was too remote; the second had now been relegated to an alternative and marginal use in the Postcommunion. This left available only the Humble Access. Cranmer regarded this theme as so vital that he took the bold measure of inserting the Humble Access actually *infra actionem*, 'within the eucharistic action,' between the Sanctus and the Consecration Prayer. In that place, it prefaced the Consecration with its sublime witness to the purpose of the rite: 'that our synful bodyes may be made cleane by his body, and our soules washed through his most precious bloude, and that we may euermore dwell in hym, and he in vs.'

It seems probable that this insertion may account for Cranmer's striking out the words 'Blessed is he that *commeth* in the name of the Lorde' from the Sanctus, on noting the repetition of the word in 'We doe not presume to *come* to thys thy table (O mercifull lorde) trustynge in our owne righteousnes, but in thy manifolde and greate mercies.' Perhaps he may have thought — correctly — that this was a sufficient paraphrase, and therefore a suitable substitute, for an expression which in its origin was a communion-time chant.

e) The Penitential Preparation: The Invitation, Confession, Absolution, and Comfortable Words were now put in the next nearest available place, namely before the *Sursum Corda*; and the Exhortation was moved from its former location after the sermon to precede this block, and to reenforce it with its hortatory emphasis on the need of penitential preparation for Communion, and likewise to give a further underscoring to the 'Incorporation' theme.

This arrangement made this section a preparation for the Consecration as well as the Communion. This order of thought is entirely appropriate psychologically, and structurally it is faultless. It may be noted that the Greek rites, which do not happen to possess a formal *Confiteor* anywhere, do have its equivalent in penitential prayers at precisely this part of the service.

This plan has the merit of not carrying the mind down into a long 'Valley of Humiliation' after the heights of feeling which have been reached in the Prayer of Consecration. This may well turn out to be a permanent improvement. The only liturgy which has attempted to reverse this action of 1552, and restore the penitential section to a place after the Consecration, is the Scottish. And perhaps one important reason why the Scottish Liturgy has never been able completely to supplant the English, even in its own domains, may be the sense of a prolonged anticlimax produced by such an arrangement.

f) The Prayer for the Church: When Cramer found it necessary to make a place for the Humble Access immediately before the Prayer of Consecration, he thereby had to displace the Prayer for the Whole State of Christ's Church which occupied that position in 1549. This was no loss; on the contrary, it resulted in a striking structural improvement. In the First Prayer Book, Cranmer contented himself with following the order of his Latin original, pretty much as it came. The Mass has the peculiarity of interpolating the Intercessions for the Living between the *Sanctus* and the proper continuation of the Thanksgiving; and again toward the end it digresses to take in the Commemoration of the Departed. Even in 1549 Cranmer felt the irrelevance of this arrangement, and consolidated the two intercessory blocks into the Prayer for the Church preceding the Consecration Prayer. But it was obvious that this material had no organic contribution to the developing progress of the rite; and he may have been glad of an excuse to seek a more logical place for it.

In doing so, he was exceedingly fortunate. He succeeded in restoring it to the most primitive place of all, where it is found in the first description by Justin Martyr in the second century.

It appears that the Intercession originated in the 'Morning Prayer' part of the Liturgy, rather than in connection with the Eucharistic Oblation proper. Justin seems so to describe it in his outline of the Sunday Eucharist. But if so, it had already formed unbreakable ties of thought with the action of the Offertory, since when the normal 'Ante-Communion' of the Sunday service was displaced by the ceremonies of a Baptism, Justin indicates that the following Baptismal Eucharist nevertheless began with the Prayer for the Church.

All historic liturgies retain traces of an Intercession before the Offertory: though all of them except the Gallican also transfer this matter more or less in duplicate to the prayers of the Anaphora. Now the Gallican Rite had been extinct in France since the end of the eighth century. But in much of its former domain throughout North Europe, it left a legacy of its original structure in the form of a 'Bidding Prayer' in the vernacular, inserted after the Sermon and before the Offertory. This was the case in England: and when Cranmer looked about for a suitable place to put his Great Intercession, he found this one which was already familiar to the people in their own tongue.

This feature therefore is now home in its original place:[14] and on the whole, much the best place. The Scottish Liturgy has transferred it to follow the Consecration Prayer, in direct imitation of the Greek liturgies. But this is not at all successful, since it adds further weight to the anticlimax of the other post-consecration devotions already mentioned.

---

14. It is perfectly possible that Cranmer was quite aware of this, and that the appearance of the first printed edition of the works of Justin Martyr in the year 1551 may have put it into his mind to bring his service of 1552 into conformity with that earliest description of the primitive Liturgy as to the placing of the General Intercession.

g) The Decalogue and the Gloria: One more transposition of parts was not due to the foregoing factors arising from the removing of matter between Consecration and Communion, but was the result of a new addition to the service.

The Second Prayer Book adopted a characteristic Calvinistic feature in the form of penitential introductions to both the Daily Offices and to the Liturgy. The source of both seems to have been the forms published in 1551 for the use of two congregations of foreign refugees — the *Liturgia sacra* of Valerand Pullain, and the *Forma ac ratio tota ecclesiastici ministerii* of John Laski. Both of these were derived from Calvin's Genevan scheme. Both embodied the recitation of the Decalogue in connection with a Confession and Absolution.

Cranmer in 1552 did not remove his Confession, etc., to the beginning of the rite — quite justly, since the force of this feature in the Liturgy is its preparation for the sacramental action, not the general service. But he did adopt the familiar use of the Decalogue as a preparation for private confessions, for the purpose of presenting it at the beginning of the service as the basis of an Examination of Conscience, which would give a realistic content of actual contrition to the General Confession later on. That this was what he had in mind is shown by the words which he wrote for an Exhortation in this Prayer Book, and which we still retain on pp. 86 ff. of ours: 'The way and meanes therto is: First to examine your liues and conuersacion by the rule of gods commaundementes, and whereinsoeuer ye shall perceiue your selfes to haue offended, either by wil, word, or dede, there bewaile your own sinful liues, confesse your selfes to almightie god with ful purpose of amendment of life.'

The Decalogue was inserted in the service so as to absorb the Ninefold *Kyrie eleison* of 1549. This rather unusual device was ultimately derived from the use of the so-called 'farced *Kyries*' before the Reformation; and perhaps more immediately, from Luther's metrical version of the Decalogue with responds of 'Kyrioleys.'

Now the distinctive Litany-Respond of 'Lorde haue mercy vpon vs,' etc., gave this setting of the Decalogue the intrinsic form and character of a Litany: a fact which the Scots later recognized by finishing it off with a proper Litany-Collect for grace to keep the Commandments, taken from the English list of Collects employed to conclude the 'Ante-Communion.'

It is curious that this move precipitated a conflict of ideas which first arose almost exactly one thousand years before: but this time with a precisely opposite result.

In the century or so before the time of Gregory the Great a Litany form was introduced into the beginning of the Roman Mass. Like all litanies, it was of Syrian provenance, terminated with triple *Kyries*, and led up to a summary Collect. This Collect was already in the service. Its original form was that of fixed Collect in the Alexandrian Rite, which Serapion called 'The First Prayer of the Lord's Day,' and the Coptic Church still names 'The First Prayer of the Morning.' In the early Western manner, its Roman form was made that of a prayer variable with the occasion — 'The Collect of the Day.' It was assimilated to be the terminal Collect of the Litany. That, incidentally, is why in so many cases our 'Collect of the Day' is such a general kind of prayer: this Collect had to be comprehensive rather than specific if it was to serve as a broad summing up of that sixth-century Litany.

But in the course of that century, the *Gloria in Excelsis*, formerly a Hymn at Matins, began to be introduced into this part of the Liturgy on festal occasions. The supreme rejoicing quality of that canticle brought it into sharp contrast with the almost penitential tone of the supplications of the Litany. The result was that the Litany was dropped from ordinary use. It left behind it only its terminal *Kyries*, which it had brought in untranslated from its Greek original. Thus the existence of the *Kyrie eleison* in the Roman Mass is not a survival of the use of the Greek language for the entire liturgy in that center in the earliest days, but a vestige of an imported feature which came and went. Gregory the Great bears witness to the disuse of this liturgical litany, and its curtailment to the *Kyries* alone.

Now, in the sixteenth century, the introduction of what was an intrinsic Litany-form in this setting of the Decalogue, with still more emphatic penitential implications, brought in exactly the same collision of mood in the two features, which would have occurred in direct sequence with each other if Cranmer had left the *Gloria* where it was, after substituting the Decalogue for the *Kyries*. This time, it was the *Gloria* which was displaced. Cranmer removed it from its ancient location to the only other context in the service where it could be used without rhetorical abruptness. After the Post-Communion Thanksgiving, with its concluding 'be all honour and glory,' the opening acclamation, 'Glorye be to god on hygh' formed a perfectly smooth and logical verbal connection. That it was not an organic, nor indeed, a useful, ingredient of the service at this point was a consideration which did not occur to Cranmer: that was a fact which could be brought into prominence only by the test of continued use.

4. The Teaching of the Second Prayer Book

It might be thought that all these radical changes, which so greatly altered the *appearance* of the service from the old Mass, would have had the result of transforming it into a purely Protestant rite — perhaps to the extent of disqualifying it from any position in the lineage of the historic liturgies. This, of course, is precisely what the Church of Rome has always claimed about it.

Nevertheless, the alterations had surprisingly little effect upon the teaching which it contained and conveyed. It might be disconcerting to find the *Gloria* transported from one end of the service to the other: but it did not alter doctrine by a particle that it was. Every mention of a verbal Oblation of the holy Gifts was suppressed: which did not affect the fact that they were offered, and that indeed the rite could not be performed without doing so. The long central prayers of

Consecration were drastically curtailed: but the results of that were to lighten them of a considerable load of irrelevancies, and to concentrate attention upon those essential constituents which Cranmer's stubborn conservatism refused to remove from them. Cranmer himself maintained that the vital meaning of the Greek Liturgies, the Latin Mass, and the rites of both of his Prayer Books, was one and the same: and he was right. That meaning may not have been the personal rationalization which he imposed upon all these liturgical forms alike: but it was there.

True, in the service of 1552 Cranmer did all that he could to set forth the Zwinglian interpretations which he applied to the historic Liturgy. He stripped the Invocation of an explicit *Epiclesis* of the Holy Ghost, and reduced it nearly, if not quite, to the level of a prayer for a worthy Communion, rather than a form of Consecration. The Sentences of Administration dropped the explicit designation of the Body and Blood of Christ, and said only 'Take and eate this, in remembraunce that Christe died for the, and fede on him in thy heart by faith, with thankes geuyng,' and 'Drinke this in remembraunce that Christes bloud was shed for thee, and be thankfull.' It would hardly seem possible to express more precisely, not to say baldly, the idea of a mere mental commemoration.

And yet the Church of England has never for a moment accepted that obvious interpretation. Zwinglianism, in the form in which Cranmer held it, that of a contact with the disembodied Spirit of Christ by means of a thankful recollection of the Passion, has never taken the slightest root in our Church. Few, if any, of its members have ever shared the peculiar defect of Cranmer's thinking, whereby he considered that after the Ascension the actual Body of Christ was present only in heaven, under the same limitations as during his life upon earth, so that he could not be present to the souls of the faithful, whether through the Sacrament or in any other way, only in his Divinity, and by virtue of his 'grace and power.'

The 'Black Rubric' of 1552, unsanctioned by the Church, and imposed by Royal Authority, is undoubtedly of Cranmer's authorship. It states explicitly that in requiring that the Sacrament be received kneeling,

> we dooe declare that it is not mente thereby, that any adoracion is doone, or ought to bee doone, eyther vnto the Sacramentall bread or wyne there bodelye receyued, or vnto anye reall and essenciall presence there beeyng of Chrystes naturall flesh and bloude. For as concernynge the Sacramentall bread and wyne, they remayne styll in theyr verye naturall substaunces, and therfore may not bee adored, for that were Idolatrye to be abhorred of all faythfull christians. And as concernynge the naturall bodye and bloud of our sauiour Christ, they are in heauen and not here: for it is agaynst the trueth of Christes true naturall bodye, to be in moe places than in one at one tyme.

This is very illuminating on the nature of Cranmer's difficulties about the Real Presence. As was to be expected, there is an outright denial of the theory of Transubstantiation. Apart from that, this Declaration denounces two doctrines which no Catholic has ever held: the worship of bread and wine, and the Presence of Christ's *natural* Body. The Church's teaching has always been that at the Ascension our Lord's Body, as the vehicle of his Humanity, was *glorified*, raised to the spiritual level, and universalized above all local limitations: so that the Incarnate Lord is now everywhere present in his Humanity as well as his Divinity. It is not the Natural Body which is physically, materially, naturally, spatially, and locally present in the Holy Eucharist, but the Glorified Body, present metaphysically, immaterially, supernaturally, extra-spatially, and supra-locally, after the manner of a spirit.

It was precisely this failure to grasp the truth of the Glorified Body of Christ which causes Cranmer to be properly classified as a Zwinglian rather than a Calvinist in his theories of the Sacrament. Calvin had no difficulty whatever with this doctrine. Like Cranmer, he rejected the idea that there was any Real Presence *within the Elements*: but he accepted the fact of a Real Communion of the actual glorified Body and Blood of Christ within the soul of the faithful receiver. And it has always been Calvinistic, not Zwinglian, conceptions of the Sacrament which have been the 'low-water mark' of eucharistic belief in the Church of England.

There is a certain paradox in the circumstance that Cranmer's *would-be* Zwinglian formulas were perfectly acceptable to the Calvinist-minded, but that he utterly failed to put over the idea which he intended. The reason for this is the fact that as a rationalization of *any* form of the traditional liturgy — even one so curtailed, disarranged, and disguised as the rite of 1552 — Zwinglianism necessarily falls of its own weight. If the purpose of the rite is a mere mental commemoration and appropriation of the benefits of the Passion, then any sort of observance of 'the Lord's Supper' is not even an apt instrument for that objective. There is nothing in the receiving of token portions of bread and wine to recall Calvary. To find any relevance to that theme in the rite, one must have recourse to distinctly secondary symbolisms, and stress the *broken* bread and the *poured-out* wine, as possible reminders of the Body broken upon the Cross, and the Precious Blood there shed. If the desire is to make nothing but a Memorial of the Cross, then the appropriate means would be to abandon the observance of the 'Lord's Supper,' and to put on some kind of Passion Play. The next best thing would be to do as some Unitarians used to do, and meditate upon Calvary about a bare table, with no irrelevant ceremonial distractions whatever.

Therefore there is no wonder that the mere form of the Liturgy defeated Cranmer's intention. And it is significant that in the most unlikely quarters, in modern denominations which have the baldest forms for celebrating 'the Lord's Supper,' and official doctrines of a bare Memorial, or even no stated teaching on the Sacrament at all, one constantly finds that the devotion of the untaught people often rises to the level of a faith in some actual 'Holy Communion.'

Furthermore, Cranmer's efforts to alter the shape of the liturgy so as to exclude all belief in an Objective Presence were likewise self-defeating. The reduction of the Invocation to something little more than a prayer for a worthy communion, and the sweeping out of the way of all the prayers of the Canon following the Institution, served only to throw all the emphasis of the English Rite upon the Institution Narrative as the effective means of Consecration. Indeed, that rite ever since 1552 has symbolized Roman theories of Consecration by the Dominical Words more fully than the Roman Mass itself. In spite of the slightness of content of the English service, its constant tendency has been to develop a belief in the Real Presence — even in some cases to the extreme of the Roman theory of Transubstantiation.

In other words, Cranmer's personal opinions were certainly theologically defective, and may be conceded to have been heretical. But in spite of all he could do, his liturgy was not heretical, even in the impoverished form of the Second Prayer Book.

The Elizabethan and Jacobean Prayer Books

The foregoing conclusion is of real importance, in view of the fact that it is essentially the rite of 1552 which has continued in use in England to the present day, with no changes of order, and for the most part with very minor alterations in text and rubric. It simply will not do to vilify the service of the Second Prayer Book as a reprehensible Protestant extreme, and to pretend that a true balance was recovered in the Elizabethan Prayer Book of 1559. Actually, all the liturgies of all subsequent Anglican books are directly descended from that of 1552, with only piece-meal restorations of some of the classic excellencies of 1549.

Queen Elizabeth would have been glad to see the First Prayer Book restored, as representing essentially her father's churchmanship. This might have seemed practicable, since the Book of 1552 had been little used before the accession of Queen Mary in 1553 made a sudden end of Archbishop Cranmer and his liturgical work alike. But it was impossible, since the only clergy on whose support Elizabeth could rely had returned from their exile under Mary thoroughly imbued with Calvinistic ideas. The Book of 1552 represented the maximum they were prepared to accept.

The Queen's insistence secured only three points. The 'Black Rubric' was omitted. An 'Ornaments Rubric' restored the vestments of the First Prayer Book; though that proved unenforceable, and was replaced by Archbishop Parker's 'Advertisements' of 1566. The only point affecting the text of the service was the combining of the Sentences of Administration of the Sacrament in the first two Prayer Books. In this vital respect a balance of doctrine was indeed restored: but it was the only particular in which it was.

The Liturgy was not touched at the revision of 1604 under King James I. But the Canons of that year put a stop to the practice of some of the Puritan-minded clergy of using unconsecrated bread or wine if either species were spent before the end of the Communion. But the form indicated for a Re-consecration, taken from *The Order of the Communion of 1548*, consisted only of repeating the Words of Institution for the species in question, unaccompanied by any prayer whatever. This is simon-pure Romanism, implying a Transubstantiation at the magic formula of the Institution. Its adoption in the English Prayer Book of 1662 is the worst blot on the English Liturgy. Yet even the abortive attempt at revision in 1928 retained the reconsecration of either element by the Dominical Words, without introduction, though followed by the Invocation. The Scottish-American line is on much firmer ground, and in accord with the principles of all primitive sacrifices, in embracing the principle that a second consecration is a second celebration, that both species should be offered and sanctified by a complete Consecration Prayer.

The Scottish Liturgy of 1637

It is a remarkable circumstance that a Prayer Book which was never used has exercised an important formative influence upon all subsequent revisions of the Liturgy. This was the first Scottish Book of 1637.

In 1610, King James I restored to Scotland the Episcopate which Knox had obliterated. The 'Episcopal' following in the northern kingdom remained largely non-liturgical, following the pattern of Knox's Genevan Book of Common Order: it would not have been possible for a visitor in those days to have told whether he was in an 'Episcopal' or a 'Presbyterian' church. But soon there was a move on the part of the Scottish Bishops to have their own Prayer Book: and this undertaking was ordered by the General Assembly of 1616. The resulting draft of 1619 was not, however, published at that time. Its Communion Service was along the lines of Knox's scheme, but with the English form for the Consecration and the Communion.

In 1629, at the instance of Charles I, the project was revived by the Scottish Bishops in conference with Archbishop Laud. Laud at first was not much interested, desiring the Scots simply to conform to the English book. The first draft was actually partly in print before he suddenly awoke to the liturgical opportunity to furnish them with something much better than a carbon-copy of the curtailed English rite, namely to restore some of the riches of the First Prayer Book which had been unwisely abandoned in 1552.

Chief credit for the Prayer Book of 1637 undoubtedly goes to Bishop James Wedderburn of Dunblane, a fine liturgical scholar, if not a very judicious politician. Wedderburn would apparently have restored the whole rite of 1549. Laud succeeded in preserving the current English order of parts, except for the restoration of the Lord's Prayer, with its Prologue, and the Prayer of Humble Access, between the Consecration and the Communion. But Wedderburn carried the day for recovering also the text of the Prayer for the Church, the Consecration Prayer, and the Sentences of Administration, as in the First Prayer Book. And a considerable number of fine details in both text and rubric from his firm and delicate hand have been appreciatively adopted in later revisions.

Though the Scottish Prayer Book was authorized by the Scottish Privy Council and by Royal Warrant in 1636, the attempt to initiate its use in St. Giles's Cathedral, Edinburgh, on July 23, 1637, resulted in a riot. This incident was in fact the first act of the rebellion of the Puritans against Church and King which culminated eight years later in the subjugation of England with the aid of Scottish mercenaries, the execution of Charles I and of Archbishop Laud, and the prohibition of the use of the English Book of Common Prayer for the space of fifteen years. And thanks to these disturbances, there was no further attempt to bring the Rite of 1637 into use in Scotland until the following century.

The Restoration Prayer Book of 1662

1. Influence of the Scottish 1637

Fortunately, there was a living link between the history of the Liturgy before the Great Rebellion and that after the Restoration, in the person of Matthew Wren, who as Bishop of Norwich has cooperated with Laud and Wedderburn in the making of the Prayer Book of 1637, and who as Bishop of Ely took a leading part in revising that of 1662. It was undoubtedly due to his special interest in this direction that the alterations adopted in 1662 out of the Scottish book far outnumber all others.

It is notable that 1662 made no fundamental change in the text of the service, nor yet in its order of parts. This revision was almost entirely a *literary* recension of the basic rite of 1552. And in no case did the revisers go back of the Book of 1637, to recover matter of the First Prayer Book which was not included in the Scottish Book.

Restorations of features of 1549, through the Scottish Rite, to make good some of the impoverishments of 1552 were the following: the mention of singing the Creed; in the Offertory rubrics, a specific direction of the act of setting the Elements upon the Table; a commemoration of the Departed in the Prayer for the Church (though 1662 avoided praying *for* them); the Manual Acts at the Narrative of the Institution; even such minutiæ as the announcing of the 'holy' Gospel.

Details originating in 1637 which were now adopted in the English Rite included more meticulous rubrics instructing the Priest to turn to the people at the Decalogue, and for the people to stand at the Gospel and the Creed; and for the covering of the Elements which remained after the general Communion with 'a fair linen cloth,' and for their subsequent consumption. A beginning was made at giving titles to the component parts of the service in the rubrics, such as *The Collect* (for Purity), *The Absolution*, and *The Prayer of Consecration*. The announcement of Epistle and Gospel was extended to mention the initial verse; and the reading of the Epistle was concluded with 'Here endeth the Epistle.' The Alms were now to be collected, not brought up individually, and 'presented and placed upon the Holy Table.' The Doxology of the *Textus Receptus* of Matt. 6:13 was appended to the Lord's Prayer. Provision was made for a Second Consecration in terms of the Canons of 1604.

2. New Features

Most of the changes which were initiated in 1662 were trivial — emendations of the Exhortations, putting the Notices before the Sermon instead of afterwards, and the like. Though the ostensible reason for this revision was the conciliation of the defeated Presbyterian party, and a committee of Bishops undertook the work after an exhaustive debate with them at the Savoy Conference, the alterations in the Communion Service which resulted from the *Exceptions of the Ministers* were very few. There are three of these which merit comment.

a) The Ornaments Rubric

There was some question among the Bishops of dropping the 'Ornaments Rubric' which, the Presbyterians alleged, 'seemeth to bring back the cope, albe, &c., and other vestments forbidden by' the Second Prayer Book. None of the Churchmen used the Vestments, or wanted to. They were half minded to make the Presbyterians a concession which would have cost them nothing. But they seem to have been convinced by the Presbyterians' argument that the rubric did in fact sanction the now obsolete vestments. They declined to sacrifice the heritage of the future for a present advantage: and therefore deliberately retained the rubric, in hope of better times.

Moreover, they not only retained it, but they revised its language slightly to make it conform still more precisely with that of the Act of Uniformity. Legally considered, this alteration is of the utmost importance, since it had the effect of reenacting the regulation. Therefore the decisions of the Court of the Privy Council in 1871 and 1877, that the rubric adopted in 1661 was intended only to maintain the *status quo* of a time when the vestments were not used, and therefore that the vestments were illegal, really proposed the juridical imbecility of maintaining that a law enacted in 1661 had been repealed by an executive order (Parker's 'Advertisements') of 1566!

b) The Black Rubric

Then, the Black Rubric 'of the Declaration on Kneeling' of 1552, which had been omitted since 1559, was reinserted upon the insistence of the Presbyterians — though the Bishops observed that there was not 'any great need of restoring it, the world being now in more danger of profanation than of idolatry.' The 'Black Rubric' was approved by the Privy Council after the adjournment of the Convocation which adopted the Prayer Book — but only after Dr. Peter Gunning had amended the text by substituting 'any *corporal* presence' for 'any *real and essential* presence of Christ's natural flesh and flesh [sic] and blood.' Theologically, there is no difference, since no Catholic has ever believed in *any* kind of presence in Christ's *natural* body. Practically, this elucidation is of considerable importance, making it evident that the Church of England had completely transcended the limitations of Cranmer's thinking on this important subject, and now accepted, instead of rejecting, the idea of a Real Presence.

c) The Manual Acts

Though it was the influence of the Scottish Prayer Book which secured the restoration of the rubrics directing the Manual Acts, their content was unfavorably influenced by the ideas of the Presbyterians. Those rubrics were very simple in the First Prayer Book: 'Here the prieste must take the bread into his handes'; Here the priest shall take the 'Cuppe into his handes.' In 1637 this was expanded: 'At these words the Presbyter that officiates is to take the Paten into his hand'; 'At these words he is to take the chalice in his hand, and lay his hand upon so much, be it chalice or flagons, as he intends to consecrate.' The rubric of 1662 extended that sort of provision as to the Chalice to the other species: 'And here to lay his hand vpon all the bread.'

So far, all was in reasonable order: although the multiplication of gestures had some tendency to underscore the medieval idea that the Words of Institution, which they accompanied, were the effectual means of Consecration. The mistake was in yielding to the further Presbyterian demand for the insertion of the rubric And here to break the bread, 'at the words he brake it' in the text. It is one thing to carry out the exact pattern of the divine Institution, and imitate precisely in our ritual what our Lord did at the Last Supper, by breaking the bread *after having given thanks*: and this all ancient liturgies duly perform. It is quite another to 'act out' the Narrative of the Institution with 'mimetic' gestures, and to break the bread *while* 'giving thanks,' set off by the mere historic statement. And this no ancient liturgy has ever done, and no modern one either, except the present Coptic and the related Abyssinian and even this isolated Church directs that the broken loaf be fitted together again, 'as if it had not been broken,' in order to perform the ancient ritual Fraction at its proper place after the Thanksgiving.

The Presbyterians insisted upon it because they considered it indispensable to their idea of a 'memorial.' This is another instance of what we have said before, that the sheer form and pattern of any kind of 'Lord's Supper' rite is not even a good ritual 'memorial' of the Passion as such, and suggestive symbolic reminders of that subject must be sought in secondary and incidental ceremonies. But such values — if they have value can still be found when the liturgical Fraction is performed in its proper place.

The Liturgies of the Non Jurors

1. The Schism

There were no attempts to revise the rite of 1662 in the Church of England until the present century. But between the English Restoration and the American Revolution, there was a schism in Great Britain which gave rise to a further evolution of the liturgy, which was destined to have some important effects upon the American Rite.

After the Restoration, the lapsed episcopate was restored in Scotland; but as yet there was no attempt to revive their Prayer Book of 1637, which lay under the cloud of having been the *fons et origo* of the disasters which had befallen Church and State in England and Scotland alike. The Scottish Churchmen seemed to have quite all they could do to maintain the use of the Lord's Prayer and the *Gloria Patri*, at a time when the Presbyterian party were voicing their implacable aversion to any fixed forms whatever by eliminating even those hallowed vestiges from services which, as they performed them, consisted practically of extempore sermons from one end to the other.

But a still heavier blow was in store for the Church in Scotland — one which beggared and decimated and all but destroyed it: which put an end in that realm to the triumph of Episcopacy, which at one time seemed to be within its grasp: yet which was directly responsible for the revival of its worship, and the recovery of its soul.

In 1688, when the Roman Catholic King James II fled the country, an Act of Parliament called to the throne his daughter Mary, with her husband Prince William of Orange as co-sovereign. The new King demanded new oaths of allegiance from all officers both of the Church and State. To our minds today, imbued with the principle of 'government by the consent of the governed,' and familiar only with 'constitutional' monarchies which make a King merely a personal symbol of the authority of the people, it seems passing strange that anyone could have raised objections to such an oath. But it is not for nothing that the British speak of that orderly change in the succession to the Crown as a 'Revolution.' It marked the end of the old regime of the 'Divine Right of Kings,' and the beginning of the modern age of 'constitutional' government. And at that juncture, there were those for whom the oath of allegiance was a religious principle, and a matter of conscience. The Archbishop of Canterbury, seven other Bishops, and four hundred clergy of the Church of England refused to take the oath, and were remorselessly deprived of their positions.

This fate, which affected only a fraction of the Church of England, overwhelmed the entire Church of Scotland. Remarkable as it may seem now, it appears that at that time the 'Episcopal' following there was actually larger than the Presbyterian. The Dutch Calvinist King offered to espouse their side if they would take the oaths to him. When this was officially and almost unanimously refused, Episcopacy was formally disestablished and deprived of all public support in Scotland, and Presbyterianism was set up in its stead.

Thus while the 'Nonjurors' formed a small schism in England, as inconsiderable in their numbers as they were outstanding in their Churchmanship, in Scotland all of the former National Church which in the light of Catholic principles could be called a Church was treated as 'Nonjuring,' and forced into schism. Later on, at the height of English exasperation over the repeated revolts in Scotland on behalf of the banished Stuart dynasty, the Church of England actually disavowed the Orders of the Scottish Episcopal Church — a political gesture afterwards wisely rescinded.

2. The 'Communion Office' of 1718

In their isolation, the Scots turned for fellowship to the English Nonjurors. The latter had, after some hesitations, accepted their schismatic position, and perpetuated their episcopate. Then it dawned on them that their free status, without the sponsorship but also without the dictation of the State, had opened the door for them to do what the Church of England under parliamentary control has been wholly unable to accomplish (though several attempts to do so were started), namely to revise their Liturgy on the basis of principles, without regard to policy. Their program comprised the so-called 'Usages,' consisting of an explicit Invocation of the Holy Ghost, the Prayer of Oblation, Prayers for the Departed, and the Mixed Chalice: all of which had found a place in the First Prayer Book.

The outcome was the Nonjurors 'Communion Office' of 1718. It was chiefly the work of the English Bishops Jeremy Collier and Thomas Brett, and the Scottish Archibald Campbell and James Gadderar. This work combined the current English Rite of 1662, the Scottish 1637, and the English 1549, together with some new departures of its own.

The dominant characteristic of this service was its deliberate conformation to the structure of the Greek liturgies. A new Offertory Prayer (the analogue of the Latin *Secreta*), and the Thanksgiving for the Redemption at the beginning of the Consecration Prayer, were taken outright from the Jerusalem Antioch Liturgy of 'St. James'; the Invocation was from the older Antiochene text of the *Apostolic Constitutions*. Moreover, the Invocation was placed after the Institution, as in all Greek rites, and the Prayer for the Church after the Prayer of Consecration, in imitation of the post-consecration Intercessions of the Eastern liturgies.

Other rearrangements which affected the subsequent history of the Scottish Liturgy were the return to 1637 and 1549 for the place of the Lord's Prayer and the Prayer of Humble Access between Consecration and Communion, and directly to the First Prayer Book for putting the Invitation, Confession, Absolution, and Comfortable Words before the Humble Access.

It is of interest that the Nonjurors' service anticipated the American Book of 1892 in restoring the threefold *Kyrie eleison* as an independent feature, and also in providing for an Introit (in our Prayer Book, represented only by the General Rubric on Hymns and Anthems.) Another prophetic gesture was the restoration of the Salutation of 1549 before the *Sursum Corda*, recovered by the rites of England, Scotland, South Africa, and Ceylon in the present century. A like restoration of this Salutation before the Postcommunion Thanksgiving has been adopted only by India and Ceylon.

This rite also replaced the *Benedictus qui venit* after the *Sanctus*, as in 1549, but with its 1552 ending: much the best form, if this is to be done. This version of 1718 was proposed in the Scottish Draft Liturgy of 1889; but the Scottish since 1912 and the English of 1928 admit it only as an optional addition to the *Sanctus*, without the unifying welding of language which distinguishes the Nonjurors' rendition.

The one absolute innovation in this service was the substitution of the 'Summary of the Law' for the Decalogue. It is quite evident that the Nonjurors had completely lost sight of Cranmer's original purpose for this feature as a penitential preparation by means of an examination of conscience, and thought of it only in the light of its moralistic content. In this respect, to be sure, they were not a bit worse off than most Churchmen now alive.

3. The Evolution of the Scottish Liturgy

Obviously, no such liturgy as that of the English Nonjurors, including 'enrichments' going considerably beyond even the Rite of 1549, had any present chance of being welcomed by the Scottish Episcopal Church, which hitherto had not used any liturgy at all. Therefore Bishop Gadderar, who had himself taken a hand in making the English service of 1718, began in 1722 by reprinting the part of the rite of 1637 which commenced at the Offertory, under the title of 'The Communion Office of the Church of Scotland, as far as concerneth the Ministration of that Holy Sacrament,' and further commended it to his 'Nonjuring' brethren by the certification, 'Authorized by K. Charles I. *Anno* 1636.'

This was the first of the 'Wee Bookies,' as the Scots affectionately called the little pamphlets containing the second division of the service. And 'Wee Bookies' they remained throughout most of the definitive evolution of the Scottish Liturgy being used as supplemental to the Church of England Prayer Book, which was made available to the Scots in quantity. A complete service was not printed until 1844. The various editions were never synodically authorized, and therefore standardized, until 1912. They represented emergent custom, not legislation. They grew, as the primitive liturgies grew, by the contributions of individual leaders, and they competed with each other on their own merits. They were experimental forms which approved themselves by use, and in the end won such a unanimity as secured the adoption of their final form. This was a situation which in modern times could exist only in a small Church, closely united under external pressures: and which may well be envied by a large national Church, which is so tied by constitutional limitations as to find itself unable to license new forms for experimental use at all.[15]

The edition of 1722 reprinted that of 1637 exactly, though omitting the two Exhortations given as 'Warnings' of a coming celebration. However, from the very first Bishop Gadderar and his followers freely changed the order of parts, in the direction of the 'Eastern' pattern of the Nonjurors' Liturgy of 1718.

In 1735, two young printers, as a private venture, published the rite in the form in which it was commonly being used, with the heading: 'All the parts of this Office are ranked in the natural Order.' This edition followed 1718 in placing the Salutation before the *Sursum Corda*; in putting the Prayer for the Church (shorn of the word 'Militant') after the Consecration Prayer; and inserting the penitential preparation of Invitation, Confession, Absolution, and Comfortable Words between the Lord's Prayer and the Humble Access. Moreover, the words 'which we now offer unto thee' were interpolated in the 'Oblation' section of the Consecration Prayer. This may be from some current use: its author is not known.

In 1744, a book was published anonymously under the title 'The Ancient Liturgy of the Church of Jerusalem.' This was a posthumous work of Bishop Thomas Rattray, Bishop of Dunkeld, and Primus of the Scottish Church since 1739. It printed translations of the 'Liturgies of St. James,' and the *Apostolic Constitutions*, together with the Catechetical Lectures of St. Cyril of Jerusalem, and other documentations from Eastern sources. The most important effect of this work upon the minds of the Scottish churchmen was to convince them that the Invocation ought to come after the Institution, not before, as had been the case in all the English forms (save 1718) up to this time.

In 1755, accordingly, Bishop William Falconar of Edinburgh published a version of the service which omitted the old English 'Preliminary Invocation,' and inserted after the 'Oblation' paragraph the following:

---

15. Ed note: The mild tone of exasperation at canonical and constitutional limitations you detect here will only grow through successive years until Prayer Book Studies XV is not a study of the prayer book at all, but a thoroughgoing plea for a sensible system of "Trial Use."

> Hear us, O merciful Father, we most humbly beseech thee, and of thy Almighty goodness vouchsafe to bless and sanctify with thy word and Holy Spirit these thy gifts and creatures of bread and wine, that they may be to us the body and blood of thy most dearly beloved Son, so that we, receiving them according to thy Son our Saviour Jesus Christ's holy institution, in remembrance of his death and passion, may be partakers of the same his most precious body and blood.

This was a conjunction rather than a consolidation of the English Invocations in 1549 and 1552.

Finally, in 1764, Bishops Falconar and Richard Forbes perfected the Scottish Rite in the form in which it was known to Seabury. This has ever since remained the 'classical' form of that liturgy: its continued use being authorized in the Scottish Prayer Books of 1912 and 1929 for those congregations which had previously employed it.

This form first brought in the magnificent exorium, 'All glory be to thee,' before the initial 'Almighty God, our heavenly Father,' of the Consecration Prayer. This links the Thanksgiving with the concluding 'Glory be to thee, O Lord most high' of the *Sanctus* which precedes it, and restores, as all Eastern rites have been at pains to do, the continuity of what was once one unbroken supplication, which was interrupted when the Sanctus was first interpolated into it.

It is not known whether Falconar and Forbes realized that the words 'according to thy Son our Saviour Jesus Christ' holy institution, in remembrance of his death and passion,' in Cranmer's 'Preliminary Invocation' of 1552, were an *intentional* salvaging of the Commemoration which had been diplaced in that rite: 'according to the institution of thy dearly beloved Son our Saviour Jesus Christ, . . . having in remembrance his blessed passion, and precious death.' But it is apparent that they realized that when the two passages were brought into juxtaposition, by placing the 'Invocation' of 1552 directly after the restored Oblation-Commemoration section, there was an indefensible duplication and repetition. They therefore canceled the insertion of 1552, and produced something quite close to the formula of 1549:

> And we most humbly beseech thee, O merciful Father, to hear us, and of thine almighty goodness vouchsafe to bless and sanctify, with thy word and Holy Spirit, these thy gifts and creatures of bread and wine, that they may become the body and blood of thy most dearly beloved Son.

This brings us up to the situation prevailing at the time of the adoption of the first American Prayer Book in 1789. The further developments of the Scottish rite in the nineteenth and twentieth centuries will be noted later.

The American Revisions

The First American Prayer Book

The current Prayer Books of the Church of England, from 1559 to 1662, had, of course, been in use in the Church in America before the Revolution. After that event, the only necessary change in the Communion Service was the obvious one of dropping the fixed Collect for the King which preceded the Collect for the Day, together with the corresponding suffrages for the King in the Prayer for the Church Militant. And in fact, the alterations in the English rite were relatively few. They fall into three classes: those contributed by the Scottish Liturgy, those retained from the 'Proposed Book' of 1785, and a handful resulting from local conditions.

1. Scottish Contributions

In 1784, when Samuel Seabury, unable to overcome the inertia of the English Bishops, received consecration as the first Bishop in America from the hands of the Bishops of the Scottish Episcopal Church, he entered into a concordat with them to recommend the adoption of the Scottish Communion Office of 1764 by the infant American Church. In 1786, he issued the text of such an Office, 'recommended' to his own Diocese of Connecticut, which in all but a few minor phrases was identical with the Scottish.

The rite of 1764, like its predecessors, was a 'Wee Bookie,' beginning with the Offertory. The same was true of Seabury's diocesan rite. For the introductory 'Ante-Communion' passages, the Scots followed the order of the English Book of 1662 in the main, though with free variations according to local custom. This first part of the Scottish service was never printed until 1844, and its exact contents as actually used is a matter of conjecture. Indeed, the first American Prayer Book of 1789 is one primary witness for the usage current in Scotland in 1764. This first American rite bears testimony to the following Scottish features:

1. The 'Summary of the Law,' permitted as an optional addition to the Decalogue, reflects the known Scottish custom of using it as an alternative: dating from the Nonjurors' Office of 1718, which had substituted it absolutely for the Decalogue.
2. The Collect for grace to keep the Commandments,[16] taken from the former list of votive Collects printed after the service (corresponding to those now

---

16. Ed note: O ALMIGHTY Lord, and everlasting God, vouchsafe, we beseech thee, to direct, sanctify, and govern both our hearts and bodies in the way of thy commandments; that through thy most mighty protection, both here and ever, we may be preserved in body and soul; through our Lord and Saviour Jesus Christ. *Amen.*

on p. 49 f. of our present Prayer Book), which the Scots were in the habit of using in preference to the English Collect for the King. This had the merit of finishing off the essential Litany-structure of the Decalogue with an appropriate Litany-Collect.

3. The response, 'Glory be to thee, O Lord,' after the announcement of the Gospel, was in the First Prayer Book, but had been omitted in England since 1552; but it had been revived in the Scottish 1637 and the Nonjurors' 1718.

It is not of record that Bishop Seabury even suggested that the new American Church should adopt the Scottish order of parts of the Communion Service, with its radical rearrangement of putting the Intercession, the Lord's Prayer, and the penitential preparations for Communion, after the Consecration Prayer — though his diocesan rite followed that order. If he did make this suggestion, he did not press it, as it was immediately evident that the utmost obtainable at that time would be the adoption of the Scottish Prayer of Consecration. Bishop White, who was perfectly content with things as he found them, saw no great need even for that; but, as he mildly observed, it apparently 'lay very near to the heart of Bishop Seabury,' and acquiesced, with his customary political astuteness. There is little doubt that if he had not done so, there would have been a new 'Nonjuring' schism in Connecticut.

The man who was chiefly responsible for carrying the General Convention of 1789 for this point was Dr. William Smith of Maryland, President of the House of Deputies, and himself a Scotsman by birth. He had been President of the preliminary Convention of 1785, and had then joined with Dr. William White in framing the 'Proposed Book' of that year. But the next year, he took up Bishop Seabury's new diocesan rite with his own Convention in Maryland. There it was at once recognized that the Scottish Invocation, with its expression 'that they may become the body and blood of thy most dearly beloved Son,' involved such a shift of emphasis as to amount almost to a change of accepted doctrine: and the Convention recommended the restoration of the familiar words of the English Book, 'that we, receiving them according to thy Son our Saviour Jesus Christ's holy institution, in remembrance of his death and passion, may be partakers of his most blessed body and blood.'

This recommendation of the Maryland deputies was accepted by the General Convention. It is recorded that it was Dr. Smith's solemn and impressive reading of the proposed Prayer of Consecration which secured its adoption by acclamation by a House most of whom, like Bishop White, had never felt the need of any change.

The Maryland people and this first General Convention were quite right in refusing to alter the existing balance of doctrine expressed in the form previously in use, which corresponded exactly to the range of permitted opinion then prevailing in the Church: and they were right in considering that this balance would have been altered if the Scottish prayer had been taken just as it stood. It was, however, distinctly unfortunate that they did not realize that when they insisted on restoring the English phrase, as inserted in 1552, and *also* proceeded to adopt the Scottish revival of the Commemoration of 1549, they were incorporating doublet forms of the same essential thought, at the closest possible interval, and in nearly the same words. This was a definite backward step — a reversion to approximately the state of development of the Scottish form of 1755 — and a liturgical blunder which should now be redressed. In fact, it has been redressed in all recent Anglican revisions except our own. From England to Ceylon, these revisions have removed the interpolation of 1552, with the exceptions of South Africa and India (1952), which retain it, but at a considerable distance in the prayer, namely before the Institution, where 1552 placed it.

Finally, it is of considerable importance that the first American Prayer Book followed the Scottish 1764 in the provisions for a Second Consecration in case either of the Elements should be exhausted before all have communicated, by requiring the use of the Consecration Prayer from its beginning through the Invocation. This corrected Cranmer's error in 1548, followed by the Canons of 1604, and the Prayer Book of 1662, of permitting 'Consecration in One Kind,' and the use of the bare Narrative of the Institution, without prayer of any sort, as a Formula of Consecration.

2. Influence of the 'Proposed Book'

The treatment of the Communion Service in the 'Proposed Book' of 1785 had only one point in mind, namely the elimination of matter which was duplicated when Morning Prayer, Litany, and Holy Communion (or more usually 'Ante-Communion ') were said as one continuous service, as had been the English custom ever since the Puritan Archbishop Grindal had ordered that 'accumulation' in 1571. Since it was assumed that the Communion would never be used separately, the initial Lord's Prayer and the Creed were dropped absolutely from the service of 1785, and the 'Ante-Communion' came to an end with the Gospel, instead of the Prayer for the Church Militant, as in England.

This deletion of the Nicene Creed from this service, and therefore from the Prayer Book entirely, was one main reason for the hesitations of the English bishops about conferring the Episcopate upon the new American Church. Accordingly, the General Convention of 1789 made haste to restore it, by this rubric: 'Then shall be read the Apostles', or Nicene Creed: unless one of them hath been read immediately before, in the Morning Service.' Neither Creed was printed in the text of the Communion service, but both were given in both Morning and Evening Prayer. The latter was completely unprecedented. If it was a gesture to prove that the American Church had no prejudice against the Nicene Creed as such, and that its omission from the Proposed Book had been only an inadvertence, it was doubtless successful. But we have not heard that it has ever been used at Evening Prayer.

As to the initial Lord's Prayer, it was now specified that it might be omitted here if Morning Prayer had been said immediately before.

3. Influence of Local Conditions

a) The Place for Beginning the Service: Some circumstances peculiar to a new Church in a new land gave a different turn to some minor particulars.

The rubric of 1552, 'The Table . . . at the Communion tyme . . . shall stande in the body of the Churche, or in the chauncell, where Morninge Prayer, and Eueninge prayer be appoynted to bee sayde. And the Priest standing at the north-side of the Table,' etc., had marked a revolt of the Puritans against the idea of a fixed 'Altar' again the East wall of the church, and their attempt to substitute a true movable 'table,' 'with legs,' which 'at the Communion tyme' should be brought down to the head of the nave in small parish churches, or into the midst of the choir in large churches and cathedrals — where the Daily Offices were often read to a congregation, all of whom could be seated in the choir. This 'Table' was placed at right angles to its former position, with its long dimension in the axis of the church: and the rubric directed the Priest to take his stand on the 'North' ('Cantoris' or 'Gospel') side of it.

This innovation never commended itself to many clergy, and Archbishop Laud succeeded in making an end of it by ordering that the ' Table ' should be restored to an 'altar-wise' position in the Chancel, and fixed in its place. This rubric, though it has remained unchanged in the English books, has actually been devoid of meaning ever since, since it was never intended to apply to an 'altar-wise' Table. The extremely literal-minded perpetrated the ritual absurdity of celebrating at the north end of the altar. Even after lively debates had established the legitimacy of the 'Eastward Position,' facing the altar, the rubric was interpreted as indicating the 'Gospel' portion of its front.

In 1789, the rubric was altered to read: . . . 'shall stand in the body of the Church, or in the Chancel; and the Minister standing at the north side of the table, or where Morning and Evening prayer are appointed to be said, . . .' The slight, but peculiar, change of wording was made on account of the curious local construction of St. Peter's Church, Philadelphia. To this day this church has a 'three-decker' reading-desk and pulpit at one end of the building, and the altar at the other. The congregation must reverse the way they are sitting in the square box pews when the service passes from Morning Prayer to the Holy Communion. Bishop White, who was then in charge of the parish, asked to be spared the needless effort and disturbance of walking from one end of the church to the other merely to read the ' Ante-Communion,' as was the invariable custom in those days, and then back again for the Sermon.

b) Minister: All the rubrics of the Communion Service conform to the one just quoted in using the word 'Minister' for the Celebrant: no doubt to avoid giving offence to well-meaning people in the new country to whom the Church and her ways were little known, and the word 'Priest' unfamiliar and alarming. Certainly the Communion was never celebrated by a Deacon in our Church, as is the case among the Moravians. Nevertheless, the use of the generic term was unfortunate in a liturgical setting. Canonically, a Bishop, a Priest, and a Deacon are all 'Ministers': though the field of their respective ministerial commissions has always been carefully discriminated. The rubrics should always indicate the exact portions of the services which each may take. This was accurately done in 1549, when the Celebrant is always called 'the Priest,' and the word 'Minister' invariably refers to some assistant: and even then subsidiary rubrics draw distinctions between the 'Deacon or other Priest' who might minister the Chalice, or read the Gospel, and the Parish Clerk who might read the Epistle and the Offertory Sentences, and lead the General Confession. It was the Puritan exaltation of the importance of the ordained 'Ministry,' coupled with their denial of distinctions of grades in its Orders, which was responsible for the loose use of this word for a time in our rubrics.

c) Music: It would appear that it was the difficulty of getting the *Gloria in Excelsis* sung under pioneering conditions, when few singers were familiar with any songs of praise except metrical hymns, which prompted the permission to substitute 'some proper Hymn from the Selection' (*i.e.*, the Church Hymnal of those days). No Prayer Book since 1549 had permitted the omission of the *Gloria* under any circumstances; though the First Prayer Book had allowed it to be left out, along with the Creed, Sermon, and Exhortation, 'on the workedaye, or in private howses' — that is, on weekdays which were not Holy Days, and at the Communion of the Sick. Thus this provision of 1789, which was originally simply a concession to frontier choirs, has been very useful in enabling the American Church to conform its service to the liturgical proprieties of the Christian Year, and to the old principle that this supreme song of praise ought not to be used during Advent and Pre-Lent, or in Lent and on other penitential occasions, or indeed even on ordinary weekdays outside the Festal Seasons. Whether the substitution of a Hymn should be allowed upon normal Sundays of the year, as seems to be a rather increasing custom, is another matter.

On the other hand, the same primitive conditions appear to be reflected in a consciousness that the Communion Service, with none of its prose text sung, was barren of musical ornament, coupled by a willingness to do what could be done to remedy this situation, appearing in the modest 'enrichment' of a Hymn after the Consecration Prayer. This was sound liturgical instinct, recognizing the need of something of the order of the old Communion Anthem before the Reformation, at the distribution of the Communion. Indeed, we find hymns for use in this place in 'Tate and Brady.'[17]

d) *The Trinity Preface:* The impact of the outbreak of Unitarianism in New England by the secession of King's Chapel, Boston, may have influenced the adoption of a new alternative Proper Preface for Trinity Sunday. If anyone were troubled by the somewhat cryptic expressions which were the best Cranmer could make of the very idiomatic medieval Latin, he might substitute some plain historical statements of Christian experience. (But compare p. 353 f.)[18]

The Revision of 1892

During much of the nineteenth century, it appears that the American Church developed a stronger interest in the Prayer Book, and greater actual uniformity in its ritual (though not ceremonial) use, than had yet been attained anywhere else in the Anglican Communion. To a large degree, this was the result of the great energies which Bishop Hobart of New York threw into exalting the importance of the Church's worship as set forth in the Prayer Book, as the carrier of the Church's faith, and as the great integrating factor among all the divergent opinions and the varied objectives of its members.

Hobart, in fact, initiated a real 'Liturgical Movement,' centered in the Book of Common Prayer. There seems to be a good deal in the claim that he was the prime inspirer of the 'Oxford Movement' in England itself. The real beginning of that great revival of the faith and worship of the Church seems not to have been Keble's 'Assize Sermon' in 1833, but Hobart's visit to Oxford in 1824: on which occasion he met Newman, and appears to have imparted to him his own

---

17. Ed note: 'Tate and Brandy' is the colloquial name for *New Version of the Psalms of David* first published in 1696 by Nahum Tate and Nicholas Brady. As the name suggests, it was a metrical psalter containing paraphrases of all 150 psalms, the Lord's Prayer, and Apostles' Creed. Later editions included some select canticles and hymns; a 1796 London printing with successive editions contains a small selection of hymns at the end including the 1755 Philip Doddridge composition 'My God, and is thy table spread' labeled "For the Sacrament."

18. Ed note: The 1549/1662 Preface is this: "which art one God, one Lord, not one only person, but three persons in one substance : For that which we believe of the glory of the Father, the same we believe of the Son, and of the Holy Ghost, without any difference, or inequality : whom the angels, &c."

The American 1789 alternate Preface is this: "FOR the precious death and merits of thy Son Jesus Christ our Lord, and for the sending to us of the Holy Ghost, the Comforter; who are one with thee in thy eternal Godhead: Therefore with Angels, &c."

The offering in this book will be this: "WHO, with thine Only-begotten Son, and the Holy Ghost, art one God, one Lord, in Trinity of Persons and in Unity of Substance. For that which we believe of thy glory, O Father, the same we believe of the Son, and of the Holy Ghost, without any difference of inequality:"

successful method of propaganda by means of tracts on the Prayer Book. Certainly Newman afterward exploited this same procedure so vigorously that his grand project was first christened, and long known, as the 'Tractarian Movement.' And it followed precisely the line of Hobart's plan of a genuine liturgical basis of doctrine, whose first principle was to take the Prayer Book seriously — to believe that the Church meant what it said when it talked to God.

In America, 'Prayer Book Churchmanship' became the aim and claim of every party, vieing with each other in their protestations of loyalty to that standard, and in their assertions that their own position best set forth its meaning and power.

But the defect of 'Prayer Book Churchmanship' — then and now — has been that with many it has a tendency to degenerate into a conservative complacency with 'our incomparable liturgy,' to debase the ideal of Uniformity into a fetish, and to set its face against even reasonable improvements.

This was the chief obstacle to Dr. William Huntington's valiant efforts for the revision of the Prayer Book in the latter part of the century. In the controversies over ceremonial in the 1860's and '70's, both sides had appealed to the text of the Liturgy as a fixed and final authority. Those controversies were of such recent and poignant memory that Dr. Huntington felt constrained to assure the General Convention of 1880 that in case such permission to launch a movement in favor of revision as was asked for was granted, no attempt would be made seriously to change the Liturgy proper, namely, the 'Office of the Holy Communion.'[19] Accordingly, the amendments to this service actually adopted in the Prayer Book of 1892 were very few.

1. Influence of the Scottish Draft of 1889

The majority of the changes, including all those that involved any alteration in the actual text, are identical with proposals in the Scottish Draft Liturgy of 1889. Their adoption is to be attributed to the initiative of Dr. Samuel Hart, whose activity on the Revision Commission was second only to that of Dr. Huntington, and who, as a Connecticut Churchman, had kept in close touch with the current developments in the Scottish Church. These comprise:

1. The initial Lord's Prayer was shorn of the Doxology which had been appended to it in 1789.
2. The 'Summary of the Law,' which in 1789 had been presented by the rubric as only an optional addition to the Decalogue, was now allowed as a substitute for it, except at one service each Sunday. There is evidence for this alternative use as a custom of the Scottish Church as far back as 1718, the same year that

---

19. W. R. Huntington, *A Short History of the Book of Common Prayer* (N.Y.: Whittaker, 1893), 135.

the English Nonjurors printed their 'Communion Office,'[20] which originated the use of this formula, and employed it to supplant the Decalogue on all occasions. A good many American clergy had followed the Scottish lead in using it as an alternative instead of the supplement which the rubric of 1789 had authorized. The Scottish Draft of 1889 now permitted the alternative at any time, and the American Book of 1892 with the above limitation.

3. The 'Lesser Litany' of *Kyrie eleison* was now inserted after the 'Summary.' This feature of 1549 had been restored in the Nonjurors' rite of 1718, but in an anomalous place, before the initial Lord's Prayer. The Draft of 1889 first proposed it for this place.

4. The second and third Exhortations, comprising the little-used 'Warnings' of a future celebration of the Communion, were relegated to the end of the service — where unfortunately they have been increasingly disused.

5. Five new Offertory Sentences were incorporated from 1889. Four of them had been in the Scottish line since 1637. The last two in our list ('Thine, O Lord, is the greatness,' and 'All things come of thee') had been separated from the rest by a rubric specifically designating them for use at the Presentation, since the Scottish service of 1764. No doubt our Prayer Book of 1892 intended them for such employment, though the ritual point was not made clear by rubric.

6. The *Sanctus* was detached from the end of the Preface to form a paragraph of its own.

7. In like manner, 'The Invocation' section of the Consecration Prayer was given a new paragraph after 'The Oblation.'

2. Other Changes

The other alterations of 1892, which were not indebted to the Scottish Draft of 1889, were these:

1. The 'Long Exhortation' was now required only once a month. This is the provision of the Nonjurors' rite of 1718.

2. The text of the Nicene Creed was printed in the Communion Service. The Apostles' Creed (though not printed here) could still be substituted for it, as before. And though both Creeds could still be omitted from the Communion if either of them had just been said in Morning Prayer, the rubric now required the use of the Nicene Creed in the combined service upon the five greatest festivals.

---

20. John Dowden, *The Scottish Communion Office*, ed. H. A. Wilson (Oxford: The University Press, 1922), 145.

3. The use of the Offertory Sentences was extended to 'any other occasion of Public Worship, when the alms of the People are to be received.'
4. A Hymn or Anthem was authorized 'when the Alms and Oblations are presented.' This was, in principle, a restoration of the *Offertorium* of the service before the Reformation.
5. The then recent controversies over ceremonial left just one trace, in a new rubric stipulating that 'sufficient opportunity shall be given to those present to communicate.' This was designed to ban any celebrations at which the clergy did not permit any communions.

The Last Revision of 1928

The extreme conservatism which took alarm at any 'serious' change in the Eucharistic Liturgy in the Revision of 1892, and which limited improvements adopted then to a very scanty list, by that very fact left over a considerable amount of 'unfinished business' in the form of unsatisfied demands. Less than 25 years later, there was an insistent call for a further revision.

The experience in the use of the considerably altered Daily Offices in the Prayer Book of 1892 had shown that the idol of Uniformity could be thrown down, and a very fair amount of variety and flexibility introduced into the services, without the Church's coming apart at the seams. The Revision Commission found itself flooded with suggestions for similar treatment of the Communion Service.

And similar treatment it turned out to be. Quite a list of alterations of the framework, the arrangement, and the incidental decorations of the rite were approved; but the Commission was very chary of proposing any real changes in the basic text of the service: and conservative resistance rejected all but two or three small points out of those which it did propose.

By far the most important source of the amendments adopted in the American Prayer Book of 1928 was the attempt to revise the Prayer Book of the Church of England, which had been initiated in 1906, completed and passed by the Convocations in 1920, then renegotiated before the new Church Assembly for eight more years, until it wound up with the equivocal situation of having been accepted by the Church, but rejected by Parliament, in 1928. The thorough and far-reaching proposals of this book received extensive consideration by the American revisers. And, as we shall see, these English findings were to a very large extent dependent upon the Scottish line of liturgies since 1637.

Let us examine the changes in our last revision in the order of the historic strata from which they were ultimately drawn, noting the British sources which immediately brought them to the attention of our revisers.

1. Restorations of Pre-Reformation Features

The year 1928 marked the first time any English or American revision went back to the First Prayer Book, and even to earlier Latin origins, for restorations of desirable features which had not been included in the Scottish revision of 1637.

The reversions to Latin sources were these:

1. The English and American (followed in 1938 by Ceylon and India in 1952) give the respond, 'Praise be to thee, O Christ,' after the reading of the Gospel. This is an exact translation of the modern Roman *Laus tibi, Christe*, now said by the server at Low Mass. It was not in the Sarum rite at all. It is of relatively recent employment even in the Roman: the older Western use being to reply *Deo gratias*, 'Thanks be to God,' as to the lections in the Breviary. This is still the respond after the so-called Last Gospel.'

   The Anglican source of this feature was in the Scottish 1637, which had 'Thanks be to thee, O Lord.' This seems to be a conflation of the two variant forms, *Laus tibi, Christe*, and *Deo gratias*, which were still to be found in contemporary Continental usage when this revision was made. The Scottish, South African, and Indian (1933) liturgies retain some variant of the form of 1637. But the form which eventually won out in Roman use is more distinctive.

2. The breaking up of the long and heavy Prayer for the Whole State of Christ's Church into the short paragraphs of its constituent units of thought, which has been effected in all Anglican revisions, beginning with the Scottish Draft Liturgy of 1889, is really a reversion to the Canon of the pre-Reformation service. This Canon was a chain of Collects, not the single uninterrupted Intercession into which Cranmer remodeled it, after the standards of the Greek liturgies. Cranmer's admirable integration of the abrupt, incoherent structure of the Latin remains. But the manner of the Latin presentation had its merits too, in its superior emphasis upon the individual points, one at a time.

3. The Scottish Draft of 1889 proposed a translation of the Sarum Proper Preface for the Epiphany, which has been adopted by all subsequent Anglican revisions.

4. The Sarum Rite used the Proper Preface for the Nativity upon the Purification and the Transfiguration, as feasts of the Incarnation — though for the Annunciation it substituted the Preface of the Blessed Virgin. All recent revisions have sought for Proper Prefaces for these three festivals. The English and South African rites assign to the Purification and Annunciation our present Christmas Preface, which was composed in 1549, and offer a new composition for the Transfiguration. The Scottish and Ceylon liturgies have the Christmas Preface on the Annunciation, and new forms on the other two. The American solution was to return to Sarum for a paraphrase of the original Preface of the Incarnation (*i.e.*, the Sarum and Roman Preface

for Christmas), on all three feasts. This has been followed by the Indian rite to the extent of providing a more literal but less desirable translation of this Preface on the Purification.

5. All recent revisions have corrected the Preface for Trinity Sunday by conforming it more closely to its Sarum original. Cranmer in the First Prayer Book had made rather heavy weather of this form, leaving it with an aberrant beginning and ending, omitting the last sentence of the Latin entirely, and rather loosely paraphrasing the remainder. Nothing had been done to it since the Second Prayer Book provided it with a conventional ending. The last revisions have restored also a normal beginning by incorporating from the Latin, 'with thine only-begotten Son, and the Holy Ghost.'

The change of one small word (indeed, of one letter!) in the American form has proved something of an irritant to the overscrupulous. 'Without any difference *of* inequality' is surely a closer paraphrase of the original *sine differentia discretionis* than 'or inequality.' There was no real error even in the old phrase, since the 'difference or inequality ' refers to the 'glory,' not the essential Being, of the respective Persons of the Holy Trinity. But since some people succeeded in getting a confused impression that it was intimated that there was no 'difference' in the Persons — which of course would be pure Sabellianism the revisers deemed it well to make it clear that the meaning is that there is no 'difference of [*i.e.*, in point of, or in the nature of] inequality.'

6. The American revision pioneered in permitting a Hymn or Anthem between the Epistle and Gospel, in the place where Cranmer had not found it practicable for him to follow the Sarum provisions for a Gradual Anthem or Sequence Hymn. This feature has been copied in the rites of India and Ceylon.

7. America also took the initiative — and this time it stands alone — in allowing the insertion of the Bidding Prayer after the Creed. It was Sarum use to have this interesting variant of the General Intercession in the vernacular at the principal Mass on Sundays. The fact that it duplicated the matter of the Intercessions in the Canon did no harm whatever, since the people did not understand the Latin prayers anyhow. But now that the Prayer for the Whole Church is in English, and moreover has been transferred to a place in the service which is very close to that proposed for the Bidding Prayer, it does not seem at all useful to have these absolute doublets in the same service.

It may be that our revisers had in mind that it could be used with the 'Ante-Communion,' which in our rite ends with the Gospel, so that the accumulation of two General Intercessions would not occur. Or it may be that they were mindful of the rubric prefixed to the Bidding Prayer, permitting the officiant to 'omit any of the clauses in this prayer, or [to] add others, as occasion may require': so that this form may have been offered here as a model and framework for presenting a considerable number of special intercessions together, in a systematic yet perfectly free-handed manner. In any case, very little use has been made of this provision.

2. Restorations of Features of the First Prayer Book

1. All recent revisions follow the Scottish Draft of 1889 in expunging the obsolete and unworkable initial rubric of 1552 about the Celebrant's position at the north side of the Table[21] at the beginning of the service, in favor of some form of the rubric of 1549. The First Prayer Book directed that he should be 'standyng humbly afore the middes of the Altar' for the Lord's Prayer, Collect, and *Kyries*, but 'standyng at Goddes borde' for the *Gloria in Excelsis*. The Scottish and South African have 'at the Table'; and the English 1928 is to the same effect, though in the second phrase of 1549, 'standing at God's Board.' The American is perhaps a little closer to Cranmer's language, and certainly to his intent, in saying 'standing reverently before the Holy Table'; though Ceylon has expressed his purpose more unmistakably, by saying 'at the foot of the Altar.'

    It is of course the fact that the opening part of the Liturgy is the analogue of the old Sarum Preparation, said below the altar steps. Some of our clergy are giving this interpretation to the perhaps intentionally vague rubric of our present Prayer Book, by saying the exordium of the service through the Summary or the Collect of the Commandments below the altar steps, and going up to the altar for the Collect of the Day. They are on sound historical ground in doing so.

2. The English revision, followed by the South African, presents the Decalogue in what Dr. Srawley calls 'a shorter form (without the comments and explanations added in Exod. xx, many of which apply to the temporary conditions of Jewish life.'[22] This is the form in which the Commandments are found in the *Bishops' Book* of 1537, the *King's Book* of 1543, and the Catechism of the First Prayer Book: thus constituting a return to the standards of the Prayer Book of 1549, though the Communion Service of that Book did not contain them. The short form is reminiscent of the way in which the Commandments are cited in Mark 10:19 and Rom. 13:9. The American and Scottish rites make the shortening optional, printing the 'explanations' in smaller type.

---

21. The American rubric since 1835 has said, 'at the *right* side.' This change was made since American churches are seldom oriented; but it was intended to preserve the same idea. The word 'right' was used in it, heraldic sense: the 'dexter' side of a shield is on its *wearer's* right - though on the *left* as a spectator looks at it.

22. Clarke and Harris, *Liturgy and Worship* (N. Y.: Macmillan, 1932), 311.

3. All revisions since the Scottish 1912 restore the Salutation, 'The Lord be with you,' before the Collect of the Day, as in 1549.
4. All revisions in and since 1928 cancel the bracket, 'or, The portion of Scripture appointed for the Epistle,' upon which the Puritans had insisted in 1661, whenever the first lection of the liturgy was from some other portion of the Bible besides the actual 'Letters' of the Apostles. All save the American, however, say 'The Lesson' instead of 'The Epistle' in such case. This usage of the other Anglican liturgies is a return to Sarum, which said *Lectio Epistolæ beati Pauli Apostoli ad Corinthios*, or *Lectio Joelis Prophetæ*.
5. The 1549 rubrics directed that 'the priest or he that is appointed, shall reade the Epistle,' and after the lection was announced, 'The Minister then shall read the epistle'; and similarly, 'the Priest, or one appointed to read the Gospel,' and after the *Gloria tibi*, 'the priest or deacon then shall read the Gospel.' But in all revisions since 1552, these duties had been confined to the Celebrant — except at the Consecration of Bishops since 1662: 'another Bishop shall read the Epistle (Gospel).' The Scottish Draft of 1889 proposed, 'the Presbyter or some other Minister' for both lections. Since 1912 the Scots have had 'the Presbyter or some other Presbyter or Deacon.' However, the English 1928 declined to follow this Scottish lead of requiring an ordained 'Minister' for both lections, the English rubric explicitly distinguishing between them by saying 'he that readeth the Epistle,' but 'the Deacon or Priest that readeth the Gospel.' This is in line with the long-established English custom, before as well as after the Reformation, of allowing the Parish Clerk to read the Epistle — which after all is like any other Lesson in any service, in that no man need be ordained to read it. The American rubric does not decide that question either way, contenting itself with saying simply, 'The Minister appointed shall read the Epistle (Gospel).'
6. All recent revisions restore an explicit Intercession for the Departed to the Prayer for the Church. This feature had been in the Scottish line since 1637. Today it is most fully represented, in terms closest to the First Prayer Book, in the Scottish and South African rites, though all others afford a fairly close approximation to the thought and words of 1549: with the exception of the American, where there was indeed no actual objection to 'prayers for the dead,' but rather an excess of caution lest old Reformation phobias on that subject should be raised again. Thus there was conservative resistance to the restoration of the traditional phrases; but the entirely new expression 'to grant them continual growth in thy love and service' proved acceptable to all.
At the same time, all revisions dropped the limiting term 'Militant' from the Bidding to this prayer (adopted in 1552, in the form 'militant here in earth'), as no longer applicable to a supplication which had been enlarged again to

comprehend also the Church Expectant and the Church Triumphant. This had been Scottish use since 1735.

7. All recent revisions have placed the Lord's Prayer, prefaced by its traditional Prologue, immediately after the Consecration Prayer, as in 1549 and 1637, instead of at the beginning of the 'Postcommunion' section, as had been English use since 1552, and American since 1789.

8. Most recent revisions have restored the Prayer of Humble Access to its 1549 position immediately before the Communion, from the structurally anomalous but theologically potent location between the *Sanctus* and the Consecration Prayer which was adopted in 1552. The American rite here followed 1637 exactly, with the Lord's Prayer and Humble Access only between the Consecration and the Communion. The subsequent Scottish books interpolated the Invitation, Confession, Absolution, and Comfortable Words between the Lord's Prayer and the Humble Access, as in 1549 and 1718. South Africa has adopted the American arrangement precisely, and Ceylon approximately (interposing only *Pax* and *Benedictus*). The English revision puts the Humble Access after the Comfortable Words, before the *Sanctus*.

9. The American rite conforms to Scottish use since 1764 in reverting to 1549 by canceling the 'superfluous' repetition of 'thou that takest away the sins of the world, have mercy upon us,' which 1552 had added to the *Gloria in Excelsis*. This repetition has been interpreted as a dittography — it has even been found in some pre-Reformation manuscripts — but it is more probable that it was an intentional insertion, to preserve the text of the *Agnus Dei* intact *within* the *Gloria* which the Second Prayer Book had transferred to the end of the service, so close to the traditional place of the *Agnus* as to make it inadvisable to rehearse both of them. As in the case of the 'Humble Access,' but unlike all the other reversions to 1549 listed above, this did not get into the English revision — nor in any later one except that of Ceylon. This reluctance to correct the text of the *Gloria* has been concomitant with a reluctance to readmit the *Agnus*, which has been restored only in the rites of Scotland, India, and Ceylon. This would naturally tend to persist until the *Gloria* is restored to its original place at the beginning of the service — which has been done only in India (1933) and Ceylon.

3. *Contemporary English Contributions*

Other features of our last revision which seem to have been drawn from the revision which was going on in the same period in England are as follows. They are all modern, none of them anteceding the Scottish Draft Liturgy of 1889.

1. The Decalogue is now required at only one Sunday service in each month; the 'Summary' being available as an alternative at any other time. South Africa requires the Decalogue once a Sunday in Advent and Lent; Scotland allows either the Summary or the *Kyries* to be substituted at any time; India relegates both Decalogue and Summary to a separate service of Preparation; and Ceylon eliminates both entirely.

2. Until the Scottish draft of 1889, all Anglican liturgies had retained some form of Cranmer's direction in 1549, that after the Creed 'shall folowe the Sermon.' The Liturgy is the only service at which any Prayer Book has ordered a Sermon, or even assigned a place for one within the service. The intent of Cranmer's mandatory phrase was that the opportunity for the instruction and edification of the people should not be missed at what had always been, and he assumed always would be, the principal service of public worship. When the Liturgy later came to be replaced for the most part by Morning or even by Evening Prayer as the chiefly attended services, it became the custom to append sermons to those offices also (although the rubrics have never mentioned them), in accord with Cranmer's purpose for a Teaching Church. But when early celebrations were multiplied in the nineteenth century, the original conception did not apply to this rubric in the Liturgy, and it was largely ignored. There was, however, some uneasiness on the part of many at taking upon themselves to pronounce that such an imperative rubric did not apply; and some literalists considered that it required them to give at least a minimal 'allocution' at every celebration.

    Accordingly, the draft of 1889 took account of the changed conditions by directing, 'If there be a Sermon, it followeth here.' This is the present Scottish. The American rubric puts it, 'Then followeth the Sermon.' It is to be noted that this is the only *indicative* rubric in our Prayer Book: it is a descriptive statement, rather than a requirement. England, followed by South Africa and Ceylon, says, 'Then may follow a Sermon.' The effect of all three forms is the same; but it might appear that either the Scottish or the American comes nearest to what Cranmer was trying to convey, namely not only that 'This is the place in the Liturgy for the Sermon, on the occasions when there is to be one,' but also, 'The Liturgy is the one service which is entitled to contain a Sermon, as an integral part of it.'

3. The American service cancels twelve of the former Offertory Sentences, comprising two which go back to 1637, and ten which have stood in the Anglican books since the First Prayer Book. These consisted of those which seemed to allege 'unworthy' motives and inducements for almsgiving, and those which made a plea for the support of the clergy. Six of these Sentences were dropped in the English revision, and all twelve in the Scottish.

4. The 'Long Exhortation,' required once a month in our Prayer Book of 1892, is now demanded only on the first Sundays in the seasons of Advent and Lent, and upon Trinity Sunday. This appears to have been suggested by the English book's assigning it to be read 'at the least on the fourth or fifth Sunday in Lent.' The Scottish rite since 1889 has left it wholly optional, 'at the discretion of the Presbyter.' The liturgies of South Africa, India, and Ceylon do not use it at all.

5. The English revision is the only one besides the American that provides for the insertion of special Biddings of particular intentions before the general Bidding 'for the whole state of Christ's Church.' Their rubric is, 'The Priest may here bid special prayers and thanksgivings'; ours, 'Here the Priest may ask the secret intercessions of the congregation for any who have desired the prayers of the Church.'

6. The very lengthy Proper Preface for Whitsunday was newly composed for the First Prayer Book by a conflation of Acts 2:2–4, John 16:13, and 1 Peter 2:9. Our modern age has felt a little dubious about the actual relevance of some of the picturesque descriptions of the external manifestations of the Pentecostal experience, namely 'with a sudden great sound, as it had been a mighty wind, in the likeness of fiery tongues,' and 'the gift of divers languages.' The Scottish Prayer Book of 1912 adopted an entirely new composition, of distinctly pedestrian quality. All the more recent revisions save our own have returned to some form of the Sarum Preface. But that ancient 'Leonine' form has two defects. Most of it is given over to a reiteration of the meaning of the Ascension, and very little is said about the Holy Spirit — so little that the English version was constrained to supplement it by concluding with the last clause of Cranmer's form. And secondly, the Sarum language is bombastic Italian rhetoric, in the style of the pretentious *Præconium Paschale* at the Blessing of the Font on Easter Even; and the translators added to it some rather high-flown embellishments of their own.

Therefore the American revisers rejected the neo-Sarum form, and contented themselves with pruning Cranmer's version of the phrases quoted above, though they retained the rest of his vivid scriptural language. The Scots seem to have shared something of the American dissatisfaction with the new English imitation of the Latin version, since they accepted it only as an alternative to Cranmer's composition (modified only by saying 'tongues' instead of 'divers language ' — none too happily, since they kept the previous fiery tongues,' so that the echo of the word is also a clash of meanings) — though they dropped their own attempt of 1912.

7. All recent revisions have adopted a new Proper Preface for All Saints', in some variant of that originating with the Scottish Draft of 1889, based upon an admirable conflation of Heb. 12:1 and 1 Pet. 5:4.

4. Scottish Contributions

We have already noted under the restorations of features of 1549 that we owe to the Scots, but not to the English, the place of the Prayer of Humble Access, and the corrected text of the *Gloria in Excelsis*. Other American indebtednesses to the Scottish line, since they were not adopted in the English Book of 1928, are these:

1. We have seen that in 1662 Cranmer's peculiar phobia about the 'Minor Oblation' at the Offertory was quietly shelved by directions for the priest to 'present and place' the Alms, and to 'place' the Bread and Wine, 'upon the Table,' in language taken from the Scottish 1637. Our last revision had further recourse to this same source for the fuller phrase, 'shall then *offer*, and shall place upon the Holy Table, the Bread and the Wine.'
2. The Scottish liturgies since 1889 have relegated the 'Long Exhortation,' as a seldom used feature, to be printed after the service. We have done the same; though the English book retains it in the text of the rite.

5. Features Originating in the American Rite

It will have been observed in the foregoing analyses that our American revisers, though they paid the utmost deference to our own two 'Mother Churches' in England and Scotland, and were eager to avail themselves of the great stores of devotional learning in both countries, were not content to follow their lead slavishly in all particulars, but considered each question which they raised upon its own merits, and decided upon it according to their own judgment. We have noted a number of instances where it appeared to our revisers that the British censors of the Liturgy had asked the right questions, but had not found the right answers. In such cases, the independent American solutions have every right to be regarded as original contributions to liturgical reform — even though we have found it convenient to consider them as having been occasioned in the first instance by British attempts to amend the inadequacies which they found in the Liturgy as it had come down to them. Such are our distinctive form of the Intercession for the Departed; the restoration of the Sarum Proper Preface of the Nativity for the three feasts of the Incarnation; and our revision of Cranmer's Preface for Whitsunday.

We have also noted two other restorations of Sarum features entirely ignored by the British revisers, namely a Hymn or Anthem for the Gradual, and the Bidding Prayer.

Other instances where the American revisers were thinking on independent lines, and made definite new departures, are these:

1. The permission to insert special intercessory Collects after the Creed. England permits such Collects after the Intercession, or before the Blessing;

Scotland, South Africa, and Ceylon before the Blessing; and India allows the insertion of clauses of intercession or thanksgiving within the Litany which that rite has inserted before the Collect of the Day. It may be observed here that none of these provisions is liturgically sound, or satisfactory in operation; and that further consideration of this problem is needed.

2. Three entirely new Offertory Sentences were added: Matt. 25:40 for charitable occasions, and Rom. 10:14 f. and Luke 10:2 for missionary offerings.

3. The initial Lord's Prayer was made optional at all times — not merely when preceded by Morning Prayer, as in 1892. This has been adopted in the Scottish Liturgy of 1929. India (1933) and Ceylon omit it entirely.

The latest Scottish book also adopted the 'sufficient opportunity' rubric of the American 1892. This is mentioned here because these two particulars seem to be the only demonstrable examples of any influence of American contributions upon the Scottish revisions. The English do not appear to have paid any attention whatever to any amendments which originated on this side of the water.

6. Defeated Amendments

The account of our latest revision would not be complete without taking note of two proposed 'enrichments,' both of which were restorations of features of the First Prayer Book, which received preliminary approval of one General Convention, and seemed certain of adoption, but which were defeated at their final consideration.

The *Agnus Dei*, eliminated in 1552, has, as we have observed, been restored in Scotland, India, and Ceylon. Passed by our General Convention in 1925, it failed of enactment in 1928 from the sheer accident that so many Bishops had been called back to their dioceses toward the end of a protracted session, that the negative vote of only six conservative Bishops caused the proposal to fall short of the 'constitutional majority' of all Bishops having jurisdiction, which is required for final action upon any change in the Prayer Book. However, the permission to use 'a Hymn' at this point of the service remained; and as the Agnus is certainly 'a Hymn,' it continues to be legal to sing it here — as had been a fairly widespread custom in the Church before the amendment was brought forward. Its legitimacy is attested by its inclusion in the musical settings of the Communion Service in the official Church Hymnal, before and afterward.

The *Benedictus qui venit*, likewise missing since 1552, was restored in the Nonjurors' service of 1718, proposed by the Scots in 1889, and adopted as a permissive addition to the Sanctus by England in 1928 and Scotland in 1929. This proposal also passed the General Convention of 1925. But before it came up for final action, some premature jubilation on the part of certain partisans, alleging an unhistorical rationalization of this feature as an acclamation of a coming Eucharistic Presence, caused some members of the Revision Commission itself to turn against it, and to defeat its adoption by direct attack. Accordingly, the Hymnal Commission withdrew its previous sanction of it by excluding it from the next revision of the Hymnal.

Other Anglican Revisions

In the foregoing analysis of the sources of the text of the American Liturgy in 1892 and 1928, we have had occasion to take note of features of the contemporary English and Scottish revisions, and also to draw comparisons with changes of the text which have been made after that time in other branches of the Anglican Communion. It remains to give some account of these other Anglican developments.

The Scottish Liturgy

In the nineteenth and twentieth centuries, the Episcopal Church in Scotland continued to maintain the lead in liturgical reform which it had held since 1637. Though small, and poor, and for part of this time still under the cloud of its former 'Nonjuring' associations, it had two great tactical advantages over the neighboring Church of England. It was entirely autonomous, free from the State control which so hampered the development of the Prayer Book in England. And it was compact, more homogeneous in its Churchmanship than any other national body in the Anglican Communion, and largely lacking in extremes of partisanship in either direction.

The chief division of sentiment in the Scottish Church was more a matter of inherited custom than of principle. The Church as a whole employed the English Prayer Book of 1662. The distinctive Scottish Liturgy of 1764 existed only as a supplementary pamphlet (a 'Wee Bookie'), containing the part of the service beginning with the Offertory — together with a body of unwritten customs covering variants in the preliminary portions of it. The use of this rite was largely confined to the Highlands, the populous dioceses of Edinburgh and Glasgow adhering to the English use. A determined effort led by Dr. Charles Wordsworth, an English schoolmaster who in 1852 became Bishop of St. Andrew's, sought to bring the Scottish Church into complete conformity with the Church of England. The Canons of 1863 for the first time gave legal priority to the English Communion Service, and placed the native Scottish Rite under disabilities which might eventually have extinguished it to the vestigial status which the Mozarabic occupies in Spain.

Yet the 'faithful remnant' of the Scottish tradition produced a succession of eminent liturgical scholars, who were in truth 'the lights of the world in their several generations.' The first of these in this period was the Rev. George Hay Forbes (1821–1875), who was a collaborator with Dr. J. M. Neale of England in the investigation of liturgical origins, and a prophet much in advance of his time in the field of liturgical reform. His ideas on the revision of the Scottish Liturgy appear not only in his own parochial Use of 1862, but dominate the service of 1844 attributed to his father and brother, and also that which was published by Bishop Torry in 1849.[23] Many of these changes have been accepted in the more recent Anglican books, and more of them deserve consideration in any future revision.

The ripe fruition of this Scottish School was found in John Dowden, Bishop of Edinburgh, a deeply learned scholar, and a wise and kindly ecclesiastical statesman. His *Workmanship of the Prayer Book*, and his *Further Studies*, made most important contributions to the origins of many overlooked details in the English Prayer Books, and thus won most respectful consideration of his classical work on the Scottish Liturgy. His influence was paramount upon the revision attempted in 1889, and upon that accomplished in 1911, although he did not live to see the latter adopted.

The Scottish Draft Liturgy of 1889, to which frequent allusion has been made, for the first time proposed a text of the entire rite. When the Provincial Synod submitted it to the Diocesan Synods, it was found that the memories of the controversies between Forbes and Wordsworth[24] were still so alive that anything like unanimity was not obtainable, and the matter was dropped for the time. But this Draft has proved almost as valuable as the Scottish Book of 1637 as a mine of suggestions for subsequent revisions.

In 1911, however, the Scottish Church had no difficulty in adopting an entire Prayer Book, consisting of the English Book with permitted variations, including a complete Eucharistic Liturgy. In 1918, when both England and the United States were actively engaged in revising their Prayer Books, Scotland reopened the matter again. In 1925 the Scotch suspended work, pending the outcome of the English undertaking. After the failure of the English Book to obtain the sanction of Parliament, the Provincial Synod finished off the Scottish Book, and referred it back to the Diocesan Synods and to the new Consultative Council representing the laity of the Church. These constituent bodies accepted it with almost unanimous votes, and the Provincial Synod formally adopted it in 1929.

Some of the characteristic contributions of this latest Scottish Liturgy have been noted already, and more will be cited later. In general, the influence of the Scottish rite has been predominant upon all recent Anglican revisions. Its outstanding feature is its 'Eastern' structure of the Prayer of Consecration, with the Invocation after the Institution and Oblation: and here the Scottish order has practically swept the field. Features of the Scottish Liturgy which have exercised

---

23. John Dowden, *The Scottish Communion Office*, ed. H. A. Wilson (Oxford: The University Press, 1922) 200 f., sec. V-VII; and W. Perry, *George Hay Forbes* (London: S.P.C.K., 1927), 20–26, 45–47.

24. W. Perry, *George Hay Forbes* (London: S.P.C.K., 1927), 47–50.

little or no influence have been the restoration of the penitential devotions of 1549 before the Administration of the Communion, where the Scots stand alone, and the 'Eastern' placing of the General Intercession after the Consecration Prayer, adopted only by India.

But the Scottish Liturgy has also led the way in the restitution of many 'Western' features which had been too hastily abandoned in 1552, and even in 1549, under pressure of the Reformation phobias of Cranmer and his 'hostile friends' from the Continent. Perhaps the principal lesson to be derived from the Scottish rite is that the recovery of the primitive structure and balance of the central Consecration Prayer makes it perfectly safe to lay some of these historic bogies quietly to rest.

Revision in the Church of England

1. Resistance to Change

It may well seem to us distinctly remarkable that the Communion Service of the Second Prayer Book of 1552 should have continued in use in the Church of England for four hundred years without any essential alterations — since the changes in 1559, 1604, and 1662 touched only minor details of phraseology, affecting in all little more than a hundred words of the spoken text. This rite, in comparison with other liturgies, is both cumbersome in form, and at the same time defective in content. It possesses distinct elements of tedium, in its slow and heavy beginning with the Decalogue, and in the homiletical feature of the 'Long Exhortation' both of them required by the rubrics at every celebration. It has some serious structural defects, in the location of the Prayer of Humble Access between the *Sanctus* and the Consecration Prayer, of the Lord's Prayer relegated to the Postcommunion section, and of the *Gloria in Excelsis* transported to the end and anticlimax of the service. On the other hand, its drastically curtailed Consecration Prayer is the barest and driest form of any orthodox rite. It is indeed a sufficient liturgy, containing all the constituents necessary for a valid celebration; but it leaves much to be desired as an adequate vehicle for the Church's greatest service of worship.

These blemishes were not much felt during the more than two centuries during which the Holy Communion was administered not oftener than thrice a year in most English parishes, and when it was always celebrated in one unbroken service with Morning Prayer and the Litany. It was only when the Oxford Movement inspired multiplied celebrations, weekly and even daily, that its inconveniences became a burden; only when it stood alone, and when every word of it was weighed for its effectiveness in setting forth the great meanings borne by the rite as a whole, that its inadequacies became only too evident.

Yet though English Churchmen had followed the liturgical experiments of the Nonjurors and the evolution of the Scottish rite with interest, admiration, and even a certain envy, it was not until the latter part of the nineteenth century that it was possible for them even to think of doing anything about their own service. As an aftermath of the expulsion of the Nonjurors, the Convocations (the legislative voice of the Church) were suppressed in 1718: and they remained silenced until 1852 in the Province of Canterbury, and until 1861 in that of York.

2. *The Ritual Controversies*

By that time, new factors in the domain of worship had arisen, and absorbed all the Church's energies, in the bitter 'ritual' controversies of the 1860's and '70's.

The first generation of the leaders of the Oxford Movement had been deeply concerned with doctrine, but not at all with ceremonial. Dr. Pusey never so much as wore a stole as long as he lived. But after Newman's secession in 1845, active leadership in the Movement passed from the theologians to the 'practical' clergy, who threw their energies into exemplifying the Catholic Faith in the visible form of Catholic Worship. Few people are qualified to think in terms of basic principles: hence most 'popular' controversies have raged in terms of symbols. It is significant that the 'Catholic Revival' was never defeated on the ground of the fundamental theology of the Eucharist: the courts of England upheld the doctrines of even what Dr. DeKoven in this country apologetically admitted was 'a bald statement' of the Real Presence in the case of Bennett of Frome. But when these vindicated doctrines were clothed in the concrete forms of vestments and ceremonies, there was a different story.

The early 'Ritualists' professed strict conformity with the prescriptions of the Book of Common Prayer, and revived ceremonial plainly implied in the rubrics, which had been ignored by Puritans and Latitudinarians. First of all, they seized upon the 'Ornaments Rubric' as justifying the restoration of the Eucharistic Vestments. This was historically correct: we have noted that this rubric had been reenacted in 1662 with precisely this contingency in mind.[25] The decisions of the high secular courts which attempted to nullify the manifest meaning of this rubric were not only legally and even morally wrong — they were disastrous in their effects upon the authority of the whole ritual law of the Church of England. Up to this point, the 'Ritualists' were sincere in their aim and claim to obey that law. Those decisions, which Lord Justice Amphlett afterward stigmatized as 'flagitious,' drove them in the name of conscience to be law-breakers, in protest against an 'unconstitutional' usurpation of the State over the rights of the Church. Five clergy actually went to jail rather than to comply. Eventually the Bishops stopped the scandal of such a situation by vetoing further ritual

---

25. Page 76 f. above.

prosecutions. And this move, however equitably justified and practically necessary, was an abdication of the Church's right to regulate its own ritual. By it, the Act of Uniformity itself became a dead letter. This was more than a breakdown in control: it was a dissolution of loyalty; and it proceeded in ever-widening circles, far beyond the mere question of the Vestments.

The first wave of those who sought to express the Catholic Faith through the forms of worship maintained the principle that the traditional ceremonies accompanying that worship in the Church of England before the Reformation were still legal, where the Prayer Book did not otherwise direct. This had been unquestionably true in the First Prayer Book, which expressly (if a little grudgingly) permitted interpretative 'gestures,' and whose rubrics took for granted a familiarity with the accustomed way of rendering the pre-Reformation rites, to a degree that no service could be actually performed without a knowledge of that living tradition. And in spite of many attempts toward a more precise rubric in the subsequent Prayer Books, the latter statement remains true to the present day.

But though there are still those in England who appeal to continuity with the native English 'Use of Sarum,' and though they comprise most of those with any claim to be called liturgical scholars, they are now in the minority.[26] The greater number of the 'practical' clergy knew little, and cared less, about ultimate questions of liturgical origins. They brushed aside the structural and theological standards of the Eastern rites, as adopted by the Scottish Church, as alien, and those of Sarum as obsolete — 'British Museum ritual,' they called it. They conceived that the most effective way to exemplify the Catholic Faith was to conform to the 'Great Rite' of Rome.

This dominant group among the Anglo-Catholics were on sound ground in pointing out that the English Communion Service is in fact a 'Western Rite.' But their inference there from, that the Roman Mass (which itself is only a 'Western Rite') should be regarded as the norm, goal, and arbiter of all liturgical questions, is really not so much a necessary conclusion as it is an expression of the human tendency to follow the largest crowd. This is the same influence as absorbed the independent Alexandrian and Antiochene liturgies in the Byzantine; as extinguished the indigenous Gallican rite in France and reduced it to a vestige in Spain; and as caused the great Roman Catholic scholar Adrian Fortescue to reprimand his fellow Romanists in England for their 'excessive and uncanonical *Romanizing*' in deserting the lawful authority of their own ecclesiastical Province in order to imitate the customs of the Italian Curia.[27]

Moreover, the 'Western Rite' version of the service in many quarters did not content itself even with using the ceremonies, vestments, and music of the

---

26. Ed. note: The reference here is to scholars like Walter Frere, Percy Dearmer, and the founders of the Alcuin Club.

27. *The Ceremonies of the Roman Rite Described* (London: Burns, Oates, 1920), xxi.

Roman Mass to adorn the English text. The 'advanced' clergy went on to revive the Roman private prayers of the celebrant to accompany the elaborated ceremonies. And some priests further proceeded to supplement and even to interlard the Prayer of Consecration with excerpts from the Roman Canon. It may be noted that these measures were an admission of the poverty of the English provisions, and in themselves constituted as severe a criticism of the rite of 1552 as is represented by the Scottish line of liturgies since 1637.

Neither of the foregoing additions altered the actual rite as heard by the people, since those devotions were said inaudibly, as they were in the Latin Rite. Nevertheless, the English Book of 1928 takes exception to them by a rubric, 'Nor shall the private devotions of the Priest be such as to hinder, interrupt, of alter the course of the service.'

Eventually, however, this Romanizing went to the extreme of making an absolute breach with the text of the public service, by changing the order of parts, nullifying positive rubrical directions, and interpolating Roman features into the audible rite. Desirable or not as such importations might be (and they comprised both categories), indicative as they might be of the need of restorative revision, this method of making them on an individualistic and parochial basis was an ironical realization of the platform of the original 'Nonconformists' — those Puritans who while still members of the Church of England refused to comply with her ritual, but demanded that every 'Minister' be allowed to conduct his services precisely as he pleased.

After the collapse of the attempt of the State to dictate the ritual practices of the Church, and the abdication of administrative control by the Church authorities, the only check upon the growing anarchy was the endeavor of the individual Bishops to keep matters in bounds by personal persuasion in their dioceses. But there was one more effort to settle questions of ritual on a plane of purely spiritual authority. The two Archbishops gave judgment on a number of ceremonies on that basis in the Lambeth hearings of 1899 and 1900. Most unfortunately, they grounded their findings upon the entirely unhistorical and quite untenable premise that any action not explicitly commanded in the rubrics is expressly forbidden. Consequently, the Archbishops' 'Opinions' won little or no acceptance in the Church.

3. *The Revision of 1928*

After that fiasco, there was nothing for it but to face the task of an outright revision of the Prayer Book. In 1906, a Royal Commission appointed in 1904 reported that 'the law of public worship in the Church of England is too narrow for this generation.' It was further stated that it was necessary that this 'law should be reformed, that it should admit of a reasonable elasticity,' if there was to be any hope of achieving the paramount need 'that it should be obeyed.' Later the same year, Letters of Business were issued to the Convocations, mentioning specifically the vesture of the clergy, and more generally the whole conduct of worship, in order 'to secure the greater elasticity which a reasonable recognition of the comprehensiveness of the Church of England and of its present needs seems to demand.'

What was really the most crucial point at issue appears from the first item of the 27th Resolution of the Lambeth Conference of 1908, in laying down the general principles of Prayer Book revision: 'The adaptation of rubrics in a large number of cases to present customs as generally accepted.' This was a recognition of the fact that there had been a great shift of emphasis in the transformation of the Eucharist from a Protestant order infrequently observed to a Catholic Liturgy continually celebrated. Quite apart from individualistic extremes, this change had affected every clergyman and every parish in some degree. In many cases, the richer ceremonial had been employed for two or three generations, and acquired such an extent of prescription that any attempt to enforce the scanty provisions of 1662 would have disrupted the Church. Room had to be found for them in the official design of the Church's worship — but if possible on a permissive basis which would not coerce nor fluster the conservative survivals of a more meager age.

The work of revision was completed by the Convocations in 1920. The results were then submitted to the newly constituted Representative Church Council of the Church Assembly, which had been set up to supplement the Convocations of the two Provinces with a single legislative body integrating the whole National Church, and containing for the first time a House of Laity coordinate with the Houses of Bishops and Clergy. Instead of accepting or rejecting the labors of the Convocations as a whole, as had been expected, the Assembly insisted upon working through the whole matter over again. Seven years were consumed in this process. A great deal of popular interest was aroused. Party groups published their own proposals.

In the last six months of this time, an extraordinary agitation broke out, centering on the question of the Reservation of the Sacrament for the Communion of the Sick, with the cry that Protestantism was in danger. The result was that at the end of 1927 the Prayer Book which had passed the Convocations and the Assembly by heavy majorities, though approved by the House of Lords and by a small majority of the Churchmen in the Commons, was narrowly defeated in the Lower House by a vote which drew in Scotch and Irish Dissenters, and even a stray Parsee!

The Convocations and the Assembly went over the matter again, and effected safeguarding revisions which placed somewhat unprecedented restrictions upon the practice of Reservation. Nevertheless, when six months later they presented the Prayer Book to Parliament again, the House of Commons rejected it by an increased majority.

From one point of view, this turn of events marked some of the disadvantages inherent in the position of an Established Church, since it saw a work which had won the fullest possible approval by the Church's own legislative bodies frustrated by a political coalition in the legislature of the State, containing, as was pointed out at the time, elements 'non-Anglican, and non-English.' It must, however, be admitted that the scale was tipped in Parliament by the intransigence of some of the 'Western Rite' group of Anglo-Catholics, who opposed the new Prayer Book partly out of resentment for the novel limitations placed upon the Reservation of the Sacrament which they had long practiced, but partly also out of distaste for the Scottish and Eastern structure of the Prayer of Consecration. Such extremists were a small minority in both Convocation and Parliament: but when they joined the opposition to the new Book in the Commons, they were just as much responsible for its defeat as the die-hard Evangelicals or the Scotch Presbyterians.

The 'Prayer Book as Proposed in 1928' was therefore printed as a private venture of the publishers, not as authoritative for the Established Church. The Bishops, however, held that since it had been passed by the Church, its use in whole or in part might be permitted wherever clergy and congregations were agreed upon it. This opened up unprecedented liberties, since this 'Proposed Book' was practically a Prayer Book in duplicate, retaining nearly everything in the old ritual of 1662 as alternative to the new material.

But though some of the Occasional Offices have been widely used, conservative inertia has made the English very slow to adopt the new orders for the principal services of public worship. This has been particularly true in the case of the Eucharistic Liturgy, where the memory of recent controversies has maintained Low-Church suspicion and High-Church dislike.

But such hesitations have been entirely lacking in the other Provinces of the Anglican Communion which have carried out revisions since 1928. In Scotland, South Africa, India, and Ceylon, the achievements of the English attempt have been recognized as of very great value, and its influence has been paramount.

However, before turning to these provincial forms, it may be of service to note here some restorations of features of the First Prayer Book, and even of the pre-Reformation service, which did not find their way into the American revision of 1928, but which deserve consideration in any future revision. Most of them indeed have been adopted in later Anglican rites.

From 1549:

1. The Salutation before the *Sursum Corda*.
2. The *Benedictus qui venit* after the *Sanctus*.
3. The *Pax Domini* after the Lord's Prayer.
4. Reservation for the Communion of the Sick.
5. Provisions for shortening the service on 'work-days' which are not Holy Days, by omission of Creed, *Gloria*, etc.

Recurrences to the Sarum Mass include the following:

1. The singing of the *Kyrie Eleison* in Greek (permissive).
2. The announcing of a 'Lesson' instead of 'The Epistle,' when the portion assigned is not from a Letter of an Apostle.
3. The use of the phrase, 'the Gospel according to Saint—.'
4. The restitution of the missing word 'Holy' to the Notes of the Church in the Creed.
5. The extension of the use of the Proper Prefaces for Christmas, Easter, and Ascension from their Octaves to their Seasons.
6. The use of a separate paragraph for the Narrative of the Institution.
7. The order of the Oblation and the Commemoration reversed to conform to that of the Latin *Unde et memores*.

Provincial Revisions

The same factors of growth to the stage of self-responsibility in the course of the nineteenth and twentieth centuries which raised the principal British Colonies to the status of Dominions, and made them independent of the Parliament of Westminster, brought a parallel autonomy to the independent colonial, and even the dependent missionary, Provinces of the Church of England overseas.

The first meeting of the Lambeth Conference in 1867 resolved that 'each Province should have the right to make such adaptations and additions to the services of the Church as its peculiar circumstances may require. Provided, that no change or addition be made inconsistent with the spirit and principles of the Book of Common Prayer, and that all such changes be liable to revision by any Synod of the Anglican Communion in which the said Province shall be represented.'

It seems probable that this last stipulation envisaged the development of the Lambeth Conference from a voluntary consultative body of Anglican Bishops into some kind of international Legislature with overruling powers upon the constituent national Churches. But the evolution of this institution has been in the other direction, away from the sort of 'Anglican Papacy' which was feared by some at the time. There has never been any attempt on the part of the Conference to control the action of the Provinces.

However, the Third Conference in 1888 raised a like note of caution, advising that 'no particular portion of the Church should undertake revision without seriously considering the possible effect of such action on other branches of the Church.' The Sixth Conference in 1920 requested the Archbishop of Canterbury to appoint a Liturgical Committee to advise any Diocese or Province on matters of revision: but the Seventh Conference in 1930 discharged this Committee, since all the revisions of the previous decade had been carried out without having recourse to it.

On the other hand, from 1897 on the Bishops at Lambeth advocated a recovery of the ancient episcopal *jus liturgicum*, which in the early ages had made the Bishop the arbiter, often the creator, of forms of worship within his jurisdiction. This former exercise of the Bishop's 'liturgical right' had been much circumscribed by the canonical limitations placed upon the 'constitutional Episcopate' of post-Reformation times: so that in both England and America the only authority placed in the Bishop's hands by canon and rubric is the right to prescribe special orders of service for particular occasions. The Bishops seemed to feel that such limitations were only of a statutory order, and were to some degree an infringement upon the intrinsic 'constitutional' right of the Chief Pastor to exercise his natural leadership in the worship of his diocese.

Thus in 1897 a Resolution spoke of the right of each Bishop to 'adapt the Services in the Book of Common Prayer to local circumstances,... subject to... lawful authority, provided also that any such adaptation shall not affect the doctrinal teaching or value of the Service or passage thus adapted.' And in 1920, it was resolved that 'although the inherent rite [sic] of a Diocesan Bishop to put forth or sanction liturgical forms is subject to such limitations as may be imposed by higher synodical authority, it is desirable that such authority should not be too rigidly exercised so long as those features are maintained which are essential to the safeguarding of the unity of the Anglican Communion.'

Finally, the Conference of 1920 set forth the principles to be observed in any local revision of the Prayer Book, in terms which are admirably descriptive of all such revisions as have been made up to the present time, and which will doubtless continue to be the charter of any future changes:

a. The adaptation of rubrics in a large number of cases to present customs as generally accepted;
b. The omission of parts of the services to obviate repetition or redundancy;
c. The framing of additions to the present services in the way of enrichment;
d. The fuller provision of alternatives in our forms of worship;
e. The provision for greater elasticity in public worship;
f. The change of words obscure or commonly misunderstood.

Full advantage has been taken of all these proffered liberties in the Missionary Dioceses and the autonomous Provinces of the Church of England, in the spirit of the Resolution of 1920 at Lambeth: 'While maintaining the authority of the Book of Common Prayer as the Anglican standard of doctrine and practice, we consider that liturgical uniformity should not be regarded as a necessity throughout the Churches of the Anglican Communion.' Everywhere the ancient 'liturgical authority' of the Bishop has been wisely interpreted as an invitation to leadership, and temperately exercised 'with the advice and consent' of the local synodical authorities.

The result has been the development of a distinctive family of Anglican liturgies, reflecting much of the diversity of the historical forms of the service in the Universal Church, from the thoroughgoing 'Western Rite' of the almost completely Romanized Mass of the Diocese of Zanzibar in the Swahili vernacular, to the almost equally strong 'Eastern' emphases of the Indian Liturgy of 1933. Yet these variant rites have preserved a real unity in diversity: the Anglican quality of all of them is unmistakable, particularly in pregnant brevity of expression, and in balance of doctrine. Some of these local forms have considerably enriched the Anglican tradition by the recovery of ancient elements not utilized by Cranmer. And they have furnished a useful laboratory for trying out attractive innovations in actual practice.

1. South Africa

a) Method: The Province of South Africa embarked on its own revision in 1911, and completed it simultaneously with the Scottish in 1929. It made free but independent use of the English and Scottish proposals, with some contributions of its own. It is of special interest to us here in America on account of its method of procedure.

The South African 'House of Bishops' meets annually in Episcopal Synod. This body put out successive drafts of the Liturgy for study and criticism. When this process had had its due effect, the Provincial Synod, which meets every five years, gave the work 'general approval,' and licensed its use where desired as an alternative to the English rite of 1662. It was only after the new service had weathered this final test of employment in public worship for a sufficient period, that it was adopted and incorporated into the Prayer Book.

It was primarily this method which inspired the present undertaking of the Liturgical Commission of our Church in America, to publish the series of *Prayer Book Studies* for public consideration, criticism, and counter-suggestion.

Unfortunately, the stipulations of our written Constitution do not permit a further application of the South African procedure by licensing the proposed drafts for trial use. During our last revision of the Prayer Book completed in 1928, permission to use the new matter brought forward by the Revision Commission was widely sought, and the Commission itself was anxious to secure it. But the Canonists advised that there was no way in which this could legally be done without changing the Constitution. It might be possible to make such a change, by adding to Article X a further proviso which would permit General Convention to enact a Resolution to sanction a bishop within his jurisdiction to license the use of draft services approved by the Liturgical Commission, for such term and under such conditions as he should require, or the Resolution of General Convention prescribe.

Bold and unprecedented as such a measure might appear, there would be important values in being able to use this approach to the desired goal. It is really not possible to evaluate a proposed form of service without trying it out. Some proposals look very specious at first blush: they are what they call SOKOP in Charleston ('Seems OK On Paper') — but they need to be used exactly all of once to see that they will not work. The Liturgical Commission has had precisely this experience in its try-outs of various forms of the Draft Liturgy in closed session. Other features, however, will survive this first hurdle, but will not stand the test of repeated use: such as some of the amiable material in the English 'Grey Book,'[28] which was hailed with some enthusiasm in this country, and actually authorized for supplemental use by the General Convention of 1934; or such as some of the prayers printed in the appendix of our Prayer Book, though not actually a part of it, which speedily wear threadbare if frequently imported into the public services.

Moreover, the trial use of new services would acquaint the laity in their pews as well as the clergy in their studies with what is being proposed for the worship of the Church. They would be able to express their reactions, for or against. And perhaps the eventual consideration of the new matter in General Convention would be a less time-consuming task for that overworked body, if it were already familiar to all by such field-trials beforehand.

b) Characteristics: The content of the South African Liturgy is on the whole decidedly conservative, following the Scottish order closely. It gives the Commandments in short form only, numbered, and required to be said once a Sunday: otherwise the Summary and/or the *Kyries*. As a Missionary Church, it makes provision for dismissal of Catechumens before the Creed. In the Creed, it gives 'The Lord, The Giver of Life,' and 'One Holy Catholic and Apostolic Church.' There is a list of seasonal Offertory Sentences, and an Offertory Collect. A short form of Confession and Absolution is provided for weekdays. The Consecration Prayer begins 'All Glory and Thanksgiving be to thee,' and the commemoration of our Lord's saving Death is balanced by his Life, by saying 'didst give thine only Son our Saviour Jesus Christ *to take our nature upon him, and* to suffer death upon the Cross.' This Prayer has the peculiarity of retaining the 'Preliminary Invocation' of 1552–1662, as above on p. 60, before the Institution, and also, at the proper

---

28. Ed. Note: After the release of the English Draft Book of 1922, three partisan editions were crafted as attempts to influence the final shape of the text: the Green Book was pushed by Romanist Anglo-Catholics, the Orange Book by the moderate Anglo-Catholics of the Alcuin Club, and the Grey Book by more liberal Anglo-Catholics like William Temple (who wrote its Foreword) and Percy Dearmer.

place for an Invocation, adding 'and we humbly beseech thee to pour thy Holy Spirit upon us and upon these thy gifts, that all we who are partakers of this holy Communion may worthily receive the most precious Body and Blood of thy Son, and be fulfilled with thy grace and heavenly benediction.'

2. India and Ceylon

The Province of India, Pakistan, Burma, and Ceylon has produced *three* liturgies of the very first order of excellence, combining a comprehensive knowledge of comparative liturgiology with no common measure of judgment and literary taste and skill. Although these are the youngest of Christian liturgies, their quality makes them as worthy of attention as the oldest: and no future Anglican revision can afford to ignore some of their contributions.

a) India 1933: The Indian Rite of 1933 was the creation of the Rev. J. C. Winslow and his associates at Poona. It was licensed in 1922 by the Episcopal Synod for experimental use in the Diocese of Bombay, and in 1933 for employment throughout the Province, with permission of the Bishops of the several dioceses. It is a thoroughgoing carrying out of the Provincial Canon of 1930, 'Of the Services of the Church,' which expressed a desire 'to work towards the development of forms of worship congenial to the nature of the Indian races,' and 'to give opportunities for greater liberty of experiment in the direction of such development, but at the same time to safeguard provincial unity.'

The 'forms of worship congenial to the nature of the Indian races' were in allusion to the Eastern liturgies, versions of which had been indigenous in India long before any Roman or Protestant foot had been set in the country, in the Nestorian Mission at Malabar, which was mentioned as early as the year 527 by Cosmas Indicopleustes. After the collapse of the vast spiritual empire of the Nestorian 'Church of the East,' which once outnumbered all other Christians whatsoever, the 'Christians of St. Thomas' at Malabar lost touch with their own Patriarch, and formed a new connection with the West-Syrian Jacobites, This move brought into use a form of, the Liturgy of 'St. James of Jerusalem' — a rite which from a literary point of view has some claim to be the most admirable of historic liturgies. And it was this liturgy which Fr. Winslow's group took as the base of their construction, employing it in judicious condensation, much as Bishop Rattray had utilized its Greek form for the Nonjurors.

At the same time, the 'provincial unity' desired by the Canon of 1930 was preserved by embodying much of the structural matter of the Western forms, both Latin and English, so that the Indian Liturgy remains an authentic member of the Anglican family. Nothing could be more skilful and successful than the harmonious blending of Eastern and Western features in this liturgy.

Eastern details consist of the Preparation of the Elements at the beginning, with a Prayer of Prothesis; a Prayer of Entrance; an Enarxis Litany; a Prophetic Lesson; an Expulsion of Catechumens; the Kiss of Peace at the Offertory; a Lavabo; the Prayer of the Veil before the Anaphora; the Thanksgiving for the Creation, Preservation, and Redemption of Mankind from the Liturgy of St. James — but incorporating the South African phrase, 'to take our nature upon him'; a full-fledged 'Eastern' General Intercession within the Consecration Prayer; the *Sancta sanctis* and *Benedictus qui venit* before the Communion; words of Administration taken from the Apostolic Constitutions: 'The Body of Christ, the Bread of Life,' and 'The Blood of Christ, the Chalice of Life.'

Western features comprise the singing of the *Gloria in Excelsis* at the beginning; a Gradual Psalm and Sequence Hymn; the interpolation into the Institution Narrative of the words, 'took bread into his holy and spotless hands, and looking heavenward unto thee (*here the Priest is to look upward*), O God and Father, bles†sed, brake,' etc.; in the Invocation, 'that by his power this bread and this wine may become unto us the Bo†dy and the Bl†ood of thy Son our Saviour Jesus Christ;' and the singing of the *Agnus Dei* at the Communion-time.

b) Ceylon 1938: Meanwhile, another exceedingly intelligent development was being worked out by a committee of the Diocese of Columbo in Ceylon. It was issued for trial use in 1931 by the diocesan Synod, and sanctioned in 1938 by the Province for use in that Diocese. This rite also shows some degree of 'Eastern' influences — partly through the Indian, as in its following the 'St. James' text of the Thanksgiving for the Redemption; partly independently, as in the recasting of the Prayer for the Church into the Syrian form of a Litany. But for the most part, it employs 'Western' constituents.

Thus it incorporates the entire 'Western' Preparation, Psalm 43 and mutual Confession and Absolution, during the singing of the Introit; gives the *Kyrie eleison* in alternate ninefold form, in English or Greek, with no Decalogue or Summary; and follows this with the *Gloria in Excelsis*. The Invocation says, 'may be unto us.' The Lord's Prayer is followed by the *Pax Domini* and the *Benedictus qui venit*. The *Agnus Dei* is sung during the Priest's Communion. The Ablutions are taken at the end of the general Communion.

The tensions between Eastern and Western forms of expression work out particularly well in this form, which lacks the oriental luxuriance of the Indian 1933. It presents an able evaluation of the features of all preceding Anglican revisions, together with some distinctive contributions of its own.

c) Indian 1952: At the present moment, the Indian Church is in the process of publishing a complete new Prayer Book. And included in that work, kindly made available to us in galley-proof by the Metropolitan, the Most Rev. Arabindo Nath Mukerjee, is an entirely new version of the Liturgy, even more emphatically

'Western' in its makeup than the Rite of Ceylon.[29] This form marks a considerable reaction against the very free 'Eastern' Liturgy of 1933, and a sedulous restoration of characteristic Anglican features light-heartedly abandoned in the previous efforts in India and Ceylon. This Prayer Book is due to contain this new form of 'The Holy Eucharist,' The Order for Holy Communion' (1662), and 'The Indian Liturgy' (1933). Certainly a fair field and no favor, trying out widely different forms in active competition with each other, in the same Church!

This new Liturgy, provisionally cited throughout this book by the date of the proofs, begins with the Latin Preparation during the Introit. Then, after the Lord's Prayer and the Collect for Purity, come the Commandments, in short form, and numbered, to be said once a month: at other times the Summary and/or the *Kyries*, the latter in alternate ninefold form, in English or Greek. The Salutation may be used before the Gospel, and Alleluia may be added to the responses before and after the Gospel, except from Septuagesima to Easter Even. The Creed says, 'Through him all things were made,' 'His kingdom shall have no end,' 'the Lord, the giver of life,' 'One Holy Catholic and Apostolic Church.' 'Then may follow the Sermon.' Eleven Offertory Sentences are followed by 19 seasonal Sentences. The Bread and Wine are 'offered up, and placed upon the Holy Table.' Representatives of the congregation may bring up the Elements. 'In the meanwhile' the Alms are being collected, 'to be presented and placed upon the Holy Table,' and the Scottish Presentation Sentences are said. The Prayer for the Church includes supplications for Missionaries, and against famine; ignorantly displaces the supplication for Rulers; and has rather brief supplications for the Departed, and thanksgiving for the Saints. This Prayer may be said in Litany form. The Invitation, Confession, Absolution, and Comfortable Words must be said at least once on Sundays and Feast Days, but may be omitted at other times, if the Preparation has been said with the congregation.

Proper Prefaces are provided for Advent, the Presentation, Lent, Passion-tide, Maundy Thursday, the Transfiguration, Apostles and Evangelists, the Consecration of a Church, Ordinations, missionary occasions, the founding of a Diocese, common Sundays, and requiems, besides all those now in our Prayer Book.

After the *Sanctus*, the Prayer of Consecration begins 'Holy in truth art thou, and blessed in truth,' and includes the words, 'to take our nature upon him' (South African) and 'renew thine image within us ' ('St. James') — both in the Indian 1933: the rest of the text of this Thanksgiving follows the English 1928. The South African rite is followed in inserting the passage 'Hear us,' the Invocation of 1552–1662, between this Thanksgiving and the Institution. But in the proper place for the Invocation, after the Oblation, the petition is 'to send down thy holy and life-giving

---

29. Ed. Note: The Church of South India was created in 1947 through a union of Methodist, Presbyterian, and Congregationalist church bodies with the Anglican provinces in Southern India and Ceylon (now Sri Lanka). Thus, the draft Eucharist mentioned here is that which would appear in the 1963 *Book of Common Prayer* of the Church of South India.

Spirit upon these thy gifts, to hallow this oblation of the Body and Blood of Jesus Christ our Lord; entirely desiring thy fatherly goodness to accept upon thine altar on high this our sacrifice of praise and thanksgiving,' etc. This most extraordinary expression does actually 'offer Christ,' as the Roman Mass does not, and as no other liturgy has ever done. Cranmer would have excommunicated them!

The Lord's Prayer is followed by the *Pax*, the *Benedictus qui venit*, and the *Agnus Dei*. After the Humble Access, there is a short Bidding to Communion, with permission to omit the second half of the 1559–1662 Sentences of Administration. The Ablutions may be taken at the end of the general Communion, or after the Blessing. The Thanksgiving is prefaced by the Salutation and a short Bidding. The *Gloria* may be omitted on the Sundays in Advent and from Septuagesima to Palm Sunday, and upon weekdays which are not Holy Days, except that it must be said every day from Easter to Trinity Sunday. A so-called 'Post-Communion Prayer' may be said before the Blessing. Twenty-five alleged 'Post-Communion' prayers are printed after the service. Out of the entire lot, exactly one is qualified to serve as a true Post-Communion. The rest are fair-to-middling 'Super Populum' prayers.[30]

This latest-born of Anglican liturgies is somewhat stiff, and has rather too much of the aridities of the English 1662, too much also of the copying of Roman standards, to win many adherents in this day and age. The Indian 1933 and the Ceylon 1938 are much better representatives of the latest stage of Anglican liturgical development. And such of their features as are not obviously of purely local significance and value merit most serious consideration in any American revision which would take due account of the possibilities of its work.

Conclusions

The foregoing review of the evolution of the Eucharistic Liturgy in various times and places has provided us with a convincing picture of unity in diversity. Its organizing principles, the integral design of its grand religious action, its fundamental theological and devotional import — these characteristics are primordial, in its apostolic beginnings: and they have never changed. But throughout its history, the details of the rite have shown infinite mutability in length, in order, and in expression — yet without being able to destroy or even appreciably to distort the intrinsic meaning of the whole. So long as the Eucharist continues to be celebrated by whatever rite, the sheer force of what it does makes its witness imperishable.

This quality of essential unity, without any need for the shackles of uniformity, is particularly in evidence within the Anglican family of liturgies. From the time of Cranmer, the English rites have been the heirs of the liturgical traditions

---

30. Cf. p. 314 ff.

of both East and West, combining and harmonizing their vital contributions, and embodying the devotional richness of the ages with much of the creative freshness of the Primitive Church. We have seen how some Provinces have been able to approach either the Eastern or the Western pole of emphasis in the text of the liturgy, without losing the distinctive values of the other standpoint, and therefore without ceasing to be characteristically Anglican.

Very many changes, covering nearly every possible feature of the rite, have been urged upon the Liturgical Commission, for the better adapting of our existing service to the varied needs of the present day. We have found that the evaluation of these suggestions falls into much better perspective when we have examined just what has been done with such proposals in the numerous recent Anglican revisions.

But beyond that, we have sought to apply all that could be gathered of present knowledge and experience to the best attainable expression of the purpose and meaning of the rite as it has come down to us. This led us to a comparative study of all the Christian liturgies, historical and contemporary. Since we do not have a Basil or a Cranmer to write new prayers, nor even a Johann Burchard to devise more perspicuous rubrics, for the most part we have not attempted to insert any innovations of our own. The most practical method we have found to be an attempt at a better utilization of existing Anglican material, duly adopted and tested in practice in the Prayer Books of other branches of our Church in full communion with our own. Just as our first American Prayer Book of 1789 drew upon the Scottish Liturgy of 1764, as our Book of 1892 took features of the Scottish Draft Liturgy of 1889, and as our last revision in 1928 availed itself of the revisions then going on in England and Scotland, so now we have not only restudied these and other past achievements of liturgical construction, but we have given careful attention to the rituals in successful use in some of the other Provinces of the Anglican Communion.

Part Two: Proposals For The Revision of The Liturgy

General Considerations

1. *The Need of Revision*

a. Insufficiency of the Last Revision: It is very apparent that a revision of our Eucharistic Liturgy is considerably overdue. Every other branch of the Anglican Communion which has undertaken to bring its Prayer Book up to date has made radical alterations in the text of this service. All of these revisions have captured the initiative which we in America had, a little fatuously perhaps, thought that we possessed. Ever since our first American Prayer Book of 1789, we had felt a certain complacency in the superior advancement of our liturgy in comparison with the 'frozen' English Rite of 1662, and were disposed to congratulate ourselves on its various 'modern improvements' along the lines of greater richness, completeness, balance, and flexibility. We looked up to the Scottish line, which had given us these advantages, and in 1892 and again in 1928 had shown ourselves willing to accept further betterments from that source but rather conservatively withal; we did not really believe that our rite needed any alterations in its basic text, though it might gain by minor rearrangements and added detail.

Resistance to change of any sort was still nearly at its maximum in 1928. Moreover, our revision completed in that year was brought to an end before there was time to digest the rather far-reaching changes which were then being proposed in England and Scotland. The revisions made since that time in the British Dominions and Missionary Provinces have had opportunity properly to assimilate that material, and to carry on its principles to further achievements of the best presentation of our ancient inheritances for the use of our modern age. The result is that we have lost our pride of place, real or imagined, and can no longer flatter ourselves that we are in the forefront of the procession.

The natural reluctance to change language endeared by generations of devotional use which operates as a strong, and very proper, deterrent to Prayer Book revision of any kind, is particularly potent in a service so central, so charged with the highest and deepest emotions, as the Eucharist. Dr. Huntington's Committee for the revision of 1880–1892 was frankly afraid to tamper with it at all, and passed a sort of 'self-denying ordinance,' forswearing any 'serious' revision of the 'Liturgy proper, namely, the Office of the Holy Communion,' as the price of being able to secure any general Prayer Book revision whatever. Again, in 1928, while there were a few changes of arrangement, and some additions of marginal enrichments, the basic texts of such prominent features as the General Confession, the Prayer for the Church, and the Consecration Prayer, were not touched at all.

b. The Breakdown of Uniformity: Admitting all the perils and difficulties of revising the Liturgy, the task cannot be avoided. There can be no doubt as to the dangerous degree of dissatisfaction in the Church with our present service. It is not a mere question of individual idiosyncracies, as in the case of parsons who take it upon themselves to amend particular phrases according their own taste and understanding, such as changing *'punishment'* to *'correction* of wickedness and vice' in the Intercession. It is the distinctly ominous fact that large sections of the clergy are expressing their criticisms of the service in the absolute manner of refusing to follow the provisions of the Book of Common Prayer.

Many clergy all over the Church, and regardless of party, largely ignore the rubrics requiring the reading of the 'Long Exhortation' thrice a year, and of the

Decalogue at one celebration a month. The rubrics on the place for the insertion of 'Occasional Collects' are commonly either misunderstood or disregarded. The Sentences for the Administration of the Holy Communion are variously abbreviated. There is an increasing tendency to eliminate the Gloria in Excelsis upon ordinary Sundays. And many clergy bypass the 1662 rubric requiring the consumption of the surplus of the consecrated Elements after the Blessing, by taking the Ablutions at the end of the general Communion.

One group of clergy often abridge or omit the Great Intercession on weekdays, or even on Sundays when they conceive themselves to be in a hurry. They also have been known to curtail the Prayer of Consecration by leaving out the last paragraph, or even more — sometimes to an extent which raises a serious question as to whether they have left enough to constitute a valid celebration.

Another group are wont to import a Preparation and a Last Gospel, not as private devotions, but as a part of the public service. Some of them decline to obey the rubrics requiring the celebrant to kneel for the General Confession and the Prayer of Humble Access, because such ceremonies are unknown to Rome. They add the Salutation, 'The Lord be with you,' before the Collect for Purity, the announcement of the Gospel, the Offertory, the *Sursum Corda*, and the 'Postcommunion.' They have the *Kyries* sung in Greek, and transfer the *Gloria* from one end of the service to the other. They omit the Communion devotions of Invitation, Confession, Absolution, Comfortable Words, and Humble Access, from celebrations at which, contrary to the intent if not the letter of the rubric, no communions of the people are allowed.

These various kinds of ritual disobedience, of which the above are examples rather than an exhaustive list, are no doubt serious enough, since they mark the breakdown of even a reasonable degree of uniformity in that essential service which is the fundamental tie of the Church's unity. But let us lay all partisanship aside, and forego the luxury of 'viewing with alarm' the flagitious outrages perpetrated by our personal ecclesiastical opponents. Let us consider these varied infractions of our ritual law for what they really are in their origin and intent, namely as the most serious sort of criticism of the rite which we have inherited, as imperfectly adapted to manifest needs of the present day. It needs to be recognized that it is the logic of the situation, not the perverseness of a 'rebellious house,' which cries aloud for an ameliorative revision.

It is one of the paradoxes of our Anglo-Saxon democratic inheritance that we combine a quite genuine respect for the law in theory, with a frank disregard for inconvenient statutes in practice. This is not Pharisaism, but an expression of the principle that the only substantive 'law' which we recognize as having a moral imperative upon our actions is that which represents the common consent of the people. If an individual breaks that law, we consider that he is to blame, and deal with him accordingly. When the majority of the people annul the operation of a law by refusing to obey it, it obviously no longer represents the mind of the people — the law is wrong, and ought to be changed. Though it may remain on the books, it is no longer a living law, but a 'dead letter' — an unenforceable statute. Most unhappily, something of very much these dimensions has befallen the great Act of Uniformity of the Mother Church of England, thanks to the legal impasse of the frustrated Revision of 1928. It does seem that we ought to be willing to come to grips with any measures, however thoroughgoing, which may be required to meet proved needs, to put an end to any large-scale disobedience and 'nonconformity' in our own Church, and to avert the very evident dangers which are latent in such a situation of divided counsels and discordant practices.

c. The Principle of Flexibility: Of course it is manifestly impossible to satisfy everybody. It might be very readily imagined that it would be futile even to begin to try to do so, since it might be thought that the desires of opposing parties in the Church would be mutually incompatible. Yet in a surprising number of instances this turns out not to be the case. Our present liturgy makes a good deal of use of the principle of flexibility, noting normal constituents of the service which may be omitted, and other features which may be added, at the discretion of the officiant, who may lawfully mold the rite to his particular requirements without breaking its pattern. Much of the ritual disobedience which now threatens our unity is really a demand for the extension of this principle, with further rubrical provisions to meet needs which are acutely felt.

Thus it would be generally conceded that the length of our present liturgy is entirely adapted to most of its uses; that something of its present dimensions should be retained as its norm; and that not a great deal of attention need be paid to the complaints of some clergy who groan under the self-imposed obligation of a daily celebration. Yet there are some city parishes which have met with eager response to weekday services which can, with some self-sacrifice, be attended by business people, whether on their way to work in the early morning, or even at noon, in time squeezed out of their lunch-hour. For such people, there is a real need for provisions like Cranmer included in his First Prayer Book, for a celebration 'on the workedaye,' allowing the omission of such normal constituents as *Gloria,* Creed, and Comfortable Words, and reducing the rite to its briefest essentials. And on the other hand, in almost every parish there are occasions to justify the most elaborate attainable 'Cathedral' type of service, provided with the richest ceremonial magnificence and the fullest musical adornments. Now all three of these classes of celebrations, and every gradation between them, can be secured with the same basic text and pattern by judicious rubrics conveying lawful permission to choose, to add, and to omit.

What is chiefly needed in order to attain a reasonable degree of general satisfaction for all parties is a certain generosity of approach. It is perfectly possible for anyone not to care for a given 'embellishment' proposed for optional use in the service, and even for him to have a firm intention never to employ it himself, and yet to be considerate enough of the wishes of other people to refrain from trying to block its use by those who are asking for it. Just for example, there does not happen to be a single clerical member of the Liturgical Commission who has ever felt any desire to have the *Kyries* sung in Greek at his own services. But since there is a perfectly good reason why some people want this particular form, and since it is permitted in the rites of England, India, and Ceylon, it would certainly seem a little churlish of us not to propose this variant for the judgment of the Church.

Accordingly, the Commission has made a point of considering all the 'partisan' suggestions made to us carefully, upon their own merits, with no regard at all to the fact that certain people have considered them to be partisan. We have refused to let ourselves be prejudiced by their origins, or their advocates, and have examined only their potential usefulness. When they were found to have value, room could usually be made for them in the flexible structure of the rite — and that without altering in any way the meaning of the service.

d. The Balance of Doctrine: This last point is of paramount importance. The first words of the Preface of the American Prayer Book, adopted in 1789, present the keynote of the ruling principle of our worship ever since: 'It is a most invaluable part of that blessed "liberty wherewith Christ hath made us free," that in his worship different forms and usages may without offence be allowed, provided the substance of the Faith be kept entire.' That has been the foundation-stone of the work of the Liturgical Commission toward the revision of the Eucharistic Liturgy. Since the various national Churches of the Anglican family have found it practicable to permit a considerable latitude of 'different forms and usages,' while remaining in the most cordial intercommunion with each other, we have considered it desirable to make many of those variants available within the structure of the same service, for use within the same Church, and even within the same parish, as occasion may arise. Yet at the same time we have been constantly vigilant not to introduce any change of underlying doctrine in the liturgy that has come down to us. And more than that, we have diligently sought to avoid altering the existing balance of doctrine. To do so would restrict the comprehensiveness of the Church. Our objective has been a greater liberty for all, not a narrower *locus standi* for any.

A crucial example, which brings to light about the only instance where we found any real difficulty in harmonizing the desires of opposing parties, appears in the wish of one group to see the Invocation expressed in more definite and 'operative' terms, and the objections of another circle to the admittedly scriptural language of the Prayer of Humble Access as being only too harshly definite. It is obviously impossible to satisfy both factions. It would involve a serious upset of the present balance of doctrine to give in to either. The Invocation cannot express the doctrine of the Objective Real Presence in such terms as to leave no room in the Church for those who happen to be vague on that subject, but have a firm grasp on the subjective truth, and sincerely believe in a Real Communion. Yet the Humble Access ought not to be watered down until it takes away from those who value it what they feel to be a great devotional confirmation of their faith. Therefore, though for other reasons we are proposing certain modifications of the language of both passages, we have done our best to leave their theological meanings exactly as they are.

The general fact is that the comprehensiveness of the Church, especially as expressed in the latitude of belief about the Eucharist which is permitted by all the Anglican liturgies, is something much more than an expression of the celebrated Anglican 'genius for compromise.' It is based upon a recognition of the fact that the Sacraments are exactly what the Greeks have always called them, namely 'Mysteries.' They are realities which we experience, but which are beyond the capacity of the human mind completely to comprehend. This is exactly what we should expect, since they are 'extensions' of the Mystery of the Incarnation, of which precisely the same statement is true. No formula which the wit of man has ever devised for the explanation of the Eucharist is wholly and exhaustively true. On the other hand, there is no such explanation that has not proved to be the only avenue of approach to its reality which is open to some type of mind. And certainly it is not for us to shut any of these doors against those who seek the Presence of the Lord.

2. *The Title of the Service*

The general title of the service ought to be clearly expressive of its distinctive character and content; it should be inclusive of the particular emphases given it in the Church, and present those emphases in an impartially balanced form; and it should furnish a convenient term of reference by which to speak of it in uncontroversial connections.

1. In the First Prayer Book: The title which Cranmer affixed in the First Prayer Book quite evidently had those objectives in mind. It read:

THE SVPPER OF THE LORDE,
AND THE HOLY COMMUNION
COMMONLY CALLED THE MASSE.

This combined the Reformation slogan of 'The Lord's Supper' with the familiar pre-Reformation designation of 'The Mass.' It threw primary emphasis upon 'The Holy Communion' as the *terminus ad quem* of the action, as both Catholics and Protestants would admit. And it retained the useful handle of 'The Mass' as a term of reference.

Yet two of these three terms were not really fortunate choices. One of them was almost immediately dropped; and in the light of present knowledge, it appears that the other ought to be also.

a) *The Mass:* The word 'Mass' has a rather peculiar, and entirely undistinguished, origin. It is derived from the Deacon's proclamation, *Ite, missa est* --'Go, [the congregation] is dismissed.' In medieval Latin, the participial form *missa* was used as a verbal noun, for *missio* or 'dismissal.' Now there were two Dismissals in the service, that of the Catechumens after the Lections, and that of the Faithful at the end. So by the figure of speech known as *metonymy* (the transfer of the name of a part to designate the whole), the terms 'The Mass' (Dismissal) 'of the Catechumens' and 'The Mass of the Faithful' were assimilated to be handy terms of reference for the two divisions of the rite which concluded with those Dismissals. And when the Dismissal of the Catechumens fell into complete disuse, the word was applied to the whole service.

Thus this word, which is now overloaded with semantic connotations, proudly esteemed by some and detested by others, started out as the most nearly meaningless term ever employed. It has completely lost its original denotation, and exists only upon the connotations which it has acquired. In other words, it means only what its users — or hearers — understand it to mean.

For a long time, its connotations were only of a 'celebration' of any sort. To this day, the word 'Messe' in German is applied quite indifferently to the Eucharistic Liturgy, or to a village fair! And, in the light of Cranmer's known views upon the Liturgy, it would seem certain that in 1549 he retained it only in the general and neutral sense of 'the celebration of the Sacrament.'

However, late medieval times provided it with the very significant connotation of 'The Eucharistic Sacrifice': and this meaning is now accepted as its primary significance. Anglicans who now employ it do so in that sense. It seems perfectly possible that Cranmer did not mean to exclude even this meaning, if it were rightly understood, since he certainly regarded the Eucharistic Sacrifice not as something to be denied, but to be defined. It was not until the Council of Trent that the Church of Rome officially declared the Mass to be 'a sacrifice truly *propitiatory.*' Cranmer did reject that concept. It has never had any recognition in our Church; and it is not what the vast majority of Anglicans who use the term mean by it. Unfortunately, it is just what those who do not use it understand by it. Hence the use of the word is the source of considerable friction and mutual miscomprehension. In any case, it is very inconvenient to be continually explaining that we are employing it only in its early medieval sense, of a Sacrifice which is Eucharistic, but not Propitiatory. So it is quite impracticable to suggest any official recognition of it: this in spite of the fact that as a term of reference it is more handy than any other.

Further, it may be observed that the liturgical scholars of the Roman Church are not fond of the word 'Mass,' but show an increasing tendency to employ the far more distinguished and significant term 'Liturgy' in the titles of their books.

b) The Lord's Supper: The expression, 'The Lord's Supper,' was strongly featured by all the Reformers. The phrase occurs only once in Holy Scripture, in 1 Cor. 11:20: 'When ye come together therefore into one place, this is not to eat the Lord's supper.' St. Paul was speaking of what was then an undivided observance of *Agapé* and Eucharist; and the gravamen of what he says is a criticism of the Corinthians for treating as a *common* meal what they ought to remember is also a *sacred* meal. In the strict sense, the expression has no application to an observance which does *not* contain a meal. It is properly used only with a reference to the Last Supper itself (as in the Roman title of Maundy Thursday, *Feria quinta in Cœna Domini*), or as St. Paul does, to a combined *Agapé*-Eucharist. It may also be used descriptively, with certain expressed or understood limitations, for such forms as in the *Didaché*, which preserves so much of the rite of the Last Supper as affects the Sacrament.

While it is also true that the Fathers occasionally refer to 'The Lord's Supper' when they wish to substantiate the identity of the action of the Catholic Liturgy with that of the Last Supper, it was never a term for the Liturgy alone before the Reformation. The Reformers seized upon this *hapax legomenon* of Scripture to draw an entirely new contrast of their own invention between the communion-feast which they considered the Eucharist to be, and the 'Sacrifice of the Mass' which they maintained that it was not.

Since then, the modern investigations of liturgical sources, of which some account has been given in Part I of this Study, have entirely appropriated this expression to yet another contrast, namely between the 'Last Supper' type of table-prayers, and the developed structure of the Liturgy. From that historical point of view, it is distinctly misleading to speak of 'The Lord's Supper or Holy Communion' in the title of the service.

We can still continue to refer to 'the Sacrament of the Lord's Supper' (as Article XVIII and the Catechism do), for the purpose of maintaining, with the Fathers, the eternal unity of the Sacrament which Christ ordained to be observed until his coming again. That idea, and that witness of the Church, will by no means be lost to the Prayer Book if we remove the expression from the title of this service.

One additional reason of some weight for dropping the phrase from the title is that it is quite useless as a term of reference. It is impossible to form a plural of it without being comical: one cannot speak of a parish's having 'three early Lord's Suppers on Whitsunday!'

2. The Present Title

The title we now use has remained unchanged since it was adopted in 1552: 'The Order for the administracion of the Lordes Supper or holy Communion.' It has several distinct shortcomings.

a) The Order for: No doubt the expression 'The Order for' was in imitation of the 'Orders for' the offices of Morning and Evening Prayer, already in use in 1549. One effect of it is to break down the distinction between the Liturgy *par excellence* and those other 'regular services of public worship.' In 1552, it was probably intended to do just that.

Beyond that, the term is an inconvenience to liturgical students, one of whose first tasks is to learn to discriminate between an 'Order,' which sets forth a structural plan of a service which may vary in nearly all its constituent parts, and a developed 'Liturgy,' which prescribes a fixed text of at least a Canon or Anaphora. In this exact use of words, the phrase is accurate for Morning Prayer, but it does not apply to the Liturgy.

b) The Holy Communion: We have noted that the equating of the expressions 'The Lord's Supper,' and 'The Holy Communion,' however justified when we are maintaining that we now are partakers of the same benefits as the Apostles at the Last Supper, is a source of confusion in a title.

The term, 'The Holy Communion,' is quite unexceptionable. Strictly speaking it applies to the actual reception of the Sacrament, or to the part of the service in which that Sacrament is administered. The Church of Rome uses it quite as frequently as we do, but only in those restricted senses. Its employment as a designation of the service as a whole is just such a metonymy as the Roman use of the word 'Mass.' Certainly such a metonymy is quite as justified, and infinitely more meaningful. We, have no cause to be ashamed of it on any ground.

This expression also furnishes a 'term of reference' which is acceptable for most purposes. In that respect, however, it has two limitations. We cannot speak of 'Communions' without leaving some uncertainty as to whether we are talking about the number of services, or of communicants. Hence if we mean 'services,' we usually desert the word in favor of saying 'celebrations.'

And this need for importing a term which is not in the title points to the second defect. The present designation speaks only of 'the *Administration* of the ... Holy Communion.' This is perfectly accurate: the Holy Communion, as such, is something which is *administered* and *received*, rather than something which is *celebrated*. It is true that the rubrics of even the First Prayer Book spoke indifferently of the 'ministracion' and the 'celebracion' alike of 'the Lordes supper' and 'the holy Communion.' This also can be defended, as the sort of verbal shortcut which we are constantly taking, assuming for granted an intermediate step which is not expressed. Nevertheless, this telescoping of thought has the disadvantage of obscuring the underlying fact, that the Sacrament of the Holy Communion can only be administered from a Eucharistic Sacrifice which has been celebrated. The omitted step throws the phrase out of proper balance, with all its emphasis upon the *administration*, none on the *celebration*.

3. The Scottish Title

Evidently due account was taken of the foregoing considerations in the proving-ground of the small, consentient, and independent Episcopal Church of Scotland: for their Prayer Book since 1912 has supplied the service with the really adequate title of 'The Scottish Liturgy for the Celebration of the Holy Eucharist and Administration of Holy Communion.' Here for the first time we have a designation which attains what Cranmer was trying to achieve in the days of the First Prayer Book, a form which is distinctive, balanced, and usable.

a) The Liturgy: 'The Liturgy' is a specific, esteemed, and impartial term for the form of the service. It is entirely neutral in its implications, since its original and etymological meaning is literally 'Public Service.' All branches of the Eastern Churches employ it exclusively to designate this service. While it is true that English usage has generalized it again to take in any fixed form of public worship, its distinctive use as denoting the service for the Eucharist par eminence is well known to the literate, and this proper understanding of it can with little effort be restored in the minds of everyone. It affords a convenient term of reference to this service, whether in rubrics or in exposition, where we are now compelled to resort to various awkward circumlocutions.

b) The Eucharist: In like manner, the word 'Eucharist' has equal value in expressing the content of the rite. It is as ancient as any term which can be used, being found in the *Didaché*, and having its roots in numerous texts of the New Testament itself — notably Matt. 26:27, Mark 14:23, Luke 23:17, 19, 1 Cor. 11:24 and 14:17, Phil. 4:6, and 1 Tim. 2:1. Though at one time it was something of an exotic in our language, it is now in constant use in some quarters, and is generally understood everywhere. The Prayer Book already contains it, in the Office of Institution. It is the only expression for the essential character of the service which has been universal in all ages, in all parts of the historic Church: and which at no time or place has been beclouded with deforming misconceptions or invidious connotations of any kind. It fills in the gap which has been noted in our present title with a description of the kind of Sacrifice which is 'celebrated,' in positive and entirely noncontroversial terms.

Once this 'Celebration of the Holy Eucharist' has supplied an expression of the corporate and objective action of the Church, then the 'Administration of the Holy Communion' falls into its proper place, completing the description by indicating the personal and individual participation which is the objective of that action — without which indeed it cannot be fully corporate, performed *by* as well as *for* the whole company of the faithful.

Again, this second phrase preserves the most common 'term of reference' which we now employ. Anyone may continue to speak of the service as a whole as 'The Holy Communion,' in case he should find 'The Liturgy' too unaccustomed, or 'The Holy Eucharist' too precious.

3. Subtitles

The Scottish Prayer Book of 1637 began the good work of giving subtitles to the constituent parts of the services in the rubrics. This device obviously has great practical advantages, both for cross-references to other portions of the services in the rubrics, and for devotional instruction and exposition of the Prayer Book offices.

All the recent Anglican revisions exploit this procedure still further, by marking the major divisions of the various offices with headings in small capitals — this in addition to the former captions of individual features in italics, or embedded in the text of the rubrics. The Liturgical Commission has adopted this method in its recommendations for all services throughout the Prayer Book. And we have endeavored to carry it out clearly and consistently in the Liturgy, for not only is the overall organizing structure of the whole rite of paramount importance for a right understanding of the great action, but there is no constituent detail which is without its distinctive significance.

This undertaking must be executed thoroughly, and not on the more or less hit-or-miss basis which is shown in our present service. On p. 73 of the Prayer Book, it is very well to have the heading *The Collect*, to designate the Collect alluded to in the previous rubric; but in practice we always speak of it as 'The Collect for Purity,' in order to distinguish it from 'The Collect of the Day.' Likewise, on p. 323 the rubric alludes to 'The Prayer of Humble Access': yet that prayer on p. 82 is not so entitled — though it is in the Scottish Liturgy.

The major subtitles of the Communion Service in the English Revision of 1928 are: The Introduction, The Ministry of the Word, The Offertory, The Intercession, The Preparation, The Consecration, The Communion of Priest and People, and The Thanksgiving. Analogous subdivisions, with some variations, appear in the liturgies of Scotland, South Africa, India, and Ceylon.

Without going into all the pros and cons of this scheme, it may suffice to say that we have come to the conclusion that it errs in both directions: it is too detailed to give a lucid idea of the main movements of the service; and at the same time it is not detailed enough to give names to all the constituents which it is desirable to designate.

It is a rather curious circumstance that the radical rearrangements of the Communion Service of 1552 gave it, and its descendants to the present day, very much the same structural shape as that of the Eastern Liturgies. The Greek rites are composed of four major divisions: The Prayers of the Catechumens, The Prayers of the Faithful, The Anaphora, and The Holy Communion. Our service naturally falls into the same four chief movements. Two of the Greek descriptions are not usable, being technical terms requiring more explanation than they are worth. To secure expressions which are readily understood, we are proposing to substitute headings from the contemporary Anglican books. We suggest:

I. THE MINISTRY OF THE WORD, from the beginning through the Lections, Creed, and Sermon.

II. THE OFFERTORY, comprising the Offertory, Intercession, and penitential preparation for the Communion.

III. THE CONSECRATION, from the *Sursum Corda* through the Lord's Prayer.

IV. THE HOLY COMMUNION, to the end of the service.

Then, within this general framework, we consider it very desirable that each constituent feature should have its own title in italics. Some few of them do now; some others are named in the small type of the rubrics. But if each feature has its own designation, it will serve as a most convenient 'handle' to pick up each item from the page in the instruction of 'the youth and others' in the 'Liturgy of the Church;'[31] — as well as conveying its own teaching on the parts of the service to all who use the Prayer Book.

Thus on p. 75 we have a sort of clot of rubrics covering the Collect, Epistle, Gradual, and Gospel. At present, they are little more than a stumbling-block to the laity who are following the book. The two responds at the Gospel stand out on the page in much more prominence than the major constituents at that point. The arrangement of this matter in the Draft Liturgy makes clear to the eye and the mind what the important elements are, and the relation between them.[32]

4. *The Order of Parts*

For the most part, we are not proposing changes in the familiar order of the elements of the service. We may or may not agree with the reasons which prompted the radical rearrangements of the Second Prayer Book: but nearly all of them have approved themselves in use where they now are, as constituting a rational and

---

31. Canon 45, sec. 2 (a).

32. Cf. p. 359.

satisfactory pattern. It does not seem desirable, for example, to follow the Scottish Rite in putting the Intercession between the Consecration Prayer and the Lord's Prayer, and the penitential preparation immediately before the Communion.

1. The Beginning and Ending of the Service: But the attention of the Liturgical Commission has repeatedly been drawn to rather widespread dissatisfactions with the beginning and the ending of the Liturgy. Neither passage is as clear-cut, facile, and concise as is to be desired. The service is distinctly slow in getting under way; and at the other end, it seems difficult to get it stopped!

The natural instincts of devotion which throughout history have sought to embellish the liturgy with adornments have always been particularly busy with the preparation and the conclusion of the rite. As early as the fifth century, the Church of Constantinople prefixed a Preparation of the Elements in a service of 'Prothesis,' which by the sixteenth century had been elaborated until it was almost a liturgy in itself. And this Church added on to the end a trail of concluding devotions, the distribution of holy bread, individual parting benedictions, and final prayers in the sacristy.

During the medieval period the Church of Rome evolved an extended Preparation of the Ministers, consisting of pre-Communion prayers, prayers of vesting, the 43rd Psalm, mutual Confession and Absolution, *preces*, and Collect. Originally, all of this was said in the sacristy; most of it was still said there in the Use of Sarum; but in Roman custom the portion beginning with the Psalm came to be used before the altar, and thus invaded the public service.

Similarly, the Deacon's proclamation, 'Go — the congregation is dismissed,' once ended the Roman Mass: compare Dom Gregory Dix's amusing but accurate paraphrase, 'That's all, gentlemen; good morning!' But there have been continual accretions at this point. The Roman Rite now adds the afterthought of the prayer *Placeat*; then a sacerdotal Benediction, borrowed from the bishop's blessing of his people as he goes out in the recessional; then the Christmas Gospel, formerly a private devotion of the Celebrant on his way back to the sacristy, now another invasion of the public service. Since 1884, prayers in the vernacular have been prescribed after Low Mass — *Ave Maria, Salve Regina*, 'St. Michael the Archangel, defend us in battle!' At present, the *Benedicite*, the 150th Psalm, *preces*, and collects, are prescribed for the Celebrant to say during his return from the altar. Some day those might get into the public service also.

In the nature of things, there can be no limitation upon, the right of the Celebrant to say as many private devotions as he finds edifying — always provided, as the English Book of 1928 sensibly observes, that 'they shall not be such as to hinder, interrupt, or alter the course of the Service.' Late medieval times brought a good many such prayers into the text of the Mass, to accompany necessary actions during the service, which they adorned without protracting it at all. And as purely private devotions, said inaudibly, they were not properly part of the public rites as such. We have observed that Cranmer did not include them in what he designed to be a 'Book of *Common* Prayer.'

It is rather another matter when such devotions are added on to the public service at the beginning and ending, so that their ceremonies, and (in a service in English) their text, become a part of the accepted pattern. The Liturgical Commission records that it has had requests for the addition of the 43rd Psalm, etc., at the beginning of the Liturgy, and a 'Last Gospel' at the end. We do not feel able to recommend that any sanction be given to such features. We consider that at the present juncture it is more important to simplify the stated beginning and ending of the Liturgy, than to add a further overload to those portions. Such additions are certainly in no way illegal, since no limitations can be placed upon devotions performed before a given service begins, or after it ends. We do not advocate their incorporation into the public service, but propose to leave them in their present status of private devotions.

It is true that the text of a Latin type of Preparation before Mass is included in the Diocesan Uses of Zanzibar, Nyasaland, and Antigua, as well as in a new Western Rite version of the Liturgy incorporated in the Prayer Book of the Church of India, Pakistan, Burma, and Ceylon which is now on the press — offered alternatively with the Eastern Indian Rite, of which an account has been given above. On the other hand, it is reported that the conference of 48 Roman Catholic liturgical scholars held in 1951 at Maria Laach to consider revision of the Roman Missal recommended that the Preparation of the Ministers, if said at all, be said on the way from the sacristy, and that the public rite should begin with the Introit. (*The Living Church*, November 9, 1952, p. 12). Evidently this conference of Roman scholars is of the same mind as our Liturgical Commission on this subject.

a) In the First Prayer Book: The First Prayer Book presented both the beginning and the ending of the rite with admirable clarity and directness. The Choir sang a whole Psalm 'for the Introite (as they call it),' instead of the brief verse or so to which this feature had been curtailed. Meanwhile, the Clergy entered, and the Priest said the prefatory Lord's Prayer and Collect for Purity, 'standyng humbly afore the middes of the Altar' — i.e., on the floor of the Chancel before the altar steps, where he had been wont to say the old *Præparatio ad Missam*, of which these two prayers were all that was left. Then the Priest said the Introit Psalm: apparently to himself, while the Choir was completing the singing of it, after the later medieval pattern which had the Priest repeat the choir parts along with his own proper parts of the service, at High Mass. Then *Kyrie eleison* was said or sung in English in ninefold form. The rubric continued: '*Then the Prieste standyng at Goddes horde shall begin,* Glory be to God on high. *The Clearkes.* And in yearth peace,' etc. The Salutation, and the Collect for the Day, followed immediately.

At the conclusion of the service, after the general Communion there was another Salutation, and the new prayer of Thanksgiving as a fixed 'Postcommunion Collect.' Whereupon at once, and without any other protractions, the rubric directed that 'the Priest turning hym to the people, shall let them depart' (*Ite, missa est!*) 'with this blessing': a very direct and satisfactory ending.

The structural vigor and sense of artistic form displayed by Cranmer's beginning and conclusion of the service are such that the more we have considered these questions, the more we have been convinced that we cannot possibly do better than to return to substantially the arrangements of the First Prayer Book. The substitutions and dislocations effected in the Second Prayer Book, and certain additions since, seem to have proceeded along mistaken lines. But they pose problems of their own as to what to do with the added material.

b) The Decalogue: The basic factor which wrought confusion on the beginning and ending of the service alike in the Second Prayer Book was the Puritan insistence upon having some kind of penitential introduction to the rite.

In 1549, Cranmer had a Confession and Absolution immediately before the Communion of the people. The Puritans wanted everything out between the Consecration and the Communion. We have seen that Cranmer was willing to do so, but made a point of taking some constituents which he considered integral to the meaning of the action, notably the Commemoration, the Humble Access, and the Confession and Absolution, which had occurred after the Consecration in 1549, and putting them as soon as possible before it.

But he also thought he saw a way to meet the Puritan desire for a penitential beginning by inserting the recitation of the Ten Commandments at the opening of the service. The Decalogue was familiar to everyone at that time as the basis for an Examination of Conscience before a private Confession. He took it for granted that everyone would use it in that accustomed sense, so that they would have something real to confess when the time came for the General Confession. He may very well have thought that this process might so enhance the value of the General Confession and the actuality of the following Absolution to a degree which would make the practice of private Confession superfluous in all ordinary cases. If so, his device was only too successful. Private confession did drop out of general practice in the Church, save for exceptional cases of conscience. And with it there lapsed the once universal knowledge of the particular function of the Decalogue as presenting systematic categories of transgressions for the purpose of self-examination.

Cranmer inserted this feature in a quite ingenious way, absorbing the former multiple repetitions of *Kyrie eleison* into litany-like responses of 'Lord, have mercy upon us, and incline our hearts to keep this law.' The added phrase seemed to throw the emphasis upon future obedience of the Commandments, rather than a searching of heart for a past infraction of them. This is sound theology: Penitence is saving precisely because it is a resolve for the righteous future, rather than remorse for the irrevocable past. Nevertheless, it had a distinct tendency to disguise, and eventually succeeded in obliterating, Cranmer's original organic purpose for the use of the Decalogue in the service for the examination of past sins, which we have noted that he explained so perspicuously in his Exhortation.[33]

Without a clear knowledge of that purpose, the Decalogue is purely hortatory in form and moralistic in content. Much has been made of it from that point of view: everyone knows Gladstone's claim that the law-abiding character of the English people is attributable to the constant rehearsal of this Law of God at every celebration of the Communion in the Church of England. The Nonjurors certainly thought that its purpose was only moralistic, when they introduced the recitation of our Lord's 'Summary of the Law' as a substitute for the Decalogue. For admirable as the Summary is as an expression of an ethical goal, it is certainly not in the least adapted to use for an Examination of Conscience: that idea was never in the mind of the Nonjurors, or of anyone else.

Once sight had been lost of Cranmer's intention for the organic function of the Decalogue in the service, it was left lacking in real rationale. It has even been fatuously explained as 'a fixed Old-Testament Lesson.' And the clergy have increasingly felt it to be a burden. The Nonjurors in 1718 boldly eliminated it. Scottish use since 1764 conservatively retained it in the text, but allowed the Summary as an alternative at any time. The American rite of 1789 still more conservatively presented the Summary as an optional *addition* to the Decalogue: but a good many clergy followed Scottish use in employing it as a substitute. Our Book of 1892 authorized the substitution, except at one Celebration each Sunday: a provision followed by the Canadian Prayer Book of 1921, the Irish of 1926, and the English draft of 1928. The American revision of 1928, followed by the Indian 'Western Rite' form of 1952, requires the Decalogue only once a month. The South African of 1929 reduces the requirement to the Sundays of Advent and Lent. The Ceylon rite of 1938 eliminates it completely.

The trend is unmistakable. In all branches of the Anglican Church, the Decalogue is on the way out of the Liturgy. And this is even more true in actual practice than in the letter of the rubrics. The trouble with that 'once in a while' type of rubric is that it is largely ineffectual. Even clergy who have every intention of observing such directives may forget to keep an eye on the Calendar, or may actually start a given service with a firm intention of putting in such an infrequent feature, and then once in the swing of the accustomed rite may overpass the proper place for it in spite of themselves. And some other clergy may elect

---

33. Cf. p. 175 above.

to ignore the provisions entirely. Many Seminarians, assiduous communicants in their home parishes, have told us that they have never heard the Decalogue rehearsed in the Liturgy in their lives.

c) An Office of Preparation: This breakdown in practice which has all but eliminated the Decalogue from the Liturgy seems to us a serious matter. It may indeed be inevitable that this feature, inserted in the service for a quite definite function, should not be found profitable when all knowledge of its original purpose had been lost. Yet apart from that, it has such distinct values of its own, so deeply rooted in our Anglican inheritance, that we should wish to see its public use enhanced, rather than further curtailed.

During the Middle Ages, the instruction of the people at High Mass was carried out not so much by sermons, as by systematic expositions of the Creed, the Lord's Prayer, and the Ten Commandments. And these three great themes furnished the content of the Catechism for instruction for Confirmation in the First Prayer Book. In our own country, many of our old 'Colonial' churches display these three basic formulas emblazoned upon panels of the chancel in perpetual reminder of the foundations of the Cult, Creed, and Conduct taught by the Church.

We therefore do not propose to drop the Decalogue entirely from the Liturgy, as the Rite of Ceylon does, but to keep it available in the accustomed place in the service for those who wish it there. At the same time we consider that the decline of this feature has now proceeded so far, and the forces which have caused its desuetude are still so potent, that there seems little possibility of reversing the trend. We do not see any way to conserve, still less to augment, its use as a part of the Liturgy. The most mandatory rubrics would simply not be obeyed.

But we believe we can bring the Commandments to a new prominence in a new use, with their ethical values recovered and enhanced, by incorporating them, with some other important and neglected matter, into a new *Office of Preparation for the Holy Communion*, to be printed before the Liturgy proper. The idea of this Office is derived from the Indian Liturgy of 1933. Preparation Services have long been used in the Church, particularly before Corporate Communions and the great Festivals. And the materials we have in mind are certainly admirably adapted for this purpose.

We have observed before that the mislaid key to Cranmer's intent for the function of the Decalogue in conjunction with the Liturgy is to be found in what is now our Second Exhortation, beginning on p. 86 of our Prayer Book. This is the so-called 'Warning,' or announcement of a coming celebration of the Sacrament. Its rubric commands that the Minister shall '*always* . . . upon the Sunday or Holy Day immediately preceding . . . read this Exhortation following; or so much thereof as, in his discretion, he may think convenient.' This rubric is quite generally obeyed — but in so *pro forma* a manner that, though the forthcoming celebration is punctiliously (and usually quite unnecessarily) announced, the actual message of the Exhortation is left undelivered. What most clergymen 'think convenient' to do is to say, 'The usual celebration of the Holy Communion will be held next Sunday morning at eight o'clock.' The Exhortation itself is almost never heard. What is more, it is manifest that it never has been — else its plain and forcible expressions upon the use to be made of the Ten Commandments would not have fallen so utterly out of the minds of the members of the Church.

Yet this Exhortation contains unique and invaluable instruction upon the necessity, the nature, and the methods of a proper devotional preparation for the reception of the Holy Communion; and upon the effective means of attaining a realizing contrition, so as to achieve the benefits of the Ministry of Reconciliation. By incorporating the substance of this Exhortation into the new *Office of Preparation*, this valuable matter will be brought into a new importance and an increased use.

The practical application of this Exhortation to the purpose in hand comes at the beginning of its second paragraph. The order is therefore rearranged, so as to present this point as a separate Bidding leading up to the Decalogue, and making unmistakable the use of the Commandments as the basis for a realistic Examination of Conscience: so as to set forth precisely the setting, meaning, and functional purpose of the liturgical use of the Decalogue, for lack of which it has withered on the vine.

Then the Commandments are given in the short form only,[34] as in the English, South African, and Indian (1952) forms, omitting the homiletical additions which our present Book prints in small type. And the Commandments have been given numbers, as in our Offices of Instruction, and the South African and Indian Liturgies.

The Commandments are supplemented, but in this setting of course never supplanted, by our Lord's Summary of the Law, with its positive terms and its inexhaustible challenge to moral effort. Then the text of the proposed Office concludes with the Scottish and American 'Litany-Collect' for grace to keep the Commandments,[35] and a rubric permitting the addition of the Confession, Comfortable Words, and Absolution, from the Liturgy.

Further flexibility for the use of this outline as an office of devotion is drawn from the provisions of the Indian Rite. The second rubric before the Office allows the Priest to make an address of his own instead of the Exhortation, and to suggest questions based upon the Commandments and upon 'The Law of Love' for use in the self-examination instead of using the Decalogue in its strict Litany-form.

We have not followed India in proposing that this Office be required before every celebration of the Liturgy. On the other hand, the inclusion of the neglected

---

34. Cf. p. 201 f.
35. Cf. p. 191.

Exhortation expresses the universal need and obligation for personal preparation for the reception of Holy Communion: and we have added the suggestion that the Office may be profitably employed privately for that purpose when it is not used corporately.

The fourth rubric indicates that the content of this Office, beginning (quite indispensably) with the Bidding, and concluding with the final Collect, may be inserted in the Liturgy in place of the Summary, *Kyries*, and *Gloria in Excelsis*; and intimates that such substitution might be especially in order in penitential seasons. Thus this matter is preserved as a part of the Liturgy for all those who want it.

This expedient also avoids printing out in the text of the Liturgy an optional feature which is relatively seldom used. The presence of any such 'occasional' constituents within the normal rite simply makes for the confusion of newcomers to the Church, and for the inconvenience of everyone at a usual service. Previous Prayer Books removed the Exhortations to a place after the text of the service for precisely those reasons; and, as we shall see, contemporary Anglican books do the same for the Proper Prefaces.

We may note that in the Exhortation, we have put 'life-giving' instead of 'comfortable.' The latter is a word which has completely shifted its meaning since the Prayer Book was first written — though the fact is not recognized, as it is in the case of the word 'prevent,' since 'comfortable' still makes good sense in all of its contexts. The trouble is, that it is an entirely different sense. 'To comfort' once bore a very active meaning, signifying 'to strengthen' us so that we might triumph over our difficulties; now it is passive, 'to console' us in supine resignation under their burden. Here, and throughout the Liturgy, we have sought for some more positive expression for this word, to restore its original force in the particular setting.

Similarly, in 'The Bidding' the phrase which Cranmer inserted in 1552, 'to examine your liues and conuersacion' has been altered to 'lives and conduct': since while the word 'conversation' is as much alive as it ever was, its use in the sense of 'manner of living' is absolutely extinct.

Finally, we propose to restore from the First Prayer Book the words 'let him go *to some discreet and learned Priest*,' and from the other Anglican books from 1552 'that *by the Ministry of God's holy Word* he may receive *the benefit of Absolution, together with* such godly counsel and advice,' etc. These provisions are to be found in every other Anglican Liturgy except our own. They were even retained in the American 'Proposed Book' of 1785, though they have been missing from our line since 1789. It seems a pity to lose the testimony, which the other Anglican books underscore by repeating the phrase twice over, that 'the Ministry of God's holy Word' is a truly evangelical 'Ministry of Reconciliation,' grounded in the Apostolic Commission of St. John 20:22 f. Even Luther exalted Absolution into virtually a Third Sacrament. And since this is the consensus of all the rest of the Anglican Communion, and represents a general agreement as to permitted faith and practice in our own Church today, there really seems no reason for being timid about proposing the restoration of these expressions.

d) The Gloria in Excelsis: In considering the changes made in the Second Prayer Book, we noted that the introduction of the Decalogue at that time had the regrettable effect of depriving the opening passages of the rite of another valuable ingredient in a way which also wrought havoc upon the former simple and effective conclusion of the Liturgy. The *Gloria in Excelsis* was ousted from the commanding position it had occupied at the exordium of the service, because of its incompatibility of tone with the new Decalogue-Litany, and was inserted after the Postcommunion Thanksgiving, where it could be brought in with a smooth literary conjunction with its context.[36]

Now easy transitions are admirable; and the Prayer Book of 1552 was certainly a model of them. But there are other considerations of fundamental structure which are of still greater importance: and the placing of the great chant of the *Gloria* in the peroration of the service is unhappily in conflict with one of the most basic of such organic principles.

It is a necessary characteristic of every literary form, and still more of every dramatic action, that it must begin at a base-line which marks a zero point of feeling; that it should rise at an accelerating rate to a high point of emotion which marks its climax; and then that it should make a short and swift descent to mother earth again. The portion known as the 'anticlimax' — that return to the base; Browning's 'resolution to the C-major of life' — is an indispensable part of the art-form. But it must be noted that it is indispensable that this movement be *short* — the briefer the better.

It follows that the place at which the Second Prayer Book sought to interpose the *Gloria* is entirely unsuited to that feature. The service is definitely on the downward arc of its parabola. The sooner it can be brought to an end after it has attained the goal of its essential action in the administration of the Communion, the more satisfactory is the effect. It is no place to try to tower up to yet another climax. The use of the *Gloria* here has three results: it impairs the effective ending of the service; it degrades the *Gloria*, depriving it of most of its power and appeal; and it correspondingly impoverishes the whole opening movement of the Liturgy.

No one who has ever heard the Latin Mass sung will ever forget the thrilling impact of this great song of praise, the way in which it bears the worshipers upward upon the wings of angels, and the high level of solemn feeling upon which it establishes the *Missa Catechumenorum*, the non-sacramental introduction

---

36. Cf. p. 176.

to the Liturgy. Without the *Gloria*, the whole Anglican 'Ante-Communion' suffers severely in comparison with the corresponding passage in the Roman service, for lack of the emotional elevation which imparts to the latter its worshipful quality. The substitution of the 'below zero' beginning of a Decalogue Litany in place of the *Gloria* was a very great grading down of that part of the Liturgy which in itself is simply a 'general service of public worship,' until, if anything, it is inferior in its effect to Morning Prayer.

Dr. Srawley senses this:

> The omission of the Introit, the transposition of the *Gloria in Excelsis* to the post-communion, and the introduction of the Commandments, with the *Kyries* as a refrain, . . . impart to this introductory portion of the service a penitential and subjective character, whereas in the older rite the use of psalmody . . . and the singing of the *Gloria in Excelsis* introduced the element of worship at an earlier stage in the service. In this respect the earlier Lutheran rites and the present Swedish service follow more closely the older forms. The Prayer Book service thus begins on a low tone, and the element of praise and thanksgiving . . . is held back until the *Sursum Corda* and Preface.[37]

On the other hand, when the *Gloria* is intruded into the inevitable downward movement of the 'anticlimax' of the Liturgy, its splendor is dimmed and dulled; instead of a lift, it is a dead weight, an impediment in the smooth, sure, downward rush of the stream. There is a distinct consciousness of this situation in the minds of our clergy, as is evidenced by the increasing number of those who avail themselves of the rubrical alternative of substituting a Hymn at this point. That rubric, which is peculiar to the American service, is a fortunate circumstance in permitting us to conform to traditional ritual propriety by eliminating the *Gloria* in Advent, Lent, the Ember seasons, and the weekdays of Epiphany- and Trinity-tides: but it is a distinct abuse to omit the *Gloria* upon other Sundays, or upon the weekdays of the 'festal seasons' of Christmas-and Easter-tides.

For every reason, then, we propose that the *Gloria* be restored to the beginning of the great action, as in the First Prayer Book. This is the only place in the Liturgy where the *Gloria* actually does anything for the service. It is also the only place which does justice to the *Gloria*. But we suggest it only as a festal feature, with rubrics to insure that it will be used on the occasions to which it is traditionally appropriate, and will be omitted without substitute at other times.

The Spanish translation of the Prayer Book authorized by the Church of England, the Indian Liturgy of 1933, and the diocesan uses of Zanzibar and Nassau (the latter of which follows the Book of 1540), all restore the *Gloria* to its

---

37. *Liturgy and Worship*, p. 309.

original place; Ceylon allows either location of this feature. The adoption of this very desirable reform in other Anglican books seems to have been impeded by the lawlessness of those who would not wait for the orderly processes of revision, but made the transfer on their own authority. Unfortunately, in the minds of many this has colored the practice of '*Gloria* At Beginning' with a certain implication of partisanship. In fact, no partisan principles whatsoever are involved. This is a clear case for considering the question on its merits: and since the arguments are all in favor of the restoration of the *Gloria* to an original place which is on every count the best place, it would seem only common sense to do so.

The Ministry of the Word

As we have noted, the British revisions use this subtitle, but confine it to the portion from the Epistle through the Sermon. They preface it with another section labeled 'The Introduction,' extending through the Collect of the Day. Since they retain the Decalogue, etc., there may be some reason for a separate division for those 'opening exercises.' We propose to reduce all that to the Collect for Purity, the Summary, the *Kyries*, and (on festal occasions) the *Gloria in Excelsis*. There seems to be no compelling reason to draw any line of distinction between this brief vigorous beginning and the following Collect, Epistle, Gradual, Gospel, Creed, and Sermon. Everything in this whole group is either in the words of Holy Scripture (the dominant feature of this movement of the rite), or is based directly upon them. Hence we propose the British title as a conclusive overall description of the whole.

1. The Introit

The General Rubric on p. viii of our Prayer Book authorizes a 'Hymn or Anthem' before any service. Since a chant during the procession to the altar before the Holy Liturgy was undoubtedly the parent of this kind of provision, it appears seemly to recognize that fact by a specific rubric mentioning the Introit. Another Committee of the Liturgical Commission has worked out a comprehensive set of Proper Anthems, available for use at the Introit, Gradual, Offertory, and Communion, on the Sundays and Holy Days of the Church Year.[38] The acceptance of that particular scheme, and its integration to the conduct of the service, is something still to be developed. But whether or not that project is accepted, there is no harm, and no change in the present situation, in this kind of a permissive rubric; which, incidentally, applies equally well to the use of a 'Processional Hymn' before the service, for those who prefer that American custom.

---

38. M. C. Stone and R. F. Brown, *Anthems for the Day* (N. Y.: Oxford University Press, 1952).

2. Preliminary Provisions

The present first rubric before the service is retained without material changes. The mention of the Lord's Prayer, with the permission to leave it out at discretion, is dropped. Properly speaking, the initial Lord's Prayer has never belonged to the public service, being a vestigial survival of the Priest's Preparation. It seems like a good opportunity to conform to Cranmer's general principle of not specifying the content of the Priest's private devotions. And there is really little point in directing the Priest to say the Lord's Prayer, and then immediately adding that he does not need to do so unless he wants to. It does equally well to say nothing about it — naturally leaving the Celebrant at perfect liberty to put it in if he desires it.

The Scottish Liturgy since 1637 has added to the provision for 'a faire white linen cloth,' a further mention of 'other decent furniture, meet for the high mysteries there to be celebrated.' Such language is attractive to some minds, distasteful to others. In any case it is another matter which may safely be taken for granted. But there remains a real point in retaining the direction that 'at the Communion-time the Holy Table shall have upon it a fair white linen cloth,' because of its plain implication that this cloth should not be left upon it at other times — else it will not long remain either 'fair' or 'white'!

The rather indefinite direction standing 'reverently before the Altar,' may very well remain. Historically considered, all rubrics are simply descriptive of the customs which are universal in an existing rite. In other words, the service itself came first, and the rubrics indicating how it was wont to be performed came afterward. Of course, once established, they have their own value and authority, as conservative of the accustomed service.

Now in this case, custom has not settled itself in our Church to anything like uniformity. Whether the initial Collect for Purity is said on the pavement, at the midst of the altar, or on the Epistle side, varies with the preferences of the Celebrant. No one of these customs is so indisputably right as to be commanded, none sufficiently wrong as to be excluded. Until there is general agreement on this point, there seems to be no need to try to dictate a settlement.

It will be observed that we suggest saying 'the Holy Table' in the rubric about its covering, but 'the Altar' in that referring to the place to begin the service. Cranmer in the corresponding rubrics of the First Prayer Book said 'the Altar' and 'Goddes borde,' and thereafter always 'the Altar.' The Second Prayer Book made it 'the Table' throughout; and so it remains in the English 1662, except for 'the holy Table' at the Offertory, and 'the Lord's Table' before the Preface. The Scottish Liturgy has 'the Holy Table' throughout, save for one occurrence of 'the Lord's Table' at the Presentation of the Elements, and 'the Altar' before the Humble Access: the last-named having got it in 1764. The Indian Liturgy says 'the Altar' throughout; so does that of Ceylon, except for 'the Holy Table' at the Offertory, and 'the Lord's Table' before the Humble Access.

The plain fact of the matter is that the old Puritan assault upon the very idea of a Christian Altar has utterly died out in our Church, and is lost to the memory of all but the learned. The word is used in our Office of Institution, and we use it constantly and exclusively in our common speech. No one ever alludes to 'the Holy Table,' unless he is consciously quoting a rubric. There does not seem the least reason for sanctimoniously excluding this universal term from the rubrics, where it is often the simplest and most obvious word that can be employed.

However, it would be a mistake to supplant the former language completely. There is no sense in making a proposed change even look like a partisan gesture, when it is actually nothing of the kind. Moreover, the retention of both phrases would be an excellent way of preserving the witness of Holy Scripture which was the basis of the early Church's adopting the term 'altar' in the first place, in St. Paul's equating of the function of the pagan altar (note that he calls that a 'table') with that of 'the table of the Lord.'

To use the two phrases intelligently, and not merely at random as in the other recent Anglican books, it would seem well to say 'the Holy Table' when we are thinking of the function of its horizontal surface, as in this rubric about its covering, and again when the oblata are to be placed upon it; but to say 'the Altar' when we are alluding to its structure as a whole, as the center of the ritual action, and indicating the position of the Celebrant in relation to it.

The new third rubric makes provision for the beginning of the Liturgy in conjunction with the use of the Litany.

We have noted that all litanies are 'periodic' in their structure, so as to lead up to and find their completion in some sort of summary terminal Collect[39] When the Litany is employed as a separate service, this Collect is the prayer 'We humbly beseech thee' (p. 59); but when it is used as prefatory to the Liturgy, the terminus is the Collect for the Day. Rome still retains this connection when the Litany is an integral part of the Mass, as at the Consecration of Churches and the vigils of Easter and Whitsunday. On these occasions, the concluding *Kyries* of the Litany coalesce with those of the Mass, and lead (after an interpolated Gloria) to the Collect of the Day.

As far back as 1911, the great Anglican liturgiologist Dr. W. H. Frere recommended that when the Litany is used before the Liturgy, everything after the *Kyries* be omitted from the Litany, and everything before the Collect from the Liturgy.[40] Moreover, Cranmer in his Ordinal of 1550 was so conscious of the organic connection of the Litany with the proper Collect of the Liturgy that he made the Collect of the Ordering of Deacons to follow the Litany immediately — though it did not occur to him to prune the Litany of superfluities in this connection. Still more, in the Ordination of Priests and the Consecration of Bishops,

---

39. Cf. p. 175 f.

40. *Some Principles of Liturgical Reform* (London: Methuen, 1911), 156 ff.

he omitted the proper liturgical Collect entirely from its place before the Epistle, in order to insert it after the Litany, which in those services occurred respectively after the Gospel, and after the Creed. Without lingering on the latter pair of anomalies, whose only importance is the *a fortiori* argument which they bring to the general principle, it may be remarked that the rite of the Ordering of Deacons at the present day is an excellent argument for the merits of Cranmer's original structure, and yet more for those of Frere's suggestion. In the service as now performed, it does seem like a waste of time and energy to see the proceedings acquire a quite fair amount of momentum in the Litany, and then to come to a dead stop, and start all over again with the preliminaries of the Liturgy, in order to work up again to the Collect of the Day.

The same thing is true of any use of a Litany before the Liturgy. But there is no apparent need to try to extend this method to the employment of the Liturgy in immediate succession to any other service, such as the Burial Office or a Marriage: since the proposed omission of the Lord's Prayer and the Decalogue, would now make the exordium of the Liturgy brief and not at all burdensome. And there is no point in dropping the *Kyries*, except when and because they are used in the Litany; nor yet in excluding the *Gloria in Excelsis* from occasions to which it is appropriate.

3. The Collect for Purity

As far back as we can obtain any information, it has been characteristic of the Christian Liturgy to begin the public service with a mutual Salutation of the Celebrant and the People. In the Greek rites this was and is in the form 'Peace be to all,' derived from the Semitic salutation — the immemorial *Salaam* of the East. Only in one place — before the *Sursum Corda* — does the 'bridge Church' of Alexandria provide the meditating form, 'The Lord be with all,' which intimates the origin of the Western version of 'The Lord be with you.' In all regions alike, the people replied, 'And with thy spirit.'

This mutual greeting effectively 'called the meeting to order,' and put the assembly on the alert to take up their part in the action of worship. This device was so useful for that purpose that the Liturgy went on to repeat the Salutation whenever a new turn of the service brought a need to summon the congregation again to take heed to a salient feature to follow. So throughout the Prayer Book we find this Salutation used to mark the points of articulation of the major divisions of the services. It is used like the 'Company, attention!' which alerts a military unit to receive a new command.

The employment of the Salutation is entirely familiar to us in other offices, though the Liturgy at our last revision had succeeded in recovering only one of the former occurrences of this feature, of which Puritan objections had stripped the rite in 1552. It seems desirable to restore it to its parent location at the beginning of the public service. It is a matter of experience, not of theory, that something is needed here, after the entry of the officiants, and after any necessary preparations, practical or devotional, have been completed, to indicate that all is now ready, and to invite the congregation to join in the actual commencement of the religious action. Many celebrants of every party are wont to add the Salutation at this point: and they have displayed a sound liturgical instinct in doing so.

The Collect for Purity was used in the sacristy in the Sarum rite to conclude the saying of the *Veni Creator* which accompanied the vesting of the Ministers, and to introduce the 43rd Psalm (which Sarum likewise held in the sacristy). This Collect did not occur in the Roman Mass. Our first record of it is in a collection of Votive Masses for weekdays made by Alcuin (d. 804); and as a Votive it has found its way into the modern Roman Missal. Whether Alcuin derived it from some unidentified English source, or whether Sarum borrowed it from Alcuin, is not known.

Apparently Cranmer recognized its essential identity of thought with the Collect *Aufer a nobis* which both Sarum and Roman rites assigned to the Celebrant as he went up to the altar before the *Kyries*, for he exchanged it with that feature, so as to open the public service as it had formerly begun the Priest's Preparation. This was good judgment. The matchless grace and power of this Collect made it something much too good to be confined to the private use of the Priest in the sacristy, and admirably qualified it for the exordium of the public rite. No more magnificent initial 'Call to Worship' is to be found in any liturgy.

4. *The Law of Love*

Through a considerable period of our discussions of the Liturgy, our Commission was minded to propose the elimination of the 'Summary of the Law' as being purely moralistic, and perhaps as even more lacking in organic function in the Liturgy than the Decalogue, which it has so extensively supplanted. But a relatively little experimental use of the proposed order of service in closed sessions of the Liturgical Commission convinced us that this move would be a mistake. In a choral celebration, the familiar sequence of Introit, *Kyrie*, and *Gloria* carries its own weight, and, as it were, furnishes its own justification. But when the service is said, there is no obvious development of thought to bind these forms together, and to lead from one to another. The *Gloria*, to be sure, even when said, is felt to be a natural reaction to what precedes it, a profoundly 'eucharistic' outburst of grateful praise to the God of All Mercy of the *Kyrie*: but what possible relevance does the Kyrie bear to the Collect for Purity? It is apparent that Cranmer felt something of the sort, a lack of *something* in the exordium of the service to justify the solemn respond of the *Kyries*, when he decreed that after the Collect for Purity, the Priest should say the Introit Psalm, even though the Choir had sung it during the entrance of the officiants.

It seems very probable that in the Second Prayer Book Cranmer had in mind not only the purpose of a Penitential Preparation in the insertion of the Decalogue, but the further value of confronting the people at the very beginning of the service with a numinous expression of the meaning of the worship of God. Any notion that worship is merely a psychological exercise or esthetic experience is sublimated at once by this proclamation in words of great authority into a vision of God's immeasurable Majesty, and the high calling of his will for us.

Most happily, these values for the heightening and deepening of worship were recognized and preserved by the Non-jurors when they substituted the 'Summary,' as a positive and therefore inexhaustible statement of the Law of God, with all the authority of the Old Covenant,[41] but made fully Christian by the authority of our Lord's own words.[42] As such, it remains a worthy exordium of our service of worship; and we believe it should be retained. And it fills up the lacuna of thought between the Collect for pure and worthy worship, and the respond calling upon God's mercy.

5. Kyrie Eleison

The far-reaching influence of the great Church of Constantinople in the fifth century secured the introduction into the beginning of the Latin Mass of a Litany of Byzantine type and origin. When toward the end of the sixth century this 'Enarxis Litany' was displaced by the insertion of the new feature of the *Gloria in Excelsis* at this point of the service, it left behind in the Mass the legacy of its terminal *Kyries*, which the Latin Litany had rather quaintly retained in Greek. These Greek words are therefore not vestiges, as some have thought, of the original Liturgy of the Church of Rome in that language. The Litany-form as such did not exist before the end of the third century at the earliest — by which time the Western Rite was always in Latin.

Originally, these phrases were not designed to be the penitential petitions for pardon which we might now assume, so much as acclamations of devotion. *Kyrie eleison* is a full Greek equivalent of the Hebrew *Hosanna* ('Save now!') which, unlike the Greek word, has succeeded in retaining its connotations of festal adoration. An adequate rendering of the *Kyrie eleison* of the primitive Church would perhaps be something of the order of 'Thou art the Lord, the fount of all mercy!' Certainly it was in such a sense that the pagans raised it as a shout of praise to the Emperor. The Eastern Christians appropriated it as a recurring respond to the suffrages of the Greek litanies, ending with a solemn repetition of it from three to twelve times over. Gregory the Great seized upon this use in multiples of three as symbolizing the Holy Trinity, and made this interpretation explicit by changing its second occurrence to *Christe eleison*.

In the First Prayer Book, Cranmer recognized the current custom of a Nine-fold *Kyrie* by putting the Latin numeral 'iij' (thrice) before each phrase in the Liturgy — though in the Communion of the Sick he omitted the numeral, and

---

41. The sources of the words are found in Deut. 6:5 and Lev. 19:18.
42. St. Matthew 22:37–40.

added the rubric 'without any more repeticion.' The numeral was omitted in 1552, and in all Anglican books thereafter. Nevertheless, the Church has preserved the old tradition, treating a 'threefold' or 'ninefold' form as open options. The American Hymnal provides music settings for both the longer and shorter versions. Ceylon 1938 and India 1952 make the dual permission explicit. But since people sometimes query the variation of our custom, we think it might be as well to do the like, with a rubric specifying that each phrase may be repeated thrice.'

Cranmer's translation, 'Lord, have mercy *upon us*,' is unfortunate in the last two words, which are not in the Greek, and which have some tendency to underscore the medieval understanding of the phrase as penitential in quality — as appears in the minor and mournful quality of many musical settings. Such, as we have seen, was not the original intent of the passage.

Bishop Dowden proposed that the last two words be dropped, in order to restore what he called 'the large *indefiniteness* of the original.'[43] The Scottish Liturgy of 1912 accepted Dowden's amendment, and was followed in this by the English revision of 1928. But the present Scottish of 1929 restored Cranmer's version in the Liturgy: retaining Dowden's form only in the 'Shorter Litany II' and the 'Litany for the Sick or Dying.' The American Book admits Dowden's form only to the Litany for the Dying.

The Scottish desertion of this precept of their greatest liturgical scholar was the result of experience with the new form. As soon as they tried it out, they found out just why Cranmer had appended the two extra words in the first place. He did so simply to fill out seven syllables, the same number as the original *Kyrie eleison*, so that the new English version could be sung to the inherited plainsong music. And the fact is that we do not have any music for the four syllables of 'Lord, have mercy,' any more than Cranmer did. The adoption of Dowden's certainly more faithful rendering would require that all the liturgical settings for the *Kyries* must be thrown away. Consequently, though the shorter phrase may be welcomed in some of the Litanies, we are not proposing it for the Liturgy.

The question of the adaptability of musical settings has had one further effect upon the liturgical text. In Cranmer's time, the only music available was Plainsong, which is entirely lacking in musical accent, so that all that was necessary was the adoption of a seven-syllable phrase. It is a somewhat different story when one attempts to sing the English version to strongly accented modern music, which was composed for the Greek text. Then it comes to light that the natural rhythms of the Greek and English forms are entirely different:

Lōŕd, hāv̄e | mēŕ - cÿ üp - ōń ūs̄. Ký - rï- | é ë- | lé ï- |són.

---

43. *The Workmanship of the Prayer Book* (London: Methuen, 1890, 71.

The one is dactylic, the other trochaic. And the music cannot be made to fit.

So it came about that ambitious choirmasters, attempting to render modern 'composers' Masses' at our service, found themselves almost driven to have the *Kyrie eleison* sung untranslated. And the people welcomed the little touch of the recondite: since it is true that we have sacrificed some elements of mysterious appeal by translating our liturgy from an ancient and hieratic tongue into the language of daily speech.

After all, the Greek form is not a whit more alien to an English context than it is to a Latin setting. Our liturgical texts contain other untranslated expressions — *Hosanna, Alleluia, Amen*. The titles of our Psalms and Canticles remain in Latin, and are a convenience for allusion and the practical purpose of choir-lists: in which last the term of *Kyrie eleison* is perfectly familiar to anyone who has ever sung in a church choir.

Because there is a real need for the *Kyries* in Greek in some musical settings, we find that this variant is permitted in the liturgies of England 1928, Scotland 1929, Ceylon 1938, and India 1952. Accordingly, we are proposing this alternative for the use of those who desire it.

6. Gloria in Excelsis

The case for a restoration of the *Gloria* to the place in the service which is occupied in the First Prayer Book has already been given, as has the need of a rubric defining its use as a purely festal feature.

Since we are so habituated to the use of the *Gloria* in another context, introduced and 'led up to' by the conclusion of the Postcommunion Thanksgiving, which in 1552 attracted it to that place, it may be that some people may feel at first that it occurs here at the beginning with some abruptness. But as we have intimated, the *Kyries* are really the proper introduction to the *Gloria*, which is simply a festal magnification of their theme of the praise of the Lord of all mercy. But even those who do not at once feel the true inwardness of this matter will very shortly find that the *Gloria* has a self-sufficiency of its own. This great hymn of adoration is its own justification: it needs no kind of 'radio continuity' to introduce it.

The text of the *Gloria* is unaltered from our last Prayer Book, except that the phrase 'on earth peace, good will towards men' has been conformed to the Vulgate version and the better attested Greek text of Luke 2:14, 'on earth peace to men of good will.' More than ever before, in these troubled days we are in a position to appreciate the fact that the more authentic scriptural text is likewise more rational and realistic.

7. The Collect, Epistle, and Gospel

1. Rubrics on Postures: The kneeling posture of the people indicated in the second rubric at the beginning of the service for the Collect for Purity and the *Kyries* will necessarily be interrupted by their standing for the *Gloria* whenever that is said: so it becomes necessary to specify that the people shall kneel for the Collect of the Day.

It should also be made clear that the people should be seated during the reading of the Epistle. This is something which the Prayer Book has always taken for granted; and the famous 'Declaration on Postures at Divine Service' put forth by the House of Bishops in 1832 so requires. Nevertheless, the custom of kneeling during the Epistle at a 'low celebration' has crept in, and seems to be increasing among those on both sides of the ritual fence. It must be pronounced to be an abuse.

It is true that Roman Catholic congregations kneel for the Epistle at Low Mass. But that is for the sole reason that there this feature is read in an unintelligible voice, in an unknown tongue, and without turning to the people, so that they have no way whatever of telling when the Epistle begins, or when it ends. On the contrary, at High Mass, where the ceremonies make it stand out in the service, they are seated. Since we have the advantage of recognizing the Epistle under all circumstances, the Roman precedent does not have any application to our usage.

Quaintly enough, this 'corrupt following' of Rome is defended also by low-church literalists on the ground that it is commanded by the present rubrics, since the first rubric of the service requires the people to kneel, and no other direction is given them until they are told to stand at the Gospel. This, however, is just another illustration of the fact that rubrics are seldom *exhaustive* in their provisions. On this assumption that they do cover everything, the congregation ought to be standing up during the Gospel, the Creed, the Announcements, the

Sermon, the Offertory, the Prayer for the Church, and the Invitation to the Communion; since they are ordered to stand for the Gospel, and no further instructions are given them until both a written and a spoken rubric direct them to kneel for the General Confession. While such an absurdity as that has not yet put in an appearance, one never can tell when it might. At all events, it does seem desirable not to leave any doubt at any point as to the proper posture of the congregation.

In the same way, the same rubric seems to call for an attempt to put a stop to the equally manifest abuse of the Minister's reading the Epistle with his back to the people. No Church has ever so read any lections, except the Roman, and some Anglican imitators. Even in the Roman Mass, this custom does not represent their ancient practice, but a medieval deformation of it. Originally they read the lections from an ambo or lectern, facing the people. Fortescue says: 'The tradition of reading the epistle from the south ambo remains in that the subdeacon still reads it on the south side. *His position toward the altar is quite anomalous, since he is reading to the people.* It appears to have begun with the disuse of the ambo.'[44]

Fortescue does not go into further details, which seem to be as follows: In the most ancient form of the service, which was High Mass, the Celebrant had nothing to do while the Ministers were reading the lections but to listen to them. When in the ninth century the new rite of Low Mass was invented, he had to read everything, the parts of the Ministers and of the Choir as well as his own. This had the incidental effect of underscoring the importance of the liturgical propers, so that the Priest at High Mass felt he had not fully discharged his sacerdotal functions unless he read them there too. Naturally, he read them to himself from the Missal upon the altar, while the Ministers were singing them from the ambos. And this in turn reacted upon Low Mass, so that the Celebrant did not bother to turn to the people then. Finally, this reacted again upon High Mass, where the Subdeacon imitated the position of the Celebrant and rendered the Epistle facing the altar.

But in our service, where the Epistle is always read to be heard, there does not appear to be any virtue in copying the Roman degeneration of the original intent of the feature, and the obvious principles of liturgical propriety. In general, we have been very chary about taking sides between divergent ceremonial customs, where each variant is equally reasonable and innocuous. This means that a good many rubrics have to be left discreetly vague as to the Celebrant's postures and actions, in order not to put ourselves in the ungracious and indefensible position of trying to impose our own preferences in matters where the Church has come to no agreement. But this does not mean that we must hold our hand when we are confronted with ritual uses which are not rational and justifiable.

2. *Forms of Announcing Lections:* The present method of announcing the Epistle and Gospel is not satisfactory, and has given rise to annoying diversities of use.

In the first place, it is not clear why there should be two different formulas for announcing the lections at the Offices and at the Liturgy. In the first case, the order is verse — chapter — book; in the second, chapter — book — verse. The Roman method was to read the lections of the Breviary Offices without title; and at the Mass, to announce only the book. Our forms for both go back substantially to the First Prayer Book, although the initial verse was not specified until 1637 and 1662.

---

44. *The Mass* (London: Longmans, 1944), 264.

If our people had the Scotch Presbyterian habit of bringing their bibles to church, and turning up the proper lections in order to follow them in their own copies when they were read, there might be some use in announcing chapter and verse. Since this is not the case, it does not appear that any valuable purpose is subserved by the form of the announcement. Certainly there is none at all at the Liturgy, where the whole text is printed out in the Prayer Book, with headings giving the reference for those who wish to verify details.

For both Epistle and Gospel, it ought to suffice to announce only the Book. And this would bring to an end the distasteful tautologies perpetrated by most clergy at present, when they say 'The Epistle is written in . . . the Epistle of,' and 'The Holy Gospel is written in . . . the Gospel according to.' The tradition of this sort of insertions has arisen from a desire to fill in the skeletal formulas in the fullest and clearest way, from the titles of the books in the Authorized Version. Yet it marks a corruption of what the makers of the Prayer Book had in mind. This can be verified by comparing the curious 'narrative rubrics' in the successive Ordinals from 1550 through 1892. For instance, take the Gospel at the Ordination of Priests, from 1662 to 1892:

Rubric in the Liturgy:	*Rubric in the Ordinal:*	*Form intended:*
The holy Gospel is written in the ___ chapter of ___ beginning at the ___ verse.	After this shall be read for the Gospel part of the ninth chapter of St. Matthew, as followeth. (S. Matth. 9:36.)	The holy Gospel is written in the ninth Chapter of St. Matthew, beginning at the 36th verse.

Yet the mistaken tautology of saying The Holy Gospel is written in the — Chapter of the Gospel according to —[45] has got into the Scottish line since their Draft Liturgy of 1889, and has infected the English 1928 and the rites of Ceylon and India 1952 though rejected by South Africa and India 1933. We consider that the form we are proposing accomplishes what these revisions are seeking to achieve, without the unhistorical and objectionable duplication of phrases.

It seems regrettable that the form we suggest for announcing the Epistle has to be so flexible, and to throw so much responsibility on the officiant. We did not see any way of evading this situation, or of devising simpler and more rigid prescriptions which would leave room for the varying appropriateness of such forms as:

The Epistle of St. Paul to the Romans.

The first Epistle of St. Paul to the Corinthians.

The Epistle of St. James.

---

45. England and Ceylon add 'Saint.'

The first Epistle of St. Peter.
The Epistle to Titus.
The first Epistle to Timothy.
The Epistle to the Hebrews.
The Lesson from the Book of Acts, Revelation, the Prophet Joel, etc.

Our 1928 revision relieved us of the awkward apologetic locution of 'The Portion of Scripture appointed for the Epistle,' for use on the occasions when some other kind of lection supplants the accustomed part of an actual Letter of an Apostle; but it reduced us again to the logical absurdity of proclaiming as an 'Epistle' something which was nothing of the kind, to which the Puritans at the Savoy Conference raised their objections. All the recent British revisions except the South African substitute 'The Lesson' in such cases. This is really a reversion to pre-Reformation standards: the Latin idiom making it equally easy to say, 'Lectio Epistolæ beati Pauli Apostoli ad Corinthios,' 'Lectio Danielis Prophetæ,' or 'Lectio libri Genesis.' But it was always a 'Lesson.' It would seem awkward and unnecessary for us now to prefix that locution to the announcement of the Epistle; but it is a perfectly correct substitute to introduce another passage from the Old or New Testaments.

3. *Laus tibi:* The revision of 1928 put in tentatively and permissively the respond of 'Praise be to thee, O Christ,' after the reading of the Gospel. It seems to have been universally accepted and used. There seems no reason therefore why the 'may' of the present rubric should not now be made to read 'shall.' Uniformity of practice is surely to be encouraged, when there is no motive for allowing variations.

8. The Creed

1. Rubrical Provisions: In its original Roman use, the Creed has always been a festal addition to the Liturgy, not a daily essential. And Cranmer's First Prayer Book allowed the Creed to be omitted 'on the workedaye ' — i.e., on weekdays which were not holidays. This precedent has been followed in all the recent British revisions, except the Indian. There seems to be every reason for providing for weekday celebrations which, if desired, may be in the briefest possible form, especially for the benefit of city churches where such services can be attended by people on their way to work — but only if they do not last too long.

Likewise, there is no need for having two Creeds said in a combined service, as the American Church has recognized from the beginning. This, however, will be taken care of by a rubric in Morning Prayer permitting the omission of the Creed from the former service, when the two are said together.

If the Creed is to be required only upon Sundays and festivals, there does not seem to be any reason for continuing the permission to substitute the Apostles' Creed for the Nicene in the Liturgy. The American Church has always stood alone in that provision: no other branch of the Anglican Communion has ever considered having anything but the great Creed in the great service.

2. *The Text:* While it is obviously undesirable to make any extensive changes in a form which everyone knows by heart, there are a few minute points, considerably more important than their size would indicate, which can be cleared up with a minimum of disturbance.

1. The Latin use of the Creed makes a distinct stop after the words, 'I believe in one God.' The Priest precents this phrase at High Mass, after which the Choir sings the rest. All the English books had a comma at this point until the revision of 1662. Even after that, many editions continued to contain the comma. This included the Oxford edition of 1775, which was in the hands of White and Smith when they were making up the first American Prayer Book of 1789. Hence the comma was preserved in all printings of the American book until the Standard of 1844 removed it, to conform with the official English text of 1662.

   We propose to restore here a punctuation-mark — preferably a colon. It may be that the original intent of the Creed was to confess belief in one God-the-Father, *and* in one *Lord* Jesus Christ, *and* in the Holy Ghost — who *also* is *Lord*. Such a reading teaches faith in the Trinity, but it leaves a real difficulty in apprehending the Unity of God. The punctuation with a stop after the word 'God' emphasizes the Unity first of all; then sets forth in due order of precedence the place of Father, Son, and Holy Ghost within that Unity. This interpretation is to be preferred. It is a safeguard against the naive Tritheism which many of our people unconsciously believe. And it preserves in a recognizable form the primal Jewish Creed which was the germ of our own confession: 'The Lord our God is one Lord' of Deut. 6:4, explicitly quoted by our Saviour in Mark 12:29.

2. 'Begotten of *his* father' is peculiar to the Anglican version: the 'his' is not in either the Greek or the Latin texts. We think it would be a gain in dignity as well as authenticity to return to the original, saying 'Begotten of the Father.'

3. The expression 'God of God' is missing from the Creed as accepted at Chalcedon, which is the text followed by the Eastern liturgies. The West restored it, as in the form adopted at Nicæa.

   Bishop Dowden was no doubt right in saying that '"of"' was a better rendering of *de* (*ek* in the original) in the sixteenth century than it would be now.'[46] He went on to intimate that our phrase is commonly misapprehended as meaning 'supremely God.' Yet he said that it will not do to render *ek* by 'from,' or 'out of,' because of the incorrect suggestion of separation conveyed by those words. His recommendation that the phrases be punctuated 'God, of God, Light, of Light, Very God, or very God,' undoubtedly represents the delicate emphasis with which they ought to be read. It is proposed by us for consideration: though it is an unusual refinement, such as generally escapes the rather approximate rendering of the spoken words which we are able to effect by punctuation; and it is probable that many people will consider it to be over-finicky. One must, however, agree with Dowden that 'it will be acknowledged by everyone who has had much experience in teaching the young and the uninstructed that the use of this preposition confuses the sense, and is, in fact, often suggestive of strange notions.' Something really ought to be done about it; and Dowden's amendment has the merit of clarifying it by changing the punctuation, without tampering with the text.

4. '*Through* whom all things were made' seems a preferable translation. Current usage tends to say 'by' only when we are speaking of direct action; for action through an agent we usually say 'through.' In the primary scriptural sources of this statement in the Creed, the King James version says 'by' in both Col. 1:16 and Heb. 1:2; but in both cases the Revised Standard renders the same preposition used in the Creed as 'through.' And the change would obviate the confusion which has been observed in the minds of learners of the Nicene Creed, who, mindful of the initial statement, 'the Father Almighty, Maker of heaven and earth,' are prone to misinterpret the assertion about the Son, 'Being of one substance with the Father; By whom all things were made' as referring the making of all things again to the *Father*. The punctuation alone has proved insufficient to dispel the misconception: but the substitution of the word ought to clear it up. The Indian Rite of 1952 adopts this amendment.

5. Our present 'The Lord, and Giver of Life' translates the Latin 'Dominum et vivificantem.' The Greek original, however, is 'To Kyrion, to zoopoion.' The intent of the expression is to give supreme emphasis to the acclamation of the Holy Ghost by the divine title of Lord — an emphasis obscured by bracketing it with the attribute of 'the Lifegiver.' Therefore the Irish Prayer Book of 1878 inserted a comma after 'Lord': and this has been followed by the American and Canadian uses. But all the more recent Anglican revisions have adopted Dowden's suggestion to make the phrase read, 'The Lord, The Giver of life.' This is in exact correspondence with the Greek; and, as Dowden remarks, 'Very solemn and dignified would that form be.'[47] Incidentally, the capitalization of the word 'Life' here, and at the end of the

---

46. *The Workmanship of the Prayer Book* (London: Methuen, 1899), 107.
47. *The Workmanship of the Prayer Book* (London: Methuen, 1899), 108.

paragraph ('And the Life of the world to come'), seems to be entirely adventitious, and is peculiar to the American Prayer Books. It may be that the idea was to contrast spiritual life, or even 'everlasting' life, with mere physical being. But as the absolute use of the word in both contexts clearly indicates *all* life, the distinction does not seem worth preserving.

6. 'Who proceedeth from the Father *and the Son*' marks a purely Western insertion. It dates from the Third Council of Toledo in the year 589. It is interesting that the last struggles of the reconciliation of the Visigoths in Spain from Arian to Catholic Christianity eventuated in this little piece of 'super-orthodoxy,' going beyond the formulas regarded as sufficient by the great Councils. This 'Filioque' has been one of the controversial points between East and West. By this time, both sides understand each other. The East does not deny that the Spirit is sent by the Son (John 15:26, 16:7); the West does not deny that the Spirit proceeds primarily from the Father as first source and *Fons Deitatis*. East and West are agreed that 'from the Father, *through* the Son' represents the approximate sense in which the Western expression should be understood. But it does not seem advisable to propose the modification of the phrase, which would not be completely accurate, and would only be disturbing. On the other hand, the omission of the phrase as a gesture of amity toward the Greek Churches could hardly be expected to accomplish anything substantial in that direction, whereas it would deprive us of a real enrichment of the thought of the Creed, of which we are in legitimate possession.

7. It appears that the authors of the First Prayer Book omitted the word 'Holy' from the Nicene Creed, because it happened to be missing from current editions of the Acts of the Councils which they had consulted to verify the text.[48] This turned out to be an excess of zeal: the word is authentic. As it is now, the four 'Notes' of the Church are nowhere found in one place: the Offices of Instruction are reduced to inquiring, 'How is the Church described in the *Apostles and* Nicene Creeds?' All the latest Anglican revisions restore the omitted word.

8. We also propose to conform to the original text of this Eastern Creed by restoring another missing word in the clause, And 'I believe *in* One, Holy, Catholic and Apostolic Church.' The word is lacking (though implied) in the version of the Creed in the Missal, though it is found in other Latin translations. It is desirable that the Greek reading be replaced. Our present phrase does not convey the intended sense. To say that 'we believe one . . . Church' is no more than to say that we admit that it exists: cf. Cranmer's translation of the Apostles' Creed in his *Annotations upon the King's Book*, 'and *that there is* an holy Catholick

---

48. *The Workmanship of the Prayer Book* (London: Methuen, 1899), 104 f.

Church.'[49] 'To believe *in* it makes *the Church the object of its own Creed*, an integral and indispensable element of its own Gospel to the world. It has always been the distinguishing contention of Anglicanism that this is true: that Holy Church is absolutely essential for the proclamation of the Gospel, the effective extension of the Incarnation, and the individual appropriation of the Redemption. It is in realization of this position that we call ourselves by preference, and with instinctive correctness, 'Churchmen.' We therefore advocate this small but weighty change, not only in the name of verbal accuracy to represent the primordial text, but for the sake of a fundamental theological verity.

9. One suggestion has been advocated, which we have found ourselves unable to recommend. This was that we should conform to present Eastern custom by saying 'We' instead of 'I' in the five places where the first person perpendicular' occurs. The Eastern Orthodox Church advocates this form as proclaiming the corporate faith of the Universal Church, and professes to find the Western version to be individual, reducing the consentient witness of the Church to the level of personal opinion. Like most disagreements between East and West, this polemical point is more a matter of form than of fact. Besides, it is historically unsound. The original texts of the Greek Liturgies of 'St. James' of Jerusalem-Antioch, of 'St. Mark' of Alexandria, and even of the Byzantine manuscripts as late as the sixteenth century, all say 'I believe.' The 'We believe' locution is found in the Acts of the Council of Nicæa. The Nestorians, Armenians, Copts, and Abyssinians, all of them a little self-conscious about their orthodoxy, adopted the exact text as promulgated by the Councils, which naturally and properly used the collective 'We.' And the modern Byzantine, made also self-conscious about matters of verbal accuracy by conflict with the variant use of the West, has done the same. It is interesting that the Syrian Jacobite liturgy directs each of the congregation to say 'I,' and reserves the collective 'We' to the celebrant.

It might be worth adventuring the change, if we could be sure that everyone would take it in the proper way, of emphasizing the obligation of the corporate historic faith of the Church upon each of them individually. But that idea is really better conveyed by the present 'I believe.' Almost certainly there would be those who would think lightly, 'Oh yes, "we believe," as a body and in general; personally, I reserve the right to my own opinions!' This would be too much on the order of the old Senior Warden, of whom it is reported that he did not believe in the Resurrection; but since he did not believe in the inerrancy of the Bible either, he had no objections to saying the Nicene Creed, but with his own scornful inflection: And the third day he rose again — *according to the Scriptures!*' Since such an alteration would certainly be disconcerting, and quite possibly dangerous, we are not advocating it.

---

49. *Remains* (Oxford: The University Press, 1833), II. 65.

9. The Announcements and the Sermon

1. Special Intercessions: The first rubric on p. 71 is retained, and we have added to it, 'and special Intercessions may be made here,' in lieu of the second rubric, which is not well thought out, in its application of historical precedent.

The medieval Latin services interpolated into High Mass at this point a considerable accumulation of devotions, instructions, and intercessions in the vernacular. This feature was known as the *Prone* — a curious old word which may be derived from the Latin *præconium*, but which has nothing to do with the idea of a 'prostration.' Our present Announcements and Sermon are a survival of this portion. Indeed, to this day, special Intercessions are sometimes bid from the pulpit before the Sermon at the Latin Mass.

Therefore it is quite in order to propose such special Intercessions in our service at this point. The 'Announcement-time' is a somewhat informal interlude in the rite, at which anything of special current interest may legitimately be brought to the attention of the congregation. This is especially true at a choral service, when the Priest normally comes down to the reading-desk in the chancel to make the announcements. Then he can inform the people as to the person or object for which their prayers are desired — since an untitled 'prayer for the sick or the departed' leaves the congregation wondering just who is sick or dead well past the time when they should have been joining in the intercession for them — and it is quite convenient for him to kneel there, and lead the congregation in the appropriate prayers. Or of course this rubric can equally well be obeyed by bidding and saying the prayers from the pulpit before the Sermon, *more romano*. For such use, so much of the present provisions may well be retained.

But the structural defects of the present rubric become apparent at a low celebration. At this service there are usually no Announcements or Sermon, and the Priest does not leave the altar. In that case, there is a distinct awkwardness, and a sense of inconsecutiveness, in interposing the Intercessions between the Creed and the Offertory. They seem irrelevant to that part of the service.

Hence there is a somewhat general tendency to ignore the plain distinctions made by this rubric on p. 71, which permits the insertion of special prayers of Intercession at this point, and the first rubric on p. 74, which authorizes the use of special Biddings — *not interpolated Collects* — prefixed to the general Bidding of the Prayer for the Church, and to put in any 'Occasional Prayers' at the latter place.

It appears to us that both places have their merits for the addition of these Intercessions, according to circumstances, and we propose to sanction both. But there is no question in our minds that this is the one place in our services where the 'Bidding Prayer' on p. 47 f. is not wanted, since it is an absolute duplication of the matter of the Prayer for the Church. It may be an acceptable *substitute* for that form of General Intercession; but both should not occur so close together in the same service.

2. *The Place of the Sermon:* We have retained the 'indicative' rubric, 'Here followeth the Sermon,' as perhaps the best expression of what it is trying to convey, that the Sermon has a place within the Liturgy by right, and that when it is preached, this is the place for it.[50] This in spite of the fact that this form is just a shade too subtle for general comprehension, so that some clergy do not notice the 'indicative' form, and are under the impression that a Sermon is required. For them, the Scottish expression would be clearer.

The Liturgical Commission has received some suggestions that the Sermon should be put immediately after the Gospel in our rite, as it is in the Roman Mass.

The Sermon was originally an exposition of the liturgical Gospel: and it is represented that were it brought into immediate conjunction with the Gospel, it might help to make some sermons less irrelevant to their occasion and setting than is the case now. If this were true, it might be an almost irresistible argument. But it seems probable that the present situation arises more from the idiosyncracies of some preachers than from the structure of the service. And the fact is that in actual use the Creed is so intimately tied to the Gospel, the whole content of which it summarizes, that it is not felt to be an interruption of this division of 'The Ministry of the Word.'

Similarly, it is true that the Eastern rites put the Creed into the following section of the service devoted to 'The Prayers of the Faithful.' But this was because in the ancient liturgies the Creed was part of the 'Discipline of the Secret,' not to be rehearsed in the hearing of the Catechumens, who were dismissed after the Sermon. This has no application to present conditions — at least outside of South Africa and India, where the ritual of the old Catechumenate has been revived for the discipline of primitive heathen converts. In our service, where we are so accustomed to making the grand choral respond of the ecumenical Christian Creed to the solemn proclamation of the liturgical Scriptures, accepting, applying, and professing the Gospel message, it does not seem desirable to separate the Creed from its familiar connections of thought.

The Offertory

1. The Question of Order

The transitional movement of the liturgy between the Sermon and the Anaphora or Consecration is composed of three divisions, the Offertory proper, the Great Intercession, and the penitential preparation of the people for their participation in the Sacrifice and the Sacrament. There three themes are not a fortuitous miscellany. Different in form and tone as they are, they are linked together by the

---

50. Cf. p. 203.

common factor that they are all acts of the worshipping congregation to make ready for the central oblation of the Eucharist. They are all 'Prayers of the Faithful': and that Eastern title might perhaps be applied to them, if it were not for the fact that it seems undesirable to import an unfamiliar term.[51] Since these prayers and actions center in 'The Offertory,' we are proposing that term for the second major division of the liturgy.

The conjunction of the Offertory and the Intercession is absolutely primitive, as old as anything we know about the structure of the service. It was a most happy device of Cranmer's that the Second Prayer Book brought them together again, after they had been separated by many centuries.

We have also given the reasons for approving this same Prayer Book's transfer of the Penitential Preparation to make it an introduction to the Consecration, not merely to the act of Communion, as it had been in the 'Order of Communion,' the First Prayer Book, and the Latin originals.

Yet there seems to be some dissatisfaction with the present placing of this feature; and two suggestions have been made for other dispositions of it.

1. A Penitential Introduction to the Liturgy?: One is that it be put at the beginning of the service, after the Collect for Purity. That is what has been done in the Ceylon Liturgy, and (permissively) in the Indian of 1952. Those who advocate such an arrangement allege the analogy of the initial Confession at Morning Prayer; but the suggestion comes from those habituated to the use of the Roman 'Preparation of the Ministers.' While such an exercise may be natural enough, and helpful enough, as a private devotion of the Celebrant, we do not consider it equally adapted to the needs and capacities of the congregation, and therefore do not recommend that it be made a part of the public service. We have noted that the Roman liturgical conference at Maria Laach in 1951 proposed that this Preparation, if used at all, be confined to the sacristy.

We have already expressed our opinion that the normal beginning of the liturgy should be simplified, not enlarged.[52] We consider that while a Penitential Preparation is a most appropriate approach to the Consecration, it is largely lacking in both meaning and feeling as an introduction to the first portion of the service which constitutes merely a general service of public worship.

Moreover, the fact is that Contrition is not a spontaneous and facile emotion: more than almost any religious feeling which it is the office of the Liturgy to inspire and express, it is needful to prepare for it and lead up to it; one cannot begin cold with it. It seems that Cranmer realized this, when in 1552 he kept the Confession and Absolution in a rather late place in the service, and paved the

---

51. The Indian Liturgy uses this title, but with a different content: Creed, *Pax, Lavabo*, potential 'Prayer of the Veil,' and Prayer of Incense.

52. Cf. p. 235 f.

way for them by putting in the self-examination of the Decalogue quite a while before: while at the same time he declined to follow the lead of his Calvinistic sources by going straight on from the Decalogue to the Confession.

And finally, even if we were able to devise an exordium of the Liturgy whose effect would be genuinely penitential, instead of some such mere formality as the beginning of the Ceylon rite seems to be, the result would inevitably be just such a *grading down* of the tone of the whole first division of the service as we have seen to have been produced by the former use of the Decalogue in that position.[53]

On all accounts, it seems better that the Eucharist should begin with the notes of worship and thanksgiving, in a major key, and wait for a later and more appropriate occasion to modulate into the relative minor theme of our own unworthiness.

2. A Penitential Introduction to the Offertory?
The other proposal agrees with all that has been said as to the inadvisability of putting the Confession at the outstart of the service, but suggests that it be placed at the beginning of the tripartite division of 'The Offertory.' Admitting the complete suitability of a Penitential Preparation for the whole eucharistic action, it urges that the people's own concrete participation in that action lies in the Offertory: and therefore that their preparation of soul ought to come before that. This is acute reasoning: we have been unable to find any fault with it in theory.

But when it came to proposing to put it into practice, we met with determined opposition from several clergy groups which we consulted. They declined to believe that it could be made to work satisfactorily. Of course the crucial test of this, as of most suggested alterations, would be the full choral service, with a general congregation and all the accustomed elaborations — an early celebration, with none but intending communicants present, is so short and simple that it rather approaches the quality of private devotions, which may quite well be taken in any order. And at such a principal celebration, the 'Ministry of the Word' attains (at last) a very fair degree of elevation in the Sermon. It maintains its position on that high plateau during the Offertory, which may take some time, and be accompanied by an elaborate Anthem which represents a major contribution on the part of the Choir. Then the action proceeds without loss of momentum to the Great Intercession, the Prayer for the Whole State of Christ's Church. And the working clergy felt that if a beautiful theory of the liturgical scholars were allowed to interrupt this triumphal progress of the service by making a new start from penitential depths, the wonted pattern would be wrecked, the impetus attained would be lost, and its effectiveness would be sacrificed.

These reasonings also seem to be unimpeachable. Perhaps the conflict of these two lines of thought really reflects the interesting fact that there are really

---

53. Cf. p. 243.

several possible divisions of the preliminary part of the Liturgy, that those divisions overlap, and that though each is valid enough for its own declared purpose, it may actually be in conflict with a different classification which has another objective in mind. Thus the Liturgy of the Catechumens ends with the Sermon, the 'Ante-Communion' in all the Anglican books except the American extends through the Intercession, and the Pro-Anaphora includes everything up to the *Sursum Corda*. We have found enough unity of thought in the Offertory, the Intercession, and the Penitential Preparation to class them together under the heading of 'The Prayers of the Faithful.' But the division of the 'Ante-Communion,' ending midway in this section, has a validity of its own. Though not much used now, it enjoyed a great deal of employment for perhaps three-fourths of the history of the Anglican rites: and that has left a permanent impression upon the manner in which a principal celebration is still performed. And the Penitential Preparation, from one point of view, actually initiates a new movement in the rite. Everything preceding is addressed to the general congregation; this concerns only the intending communicants. It has no actual continuity with what has gone before; it looks only forward to the coming Consecration and Communion.

After all, the arrangement of these three features in the Second Prayer Book has stood the pragmatic test of use for four centuries, with a very fair degree of general satisfaction. During that time, it has established accustomed patterns of use which would be very hard to alter. The only liturgies which, have presumed to vary from it are those of Scotland, Ceylon, and India. We have given the reasons why those departures do not seem to us to be recommended. We came to the conclusion that we cannot do better now than to leave the present sequence as it is.

2. *The Offertory*

1. The Sentences: Before the Reformation, the Choir sang a liturgical Anthem, varying with the day, during the time that the Elements were being prepared and offered upon the altar. This *Offertorium* consisted of a text appropriate to the occasion of the Christian Year, and had no bearing on the action which was being performed while it was sung.

A characteristic simplification in the First Prayer Book took the form of dropping the special *Offertoria*, one for each day, printed in the Propers, and giving a choice of a list of twenty Sentences. The rubric was: 'Then shall folowe for the Offertory' (*i.e.*, 'instead of the old proper *Offertorium*') 'one or mo, of these Sentences of holy scripture, to be song whiles the people dooe offer, or els one of theim to bee saied by the minister, immediately afore the offeryng.' This rubric explicitly continued the custom of singing an Offertory Anthem at this point; and that custom has survived to the present day, although the English books since 1552 have made no mention of it. At first, the words of this Anthem were confined to Cranmer's twenty texts; but this base was eventually broadened. Eventually this Anthem was recognized and regularized by the American rubric of 1892: 'And when the Alms and Oblations are being received and presented, there may be sung a Hymn, or an Offertory Anthem in the words of Holy Scripture or of the Book of Common Prayer, under the direction of the Priest.'

The Second Prayer Book, which eliminated any reference to the Choir, made the Sentence said by the Priest simply the announcement of a new turn of the action of the service. The Prayer Book of 1662 made this explicit: 'Then shall the Priest . . . begin the Offertory' (note that the reference has been shifted from an Anthem to a movement of the rite), 'saying one or more of these sentences.' Ever since, the Sentences have been a Bidding to the people's act of offering.

Cranmer's original list of these Sentences in 1549, which remained unaltered in all revisions of the Prayer Book down through our first American Book of 1789, was entirely given over to the theme of the giving of money offerings for the support of the clergy and for alms to the poor. This list was primarily from the New Testament, set down in the order in which the passages occurred in Scripture, and then, the last four happening to be concerned with the subject of charity to the poor, that theme was rounded out with four more such Sentences from the Sapiential Books. Our revision of 1892 kept this whole list, and added five more from the Scottish rite. Our last revision in 1928 canceled no less than twelve of the accumulated twenty-five, including all those adducing practical, Hebraic, and (to the modern eye) 'unworthy' motives of almsgiving, and all those appealing for the support of the clergy; and added three Sentences, one for a charitable offering, two for missionary occasions.

All the recent British revisions make extensive and sometimes radical changes in the use of these Sentences. This seems a favorable opportunity to give fresh consideration to the whole subject.

What most of the recent revisions are striving for is texts which place no stress upon the mere giving of money, save as this is implied in the sacrificial giving of ourselves. This new emphasis finds particular expression in the rites of Scotland, South Africa, and Ceylon. We are proposing four new Sentences of this order. Psalm 50:14 originated in the Scottish Liturgy of 1912, and has been adopted by England and Ceylon. Psalm 96:8 has been Scottish since 1637. Eph. 5:2 and Rom. 12:1 are South African, and the latter is used in Ceylon also. All of these speak of the general theme of Oblation, and are suitable even at a celebration where there is no 'Collection.'

We propose to eliminate from the present list all the 'begging' Sentences, which magnify the theme of giving for its own sake; retaining only six which have specific force in appealing for the entirely unselfish purposes of

Charitable Offerings, and Missionary Offerings, to be so designated in 'box titles' in the margin. The first three of these go back to 1549; the last three originated in our revision of 1928, and are peculiar to the American Church.

We also design to follow the Scottish use since 1764 by printing the two 'Presentation' Sentences, 'Thine, O Lord, is the greatness,' and 'All things come of thee,' after the Offertory Rubrics following the other Sentences, with a rubric indicating that they, or some suitable Hymn, shall be used only at the Presentation. Undoubtedly the revisers of 1892 were simply taking it for granted that they would always be used in that place only, when they added them at the end of the list of Sentences. It has really been the lack of suitable 'sacrificial' Sentences which of late years has prompted some clergy to employ 'Thine, O Lord,' as a Sentence wherewith to *'begin* the Offertory' — a use for which it is not adapted, and was never intended. In fact, it was the growth of this well-meaning but unhistorical and undesirable usage which called the attention of your Commission to the advisability of some better provisions for the happily increasing number of occasions when the obtaining of a maximum 'collection' is not the dominant thought in the mind of the Celebrant.

It may also be noted that South Africa has eleven, and India and Ceylon nineteen 'proper' Sentences assigned to various feasts and seasons of the Christian Year. They are exactly of the tenor of our 'seasonal' Sentences to begin Morning and Evening Prayer: none of them has any reference to the action of the Oblation. They represent a tentative step toward the recovery of the old provision of a Proper Anthem at the Offertory of every Mass. Again we refer to the forthcoming work of our other Committee, which seeks to provide complete assignments of such liturgical Anthems for every service.[54]

2. The Rubrics. a) The History of the Ritual: The actual actions at the Offertory are covered by the rubrics. Our present provisions represent a somewhat fortuitous survival of former developments in various directions. They are neither as complete nor as clear as could be desired. This will appear in an examination of the evolution of the Offertory ritual. In the early days of the Church, each communicant brought an offering of his own portion of bread and wine, bringing it up to the altar at the Offertory. A mark of this custom is still to be found in the words 'qui tibi offerunt' in the prayer *Memento* of the Mass, along with a vestige of the former reading of the 'Names' of those who offered. This offering 'in kind' survives to this day at Milan and Lyons, and at the Roman Mass for the Consecration of a Bishop; and it seems to have endured locally

---

54. Ed. Note: As far as I currently know, this promise was never fulfilled within the *Prayer Book Studies* series.

until well after the Reformation.[55] The chief cause of its decay appears to have been the introduction of the use of unleavened bread, which ended the people's offering of their own loaves.

As the people ceased to make an offering 'in kind,' their participation in the Oblation was commuted to the common denominator of money. But this also seems to have been present in the service since the beginning. St. Paul in 1 Cor. 16:2 makes a plain reference to 'collections' of money 'on the first day of the week'; and Justin Martyr in I *Ap.* 67 brackets the distribution of the consecrated Oblations with the apportionment of the charitable contributions of the people under the Bishop's direction. All through the history of the Church, gifts of money, things, and even the title-deeds of lands, were placed upon the altar of God at the offertory-time.

The local Roman Rite kept the Offertory in its original place, immediately before the *Sursum Corda*. The Church of Constantinople, however, at an early date took to receiving the oblations of the people before the service, and preparing them on a side-table with a service of 'Prothesis,' which eventually assumed such elaborations as to be almost a liturgy in itself. The prepared Elements were brought to the altar at the offertory-time with the imposing procession of 'The Great Entrance.'

This Eastern Preparation of the Elements before the service was copied by the Gallican Rite. And after the extinction of that liturgy, traces of its customs remained in its former domain, notably in the Use of Sarum and in the Dominican Missal. In both of these uses, the Elements were made ready before the service began, at Low Mass: although at High Mass in both the action took place between the Epistle and Gospel — perhaps because this point marked the end of the Mass of the Catechumens, who in the West were dismissed before the Gospel.

In other non-Roman uses in the West, the ninth to the eleventh centuries saw the incorporation of private prayers of the Celebrant to accompany each action of the Preparation of the Elements — though these prayers are nowhere found in their present text and order until the fourteenth century. Rome adopted them, as found in the Franciscan Missal, in 1570. In the Middle Ages, this group of prayers were known as 'The Minor Canon.' They did indeed constitute an almost complete duplication of the theme of Oblation and Benediction in the actual Prayers of Consecration, and even went so far as to include one ancient element which the Canon itself did not possess, namely an Invocation of the Holy Spirit as the 'Sanctifier.'

It is interesting to note the assurance and the sound knowledge of liturgical history and principles with which Cranmer made disposition of these

---

55. Scudamore, *Notitia Eucharistica* (London: Rivingtons, 1876), I. 352.

inheritances in his First Prayer Book. He revived the coming up of the people to make their offerings, in this form:

> In the meane tyme, whyles the Clearkes do syng the Offertory, so many as are disposed, shall offer to the poore mennes boxe euery one accordynge to his habilitie and charitable mynde.

He ignored the Sarum peculiarities, and put the Preparation of the Elements at this place:

> Than shall the minister take so muche Breade and Wine, as shall suffice for the persons appoynted to receiue the holy Communion, laiying the breade vpon the corporas, or els in the paten, or in some other comely thyng, prepared for that purpose: And puttyng ye wine into the Chalice, or els in some faire or conueniente cup, prepared for that vse (if the Chalice wil not serue) puttyng thereto a little pure and clean water: And setting both the bread and wyne vpon the Altar:

He left out all the Celebrant's prayers (which in any case had no uniformity between the various diocesan Uses in England), as not properly part of the public service. With them disappeared the old Roman Offertory Prayer, varying with the day, which made a verbal Oblation of the Holy Gifts. This prayer was known as the 'Secret,' because it was said inaudibly while the Choir was still singing the Offertory Anthem; hence it also was not part of the public rite as known to the people.

But in the Second Prayer Book, Cranmer allowed the virulence of the Puritan objections to these 'sacrificial' actions of priest and people to panick him into abandoning the direction for the singing of an Offertory, the coming up of the people to make their offerings (which were now to be gathered 'by the Churche wardens, or some other by them appointed '), and all mention both of the Preparation of the Elements and of the placing of them upon the altar.

Yet of course the bread and wine had to be made ready, and brought to the Holy Table: it was radically impossible to perform the service at all without doing so. Hence the rubric of 1662 followed the Scottish 1637 in amplifying the instructions of 1552 about the collection of the Alms, and ordered that they be placed 'vpon the holy Table.' It concluded: 'And when there is a Communion, the Priest shall then place upon the Table so much bread and Wine as he shall think sufficient.'

This last necessarily implies that the bread and wine shall be prepared then and there: but it does not say so explicitly, and neither does any subsequent Anglican book. The English 1928 considerably strengthens the implication by putting in at this place the statement that 'It is an ancient tradition of the Church to mingle a little water with the wine,' which the Scottish Liturgy since 1912 has given among the General Rubrics before or after the service. The Scottish rubric is followed by the 'Western' form of the Indian Liturgy (1952). Ceylon incorporates the direction that the wine shall be 'mixed with a little pure water' into the rubric about placing 'sufficient' amounts of the Elements upon the Holy Table.' The 'Eastern' version of the Indian Liturgy (1933) does the like in the preparation of the Elements and placing them upon the altar before the service, as in the Sarum Low Mass. The last American revision, although it considerably reinforced the significance of the Presentation by embodying phrases from the Scottish rite, saying 'And the Priest shall then *offer*, and shall place upon the Holy Table, the Bread and Wine,' by removing the 'sufficient' note also eliminated the implication of the Preparation of the Elements.

The successive revisions have all likewise sought for some means to restore the feature of a *verbal* Oblation of the Gifts which was missing from the First Prayer Book, thanks to Cranmer's elimination of the Celebrant's prayers and the *Secreta* Collect. The Second Prayer Book, whose rubrics spoke only of the Alms, inserted the words to accepte our almose and' into the beginning of the Prayer for the Church which followed immediately.

The Prayer Book of 1662 added to this the words 'and Oblations.' Dowden contends that this term was not designed to refer to the Elements — that at that time the word 'Alms' designated offerings for charitable purposes, and 'Oblations' those for all other purposes.[56] This may indeed have been the intent of the revisers of 1662 although even in that case the 'Oblations' must be considered as including the Bread and Wine, which the First Prayer Book had ordered to be paid for every Sunday at the Offertory, and both 1552 and 1662 directed to be provided by 'the Curate, and the Church-wardens at the charges of the parish.' Ever since then there has been an increasing disposition to interpret the 'Oblations' as directly denoting the Elements. This became absolute in our revision of 1928, followed by the Scottish and the South African of 1929, the Liturgy of Ceylon in 1938 and that of India in 1952, which have bracketed the words '[Alms and]' as to be omitted at a celebration at which there is no collection of a money offering.

The Scottish rite, which in 1735 removed the Prayer for the Church from this place following the Offertory, in 1764 restored a verbal Oblation of the Alms in the form of a cento from 1 Chron. 29 (embodying both of the 'Presentation Sentences' of the current American rite). Since 1912, this has been appropriated to the offering of the Elements.

The South African service has recovered the one survival of the *Secreta* Collect in Anglican use, by making a rather timid exception from the form used by the Archbishop when he presents upon the altar the Bread and Wine which is offered by the King at the Coronation Service.

---

56. *The Workmanship of the Prayer Book* (London: Methuen, 1908), 175–222.

The Indian rite of 1933, as might be expected, employs an Eastern prayer at the presentation of the Oblations.

b) Present Conditions: The general tradition of what is actually done at the Offertory has maintained itself on the whole very well: but the rubrics whose task is to regulate those actions have not kept pace with it. The use of an Offertory Anthem has continued, though there was no rubrical direction for it from 1552 to 1892. The Elements have been duly prepared, though instructions for doing so have been missing, save by indirection, ever since the Second Prayer Book. The mixing of water with the wine after the habit of the Primitive Church was a partisan bone of contention in the last century: it is practiced everywhere now without question. Some of the language in our present rubrics is obsolete, without application save to past conditions; and the order of them is poorly arranged.

All the rubrical and practical problems connected with the Offertory arise from the difficulty of devising rubrics which will give clear directions for carrying out three different actions which are to go on simultaneously. At a principal service, while the Choir is singing the Offertory Anthem, the Wardens are taking up the 'Collection,' and the Priest is preparing the Elements. That is sound ritual, performing at the same time actions which in no wise interfere with each other. But our present rubrics do not do very well in taking account of these concurrent operations. There are no directions for the Preparation of the Elements, but only for their placing upon the Holy Table. And the rubric covering the accompanying Anthem (which does not appear until after the rubrics dealing with the Presentation of both Alms and Oblations) tries to embrace too much in one statement. It says that such an Anthem may be used 'when the Alms and Oblations are being received and presented.' This inexact and equivocal language tries to conjoin two different things, which ought to be treated disjunctively, namely the time of the 'receiving,' and that of the 'presenting' of the offerings, and has the purpose of sanctioning two Anthems, not one.

Consequently, it is not remarkable that there are a few points where current practice has drifted from its rubrical moorings. The rubric is quite definite which directs that the Alms-basin shall be 'presented and placed upon the Holy Table.' Some clergy decline to do so, performing a kind of 'wave-offering,' or if they do set the Basin momentarily upon the Table, remove it instantly before the Prayer for the Church. This is in intended obedience to the ancient principle that nothing should be put upon the altar except such things as are essential to the 'Sacrifice.' That is a perfectly sound principle, to which they are not giving intelligent interpretation. Historically and actually, the Offerings of the People are their integral participation in the Christian Sacrifice. It is a great mistake to treat them as a regrettable necessity, and suppress the ritual offering of them as nearly as possible. The vital motive of Stewardship, and its expression in sacrificial giving, should be proclaimed in the most solemn ceremonial expression. And moreover, since there is a verbal Oblation of these sacrificial gifts in the following Prayer for the Church, it is a matter of ritual propriety that they be left upon the altar until after that prayer.

The rubrics are also perfectly explicit in ordering that the Alms must *first* be 'presented and placed,' and then the Bread and Wine should be 'offered and placed' upon the Holy Table. This is where the lack of a rubric covering the Preparation of the Elements has given rise to some confusion. It is quite inevitable that they should be so prepared during the 'Collection.' Most clergy not only do that, but proceed to set them immediately upon the Corporal, after the pattern of the Roman ceremonies. In other words, they really 'offer' the Bread and Wine first: which has the unfortunate effect of making the apparent climax come at the following Presentation of the Alms, in what is sometimes satirically called the ceremony of 'the Elevation of the Cash'! The Ceylon Liturgy adopts this order, directing that the Bread and Wine shall be placed upon the Holy Table 'whilst the alms and other devotions of the people are received.' But the sequence of events in all the other Anglican books is superior, making the most important matter of the Eucharistic Oblations come last.

Accurately to carry out the rubrical provisions would mean that the elements should be prepared at the Credence, or perhaps at the rear of the Church in the 'Liturgical Movement' experiments, and not brought up to the altar and formally offered there until after the Alms have been presented and set down upon the Holy Table. Some people do this sort of thing now, in one form or another. But it does not seem desirable to make the rubrics so specific as to impose unaccustomed ceremonies upon the generality of the clergy, or to hinder further development of promising new departures which are perfectly legal under our present provisions. It should suffice to do what can be done to make the intent of our existing regulations a little clearer.

The supplying of an explicit rubric requiring the Preparation of the Elements at this point in the service would also bring a natural end to another divergent custom which has appeared in a few quarters, and which likewise arose from the lack of such a rubric, namely the placing of this Preparation before the Celebration begins. This was a byproduct of the Lambeth Judgment[57] on the Mixed Chalice, which held that while it was a primitive custom to mingle a little water with the wine, nevertheless this must not be done during the service, because there was no rubric to sanction it. A few people in England saw a way of complying with this quite erroneous opinion by digging up the old Sarum provision for the 'Making of the Chalice' by a brief 'Rite of Prothesis' before Low Mass. Not only was this ruling wrong in principle, but it has no authority and no bearing upon the American rite, into which a few Anglophiles have copied it.

---

57. Cf. p. 268 f.

c) *Proposed Revision of the Rubrics:* The American service makes separate provision for an Offertory Anthem, thus disentangling this feature from the confused sort of dependence which it has upon the Offertory Sentences in the British books. The sentences set forth to 'begin the Offertory' emerge into clear light as a formal Bidding to the act of offering. Since all of the Sentences which we propose will be addressed to the people, not to God, it is only logical to underscore this meaning and function of the Sentences by directing the Priest to turn to the people when he pronounces them. Most clergy do so now.

The clarification of the rubrics after the Sentences is difficult enough, without encumbering them with the rubric on the use of the Sentences 'on any other occasion of Public Worship when the Offerings of the People are to be received.' It had very much better go back again to the position it occupied in the Prayer Book of 1892, immediately before the Sentences. We consider that the rubric should be retained, even though the 'begging' Sentences have been eliminated, since most of those now proposed will still be suitable for this use at Morning Prayer, because their emphasis is still upon giving — although giving sublimated to an expression of our full participation in the Church's worship, which is always intrinsically sacrificial in its character.

The rubric on the Offertory Anthem had best come immediately after the Sentences. The qualification, 'in the words of Holy Scripture or of the Book of Common Prayer,' seems superfluous here, since it simply repeats the General Rubric on Hymns and Anthems on p. viii of the Prayer Book. In view of the great range of available anthems, of course the choice of them is not and cannot be limited to those whose text is drawn only from those two sources; and beginning students of the subject have to be told that these provisos must be taken as descriptive rather than restrictive — literally applied, they would, for instance, exclude any amount of desirable liturgical music from the Eastern Churches. And the further stipulation, 'under the direction of the Priest,' is fully covered by Canon 24, 'On the Music of the Church.' It must be remembered that any rubric on Offertory Anthems was an innovation in 1892, and the safeguarding expressions probably had to be added as the price of getting it adopted at all. Since they are fully covered elsewhere, it is not necessary that they be reiterated here.

Next, we propose a new rubric, to fill the gap which has existed since 1552: 'The Priest or Deacon shall prepare so much Bread, and Wine mixed with a little pure water, as he shall think sufficient.' Separating the Preparation from the Oblation of the Elements, instead of treating the first as implied in the second, will do something to clear up the true order of events. And it is proper that mention of the indispensable 'matter' of the Sacrament should come first of all, just as it is proper that the offering of it should be made last. The Deacon is mentioned, since from the beginning he was associated with the preparation as well as with the administration of the Sacrament. Explicit reference to the Mixed Chalice is made, as utterly non-controversial now, and a universal custom. It will afford an opportunity to explain that in its primitive origin it was a gesture of temperance, since in the days of our Lord no one not a drunkard ever drank even the mild wines of those days unmixed.

The rubric on the receiving of the Alms is retained in substantially its present form, but with the dropping of some obsolete references. Perhaps the makers of the Scotch revision of 1637 thought that by mentioning 'Deacons' as suitable persons to take up the collection, they were doing something to revive the ancient and honorable function of the Deacon as Almoner of the Church: but it would be a surprise to learn that any Deacon has ever done so in Anglican use. 'Naming the Church Wardens' is quite in order; but to say, 'or other fit persons appointed for that purpose' seems calculated to make the people notice the absence of the Wardens, and suspect an improvisation. 'Other representatives of the Congregation' would appear to be a more significant and less exceptionable phrase. Again, in 1662 the specifying of 'a decent Bason to be provided by the parish for that purpose' may have been a necessary new direction, which now is capable of improvement by simplification.

Then follows unaltered our present provision for the offering of the Elements.

We have observed that our Book of 1892 tried to do too many things with one rubric, making the provision of an Anthem during the Offertory stretch to cover also the singing of the new Presentation Sentences, which were put into the service from the Scottish Liturgy at the end of the list of Sentences, with nothing there to indicate their specific function. We propose to follow the Scottish since 1764 by printing the two Presentation Sentences here, after the rubrics, under a rubric which again conforms to the Scottish use since 1889, of using them for the Presentation of both Alms and Oblations, instead if the former alone; or allowing a suitable Hymn here.

3. The General Intercession

1. Problems of the Prayer for the Church

The form, the text, and the use of the Great Intercession of the Liturgy, which has come down to us as the Prayer for the Whole State of Christ's Church, poses some of the most considerable problems in the whole service, and perhaps the most difficult for which to find satisfactory solutions.

As it stands, it is rather the least vital, incisive, and stirring form of General Intercession in the Prayer Book. One reason for this is that its constituents, which we first find in exactly this place in the service in the vivid and concrete form of a Litany, in later rites were converted into celebrant's prayers, and transported about the Liturgy and back again. The Latin Mass saw them divided before and after the Consecration. Cranmer fused them into a single prayer in 1549, still within the Canon, but coming before the Consecration Prayer proper and in 1552 restored them to this place of their origin in a curtailed form. All that dragging about, that remelting and casting in other molds, has cost this ancient supplication much of in vigor and trenchancy; it now possesses little of the quality of 'thoughts that breathe and words that burn.' It has been remarked that 'the Prayer for the Church, originally identical with the matter of the Litany, is an old coin which has passed through many hands, and been abraded by the attrition of the ages, till it has been worn smooth and dim, while the Litany still shines sharp from the die.'[58]

These deficiencies in style and content were, if anything, even more true of the intercessory material in the Latin Canon than they were of Cranmer's paraphrase of it. He did not have much to work with. His Prayer for the Whole State of Christ's Church was based upon four Collects of the Canon: the *Te igitur*, an offering of the Oblations for the Universal Church and its rulers and members; the *Memento* of the Living, a presentation of the 'sacrifice of praise' by the congregation present on behalf of their several intentions; the *Communicantes*, a commemoration of the Blessed Virgin, with Apostles and Martyrs; and the *Memento* of the Dead, a commendation of the Faithful Departed. The content of this General Intercession of the Latin Rite is certainly very meager, in comparison with that of any Eastern Liturgy — how meager, anyone can readily see by considering its text as given on pp. 145–152 above side by side with our Litany, a form which has preserved most of the matter of the Eastern Intercessions, and may be considered as fairly representative of them. Moreover, the Latin style again and again fades off into vague rhetorical generalities, instead of intensifying itself in trenchant and vigorous detail.

Even of what the Latin original offered, Cranmer felt constrained to remove the name of the Pope, the two offerings of the Sacrifice, the catalogue of names of the Saints, and the mention of the intercession of the Saints. This left still less of the already sketchy and fragmentary Latin material, on the basis of which he could construct a Great Intercession after the Eastern pattern, and sufficiently substantial to be accepted as a fair substitute for the Latin passages it was designed to replace. It is quite apparent that such were the objectives he had in mind.

As far as sheer bulk goes, Cranmer's Prayer for the Church was impressive. In the collation given above on pp. 145 ff., it occupies 99 lines, while the translation of the Latin takes up only 63. The supplications for Rulers, and for the Faithful Departed, were very greatly expanded: so much so that both passages have been radically curtailed in subsequent revisions. Real enrichments of the impoverished Latin provisions were added in the petitions for the Clergy and People, and Those in Need, seemingly suggested by the Greek liturgies. But throughout, Cranmer echoed only too faithfully the tone and manner of the Latin style, in its diffuseness, its use of generalities instead of cogent detail, its penchant for mouth-filling rhetorical cadences which make little contribution save perhaps to

---

58. Parsons and Jones, *The American Prayer Book* (N.Y.: Scribners, 1937), 138.

'edification,' an objective which they pursue in an almost homiletical way. It may fairly be maintained that Cranmer's efforts in this last direction are on the whole more successful than those of the Latin; but that is about the best that can be said of this method.

This examination of the genesis of the Prayer for the Church explains the fact that it has been felt to be a distinct element of tedium in our service. We have noted that all the latest Anglican revisions have gone back to pre-Reformation precedents by breaking it up into paragraphs.[59] This is a little help, making it look less dull on the page, and encouraging refreshing pauses and changes of pace in its recitation. And the Liturgy of Ceylon in 1938, followed by the Indian in 1952, made the bold experiment of presenting it in Litany form, in the hope of maintaining the attention of the congregation by enlisting their participation in recurring responses to its petitions.

Neither of these measures is sufficient. Even the expedient of Ceylon, which looks attractive on paper, works remarkably poorly in practice. We found in trial use of this form that it simply seemed further to accentuate the inferiority of the contents of this prayer in comparison with the glowing and moving quality of the Litany.

Most of the suggestions for the emendation of the text which have been made to the Liturgical Commission are in the wrong direction, and would tend only to smooth flat and 'bowdlerize' still further a form whose outstanding deficiency is a lack of incisiveness. For instance, the most common exception taken to it is on the phrase about 'the punishment of wickedness and vice.' Some people boggle at the idea of 'the punishment of *abstractions*'; others seem unwilling to face the fact that sinners not only do but should undergo divine retribution for their sins. Still others roundly defend the present phrase, with some impatience at such 'soft' ideas of God's judgments, and would share Father Hebert's scorn of those who would divest the Liturgy of every uncomfortable suggestion, since they hold that 'God is nice; and in him is nothing nasty at all!' Yet the fact remains that some clergy feel the difficulty of the phrase to such a degree that they refuse to use it, and quite illegally substitute the word 'correction' for 'punishment.'

Now the mutual dissidence of opinion at this point is precisely the sort of thing which a universally required Liturgy should not occasion. Certainly this known stumbling-block should be removed — though hardly at the price of making the phrase mean less than it does now. It does not seem that this can be done by tinkering with the present language. The only effective remedy would seem to be to throw out the existing construction entirely, and approach the essential thought to be expressed from an entirely different angle: as will presently appear.

---

59. Cf. p. 198 f.

2. *Proposed Revision of the Prayer. a) The Universal Church:* A very considerable share of the blame for the tedium of this prayer is to be attributed to its prolix and diffuse exordium. The fact seems to be that Cranmer was distinctly self-conscious about his having expunged all mention of the emphatic oblation of 'these gifts, these offerings, these holy undefiled sacrifices' from the *Te igitur* in favor of a petition 'to receiue these our prayers,' and felt that he had to provide an equally weighty apologia for a Eucharistic Intercession which was offered as a purely spiritual exercise, not as a sacrificial action. This he did in the form of a citation of 1 Tim. 2:1.

This apologetic introduction is now completely superfluous. Cranmer himself transferred this prayer in 1552 to a place immediately after the Offertory, and added 'our almose' to 'our prayers' as here offered. 1662 further appended 'and Oblations.' The petition is now again an action, and does not need justification. We believe that this prayer will be far more effective if it is made to plunge at once into its proper business, without this preliminary verbiage.

Both the somewhat cryptic Latin of this passage, and Cranmer's paraphrase of it, seem needlessly wordy expansions of the essential themes of peace, unity, and orthodoxy. We think that Cranmer's expressions can profitably be condensed, and that thus room can be made for a further idea which was voiced in the Greek liturgies, as well as in the old Roman Intercessions of the *Orationes solemnes* on Good Friday, and whose importance is now again in the forefront of the Church's consciousness, namely that of the missionary extension of the Church throughout the world.

b) Rulers: A prayer for the King by name was peculiar to the Sarum Mass; it is not in the modern Roman Canon. But a supplication for Rulers occurs in precisely this place in all normal forms of General Intercession, ancient as well as modern. It must be realized that this is not an expression of 'Erastian' ideas of the primacy of the State; still less a reflection of the fact that our Mother Church of England was and is an Established Church. In the most ancient liturgies, it came as an integral part of the supplication for the Peace of the Church. It is true that after the time of Constantine, the liturgies usually assumed that the Rulers were Christian; and our present phrase, for 'all Christian Rulers,' is sometimes defended by the argument that the scope of the Intercession is limited to the members of the Church. Yet the times in which we now live have brought us again to the reluctant realization of what the Primitive Church also knew to its sorrow, that it is impossible to pray for the Church of God without regard to its environment in the World outside. Today it is certainly much more important to the welfare of the Church that Providence should restrain the tyrannous intent of a Stalin or a Hitler, than that the Queen of England should be a devout Churchwoman. The Primitive Church prayed for — Nero! And Justin Martyr calmly told the pagan Emperor Antonius: 'Wherefore we *worship* God alone; but we *pray for* you also, that with the royal power ye may be found to have a prudent mind.'[60]

We have observed that Cranmer's version of this supplication was much expanded, from the four words of the Sarum form (p. 145.23), to 64 words of English (145.20–33). It seems rather probable that this may have been deliberate propaganda on behalf of the Royal Authority in which Cranmer believed so profoundly, and, in the end, so disastrously to himself — upon which at all events he placed his whole reliance for the formidable undertaking of transforming the worship of the nation from a Latin to an English basis.

In any case, this petition was nevertheless in somewhat more primitive terms in the First Prayer Book than it is now. It began with a rather close paraphrase of 1 Tim. 2:2 — 'for kings, and for all that are in authority; that we may lead a quiet and peaceable life in all godliness and decorum' — a text which is usually incorporated in the Greek Intercessions at this point, and which expresses very well the attitude of the early Church. The Second Prayer Book inserted 'al Christian kinges, Princes, and gouernours' before the name of the King. (Note that the limitation to *Christian* kings dates only from 1552.) Then the rest of Cranmer's form is devoted to the subordinate authorities who administer justice. This remains unchanged in the British books.

The American Prayer Books since 1789 consolidated both sentences, but in such a left-handed way as to expunge the note of 'government,' and to concentrate all the emphasis upon the idea of 'administration.' Quite apart from the fallacious popular idea that in a Democracy no one is actually *governed*, the unfortunate result was that this telescoping of expressions obliterated the scriptural reference, and with it, the primitive justification and *raison d'être* for this supplication at this point, namely the function of Rulers to preserve the Peace of the Church.

We have sought to restore the original meaning of this passage by saying, 'We beseech thee also, so to direct those in authority in all nations to maintain justice and the welfare of all mankind, that thy Church may abide in thy peace.' This is the simplest and most effective expression we have been able to devise, without resorting to the unallowable expedient of borrowing forms already in the Prayer Book, notably the beautiful paraphrase of 1 Tim. 2:2 in the Collect for Trinity V, 'that the course of this world may be so peaceably ordered by thy governance, that thy Church may joyfully serve thee in all godly quietness,' or the admirably condensed expression in our second Prayer for the President in Morning Prayer, that, being guided by thy Providence, we may dwell secure in thy peace.'

---

60. I *Ap.* 17.

All the recent British revisions have been seeking for some thing of exactly this order. The English 1928, followed by the Scottish and South African 1929, the Cingalese 1938, and the Indian 1952, says:

> We beseech thee also to lead all nations in the way of righteousne and peace; and so to direct all kings and rulers, that under them thy people may be godly and quietly governed.

The Scottish, Cingalese, and Indian rites stop there; the others go on to some form of Cranmer's second sentence. But the Indian rite makes the mistake of transferring this petition to a place after the supplication for the People.

Also, as we have intimated, this discarding of the really secondary considerations about the '*administration* of justice,' in order to restore the primary emphasis of the commission to civil rulers to preserve universal human rights, and especially the great 'Fourth Freedom' of the 'Atlantic Charter,' also completely and effortlessly bypasses the current bone of contention about 'the punishment of wickedness and vice.'

c) The Clergy: The suffrage for the Clergy of the Church is excellent in form and proportion as it stands. But some of its 'terms of reference' are not quite happy.

The Sarum Mass mentioned the Pope and the diocesan Bishop only. Cranmer felt this was not sufficient, in the light of the Greek liturgies, with their long lists of every possible office an ministration in the Church. Without adventuring into all th detail, he settled for 'all Bishoppes, Pastors, and Curates' echo of the phrase 'all Byshoppes, pastours and ministers of the Churche' which he had adopted in his Litany of 1544 from Luther's Latin Litany. The 1662 Prayer Book, which corrected the Lutheran phrase in the Litany to 'all Bishops, Priests, an Deacons,' dropped the word 'Pastors' in the Prayer for the Church. The American Prayer Book, in a region where the word 'Curate' is always understood to apply only to an assistant in a parish, not, as in England, to any clergyman who enjoys any 'cure [i.e., care] of souls,' made it 'Bishops and other Ministers.' But that is not a fortunate expression either. To many minds it implies a reference to 'non-Episcopal ministries' — which, however charitable and laudable, does not happen to be in the least what this supplication is trying to say. Therefore we propose to make the same correction in what is left of the equivocal Lutheran phrase which was made in the Litany nearly three centuries ago, to the standard form of 'Bishops, Priests, and Deacons.' This step has been taken in the English 1928, Scottish and South African 1929, Cingalese 1938, and Indian 1933 and 1952.

A second misunderstanding tends to arise from the petition that the Clergy may 'rightly and duly administer thy holy Sacraments.' It seems at the best to bring an echo of Reformation controversies. It is now entirely unrealistic. If it means anything, it would appear to suggest a doubt about the legitimacy of other people's ritual practices! Some clergy have admitted to us that they had to put that idea out of their minds every time they said it. It would seem much better to say '*faithfully* administer' — an emendation which has already been made in the form in which this passage is quoted on p. 573 in the Institution Office, in the prayer which the newly inducted Rector says for himself.

Finally, 'lively Word' should be made 'living.' The old meaning of 'lively' in the sense of *alive* is obsolete: nowadays it always signifies *animated* or *vivacious*. The first American Prayer Book corrected this word to the modern form in the 'living sacrifice' of the last paragraph of the Consecration Prayer, and the 'living member' of the first Exhortation in the Baptismal Service; and there is no good reason why it should be allowed to continue to raise misleading connotations here.

d) *The People:* The next two supplications, for all the People, and for Those in Necessity, are likewise brief and concrete, and call for nothing more than verbal changes. There does not seem to be any need to specify 'and especially to this congregation here present' in the first of these. It was not in this place in 1549, being transferred to it in 1552 from its original occurrence on p. 147.56–62 above. Since it is something necessarily implied, the passage is actually more effective with out it.

We have accepted the suggestion that to say 'with *willing* heart' would be much more significant than the word 'meek': it would turn the passive idea of an unresisting teachableness; into an active attitude of eager acceptance.

In line with what we have said above on the passive and 'escapist' meaning nowadays of the word 'comfort,'[61] we propose 'to support and strengthen' instead of 'to comfort and succour.' The last word also is obsolescent in America though still understood as a literary word, and though not actually misunderstood, as is 'comfort,' it is never used in spoke English here, the public speakers have learned to avoid it usually provoking mirth.

e) *The Faithful Departed.* 1) *History:* In the First Prayer Book, Cranmer combined the prayer *Communicantes*, which recited a catalogue of the Saints in a place before the Consecration, with the last two Collects of the Canon after the Consecration: the prayer *Memento etiam* for the Faithful Departed together with some of the sense though none of the words of the *Nobis quoque* (151.243 above), which asked that the worshippers might be brought at the last to share in the fellowship of the Saints. His text has been given before on pp. 146.69–147.115: as fine a rhetorical passage as his Prayer Book contained, furnishing a magnificent peroration to his Intercession. The subsequent deletion of this passage has strongly contributed to the 'dulness' of the present Prayer for the Church which we are now trying to remedy.

---

61. Cf. p. 241.

The Continental Reformers who had taken refuge in England were keenly mindful of the fact that a revolt against the doctrines of Purgatory and the Merits of the Saints was precisely the point which touched off the Reformation. They made an uncompromising attack upon everything in the First Prayer Book which might imply or even permit such beliefs. As we have noted before, this was the one point where Cranmer yielded entirely.[62] In 1552, every bit of the supplication for the Departed, and every mention of the Saints, was eliminated from the Prayer for the Church, along with every other prayer in the book which made intercession for the Departed.

The Scottish Liturgy of 1637 restored most of the matter of 1549. The passage 'and chiefly in the glorious and most blessed virgin Mary, mother of thy sonne Iesu Christ our Lord and God, & in the holy Patriarches, Prophetes, Apostles and Martyrs' (146.75–80) was not brought back. On the other hand, the Commemoration of the Saints was further enriched by saying 'who have been the choice vessels of thy grace, and the lights of the world in their severall generations,' instead of 'from the begynninge of the worlde' at 146.74.

This book also took the bold and successful step of putting the Commemoration of the Departed in general before that of the glorified Saints, thus forming a still more successful conclusion to the whole Intercession. The Scottish form for the Departed was 'And we also blesse thy holy Name for all those thy servants, who having finished their course in faith, do now rest from their labours,' in lieu of Cranmer's passage given on 147.95–102, but occurring immediately after 146.56. It is interesting to note that Dr. William Smith, who was familiar with this Scottish passage as it appeared in the 'Communion Office' of 1764, succeeded in getting it inserted in our first American Prayer Book, in what is now the second Collect on p. 334 of the Burial Office. And the rest of the conclusion of the Intercession of 1637 was incorporated in 1892 as the last prayer on p. 336.[63]

The English revision of 1662, with one eye on 1637 and the other on 1549, made a very cautious, brief, and somewhat dry condensation of this material. The

---

62. Ed. Note: ALMIGHTY God, with whom do live the spirits of those who depart hence in the Lord, and with whom the souls of the faithful, after they are delivered from the burden of the flesh, are in joy and felicity; We give thee hearty thanks for the good examples of all those thy servants, who, having finished their course in faith, do now rest from their labours. And we beseech thee, that we, with all those who are departed in the true faith of thy holy Name, may have our perfect consummation and bliss, both in body and soul, in thy eternal and everlasting glory; through Jesus Christ our Lord. Amen.

63. Ed. Note: ALMIGHTY and everliving God, we yield unto thee most high praise and hearty thanks, for the wonderful grace and virtue declared in all thy saints, who have been the choice vessels of thy grace, and the lights of the world in their several generations; most humbly beseeching thee to give us grace so to follow the example of their stedfastness in thy faith, and obedience to thy holy commandments, that at the day of the general Resurrection, we, with all those who are of the mystical body of thy Son, may be set on his right hand, and hear that his most joyful voice: Come, ye blessed of my Father, inherit the kingdom prepared for you from the foundation of the world. Grant this, O Father, for the sake of the same, thy Son Jesus Christ, our only Mediator and Advocate. Amen.

form of 1662, which remained unchanged until 1928 in the American books, read 'And we also bless thy holy name, for all thy servants departed this life in thy faith and fear, beseeching thee to give us grace so to follow their good examples, that with them we may be partakers of thy heavenly kingdom.' This restored a Commemoration of the Faithful Departed, which had been totally missing since 1552, but still excluded any prayer *for* them.

2) The Modern Situation: But recent days have seen a complete revolution of thought on the subject of Prayers for the Dead. The Reformation phobias which were so potent in 1552 have now faded to little more than prejudices, which even that reduced form have barely lasted until our lifetimes in our Church.

The turning-point of general public opinion seems to have been the First World War. Dr. Randall Davidson, who in 1895 as Bishop of Winchester forced Father Dolling's resignation from St. Agnes', Landport, because he had set up a special altar for requiems there, twenty years later as Archbishop of Canterbury admitted that in spite of the inveterate tradition in the Church of England against Prayers for the Dead, the insistent demand of the people for intercessions for their dear ones who had fallen in the Great War could no longer be resisted, and sanctioned forms of prayer for that purpose. And on this side of the water, the mind of Christians generally as a result of those days of travail was accurately expressed by the words of Dr. S. Parkes Cadman, sometime Moderator of the Congregational Church, who in 1926 in conducting the first religious 'Question Box' on the radio, responded to the challenge, 'Do you believe in Prayers for the Dead?' by declaring forthrightly, 'Certainly: *because there are no dead.*' The words of the author of 2 Maccabees about 'the noble Judas' might apply equally well to Dr. Cadman, as 'doing therein very well, and honestly, in that he was mindful of the resurrection: for he had not hoped that they that were slain should have risen again, it had been superfluous and vain to pray for the dead' (2 Macc. 12:44 f.).

3) Recent Revisions: Accordingly, we find that all the branches of the Church of England which have revised the Liturgy in the present century have completely emancipated themselves from the Puritan tyranny to which Cranmer capitulated in 1552, and have freely restored any or all of the matter of the Intercessions for the Departed and the Commemoration of the Saints found in the rites of 1637 and 1549.

The versions in England, Scotland, South Africa, Ceylon, and India (1952) all follow the order of the Scottish 1637, by putting the Prayer for the Departed first, and then the Commemoration of the Saints as the peroration of the whole Prayer for the Church. Only the Indian of 1933 reverts to the sequence of 1549.

The English text is fairly short, retaining the 'chosen vessels' addition of 1637, transforming the former mere commemoration of the Departed into a supplication for them, and substituting the brief ending of 1662 for the long 'mystical body' passage of 1637 and 1549.

The Scottish preserves the text of 1637 entire, though following the English 1928 in incorporating a specific Intercession for the Departed. It also allows upon certain feasts the insertion of the 'chiefly' passage of 1549, mentioning the Blessed Virgin and the Saints. South Africa on the other hand omits the 'chosen vessels,' but incorporates the 'chiefly' section absolutely; and has an abbreviated conclusion like the English.

Only the American revision of 1928 displayed the slightest diffidence about restoring any of this material. We should remember, however, that the American was, in one way, the first in the field, the earliest of all these modern revisions to be completed. Nothing appears in our Prayer Book of 1928 which had not been enacted in the General Convention of 1925 — a time when the English Book was still in the state of proposals not yet adopted by the Church Assembly. And even those who were not conservatively averse to making a breach with 'Reformation principles' were understandably reluctant to take a position too far in advance of our Mother Church, and of the rest of the Anglican Communion. That situation is entirely different now, when all other branches of the Church have left us far in the rear in this important particular.

4) The Present American Form: The text of the supplication for the Departed adopted in America in 1928 was therefore highly conservative, yet at the same time distinctly constructive. The alteration consisted only of inserting in the version 1662–1892 the words 'to grant them continual growth in thy love and service.' Being entirely original, and not in traditional language, it was entirely free of the 'semantic' overtones past controversies. Simply yet very potently, it set forth the *actuality* of the life to come, since it is an axiom that 'life is growth.' It registered an effective advance upon the static picture of existence in unchanging bliss which has come dow to us from medieval times, which is nearly all that is expresse in the Roman Canon, and from which the current British re visions, fine as they are in some other respects, have not appreciably emancipated themselves; as will appear.

But in another aspect, the use of the word 'growth' is not quite so happy. Being a material metaphor, it suggests 'enlargement' as well as 'enhancement.' And the idea of an infinite continuance of the 'growth' of a finite being is ultimately logical absurdity. Or again, 'Just like America! Even the departed souls must be always "bigger and better"!'

Possibly neither of these criticisms, domestic or foreign, which have been made to the Liturgical Commission need be taken too seriously. But they do rather suggest the possibilitybe that the new phrase of 1928 may be only too concise to theologically secure. Indeed, this would rather definitely seem to be the case in the light of a further and quite serious objection that has been raised, that the conception of a 'continual growth' is in conflict with our Church's accepted interpretation of the testimonies of Holy Scripture as to 'the Last Things': that there is indeed an 'Intermediate State' after death, in which there is opportunity for purification and progress for the soul; but that this interim condition will come to an end at the final Day of Judgment which will wind up the order of this present universe, and usher in a new heaven and a new earth 'with the establishment of an everlasting Kingdom of just men made perfect' in the immediate presence of God.

Furthermore, our present form has been criticized as defective in that its emphasis is upon the supplication for the Faithful Departed alone, and lacks a separate thanksgiving for the outstanding 'victors in the strife' whom the Church acclaims as the Saints Triumphant. It may be granted that we should be missing an opportunity by not doing what all the other Anglican books have done, and including some form of the passage in the First Prayer Book, which is not only of great power and beauty, but which expresses the ultimate argument for the effectiveness of our religion from the exalted human character that it has produced, and provides us with the greatest practical inspiration for a like growth in holiness.

Finally, the point has been raised that the petition 'to give us grace so to follow their good examples' is merely moralistic, and tends to foster the too common low-level idea of religion as a matter of 'ethical culture.' There are few Anglicans who would regret Cranmer's action throughout the Prayer Book in substituting the dynamic challenge of the 'examples' of the Saints for the endless ringing of changes upon the passive reliance upon their 'merits' and 'intercessions' which we find in the Latin books. But again it may be admitted that this petition, standing alone, does not give full and adequate expresssion to all that is meant by the 'Communion of the Saints' — an idea so important that it stands as one of the articles of the Creed.

5) *Intercession for the Departed*: We propose that this passage in our Prayer for the Church be brought into conformity with all the recent Anglican revisions (save the Indian of 1933) by following the Scottish 1637 by putting first a supplication for the Faithful Departed, and then in conclusion thanksgiving for the Communion of the Saints.

It may indeed be truly maintained that our present single abbreviated and consolidated petition is primitive. To the early Church, as to Anglicanism through most of its history, the commemoration of 'All Saints' likewise included 'All Souls.' The first complete Intercession which we have, in the *Apostolic Constitutions*, offered the Oblation before God 'for all the Holy Ones who have been well-pleasing unto thee from the foundation of the world: for Patriarchs,

Prophets, Just Men, Apostles, Martyrs, Confessors, Bishops, Presbyters, Deacon Subdeacons, Readers, Singers, Virgins, Widows, Laymen, and all those whose names thou thyself knowest.'[64] It was not until after this time that distinctions were drawn in the liturgies between our departed comrades, for whom we offer our prayers and the Saints in glory, who are asked to pray for us. It is not the least necessary that such a point of view be now revived and given liturgical expression. Yet it represented an inevitable development that the later liturgies all added on to the Commemoration of the Saints a specific Intercession for departed friends. All the recent Anglican liturgies have acknowledged the need to restore that: though they have also felt the wisdom of the Scottish line since 1637 in reversing the order of the old liturgies, as represented in 1549, as giving a better integration of the constituent ideas, and putting the major emphasis where it belongs, with its climax and conclusion in the Commemoration of the Saints Triumphant.

But when we make a closer examination of the actual content of the various supplications for the Faithful Departed, it seems that they do not seem very clear as to just what they are praying for: and in some cases their expressions do not stand a critical and theological examination much better than the American formula.

The original Latin petition for the Departed was the simple but pregnant phrase that they might receive 'a place of refreshment, light, and peace' (147.105). Here the 'place' was the 'Paradise' of Luke 21:43. The 'refreshment' implied the rewards of 'a better country, that is, an heavenly,' of Heb. 11:16, and no doubt also that compensation for the blind inequalities of this life which has always been one of the chief arguments for a life to come, since God is just. The 'light' was nothing short of the perfect illumination of the Beatific Vision: 'for the glory of God did lighten it, and the Lamb was the light thereof,' as in Rev. 21:23. And the 'peace' was more than mere rest after labor — it necessarily entailed the conception of complete reconciliation and fulfilment. It must, however, be conceded that it takes a theologian to find this much in the all too elementary Latin words. To the layman, they would present little more than the idea of an eternal quiescence a concept entirely too static to have power or appeal. A liturgy in the vernacular, intended for the use of the active intelligence of modern men, should surely be more expressive.

And exactly this inadequacy appears in the English paraphrases of the Latin original, from 1549 on. It is interesting to observe that Cranmer was 'modern' enough to shy at the mention of a 'place': even if he were not conscious of the problem as to whether Heaven is a location or a condition, no doubt he did not wish to raise the question as to whether the allusion was to Heaven, or to a 'Paradise' which in his time would arouse current controversies about the medieval

---

64. Brightman, *Liturgies Eastern and Western* (Oxford: Clarendo 1896), 21.29–22.2.

Purgatory. And he reduced the rest of 'the thing asked for' to the not very fertile form of 'thy mercy, and euerlasting peace' (147.102). This is even slighter than the Latin version. But it is all that is to be found in the English 1928 and the Scottish 1929. The Indian Liturgy of 1933 makes it 'thy tender mercy and everlasting rest,' with a respond by the people, 'Rest eternal grant unto them, O Lord, and let light perpetual shine upon them.' The South African of 1929, followed by the Indian of 1952, says 'mercy, light and peace both now and at the day of resurrection.' This indeed goes back to 1549 (147.103) for a note which is sound Eschatology, and which we have noted as missing from the present American form.

We consider that we need here first of all a clear assertion of the reality of the life immortal. It should be in such a form as to carry the dynamic suggestions which are obscurely latent in the Latin 'refreshment,' but which are somewhat overstressed in the current American 'continual growth.' Then there should be an emphasis on the heavenly 'light,' in terms making explicit that this denotes nothing less than the Beatific Vision of God. The ancient petition for 'peace' must of course be included although, in view of the somewhat inordinate weight it has been made to bear hitherto, it might be as well not to put it in a position of climax. The specific appeal to the divine 'mercy,' originating with Cranmer, and universal in the British forms, is entirely in order: though we do not care much for duplicating this idea by saying 'we commend to thy gracious keeping' (a quotation of Hymn No. 224),[65] as the English, Scottish, and South African rites do, nor yet 'we commend to thy fatherly goodness' (a borrowing of the language of the Prayer for All Conditions), as do India and Ceylon.

Turning to the Eastern liturgies in search of constructive suggestions, we found there somewhat a plethora of riches, which would hardly fit into the sober strength of our Intercession. However, in the Liturgy of 'St. James' we came upon a very telling use of two verses from the Psalms, 116:9 and 4:7, which provide lucid, adequate, and scriptural expression of what all the rites are trying to say. We therefore are recommending the following petition:

> We also commend unto thy mercy all thy servants departed this life in thy faith and fear: Grant them thy peace in the land of the living, where the light of thy countenance shineth upon them.

6) *Commemoration of the Saints*: After this, the current Anglican revisions all conclude the Intercession with some form of Cranmer's Commemoration of the Saints: the Scottish in the fullest possible version of 1549 and 1637, the others with varying degrees of condensation.

---

65. Ed. Note: The reference is to verse 1 of the hymn "Now the laborer's task is o'er" from the Hymnal 1940.("Father, in the gracious keeping/Leave me now thy servant sleeping.")

We have noted that Cranmer substituted the idea of following the examples of the Saints for a petition that we might be assisted through their merits and prayers. But it has not been mentioned that the fine rhetorical peroration of the Intercession is due to his assimilating here a note from the *Nobis quoque*, 'into whose company admit us' (151.258), in the moving but somewhat diffuse form of 'that at the daye of the generall resurreccion, we and all they whiche bee of the misticall body of thy sonne, maye altogether bee set on his right hand, and heare that his most ioyful voice: Come vnto me, O ye that be blessed of my father, and possesse the kingdome, whiche is prepared for you, from the begynning of the worlde' (147.103–115): which 1662 judiciously summarized 'that with them we may be partakers of thy heavenly kingdom.'

Most of the recent revisions retain this ending of 1662, but seek to balance the theme of the 'examples' with some less inferential expression of the idea of the Communion of the Saints. This passage in the Indian Liturgy of 1933 goes considerably too far, with an interpretation of that doctrine which is current in popular devotion of a sort, but which is hardly theologically defensible: 'And we beseech thee so to unite us in their holy fellowship that they may share in the communion of this our Eucharist, and continually assist us by their prayers.' The South African has 'rejoicing in the Communion of the Saints, and following the good examples of those who have served thee here.' The conclusion of this is a fine phrase, but unfortunately one which has been appropriated from the Collect for a Requiem which we have on p. 268 of our Prayer Book.[66] The English of 1928 has perhaps the simplest and most usable expression in 'rejoicing in their fellowship, and following their good examples.' The first phrase has been taken from the Scottish and American Proper Preface for All Saints. But, as we shall see later,[67] it is not desirable in the context of that Preface, and may be better employed here.

We are therefore recommending the form of the English 1928, altered only by a word or two, on account of its concise conclusion, and its careful avoidance of the repetition of the word 'grace,' which occurs twice in 1549, and three times in the Scottish. This version incorporates the 'chosen vessels' passage of 1637, which could hardly be improved upon as an expression of the significance of this Commemoration, and is already familiar to us in the last prayer on p. 336. It seems to us to be preferable to the 'chiefly' passage from 1549, mentioning the Blessed Virgin and the classes of Saints, which South Africa has chosen in its stead. This indeed is ancient, and ecumenical in its content. We have been urged to incorporate it: but it does not seem to us to be something which it would be opportune to include in a

---

66. Ed. Note: O ETERNAL Lord God, who holdest all souls in life; Vouchsafe, we beseech thee, to thy whole Church in paradise and on earth, thy light and peace; and grant that we, following the good examples of those who have served thee here and are now at rest, may at the last enter with them into thine unending joy; through Jesus Christ our Lord. *Amen.*

67. P. 349.

required prayer of the Liturgy. Even the Scots present it only as an optional addition upon occasion. The next revision of our Prayer Book will show quite enough advance if we can succeed in catching up with all the other branches of our Communion by replacing our present inadequate and rather equivocal single supplication by a petition for the Faithful Departed, and a thanksgiving for the Saints Triumphant. Our present contribution may well be limited to making the language of these passages more lucid and significant, leaving the substantial 'enrichment' of the restoration of the ancient material to the judgment of a later time.

The Indian Rite of 1933 contributes the initial word 'Finally,' to this concluding section — we think very effectively.

Not only has the unanimous example of the other Anglican books banished any hesitation we might have felt as to proposing these rather substantial amendments at this point, but it is significant that the *Book of Common Worship* of the Presbyterian Church in the United States of America has incorporated the English 1928 form of the Commemoration of their Saints outright in the General Intercession of its Communion Service[68] - although, as might be expected, it did not abandon Calvinistic standards by including any prayer for the Departed. The times have certainly changed: there can be no doubt about that.

3. Special Intercessions

Beside the foregoing problems of the text of the General Intercession, we must take account of its attendant rubrics. These recall the question of a suitable place in the Liturgy for the insertion of the so-called 'Occasional Prayers,' i.e., of special Intercessions for particular needs.

We have noted before[69] that our present provisions for the interpolation of such prayers between the Creed and the Sermon works well enough at a choral celebration, when there are 'Announcements,' but poorly when we have neither 'Announcements' nor Sermon at a said service, and when the inserted matter comes in abruptly and without apparent relation to the progress of the rite. Moreover, we have seen that there is a rather general feeling that this is not a satisfactory place for special prayers, so that many clergy ignore the rubric on p. 71,[70] and put such supplications in before the Prayer for the Church, where the rubric on p. 74[71] sanctions the entirely different expedient of special Biddings which

---

68. Philadelphia: Board of Christian Education of the Presbyterian Church in the U.S.A., 1946, p. 159.

69. P. 260 f.

70. Ed. Note: This is the rubric mentioned: "¶ Here, or immediately after the Creed, may be said the Bidding Prayer or other authorized prayers and intercessions."

71. Ed. Note: This is the rubric mentioned: "¶ Here the Priest may ask the secret intercessions of the Congregation for any who have desired the prayers of the Church."

state the subjects or intentions for which prayers have been desired, but does not authorize the saying of specific prayers in that place.

This disobedience — which after all may be only a misunderstanding — nevertheless reflects a sound liturgical instinct, namely that the most natural and significant point in the liturgy for the introduction of 'Occasional Prayers' is in close conjunction with the presentation of the people's offerings on behalf of the whole Church. The English 1928 and the South African 1929 do just that, indicating that special prayers may be put in immediately before the General Intercession. This has the further merit of being an accustomed order of thought in Morning and Evening Prayer, where such prayers are inserted before the Prayer for All Conditions. And it is to be noted that no other Anglican rite follows the American precedent of 1928, by allowing them after the Creed — unless the South African alternative place 'before the Offertory' may be considered to reflect the American experiment.

We propose to bring to an end the confusion of thought and discrepancy of practice in our liturgy by consolidating the two rubrics authorizing special prayers in one place, and special Biddings in another, in this place before the General Intercession, saying, 'Here the Priest may say authorized prayers, or may ask the secret intercessions of the Congregation, for any who have desired the prayers of the Church.' Certainly the present rubric, permitting the prefixing of special Biddings to the general Bidding of the Prayer for the Church, has proven its value in reminding the congregation of specific things to bear in mind in their following of the text of the Intercession, and thus bespeaking their active attention and participation in it.

Careful consideration was given to a proposal that the Priest 'in his discretion' be allowed to incorporate suffrages of special Intercessions *within* the Prayer for the Church, at appropriate points. This would be historically justifiable, since there is little doubt that the Great Intercession originated by putting into invariable form such supplications as proved to be of universal and perpetual value, out of the objects for which the people made their offerings from the earliest days. It would be entirely practicable, because the Occasional Prayers which are in true Collect form need nothing more than to remove their introductions and their doxologies to provide their central petitions in a format which is usually perfectly at home in the context of the fixed clauses of the Prayer for the Church: and even those which constitute rather long prayers pose only fairly easy problems in selection out of their superfluities. It would be completely flexible, as instantly adaptable to some temporary but most pressing need as is the 'Pastoral Prayer' of the Free Churches: and thus preferable to the half measures of the South African rite, which inserts in square brackets a few supplications for missionaries, teachers, and all men in their several callings, which may be added to the normal form upon occasion. It would integrate the Occasional Prayers into the body of the General Intercession, instead of bringing them in before it in a detached form, as the English and South African have them, and as we now propose for our rite.

It might appear that this suggestion would be the perfect form for this material: but only on the hypothesis that our clergy are perfect. While students for the Ministry of the Free Churches are as carefully trained to compose an adequate 'Pastoral Prayer' as they are in the making of their sermons, and are perfected by constant practice, our men have had no such training, and are entirely inexperienced in the arts of 'extempore' prayer. The Liturgical Commission found itself reluctantly but unanimously driven to the conclusion that this measure would put too much weight upon the 'discretion' of our clergy, who have never been prepared and practiced for such responsibilities.

It may be noted that the Indian Rite of 1933 had an 'Enarxis Litany' before the Collect of the Day, in which similar liberties were granted to the officiant, but that this feature has been canceled in their current proposals of 1952:

> Then the Deacon shall say the Litany, which shall always include at least these biddings here following: and if there be any other matters, concerning which thanksgiving or prayer is to be offered, they shall be inserted after that bidding with which they shall appear most consonant.

We, however, do not propose to close the door which our revision of 1928 opened for the exercise of free prayer, and perhaps ultimately for liturgical origination, in the rubric before the Bidding Prayer on p. 47: 'And NOTE, That the Minister, in his discretion, may omit any of the clauses in this Prayer, or may add others, as occasion may require.'

By canceling the next to the last rubric on p. 71,[72] we have removed the suggestion that the Bidding Prayer may properly be used at 'Announcement-time' in the Liturgy, since experience has shown that it is most inadvisable to rehearse both of those doublet forms of the General Intercession, the Bidding Prayer and the Prayer for the Church, not only in the same service but actually one after the other, with only the Sermon and the Offertory intervening.

However, we think well of the suggestion that permission be given to substitute the Bidding Prayer for the Prayer for the Church. It is true that the flowing style of the Bidding Prayer gives it a somewhat over-ample form: on the other hand, its rubric permits its abbreviation. Its rhetoric has been felt to be actually homiletical: but that should be the case in a formula addressed to the people, and frankly intended to rouse their devotions by 'putting into their minds good desires'; undesirable as may be the usual sort of 'oblique sermon' in some of the Free Churches — like the report of one Pastoral Prayer on the religious page of the old Boston Transcript, as 'the most eloquent prayer ever addressed to a Boston audience'! And the rubric of the Bidding Prayer would permit any who so desire to try out the possibility of incorporating special supplications as part

---

72. Ed. Note: That is, the Bidding Prayer rubric just mentioned: "¶ Here, or immediately after the Creed, may be said the Bidding Prayer or other authorized prayers and intercessions."

of the General Intercession, in contexts less classically severe than those of the Prayer for the Church.

Moreover, in spite of some diffuseness of language, the Bidding Prayer in some respects is more primitive, more vital, and more comprehensive in its scope than our Prayer for the Church. We believe that its alternative use in this place is something which has real possibilities.

And this conclusion in turn has disposed us to sanction still other versions of prayers of General Intercession instead of the Prayer for the Church. We have, as we have said, after due trial, rejected the project of the Liturgy of Ceylon, of rewriting the Prayer for the Church as a Litany: but other litanies are or will be available. If the Bidding Prayer should seem too expansive, our Committee on the Litany-form has followed the Scottish Prayer Book in proposing a so-called 'Litany of St. Chrysostom,'[73] which is actually the Byzantine Liturgical Litany of General Intercession, attested for an early date by the form in which it was used in the Latin Mass before the time of Gregory the Great, which is admirably brief, pregnant, and incisive. On p. 38 of the 1949 *Book of Offices* there is a comprehensive 'Litany for the Church' which it might be desirable to use upon occasion — perhaps abbreviated to its first and third sections. Even the 'Litany for Ordinations' on p. 560 ff. of the Prayer Book might justifiably be employed upon such times as the Ember Days, Advent III, and possibly Whitsunday. All these options are indicated by the proposed rubric, 'or else, a Litany, or The Bidding Prayer, may be said here (omitting the Lord's Prayer).'

One further 'flexibility' seems desirable. There are occasions when the 'Great Litany' may be used as a solemn Procession before the Liturgy; or when the 'Litany for the Church' may be a part of the Office for the Opening of a Church (*Book of Offices*, first rubric on p. 56), again before the Liturgy; or the Litany for Ordinations may be incorporated into the 'Prayers of the Faithful' of the Liturgy at an Ordination. To avoid duplicating these in whole or in part in the Liturgy, we propose that in such combinations the Prayer for the Church may be reduced to its first and last paragraphs, that is, to the dimensions of an Offertory Collect. That much of the Prayer for the Church is essential to the structure of the rite.

And in addition, we have observed that there is a good deal of pressure for an absolutely minimal form of the Liturgy for use upon what Cranmer called 'the workedaye,' *i.e.*, upon weekdays which are not Holy Days — and that upon such occasions some clergy have been known to mutilate the Liturgy by omitting the Prayer for the Church entirely. While this certainly cannot be sanctioned, it

---

73. Ed. Note: This Litany appears on pages 37–8 of *Prayer Book Studies V: The Litany* (volume 2). Too, this mention serves as a further reminder that these initial volumes were intended as part of a comprehensive attempt even if their release was serial rather than simultaneous.

might be permitted that the first paragraph and the concluding Doxology might be employed on such weekdays, for its necessary function as an Offertory Prayer, and because it would provide, in however laconic a form, a General Intercession for the Church.

4. The Penitential Preparation

1. *The Exhortation:* We consider it desirable that the 'Long Exhortation' should continue to be required upon the three Sundays of the year now indicated as a minimum by its present rubric. The material is valuable; and it lends an interest to the pattern of the year to have certain seasons picked out for such special distinction.

But if so, it is essential that the substance of that rubric on p. 85 should be repeated at the point in the Liturgy where the Exhortation is to be used — otherwise a previous intention to insert it is apt to be lost sight of in the run of the service. Such was the experience with the provisions of 1928 which allowed the transfer of the Lord's Prayer at Morning and Evening Prayer to a position after the Creed, so that the Liturgical Commission found it had to exercise its 'editorial' powers to put in on pp. 16 and 30 a rubric which had not in fact been adopted by General Convention, namely 'Here, if it hath not already been said, shall follow the Lord's Prayer.' So in 1934 a Joint Resolution of General Convention ordered the rubric on the Exhortation duplicated on p. 75. But on the complaint of the publishers that this insertion would compel the resetting of the plates for the whole service, the Presiding Bishop ruled that this directive was a matter of Prayer Book revision, and beyond the power of a single General Convention to order. However, the next revision of the Prayer Book should certainly make this provision.

The Canadian Prayer Book of 1922 wisely adds the direction, 'the People all standing,' to this rubric. With the increasing disuse of Exhortation generally, many of our people see to have forgotten one principle of ritual propriety which at one time was known to every good Churchman, that the people should stand at attention whenever they are addressed in a formal Exhortation. We therefore propose to add this to the rubric.

2. *The Invitation:* A number of those who are interested in reducing the Liturgy to its briefest possible dimensions on some occasions, have urged that the Invitation, 'Ye who do truly and earnestly repent,' be made optional. We do not believe that this should be permitted. The form is very short, no longer than a Collect; and it is nearly perfect in its expression. It is not to be attributed to the working of chance, but to a deep underlying theological and liturgical instinct, that both the two Great Sacraments bring their participants up to a sort of Mount of Vision, whence they may survey the past, present, and future of their lives in a moment of time. In

both cases, the past and the future terms are the same — the renunciation of past evil, and a resolve for future righteousness of life; but in the Baptismal Vows the middle term, the present possession which qualifies a man for Baptism, is Faith, while in the Invitation to the Holy Communion the key to the inner shrine is Love. The omission of this feature on any occasion or for any excuse would be a great loss to the spiritual meaning of the Liturgy.

The only improvement we feel able to suggest in the beautiful phrases of this Invitation is to exchange the passive implications which are now raised by the obsolescent expression, 'to your comfort,' for something which will revive its original intent, such as 'to sustain and strengthen you.'

3. *The General Confession:* A good deal of dissatisfaction has been expressed with the text of the General Confession. Its language seems to many to be excessive, particularly in a form to be repeated by everyone at every celebration. Phrases especially criticized are 'Provoking most justly thy wrath and indignation against us,' and 'The remembrance of them is grievous unto us; The burden of them is intolerable.'

Everyone is perfectly willing to grant that there are times in the life of each one when such language, or indeed any language, would not be too much for him to apply to his own misconduct. But there are plenty of times when perhaps the worst thing of which he can think to accuse himself may be something like having made rather too crisp remarks before breakfast — for which he is reluctant to throw himself into quite such an apparent agony of contrition.

We shall not attempt any defense of the 'wrath and indignation' phrase: it is one of the very few infiltrations of contemporary medieval attitudes into Cranmer's work, and one which it is almost insuperably difficult to justify to the modern mind. But as to the rest of it, the reason for the sweeping and absolute expressions is precisely that this is a *General* Confession: not primarily a personal acknowledgment of guilt, but, the action of the whole Church confessing the sins of the whole world before God — and therewith its own corporate and individual complicity in those sins. There are many conditions in this sorrowful world this very minute of which the most just, innocent, and holy soul can only say that 'the remembrance of them is grievous unto us; the burden of them is intolerable.'

This justification is very able, and it is even conceivable that may express what Cranmer had in mind. It must be noted, however, that it is a very modern rationalization, since it has been only in quite recent times that discomfort at the excessive expressions has become vocal. The older commentators, such as Scudamore and Blunt, make no mention of it. But the nineteenth century, which saw a general elimination of the spirit of an alien Puritanism from the Anglican Churches, brought a new demand for genuineness of religious language, and a new impatience with mere religious attitudinizing. People rebelled at feeling unrealistic, or even hypocritical, in using the words which the Church put in their mouths. Even if true, the argument that the General Confession is intended only in a collective sense will not satisfy them. They are pressing for a form which any conscientious soul can really feel and mean, in personal as well as a corporate application.

One manifestation of this movement has been the adoption in England, South Africa, and Ceylon of the brief Sarum forms of Confession and Absolution — the first two with an abbreviated Bidding as well. And on p. 323 of the American Prayer Book we find similar short forms for use at the Communion of the Sick. This, in itself, was something of an absurdity, since obviously a sick communion would be about the last time to introduce an unaccustomed novelty. Our revisers did not think of that, apparently, but were looking for a place where the innovation might be tried out on a marginal basis, so as to tell whether it would be worth while to propose it for the normal liturgy.

Now all liturgical forms have a dual function: they must be impressive as well as expressive. They must be adequate to voice a given thought or feeling which one already has, and also to inspire it in one who has not yet attained it. And on both counts these simple pre-Reformation forms are too slight in content to be adequate. Cranmer knew what he was doing when he strengthened them.

Yet we believe that the force of our present Confession can be materially improved by eliminating some unnecessary or misleading phrases. We propose to drop the following: 'and wickedness,' 'from time to time, most grievously,' 'provoking most justly thy wrath and indignation toward us,' 'the remembrance of them is grievous unto us, the burden of them is intolerable,'[74] and the repetition of 'Have mercy upon us.'

We consider, however, that it would be a false economy to eliminate any of the threefold mentions of 'Jesus Christ our Lord.' Cranmer put into the Confession a balanced expression of his whole Christology. The Lord Christ is three times invoked: first as the Incarnate Son of God and Co-Creator; next as Redeemer, the minister of our remission and our reconciliation to God; finally as the goal and means of our righteousness and our conformation to his likeness.

We have tried not to wring the form too dry, and also to preserve its accustomed rhythm and its familiar words. We have ventured to change only one word out of those which we have retained: 'acknowledge and confess' is a phrase well known to us in another context, and is surely preferable to 'bewail,' a little used word which is lacking in realism.

The rubric conforms to long-standing British usage going back to 1548, in permitting the Confession to be led by the Deacon.

4. *The 'Comfortable Words.'*: The Liturgical Commission has received many requests to make the 'Comfortable Words' optional — with the undisguised intention on the part of most of the petitioners never to use them in such case.

---

74. This phrase was dropped from George Forbes' edition of the Scottish rite in 1862; cf. p. 207 f. above.

In trying to account for this rather widespread objection to this feature, it has occurred to us that one reason for it is that this passage occupies an actually illogical place in the order of thought. Cranmer derived it from the 'Consultation' of the Lutheran Archbishop of Cologne. But Hermann put these texts of scripture *first*, as a justification for the following Confession and Absolution, in exactly the way in which Cranmer in 1552 began Morning Prayer with a series of penitential Sentences.

But when Cranmer put them *after* the solemn Declaration of Absolution, they lost much of their force. The effect is as if at that point the Priest went on to say, 'My dear brethren, I have not been deceiving you. It is true that God does forgive penitent sinners; and I shall now proceed to prove it: as follows, to-wit, *viz.*'!

It would therefore appear, that if they are to be retained, they ought to come before the Absolution instead of after. We tried it out. At first the inversion fell somewhat strangely upon our ears, thanks to our familiarity with a rhythmic passage in the service. But there could be no question that the Absolution came with greatly enhanced force after the recital of the scriptural warrants for that action.

As to the appeals for making this feature optional, we see no reason to refuse permission to omit it upon weekday services, where there are strong arguments for eliminating every non-essential. But the 'Comfortable Words' are deeply beloved by many, especially of the laity. We think that for the present they ought to be required at least at the principal celebration of the Liturgy upon each Sunday.

Since the expression, 'The Comfortable Words,' is familiar to everyone as a spoken title, this is the one place where we have found ourselves unable to suggest a better rendering of the older meaning of 'comfort.' We cannot very well rename them the 'Encouraging' or Invigorating Words' — though something of that order was the original meaning of the phrase.

The last of the 'Words,' from 1 John 2:1–2,[75] really ought to be changed. 'Propitiation' is a dubious translation of the Greek word — of which indeed every available English rendering is misleading to the modern mind. However, it happens that two verses earlier in the same Epistle we find a text which conveys all of the meaning of the one we have now which is germane to the purpose here, plus a contribution of its own. 1 John 1:9 reads: 'If we confess our sins, he is faithful and just to forgive us our sins, and to cleanse us from all unrighteousness.' This has the great merit of giving the final emphasis to the positive and constructive fact that the real function of Confession, and the real benefit of Absolution, lie in the actual overcoming of sin — not a mere remission of its penalties.

---

[75]. Ed. Note: "If any man sin, we have an Advocate with the Father, Jesus Christ the righteous; and he is the Propitiation for our sins."

5. *The Absolution:* If our present form of the Absolution is susceptible of any substantial improvement, at least no proposals for doing so have been brought to our attention.

There is one minute detail which might be bettered. Its beginning, 'Almighty God, our heavenly Father,' gives a momentary impression that the Absolution is a prayer, addressed to God: while in fact, of course, it is a declaration in the name of God. It is only because we are so habituated to it, that we do not notice the conflict of implications. This could, however, he easily obviated by beginning, 'The Almighty God,' exactly as the Prayer Book does with another solemn Declaration at the Visitation of the Sick, on p. 314.[76]

The Consecration

1. Name and Contents

The great Prayer of Thanksgiving which gave its name the 'Eucharist' is the focal point of the Liturgy. It comprises the vital heart of the sacrificial action, in the solemn presentation of the Great Oblation by man, and its acceptance and consecration by God.

In the form in which we first find the text of this Thanksgiving in Hippolytus, it is a single unbroken prayer from *Sursum Corda* to Doxology.[77] Such scanty indications as have corn down to us all point to the probability that it was in North Africa, somewhere about the year 200, that the Sanctus was interpolated into this Thanksgiving, in a context first recorded in a purely literary conflation ('The Scripture saith') by Clement of Rome about the year 95.[78]

In the Eastern Churches, the portion before the *Sanctus* has continued to be called 'The Thanksgiving'; but as a designation for the whole central action they employ the word 'Anaphora' ('Offering up,' or Oblation). This Greek word is an indispensable term for liturgiologists. Unfortunately, it has no currency in popular understanding, and therefore is not available a subtitle in the Liturgy: although the Indian Rite of 1933, which was frankly remodeled after the lines of the Eastern forms, uses it.

---

76. Ed. Note: THE Almighty Lord, who is a most strong tower to all those who put their trust in him, to whom all things in heaven, in earth, and under the earth, do bow and obey; Be now and evermore thy defence; and make thee know and feel, that there is none other Name under heaven given to man, in whom, and through whom, thou mayest receive health and salvation, but only the Name of our Lord Jesus Christ. Amen.

77. Cf. Parsons and Jones, *The American Prayer Book* (N. Y.: Scribners, 1937), 161 f.

78. Cf. Parsons and Jones, *The American Prayer Book* (N. Y.: Scribners, 1937), 177. Clemens Romanus, *1 Cor.* 34.

In the West, the whole structure of the Consecration Prayer was broken up into its constituent themes, in a chain of short prayers. After the time of Ambrose and Damasus,[79] this whole series of Collect-like forms came to be known as the Canon or fixed 'Rule' for the consecratory action, in contrast alike with the former variability of every part of it, and with the changing content of much of the rest of the service.

But as late as the seventh century, the sense of an essential unity of the whole series, as in Hippolytus, had not been lost: and the heading, 'Incipit Canon Actionis,' stood before the *Sursum Corda* in the Gelasian Sacramentary. Yet after that time, the 'Deformation Period' in the West took its toll of a right understanding of the Liturgy. The term 'Preface' came into use to designate the portion before the *Sanctus*, which the Greeks called the 'Thanksgiving.' This was harmless in itself, and there is no need to consider our renouncing the use of the word 'Preface.' The Roman error lay in considering that part to be the 'Preface *to*' instead, as before, the 'Preface *of*' the Canon, and transferring the title 'Canon Missæ' to a place after the *Sanctus* and before the *Te igitur*.

Cranmer actually retained the use of the word 'Canon' in one place in the First Prayer Book: in the rubrics outlining an abbreviated form of celebration for the Communion of the Sick, after the *Sursum Corda* he notes: 'Vnto the ende of the Cannon.' But the term has not been used in any Anglican book since, and is not familiar to our people. It cannot be said to be a luminous expression in fact, any real understanding of it at all is a matter of archeological knowledge. Even for those who do understand it, it would seem to be a mistake to try to revive its use for our Consecration Prayer, which does not contain the former Offertory Prayers of Intercession which have invaded this part of the Latin Liturgy.

The 'Prayer of Consecration' originated as a term of reference in a rubric of the Scottish Office of 1637, whence it was adopted into the English line in 1662. Since then, a knowledge of the Gelasian evidence and the historic relationships of this matter has caused the revisions of England in 1928, Scotland and South Africa in 1929, Ceylon in 1938, and India in 1952, to put the heading 'THE CONSECRATION' before the *Sursum Corda*. This solution certainly is to be preferred. It undoes the medieval mistakes, and realigns our rite with the pattern of the primitive liturgies; and it furnishes a vital and significant title for a major subdivision of the Liturgy.

2. The Preface

In line with what we have said before about the function of the Salutation, 'The Lord be with you,'[80] this Salutation should now be restored before the *Sursum*

---

79. Cf. p. 140 f. above.
80. P. 247 f. above.

Corda, to mark a principal articulation of the service. This was in the First Prayer Book, and in the Scots line since 1637, and has been recovered in all the latest revisions.

All the recent Anglican books considerably enlarge the number of Proper Prefaces. Various of these revisions propose forms for Advent, Lent, Passion-tide, Maundy Thursday, Apostles and Evangelists, the Blessed Virgin Mary, Ordinations, Requiems, and the Consecration of Churches, as well as for Sundays not covered with a Proper Preface of their own. Some of these are certainly worth having: though it is a question whether it is worth while providing a Proper Preface to he used only once in a year, such as on Maundy Thursday, or the anniversary of the Dedication or Consecration of a parish Church.

Postponing the detailed discussion of such provisions, we must note here that even without such additions, the Proper Prefaces which we now have take up nearly three pages of our Prayer Book. We therefore propose to follow all the recent Anglican revisions by printing all the Proper Prefaces after the service. It is better that the Priest, who is the only one who must use them, should be put to the slight inconvenience of turning over to them, than that the whole congregation should have to hurdle several pages of unused matter in order to keep up with the service.

We also think well of the provisions of these Prayer Books in going back to the Use of Sarum in extending the employment of certain Prefaces from a mere Octave to their whole. Seasons: that of Christmas until the Epiphany, that of Easter until the Ascension, that of the Ascension until Whitsunday. It would be a great gain, for example, to keep alive the great theme of the Resurrection throughout Eastertide — when many clergy forget all about it, and treat the significantly 'white' Sundays of this great Festal Season as if they were just as much 'common Sundays' as those after Epiphany or Trinity. And similarly, the British books extend the use of the Proper Preface of all Saints (which Rome lacks entirely) to other Saints' Days not provided with a Proper Preface (if provision is made for Apostles and Evangelists), or occulted by the Preface of a Principal Feast (or 'Great Festival'), as would be the case in the Octaves of Christmas and the Ascension.

3. The *Sanctus* and the *Benedictus*

The *Sanctus* poses no present problem. But we have seen that at our last revision, the proposal to restore the *Benedictus qui venit*, as in the First Prayer Book, was defeated after a sharp controversy.[81] And indeed the whole subject is surprisingly complicated, and full of unexpected difficulties.

---

81. P. 206 above.

1. Source and Original Meaning

The form of the *Sanctus* as it first appeared in the Liturgy consisted only of the words, 'Holy, holy, holy, Lord God of hosts. Heaven and earth are full of thy glory.' This is hardly more than Isa. 6:3b. The Egyptian family of liturgies has never had anything more.

Now this phrase is so brief as to be abrupt. The rather numerous uses of this Song of the Angels in the synagogue services show a persistent tendency to expand it with some sort of appended cadence or coda. The first step toward such an expansion in Christian use appears in the Syrian Liturgy of the Apostolic Constitutions, which supplies the short coda, 'Blessed for evermore.'

The *Benedictus* seems to have been used as a communion-time chant in the Syrian sphere of influence. So we find it — if we can believe our eyes — in the *Didaché*, and so it still appears in the modern Liturgy of St. Chrysostom. And in the *Apostolic Constitutions* we find exactly the phrase 'blessed for evermore,' already used as a *coda* to the *Sanctus*, likewise appended to the proclamation 'Holy things for holy persons' after the Consecration, and further supplemented there was 'Glory to God in the highest, and on earth peace, good will among men. Hosanna to the Son of David. Blessed is he that cometh in the Name of the Lord. God is the Lord, and hath appeared unto us. Hosanna in the highest.'

At some later time, perhaps in the fifth century, it seems to have occurred to someone in Syria to query the slightly enigmatic 'Blessed for evermore' after the *Sanctus*, and to think that this might be better expressed by excerpting the *Benedictus qui venit* as we now know it from its former place in the communion-time and putting it in place of the 'Blessed for evermore.'

The idea of *Sanctus* plus *Benedictus* seems to have been to balance the Old Testament Song of the Angels, which was a proper response to the recounting of the glories of God the Creator in the preceding 'Thanksgiving' (Preface), with the New Testament welcome to God the Redeemer, as a suitable transition to the Thanksgiving for the Redemption which followed in the 'Consecration Prayer.' This was a conception of such structural value and vigor as to obscure certain non-sequiturs of thought which we shall have to consider presently; and the Greek Churches have used the combined formula ever since with perfect contentment, and certainly no danger whatever of any deformation of doctrine.

2. Western Misinterpretations

It was otherwise when this feature came into use in the West. The native Western 'Prefaces' do not celebrate the theme of Creation, but concern themselves only with some phase of the Redemption. More over, the former Offertory-materials which have infiltrated into the Canon have completely supplanted any Thanksgiving for the Redemption after the *Sanctus*. Thus the original Eastern balance of thought of Creation and Redemption, and the transition from the sphere of the

Old Testament to the New, does not appear. Lacking it, Western minds sought some other rationale of this formula.

And somewhat unfortunately, an entirely unhistoric rationale was readily suggested by the peculiar telescoping of the rite which arose as a consequence of the introduction of the 'silent Canon.' At High Mass, the Priest did not wait for the choir to finish the Sanctus, but embarked forthwith upon the prayers of the Canon. When the choir had completed the first Hosanna (note that this, which had come in with the *Benedictus*, was now attached as a *coda* to the *Sanctus*) they fell silent, for the Priest had reached the Institution, which at that time was regarded as the 'Moment of Consecration.' Then after this 'Consecration,' the choir resumed *Benedictus qui venit*, while the Priest went on with the rest of his prayers.[82]

Thus in the actual performance of the service, the *Benedictus* was transferred from a place where it was once an introduction to the whole theme of the Redemption, to a new setting where it might appear to be a choral acclamation of the Consecration. Its sense then would be, 'As the Jews hailed our Lord at this Triumphal Entry into Jerusalem, so we greet his sacramental presence upon the altar.' It is not necessary to reprobate Roman Catholics for adopting this explanation, which seems to be quite official: it is a natural and perhaps hardly an avoidable historical mistake, which follows almost inevitably from the structural defects of the Latin Liturgy, and from the deforming medieval ritual which distorted its rendition.

It may also be natural for Anglicans desirous of giving a maximum meaning to each part of the service to adopt the current Roman explanation, in all innocence of heart and mind. But it does seem to be a blunder. The Eastern Churches have never so interpreted it. The Lutherans, the Presbyterians, the Congregationalists, all of whom have restored the Benedictus, certainly do not intend anything of the sort. Our Commission who proposed it for inclusion in 1928 had never heard of this interpretation, until the premature exultation of certain injudicious enthusiasts called it to their attention.

But the distinctive Roman rationalization of this feature is certainly not its necessary significance in our service, where it would occur in something like its original Eastern context, with a real Thanksgiving for the Redemption following it. In many ways it seems a pity that these beautiful and meaningful words, so innocent in their primary historical sense, so balanced in their expression, so universally used in the Greek and Latin communions, so unquestioningly accepted even by our 'separated brethren,' adapted to so many lovely musical settings, and

---

82. Although this long-standing practice might seem to be contradicted by the rubrics of the *Graduale Vaticanum*, it has been reaffirmed by the Congregation of Rites as recently as 1921: 'After the conclusion of the Preface, the choir continues with the *Sanctus* up to the words *Benedictus qui venit*. Then the choir is silent, and adores with the rest of the congregation. After the Sacrament has been elevated, the choir continues with the singing of *Benedictus*.' Cf. Eisenhofer, *Handbuch der katholischen Liturgik* (Freiburg: Herder, 1933), II. 160. n. 26.

hence from so many points of view such a desirable 'enrichment' of our Liturgy, should have got themselves involved in so unprofitable a controversy. In the name of charity and common sense alike, we should be strongly inclined to ignore the misunderstandings of a few extremists, and to advocate the restoration of this venerable and ecumenical element of the Liturgy.

3. The Continuity of the Thanksgiving

But having come to this conclusion in principle, the Liturgical Commission found that there were still formidable difficulties in the way of such action.

The first of these is the question of the manner of its insertion. While this problem is complicated, it is not insoluble. Since the *Sanctus* first appeared as an interpolation into the former unbroken Thanksgiving, all liturgies have been at some pains to restore the interrupted continuity of thought by 'bonding in' (as Bishop Frere says) the *Sanctus* into its context by linking up the continuation of the Thanksgiving with one or another of its phrases. This the Antiochene rite did by stressing the word *holy*: 'Verily *holy* art thou and all-*holy*, most high and exalted above all forever. *Holy* also is thine Only-begotten Son,' etc. The Alexandrian put chief emphasis on the word *full*: 'Verily *full* is the heaven and the earth of thy holy glory: *Fill* also this thy sacrifice with the blessing which is from thee.' The Gallican, which by that time had the *Benedictus* also to assimilate, made it 'Verily *holy*, verily *blessed* is our Lord Jesus Christ.' Only the Roman rite, which had lost all sense of a continuous Thanksgiving through the insertion of extraneous intercessory material at this point, and is entirely incoherent here, gave no thought to this transition. And Cranmer, whose First Prayer Book was closely following the Roman, did not do so either. But in 1764, the Scottish Liturgy made a most skilful restoration of the sequence, after the best ancient precedent, but in an original manner, adapted to the context in their possession.

We should note that in 1549 the form read: 'Holy, holy, holy, Lorde God of Hostes: heauen and earth are full of thy glory: Osanna in the higheste. Blessed is he that commeth in the name of the Lorde: Glory to thee, O lorde, in the highest.' Here the first *Hosanna* of the Latin form was retained, the second paraphrased.

Then in 1552, not all the *Benedictus* was dropped. We have observed that in Roman use the first *Hosanna* acquired ties with the *Sanctus*. And the Second Prayer Book followed that pattern, but preserved the *Hosanna* in its paraphrased form: 'Holy, holy, holy, Lorde God of hostes: heauen and yearth are full of thy glory, glory be to thee O lorde most hygh.'

Accordingly, in 1764 the tie was made with the word *glory*, alike of the text of the original Sanctus and of the vestigial paraphrased *Hosanna* of the *Benedictus*: 'All *glory* be to thee, Almighty God our heavenly Father,' etc.

This fine exordium of the Consecration Prayer is something which we have inherited in all the American books, and it has been adopted in the English and South African revisions as well. And the difficulty is that if we should follow the latest English and Scottish books by permitting the insertion of the usual text of the *Benedictus* as an optional appendage to the *Sanctus* namely 'Blessed is he that cometh in the Name of the Lord Hosanna in the highest,' the painfully won verbal continuity would be destroyed again. And we do not consider that this is at all desirable.

A solution of this problem is offered by the form in the Nonjurors' Office of 1718, and proposed in the Scottish Draft Liturgy of 1889. This takes substantially the version of 1549, but with the modified ending of 1552: 'Holy, Holy, Holy Lord God of hosts: Heaven and earth are full of thy glory Hosanna in the highest. Blessed is he that cometh in the Name of the Lord. Glory be to thee, O Lord Most High. Amen.'

The trouble with that is that it would so thoroughly incorporate the *Benedictus* into our present form that the *Sanctus* as we now use it could not be employed separately. And although there was a general disposition on the part of the members of the Liturgical Commission to concede the optional use of the *Benedictus* to those who desired it, there was strong opposition to its being required of everyone.

4. The Relevance of the Benedictus

The reasons for these objections were various. Some felt the force of the contention raised by the late Dr. Easton, that while the *Sanctus* was a legitimate insertion into the Great Thanksgiving, because it was itself in the form of a prayer, the acclamation of the *Benedictus* is not a prayer, but more of the nature of a remark! This, however, is not entirely convincing, since, without going to Roman extremes of interpretation, perhaps most people feel that either it is addressed to the Redeemer, or is a kind of thanksgiving to God for sending Him into the world.

But a further exception was taken to including the *Benedictus* in an obligatory form, in the fact that while we could logically claim to be saying 'Holy, holy, holy,' etc., with the Angels and Archangels, yet we had no warrant for alleging that the Angels were also saying 'Blessed is he that cometh!'

That, however, can be argued both ways. It is true that the *Ter-sanctus* of the ancient Vision of Isaiah is echoed in Rev. 4:8; and at least since the time of Gregory the Great men have felt the inspiration of feeling that they on earth are participating in the very words of the everlasting praises of God by 'all the company of heaven.' On the other hand, it may be quite rationally considered that the construction (to say nothing of the punctuation) of the 'Therefore' paragraph of the Preface limits the application of the phrase 'with Angels and Archangels' to the action intimated by 'we laud and magnify thy glorious Name' — without necessarily asserting that our 'praising' and 'saying' must needs be in the very same words.

5. A More Appropriate Place for the Benedictus?

The foregoing lengthy discussion is a truthful account of the ins and outs of the subject as considered and debated in the sessions of the Liturgical Commission, in an earnest and unselfish effort to do justice to all known parties and points of view. This exhausting debate was finally adjourned rather than concluded by a decision to settle upon a compromise which quite possibly may have the happiness to satisfy nobody.

Though England and Scotland put the *Benedictus* in for optional use, and with no regard for the questions of continuity which we have set forth, it may be significant that the Scottish proposal of 1889, which would have given a perfectly finished setting for this feature at the cost of making it compulsory, failed of adoption in 1912; that South Africa, which usually follows Scotland closely, would have none of it on any basis; and that India and Ceylon deserted Western standards entirely for an ancient Eastern solution. It is evident that other minds have been wrestling with some of the difficulties which confronted us.

The Indian Rite of 1933 went right straight back to the Apostolic Constitutions for this version of the *Sancta sanctis*, after the Consecration and the Lord's Prayer:

And the Priest, extending the Gifts toward the people, shall say:

> Holy things for holy persons.

And the people shall answer:

> Blessed is he that cometh in the Name of the Lord.
> Hosanna in the highest.

That may be very well for a Liturgy which is avowedly Eastern in structure and text. That particular form could hardly be proposed for the Church in America. But the rite of Ceylon, which though influenced by the neighboring ritual within the same Province was considerably more conservative of its Anglican inheritances, worked out a combination which might be entirely possible. It consisted of a restoration of the 1549 feature of the *Pax Domini* after the Lord's Prayer, with the *Benedictus*, in its complete form, sung after that:

Then shall the Priest say:

> The peace of the Lord be alway with you.
> *Answer.* And with thy spirit.

Here the Priest and people shall say or sing:

> HOSANNA in the highest. Blessed is he that cometh in
> the name of the Lord: Hosanna in the highest.

Then shall silence be kept for a space.

And this solution has been adopted in the Indian Liturgy 1952.

There are several advantages in placing this feature at this point. In the first place, of course, it restores the text of the *Benedictus* to the normal service, not merely to a marginal use. It would be a real enrichment to be able to sing the setting of the Liturgy by some great composer without omissions; and the outright incorporation of this passage would doubtless encourage its choral use. Then, it is worth something that it should be brought back to its place of origin the rite, at the Communion-time. Also, at this place the formula would be cleared of past misapprehensions: since it would not be tied to the moment following the Elevation, it would necessarily be interpreted as looking toward the Communion, not the Consecration; and in that context the 'highest' meaning anyone might desire to attach to it could do no harm whether it was understood as speaking of the 'Coming' of our Lord to us, or of us to Him, it would be free of the rather disastrous twist which the peculiarities of the Roman rite have imparted to it. Finally, for those to whom it is any comfort to conform to the customs of the Roman Church, it may be pointed out that it would occur at a point closely approximating that which it actually occupies in practice at High Mass in the Roman rite, namely *after the Consecration*: which of course the structure of the Anglican rites intimate is effected by the whole great Prayer of Thanksgiving, rather than at any particular moment within it.

This is the best we have been able to do with the matter of the *Benedictus* thus far. But we hope that the whole question will be fully considered and discussed by the Church.

4. The Prayer of Consecration

The central Thanksgiving is unquestionably the most important element in the Liturgy. All the parts of the service which precede and follow it have varied in almost every imaginable manner in the historic liturgies, without affecting the fundamental unity which all rites display in concordant testimony to a descent of this feature from some sort of apostolic original.

This prayer has not been touched in America since 1789, except for the division of its last paragraph, and the correction of 'that he may dwell in them and they in him' to 'that he may dwell in us, and we in him,' in 1892. If we were to consult our own comfort, or to take counsel of political expediency, we should not wish to touch it now.

But the fact is that there is a considerable degree of uneasiness about it in the Church. Many suggestions and requests have been received by the Liturgical Commission. A number of draft revisions of it by private individuals and groups have been circulated without in any way bothering the Commission with them, and some of them have been extensively — and quite illegally — tried out in public services. Other irregularities which likewise witness to smoldering dissatisfactions include the habit of some clergy of curtailing the Prayer at the end of the Invocation. While this may lawfully be done at the communion of a very sick person, or for a Second Consecration after insufficient quantities of the Elements have been consecrated, it is highly undesirable that this be done on a normal occasion of public worship, since it arbitrarily stops the great Prayer without conclusion, Doxology, or scriptural *Amen*.

We have therefore proceeded with our appointed task of evaluating the suggestions now in hand. We have tried to determine the causes of the present dissatisfactions, and to find reasonable means to remedy them.

In a general view of the subject, we believe that our present Consecration Prayer has some conspicuous excellencies. We owe an enduring debt to Cranmer for having remade it, after the original Greek standards, into a single great Thanksgiving, out of the disjointed scraps and pieces of the Latin Canon; for restoring to it a specific Thanksgiving for the Redemption, again according to Eastern models; for providing it with an unexceptionable Narrative of the Institution, containing all that is of distinctive value in each of the four accounts of Holy Scripture, and purged of all the additions that are not in them; and for setting a standard of a classical liturgical style in English which bears comparison with the greatest masterpieces of Greek and Latin devotion of the ages. To our inheritance from the Scottish Liturgy, we owe the magnificent exordium of the Consecration Prayer, unsurpassed by any liturgy; and the parting company with the defects and mistakes of the Roman Mass from its very inception by recovering a real Invocation of the Holy Ghost, placed at the proper point of the rite, as we find it in the archetype of all liturgies in Hippolytus, and in the universal practice of the ancient East.

In the same over-all survey of the Prayer in the concentrated light of comparative liturgics, its shortcomings seem to be derived chiefly from two sources. The first is the inferior quality of the constituent raw materials which lay ready to Cranmer's hand in the miscellaneous and incoherent series of short prayers which make up the Latin Canon. He did extraordinarily well with what he had to work with. His masterly style redeemed the fourth-century crudities of their language, without sacrificing their native vigor, or overloading them with such excesses of florid rhetoric as are the bane of the Oriental rites; his deft skill overcame their abrupt lack of continuity, and wove them together into a larger unity. But he was not able altogether to transcend their three most glaring defects: 1) the poorness of their original selection out of a confusion of alternative forms in their own sources, which left them lacking in some points of the primal pattern of the rite as we find it in all the Eastern liturgies, and which on the other hand imported some irrelevancies into the Canon; 2) the dislocated arrangement of the material, which resulted from their first makers' insufficient grasp of the underlying plan and movement of the ritual action; and 3) the repetitiousness of some themes, most especially that of the Offering of the Sacrifice, which causes the stream of the whole composition to eddy around in stagnant circles, instead of flowing swiftly straight to its destination.

The other detrimental influence upon our Consecration Prayer came from Cranmer's proper, if somewhat exaggerated, fear of the current medieval doctrines of the Eucharistic Sacrifice. Somehow he came to think that these dangers could be averted if all the passages before the Consecration were absolutely divested of all sacrificial language. He transferred all such expressions in the old Latin Canon to a place after the Institution Narrative. But unfortunately, the Latin Collects in that tract were already overloaded with the theme of Oblation. In fine, Cranmer must bear a good half of the blame attaching to the 'stagnation' and lack of forward progress of the Prayer to which exception has already been taken, and which is especially marked in the concluding paragraph of our present Canon.

These considerations are more than matters of the recondite scholarship of Comparative Liturgiologists — they are a pressing and immediate concern to every parish priest. We have to deal not only with the self-importance of the hustling-bustling type of celebrant who complains at the length of the service, and perhaps expresses his rebellion by taking the axe to the end of the Consecration Prayer: we must recognize that there is a very general complaint as to the tedium of the present rite, and that much of this attaches to the Consecration Prayer itself.

There are few clergy who have not at some time overheard a person entering the church, and spying the Vessels upon the altar, saying, 'Oh dear! Is it Holy Communion this morning? Too bad — it's such a long service!' Now as a matter of fact it is not: given comparable length of Lessons, the same proportion of music, and the same duration of the Sermon, a choral rendering of the Liturgy (at least with only a moderate number of communicants) is actually just about five minutes shorter than Morning Prayer. The service is definitely not longer though it may be that it is heavier. The rather sluggish beginning of our present rite, the dulness of the Prayer for the Whole State of Christ's Church, and the time consumed in the Administration of the Holy Communion, all have their part but the greatest element of tedium undoubtedly arises from the two pages of unbroken attention during the Consecration Prayer, with its repeated reiterations of what it has already said. The changes which we have to propose in this form would say not much more than one minute in its recitation: yet it can be guaranteed that this would have the effect of lightening the service just about as much as if its total length had been reduced by ten minutes. Tedium in any service is not a product of its over-all duration, but of having too much of the same thing at a time.

And we find that this can be done, without sacrificing any significant idea or expression, by the simple process of removing duplications and repetitions, and straightening out the order of thought into a direct purposive line; as will appear.

1. The Thanksgiving

We propose to follow all the recent British revisions by making a separate paragraph of the Narrative of the Institution, as certainly befits its importance. And since we already have 'box-titles' for two of the divisions of the Consecration

Prayer, namely 'The Oblation' and 'The Invocation,' it will be well to give like titles to the other three paragraphs. Such a device makes for clarity of understanding of structure, and has further teaching value for exposition, and for convenient reference in discussion.

We have observed that it is great gain that our Liturgy has recovered a specific Thanksgiving for the Redemption, such as is found in this place in all the Eastern rites, but is missing from the Roman except as some phase of this theme may be treated in the Preface. There is, however, rather widespread discomfort at the particular terms in which the idea of the Redemption is expressed. The emphasis is wholly upon the Atoning Death of Christ; and the language is rather harshly medieval.

It is not too well known that the expressions here, which seem so 'Protestant,' were in fact drawn from unquestioned Catholic sources — namely the *Antididagma* of the loyal Cathedral Chapter at Cologne, who were protesting against the Protestantism of their Archbishop, and the staunchly Catholic 'King's Book' or *Necessary Doctrine* issued by the authority of Henry VIII in 1543. Both of these sources sought to emphasize the orthodox doctrine of the sufficiency of the One Sacrifice of Christ, against popular medieval misinterpretations of a ritual Immolation of our Lord in repeated 'sacrifices of masses' — which the soundest Catholic theologians condemned, then as now.

Nevertheless, there is a wrong emphasis here. In particular, 'satisfaction' (from the *Necessary Doctrine*) is one word too many: it is unscriptural, and unethical. The revisers of the Ceylon Liturgy have felt this, and substituted the word 'reconciliation.' But this will not do either, since in its context it would intimate a reconciliation of God to man — not of man to God — and hence would come to exactly the same thing as the word it was designed to replace. And there would be precisely the same difficulty about the word 'atonement.'

It would seem that this is a good place to effect a simplification of Cranmer's habit of piling up synonymous words. Dropping the words 'oblation and satisfaction' would obviate the difficulty, without weakening his essential point — and it must be emphasized that it is an important point, whether from a Catholic or a Protestant position. And so far from spoiling the rhetorical effect, the flow and rhythm of the sentence would be measurably improved.

In the other matter of a lack of balance, modern Western Christians have increasingly come to see something of which the Eastern Churches have never lost sight, that the Redemption of mankind was accomplished by our Lord's whole lift and work, not merely by the last act of his Passion. The liturgies which conserve the primitive tradition, from Hippolytus down, stress the entire Incarnation, in lieu of the overweening 'Western' preoccupation with our Lord's Death. In fact, in the Thanksgiving for the Redemption they all mention the Passion only in a single phrase introducing the Narrative of the Institution.

Accordingly, the rites of India in 1933 and Ceylon in 1938 conflate into the Prayer the corresponding passage of the 'Liturgy of St. James,' in the form in which the Nonjurors adopted it in 1718. Without going so far afield, the South African rite achieves very much the same balance of thought by the simple and ingenious device of inserting a phrase from the new Collect Cranmer wrote for Christmas Day, making the passage read, 'didst give thine only Son Jesus Christ to take our nature upon him, and to suffer death upon the cross for our redemption.' This expedient was doubtless suggested by the ancient Collect of the Passion said on Palm Sunday, which likewise brings in the Incarnation as integral to the Redemption, saying 'to take upon him our flesh, and to suffer death upon the cross.' The South African phrase commended itself to India and Ceylon, so that they have incorporated it into their 'Eastern' context of this passage: and India has preserved it in the 'Western' setting of its Liturgy of 1952.

It happens that this measure occurred to us before we saw the South African revision: so that we are glad of this confirmation in these other Anglican rites. But we consider it essential to put a comma after the word 'Cross,' in order to make it perfectly clear that our Lord 'took our nature upon him . . . for our redemption,' as well as that he 'suffered death upon the Cross' for that end.

2. The Institution

England in 1928, followed by Ceylon in 1938 and India in 1952, altered 'New Testament' to 'New Covenant.' The former expression conveys an entirely misleading idea to the untaught. Apart from that, we do not consider that the text of our Narrative of the Institution is susceptible of any improvement.

It is quite otherwise, however, with the 'box rubrics' covering the Manual Acts. On p. 183 f. above, we have noted that in restoring the Manual Acts, the Prayer Book of 1662 made a mistake in yielding to the insistence of the Presbyterians in the matter of giving an unhistorical and unorganic place for the Breaking of the Bread. This was eliminated in the Forbes editions of the Scottish Rite in 1844 and 1862.[83] We should certainly do the same.

Moreover, there is a good deal of feeling among Churchmen of all sorts of schools to the effect that the rest of these rubrical provisions are needlessly detailed. The First Prayer Book had only two directions: 'Here the prieste must take the bread into his handes,' 'Here the priest shall take the Cuppe into his handes.' These are all that are required at these points in the Roman Mass.

The rubrics now numbered (a) and (d), corresponding to those of 1549, are certainly sufficient. Rubrics (c) and (e) are sometimes defended as 'gestures of designation' of the Matter of the Sacrament, expressing the intention to consecrate 'all the Bread,' not merely that in the Paten, and 'every vessel in which there is any Wine to be consecrated.' But this is needless: the fact that more than one container of Bread or Wine has been 'offered and placed upon the Holy Table' is

---

83. Cf. p. 209 above. 207 f.

sufficient indication that they have been devoted to the sacramental purpose; and the taking up of the representative portions in the Paten and the Chalice at this point is enough. Rome thinks so: and there is really no need to be more Roman than Rome. As it is now, these superfluous rubrics simply encourage additional gestures of the celebrant's own invention when there is only one Paten and Chalice to consider, and when if rubrics (a) and (d) are intelligently carried out, the Priest is already 'laying his hand upon all the Bread,' and upon the only vessel 'in which there is any Wine to be consecrated.' There will always be quite enough fussy and individualistic ceremonial to be found, without having the rubrics suggesting any more.

3. Duplications of Thought

It is in the two-thirds of the present Consecration Prayer which follows the Institution that repetitiousness sets in, and the stagnant eddies to which we have alluded slow the course of the stream.

Hippolytus' original archetype was very direct. It exploits four themes in a straightforward line of development, so clearly and vigorously that his order of thought determined the lucid structure of all subsequent Greek liturgies. These are:

1. Commemoration:	'Wherefore, having in remembrance his Death and Resurrection,
2. The Oblation:	we offer thee the Bread and the Cup;
3. Innovation:	And we beseech thee to send thy holy Spirit upon the Sacrifice of thy holy Church,
4. Benefits of Communion:	that thou wouldest grant it to all together who partake thereof in holiness, unto fulfilling with the Holy Ghost, unto confirmation in true faith.'

In practice, the historic liturgies usually bracket together the first and second of these themes, and the third and fourth; and then they tie the two divisions together by repeating some form of the Oblation — just as Hippolytus does in mentioning first 'the Bread and the Cup,' and then referring to them again as the Sacrifice of thy holy Church.' The resulting form is a Commemoration-Oblation, and then an Oblation-Invocation:

> that is, the first treats of the Oblation as offered by man, and the second as accepted by God.

These natural divisions, and this functional progress of thought, have got themselves tremendously convoluted and involved in our present ritual as a result of the complicated history of their transmission to our hands. First the Thanksgiving was atomized into a series of separate variable Collects in the early general Western use. Then there was a not very intelligent choice out of these variables in the days of St. Ambrose to form the fixed 'Canon' which endured until the Reformation. Cranmer used a free hand in interchanging the place of many constituent expressions, on principles of his own. Then the Scottish line rearranged the matter after the Eastern pattern. Even the reactionary step by Dr. William Smith in 1789 figures in the picture.

Just how thoroughly the line of thought has been snarled up can best be made clear by printing out all this matter under the headings of its four fundamental themes. We will begin with the treatment of some of these same subjects in the initial Thanksgiving for the Redemption: because though we have given general approval to that division, it does affect the question of the repetition of thought in the concluding passages.

COMMEMORATION	OBLATION	INVOCATION	BENEFITS
to suffer death upon the Cross for our redemption;			
	who made there (by his one oblation of himself once offered) a full, perfect, and sufficient sacrifice, oblation, and satisfaction, for the sins of the whole world;		
and did institute, and in his holy Gospel command us to continue, a perpetual memory of that his precious death and passion, until his coming again.			
Wherefore, O Lord and heavenly Father, according to the institution of thy dearly beloved Son our Saviour Jesus Christ, we, thy humble servants,			

COMMEMORATION	OBLATION	INVOCATION	BENEFITS
	do celebrate and make here before thy Divine Majesty, with these thy holy gifts, which we now offer unto thee,		
the memorial thy Son hath commanded us to make; having in remembrance his blessed passion and precious death, his mighty resurrection and glorious ascension,			
	rendering unto thee most hearty thanks		
			for the innumerable benefits procured unto us by the same.
		And we most humbly beseech thee, O merciful Father, to hear us; and, of thy almighty goodness, vouchsafe to bless and sanctify, with thy Word and Holy Spirit, these thy gifts and creatures of bread and wine;	

The Eucharistic Liturgy

COMMEMORATION	OBLATION	INVOCATION	BENEFITS
			that we, receiving them
according to thy Son our Saviour Jesus Christ's holy institution, in remembrance of his death and passion,			
			may be partakers of his most blessed Body and Blood.
		And we earnestly desire thy fatherly goodness, mercifully	
	to accept this our sacrifice of praise and thanksgiving;		
		most humbly beseeching thee to grant that,	
by the merits and death of thy Son Jesus Christ, and through faith in his blood,			
			we, and all thy whole Church, may obtain remission of our sins, and all other benefits
of his passion.			

COMMEMORATION	OBLATION	INVOCATION	BENEFITS
	And here we offer and present unto thee, O Lord, our selves, our souls and bodies, to be a reasonable, holy, and living sacrifice unto thee;		
		humbly beseeching thee that,	
			we, and all others who shall be partakers of this Holy Communion, may worthily receive the most precious Body and Blood of thy Son Jesus Christ, be filled with thy grace and heavenly benediction, and made one body with him, that he may dwell in us and we in him.

COMMEMORATION	OBLATION	INVOCATION	BENEFITS
	And although we are unworthy, through our manifold sins, to offer unto thee any sacrifice,		
		yet we beseech thee	
	to accept this our bounden duty and service;		
			not weighing our merits, but pardoning our offences, through Jesus Christ our Lord.

A simple running of the eye down any column of this thematic analysis will show up instantly all the duplications of expressions. In fact, some of what anyone might think an over-meticulousness in shifting from one column to another was carried out to make this possible.

In particular, the passage 'according to thy Son our Saviour Jesus Christ's holy institution, in remembrance of his death and passion,' which was reinserted in the text of the Scottish form of the prayer in 1789, after the Scots had quite properly removed it, is shown to be an absolute doublet of the 'having in remembrance' passage of the original Commemoration. And the further repetition of the same theme in the clause beginning 'by the merits and death of thy Son Jesus Christ' is also demonstrated to be superfluous.

In the same way, the reiteration of the Offering of the Sacrifice after the solemn prayers have besought God's acceptance and consecrating power upon it, which is characteristic of the Roman confusion of thought, and still further over-weighted by Cranmer's transfers of sacrificial language, also stands revealed as a structural mistake. All such expressions of Oblation must be put before the Invocation, and the thought of the Prayer must not return to them afterward.

4. The Oblation

This section is a combined Commemoration-Oblation, as in all the liturgies from Hippolytus down Cranmer, with his dominant preoccupation with the 'Memorial' of the Passion, put the Commemoration in a climatic place after the Oblation. This is a departure from the order of all the historic rites; and South Africa, India, and Ceylon have reversed Cranmer's sequence to conform to them. This reversion to the original order seems to be wise, not only for that reason, but for the purpose of using the theme of the Oblation, as most of the ancient liturgies do, to bind together the Oblation and the Invocation paragraphs into a better unity of thought and continuity of expression. Moreover, it is a help in ridding the form of some of Cranmer's trailing redundancies of phrase.

We suggest eliminating the words 'O Lord and heavenly Father, according to the institution of thy dearly beloved Son our Saviour Jesus Christ.' The Thanksgiving has established the address to God the Father, and sufficiently cited the authority of the Institution, so that neither need be rehearsed again here. And both the preceding paragraphs have quite adequately identified the part of the 'dearly beloved Son our Saviour Jesus Christ' in the great action: and after all the fore going repetitions of the pronouns 'he,' 'his,' and 'himself,' we can continue to say 'he' and 'his' in this paragraph without the faintest uncertainty as to the object of the reference.

The restoration of the original structure automatically eliminates Cranmer's rather anticlimatic *coda*, 'rendering unto thee most hearty thanks for the innumerable benefits procured unto us by the same.'

Several suggestions have been received for additions to this paragraph; but we have not found ourselves able to recommend any of them. The liturgies of Scotland, South Africa, India, and Ceylon have interpolated in different ways and with varying degrees of awkwardness commemorations of the Heavenly Session and the Second Coming. These are Eastern elaborations upon the theme of his coming again 'in the Thanksgiving.' We consider the mention of it at that point to be sufficient. Neither is it necessary to speak of the Incarnation here, as several persons have suggested to us, if that subject is brought into the Thanksgiving for the Redemption, as we have recommended.

Others again have been attracted by the flexibility of the Gallican Rite at this juncture, and have suggested that other acts of our Lord's redeeming work, such as the Circumcision, Epiphany, Baptism, and Transfiguration, be allowed to be inserted on the proper occasions. But the time has gone by for that sort of thing. A very early date saw the fusion of the former 'Gallican variables' into a Canon or fixed 'Rule' of the Consecration Prayers: and in a fixed form it ought to remain.

5. The Invocation

a) The Acceptance of the Oblation: After the Oblation in Commemoration of the Redemption, the Invocation in the ancient liturgies commonly begins with a prayer for the acceptance of that Oblation. This is the last point in the Consecration Prayer at which it is legitimate to have such a petition. It was a good move that the Scots brought the Invocation to this, its primordial location, after the Commemoration-Oblation. Nevertheless, they did not use the best judgment of form and sequence when they inserted it just *before* the words 'And we earnestly desire thy fatherly goodness, mercifully to accept this our sacrifice of praise and thanksgiving.' Such an expression should have been prefixed, not affixed, to the Invocation. And this error we propose to remedy.

We have also accepted the suggestion that we should restore the note of the 'Heavenly Altar.' This was an element of the old Roman Invocation. We have noted that in that rite it had a peculiar origin, and a rather queer history afterward, giving rise to several misunderstandings.[84] Cranmer certainly did not altogether understand it himself, and presented it in the First Prayer Book in a form so obviously altered and displaced that in 1552 he simply dropped it from the rite as irrelevant.

Nevertheless, it has a grasp of an intrinsically valuable idea not elsewhere expressed. It conveys two thoughts of importance for a right understanding of the Liturgy. It lifts our minds from the camping environment of a narrow chancel, and the circumscriptions of the 'here and now,' to the glorious and illimitable expanses of the Heavenly Places. And even more, it has the momentous effect of aligning the Eucharistic Sacrifice, not with the Altar of the Cross of that historic Calvary which belongs to the far away and the long ago, but with the universal and eternal Altar of the Heavenly Intercession. Such an alignment has long been a chief contention of Anglican theologians: it would be great gain to give it direct expression in the Liturgy.

It can be done in this place, without raising again the medieval confusions as to whether it is the 'Elements, 'the Prayers' or the 'Mystical Body' which is considered as being subsumed to Heaven, by saying simply, 'to accept upon thine altar on high this our sacrifice of praise and thanksgiving.' Exactly this phrase has been adopted in the Indian Rite of 1952 — although, regrettably, it appears after the Invocation instead of before. And further, any vestiges of the misapprehensions which beclouded this phrase in time past may be neutralized by adding the appositive description, 'our bounden duty and service' a valuable and beloved expression for which no other place can be readily found, yet one which is due to be remove from the position where it now stands, in the peroration of

---

84. Cf. p. 156 ff.

the Consecration Prayer, as yet another Act of Oblation, which should not be allowed to confuse the clear-cut progress of thought by being brought in after the Invocation.

b) The Central Petition: We have seen that the expression, 'according to thy Son our Saviour Jesus Christ's holy institution, in remembrance of his death and passion,' was interpolated into the Invocation in 1552 in order to salvage the essence of the displaced Commemoration of 1549;[85] that the Scottish line in 1637 restored the original Commemoration to its proper place, in 1755 transferred the Invocation to follow it immediately, as in the Eastern liturgies, and in 1764 recognized the duplication of thought and words, and removed it;[86] finally that the first American rite in 1789 made the structural mistake of restoring the duplication.[87]

This double Commemoration must go. The Liturgy must not be allowed to say the same thing twice over, six lines apart. But how to get rid of this intolerable reiteration without altering the existing balance of doctrine, is perhaps the most crucial problem of the Consecration Prayer.

Our present Invocation does achieve such a balance of the terms expressing the subjective and the objective realities of the Sacrament, such as the historic liturgies have all possessed, and no liturgy can afford to forego. As has been intimated before,[88] it is logically impossible to 'receive' something which is not objectively *there*. On the other hand, whatever is *there* can have no saving effect until it is received and appropriated by faith.

Sacramental Theology establishes the significant fact that whereas all other Sacraments consist of two parts only — the 'outward and visible sign' and the 'inward and spiritual grace' — the Eucharist actually comprises three elements: the *Sacramentum*, which our Catechism and Offices of Instruction 'define as the outward part or sign,' which is 'Bread and Wine'; the *res sacramenti* or inward part, or thing signified,'which is the Body and Blood of Christ'; and the *virtus sacramenti* or 'the benefits whereof we are partakers,' which 'are the strengthening and refreshing of our souls by the Body and Blood of Christ.'

Among ancient liturgical forms, Hippolytus alone makes no mention of the *res sacramenti*: his Invocation does not pray that the Bread and Wine may be made to be for us the Body and Blood, but goes on immediately to the *virtus* or Benefits. All historic liturgies, however, are at pains to make explicit mention of the *res*, with an antithetical balance of expression of the *sacramentum* of the Bread and Wine and the *res* of the Body and Blood. Yet in all the liturgies, the *virtus* of the Benefits constitutes the goal and objective of the action.

---

85. P. 171.
86. P. 188 f.
87. P. 190.
88. P. 163.

The only liturgies which go to the length of specifying a definite *change* in the Elements are those of 'St. Chrysostom,' and two minor lines which show Byzantine influences, namely the Anaphora of Nestorius, and a few Gallican Invocations. This, incidentally, accounts for a certain recalcitrance on the part of the extremists in the Eastern Orthodox Church, who are disposed to deny that our present American Liturgy has a 'valid *Epiclesis*,' because it does not ask in so many words that the Bread and Wine may be *made* to be the Body and Blood. This may be considered for what it may be worth. It is certainly worth *something*, since obviously clarity and precision of statement is much to be desired at such a vital point of the service. On the other hand, it really might appear to be a bit doctrinaire to deny all efficacy to a form which happens to be a little vague and roundabout in its expressions, as is the case with our present Invocation: especially in view of the fact that a rigid application of the Byzantine footrule would completely disallow the Anaphora of Hippolytus, and cast grave doubts upon some other historic forms.

But the really remarkable circumstance is that the Roman Rite is utterly lacking in any language whatsoever as would imply any such physical change 'in the Elements' as is suggested in the Invocation of 'St. Chrysostom.' The Roman expressio 'ut *nobis* Corpus et Sanguis fiat,' points directly away from any such an affirmation of Transubstantiation as we should certainly expect if that doctrine had been held in the day when the Roman Liturgy was being formulated. Obviously it was not so held then. Explicit expression is given to the subjective reality. The objective factor, which is implied rather than stated, consists at most of a 'mystical' change of values.

All the available evidence concurs in suggesting that the idea of a literal Transubstantiation was unknown to primitive Roman doctrine, as it was no part of the primitive Roman liturgy; but that it originated on Gallican soil, where it did receive liturgical expression,[89] and from thence infected the thinking of the Church of Rome.

Cranmer in the First Prayer Book found the Latin phrase perfectly acceptable, and translated it directly, if none too forcibly, as 'that they *maye be vnto vs* the bodye and bloud.'[90] The English revision of 1928 found it could do no better than to restore this. This English form is followed by Ceylon. India in 1933 rendered it 'become unto us,'— a somewhat stronger, if not necessarily a preferable, rendering of the Latin *fiat*. The Scottish line since 1764 has been ultra-Roman in bluntly saying 'may become the Body and Blood.' It was this excess of zeal which doomed the acceptance of the Scottish phrase in the first American Prayer Book in 1789.

---

89. *Missale Gothicum* viii, xx, lxv; *Missale Gallicanum* xvii; *Missale Francorum* viii. Cf. C. Gore, *The Church and the Ministry* (London: Rivingtons, 1889), 367, for the manner in which the last-named passage was corrupted, completely altering the original meaning of the present Roman Ordination of Priests.

90. P. 61

It will be observed that all these revisions which have been named take the obviously necessary step of canceling the interpolated *Anamnesis* of 1552; and then, seeking to retain the inherited tradition of an equipoise of subjective and objective expressions, return to some form of the simple, direct, and balanced language of the Latin original. And the ones which do this best, we consider to be those which do it most absolutely, by restoring the form of the First Prayer Book. After experimenting with a considerable variety of qualifying phrases, substitutions, and paraphrases, the Liturgical Commission has come to the same conclusion.

c) The Holy Spirit: The First Prayer Book besought God to bless and sanctify the Gifts 'with thy holy spirite and worde.' Apparently it was Cranmer's intention to comprehend and harmonize the current theories of the Consecration by indicating the Holy Spirit as the agent, and our Lord's 'word' of Institution as the means. The Scottish rite of 1637 made the phrase 'thy word and holy Spirit.' The American Standard Book of Common Prayer of 1793 initiated the capitalization of 'Word' — thus bringing in an entirely new idea of a dual Invocation of the Second and Third Persons of the Holy Trinity. But the Scottish line beginning with the Proposed Book of 1889 (here following the Forbes edition of 1844 — cf. p. 111 above) simply omits 'word and': and this version has been copied by all later Anglican revisions save the American 1892 and 1928. We think we should get in line with this unanimous consensus.

However, we do not believe that it has been so fortunate that all these revisions except the American and the Indian 1952 have added the words, 'upon us and upon these thy gifts,' etc. This is a feature which dates from the Scottish 1912, and stems from an inspiration of Bishop Dowden's.[91] Unfortunately, Dowden did not have before him all the information now available as to the texts of the Greek rites, and overstated the supposed universality of the phrase in the early Eastern liturgies. It is not found at all until after the time of the *Apostolic Constitutions*. It seems to have originated in the Liturgy of St. Basil, and to have spread from that to the rites of 'St. Chrysostom' and 'St. James,' and, through the borrowed Byzantine Anaphora of St. Basil, to the Coptic liturgies in Egypt, and to have even corrupted some manuscripts (including that of the *Textus Receptus)* of the Greek 'St. Mark.'

Thus the use of the interpolated words 'upon us' is not really primitive; and we do not consider it to be particularly useful. The most ancient forms, beginning with Hippolytus, mention 'fulfilling with the Holy Ghost' as a consequence of receiving the Holy Communion — not as a condition precedent for its consecration. If it would mean anything in our service which on the whole we take leave to doubt — it would seem to call up the old Puritan slogan that the formula of

---

91. *The Scottish Communion Office*, ed. H. A. Wilson (Oxford Clarendon, 1922), 164.

Consecration consists of *verba prædicatoria*, not *verba consecratoria* that is, it is addressed to the faith of the participants, and is not to be thought of as having any effect upon the Sacrament. The proponents of this addition do not seem to have properly thought through its implications.

6. The Supplication

It is in the concluding paragraph of our Consecration Prayer that the eddies of thought, the duplications of phrase, and the lack of a straightforward purposive plan, are most in evidence, and where wanderings of mind and an oppressive sense of tedium are most experienced.

The ancient Eastern liturgies customarily go straight on without a break from the Invocation of the Spirit to consecrate the Sacrament to an expression of the purpose for which that consecration is effected, namely the Benefits which it is to bestow upon the communicants — in other words from the *res sacramenti* to the *virtus sacramenti*.

Doubtless we could do the same, and could bring the Consecration Prayer to an end with considerable brevity, by appending a very few phrases expressing the Benefits, added to the conclusion of the Invocation. There are two reasons against this. For one thing, the Invocation is a very difficult and delicate matter, poised in a very sensitive balance of its teaching. It seems to us preferable to express the operative consecratory action of the Holy Spirit in the simplest and most unexceptionable terms available, and not to risk making it misapprehended as merely a prayer for a good communion by lumping it together with the Benefits.

Then also, our last paragraph includes considerably more than a mere list of Benefits. It contains two passages which are distinctive — it would not be too much to say quintessential — of the Anglican Liturgy: namely the Offering of Ourselves, and the interpretation of the experience of the Communion as an incorporation and an abiding indwelling in Christ. These two themes are the very greatest of Cranmer's contributions. They more than make up for the heretical cast of his personal conceptions of the Sacrament as a subjective Memorial rather than an objective Presence, and for any of his minor mistakes of omission or commission in his rendering of the Liturgy. They are indispensable for the full force and meaning of the Consecration Prayer, as any priest will realize who has had to use it in its curtailed form, stopping with the Invocation, at a Communion for the Sick.

It might seem that the inclusion of the Offering of Ourselves at this point would infringe the principle laid down above, that all expressions of Oblation should precede the Invocation — it will be recalled that we have transferred the initial petition of this paragraph, 'to accept this our sacrifice of praise and thanksgiving,' as well as its final 'to accept this our bounden duty and service,' to the beginning of the Invocation for that reason. Dom Dix recommends that the

Offering of Ourselves be transferred to some kind of prayer at the Offertory. It would not be out of place there, or incorporated into the Prayer for the Church, which is itself an Offertory Prayer. Nevertheless, it has a distinguishing value where it is. We are here offering not what we have, but what we are — moreover not in our own righteousness, but as accepted in the Beloved. The purport of this supplication at this point is very much on the order of that 'fulfilling with the Holy Ghost' which we find here in Hippolytus and in many Eastern liturgies as one of the Benefits of participation in the Holy Communion.

We therefore recommend that this Oblation of Ourselves be made the exordium of the final paragraph, which, because of the scope of its contents, may perhaps be designated simply as 'The Supplication.' Then this can be followed by a consolidation of the now scattered Benefits of a worthy Communion; 'humbly beseeching thee . . . that . . . we, and all thy whole Church, . . . may worthily receive the most precious Body and Blood of thy Son, . . . that we . . . may obtain remission of our sins, and all other benefits of his Passion, . . . be filled with thy grace and heavenly benediction, and made one body with him, that he may dwell in us, and we in him.'

The Eucharistic Doxology should follow at once. 'And although we are unworthy, through our manifold sins, to offer unto thee any sacrifices; yet we beseech thee to accept this our bounden duty and service' is yet another Oblation of the Sacrifice, and is surely to be avoided in this place. Also, the themes of humility and unworthiness, however appropriate to the immediate preparation for the reception of the Holy Communion, are distinctly anticlimatic in the peroration of the great Consecration Prayer. They are best left to the Prayer of Humble Access.

7. *A Parallel Development*

It has been a matter of considerable interest to us to discover, after the foregoing discussions of the Consecration Prayer had all been worked out, that the Presbyterian Church in the United States of America had come to surprisingly similar conclusions. Starting with the same data in Comparative Liturgics, they arrived at a form of very much the same size and shape that we have. With the permission of their Board of Christian Education, which holds the copyright of their Book of Common Worship, of 1946, their form is given here for comparison:

> All glory and thanksgiving be to Thee, Almighty God, our Heavenly Father, for that Thou, of Thy great mercy, didst give Thine only Son Jesus Christ to take our nature upon Him, and to suffer death upon the cross for our redemption; who made there a full, perfect, and sufficient sacrifice for the sins of the whole world and did institute and, in His

holy Gospel, command us to continue a perpetual memorial of His death and sacrifice until His coming again.

Wherefore, having in remembrance His Incarnation and holy life, His Passion and precious death, His Resurrection and glorious Ascension, and His continual intercession, we Thy humble servants, pleading His eternal sacrifice, do set forth, with these Thy holy gifts, which we now offer unto Thee, the memorial Thy Son hath commanded us to make.

And we most humbly beseech Thee, O merciful Father, to bless and sanctify with Thy Holy Spirit both us and these Thy gifts of bread and wine, that the bread which we break may be the communion of the body of Christ, and the cup of blessing which we bless, the communion of the blood of Christ.

And here we offer and present unto Thee ourselves, our souls and bodies, to be a reasonable, holy, and living sacrifice; and we beseech Thee mercifully to accept this our sacrifice of praise and thanksgiving, as, in the communion of all the faithful in heaven and on earth, we pray Thee to fulfill in us, and in all men, the purpose of Thy redeeming love; through Jesus Christ our Lord, by whom, and with whom, etc.

Being in the Calvinistic tradition, this Consecration Prayer does not recite the Institution within the Prayer. Otherwise, there are some remarkable homologies with the form which we propose.

Its first paragraph of Thanksgiving for the Redemption follows the Scottish version, but takes the same pains that our draft revision has done to redress the excessive emphasis of Cranmer upon the sacrificial Death of Christ by adding the expression 'to take our nature upon him' from the South African rite, and by dropping the words 'oblation and satisfaction.' It even goes farther than we have in eliminating also 'by his one oblation of himself once offered.'

The second paragraph again does what we have done in following the English revision of 1928 by putting the Commemoration first, and the Oblation afterward, and in pruning it of trailing phrases which still linger on in the Anglican versions.

The third paragraph drops the questionable Invocation of the 'Word,' and confines itself to a simple expression of the *Res sacramenti* — which in this form is put in terms of 1 Cor. 10:16.

The last section resembles our draft in beginning with the Oblation of Ourselves, and in avoiding a penitential anticlimax. Rather surprisingly, it does not affirm any particular Benefit of Communion, which one might expect to see strongly featured in a Calvinistic form, and it shies away completely from Cranmer's supreme conception of an 'Incorporation' into Christ; contenting itself with a very general expression of 'the purposes of Thy redeeming love' — somewhat unexpectedly reinforced with a mention of the Communion of the Saints.

This Prayer embodies two additions found in the Scottish and South African versions which we have rejected, namely 'All glory *and thanksgiving*' at the exordium, and the petition that the Holy Spirit might 'bless and sanctify . . . *both us and* these thy gifts.' And it offers some contributions of its own in the Commemoration, of 'His Incarnation and holy life,' 'His continual intercession,' and 'pleading His eternal sacrifice,' which we did not find it necessary to admit, at least in that form, though the underlying ideas are otherwise expressed in the form which we do propose.

Putting aside any questions of the theological implications of this Presbyterian form, which do not concern us, it must be acknowledged that this Consecration Prayer has a simplicity of plan, a clarity of expression, and a forceful directness and economy of movement, which make it distinctly superior to our present American text — at least as far as it goes, and within the somewhat more limited gamut of ideas which it covers. Evidently it was inspired by the same objectives which we have had in mind in our construction of the Draft Liturgy, and has arrived at remarkably comparable results. The existence of such a piece of work is a strong argument for the adoption of something along the lines of what we have worked out. We simply cannot afford to let our Presbyterian brethren make better use of the valuable materials, new and old, which have been attained in the latest revisions of the Liturgy by our sister Provinces of the Anglican Communion.

5. The Lord's Prayer

1. Relation to the Consecration

Roman liturgiologists consider that the Canon comes to an end with the Doxology appended to the *Nobis quoque*, and that the Lord's Prayer, which follows, begins the new section of 'The Holy Communion.' This conception seems to reflect an ancient tradition surviving from the days before the seventh century, rather than to be an accurate description of the structure of the Mass as it left the hands of Gregory the Great.

The Lord's Prayer appears to have come into the Liturgy in the first instance by being interpolated into an already existing prayer preparatory to Communion, of much the same content as our present 'Humble Access.' The Prologue, and the so-called *Embolismus* with its concluding Doxology, are vestigial survivals of the substance of this prayer in the Roman rite. It was Gregory the Great who moved the Lord's Prayer from a position after the ritual Breaking of Bread to a place, before that feature, and therefore in immediate sequence with the Consecration Prayers, and even claimed apostolic authority that this should be so.[92]

---

92. *Ep.* ix. 12. What grounds Gregory may have had in mind for this assertion, are not known. But it is worth noting that the schoolboy mistranslation of his pregnant words as claiming that the

Ever since that time, the Western Rites have always considered that there was a close tie between the great Action which our Lord commanded, and the great Prayer which he gave to his disciples. And therefore it is not remarkable that England, Scotland, South Africa, Ceylon, and India in 1952, all include the Lord's Prayer under the division of the service which they entitle 'The Consecration.'

There have even been attempts at a still closer union. In 1796, the Scottish Bishop Abernathy-Drummond proposed a form to incorporate the Lord's Prayer absolutely into the end of the Consecration Prayer, without any intervening Doxology.[93] This same suggestion has been made spontaneously from a few quarters to the Liturgical Commission — by which it has been disapproved.

Yet since the Lord's Prayer follows the Consecration Prayer at once, without any pause or even any change of posture of the celebrant, it would seem only logical for us to follow the other Anglican revisions by including the Lord's Prayer under this part of the service, and beginning the following section entitled 'The Holy Communion' after it, when there is an obvious change of direction in the liturgical action.

2. The Prologue

All the Anglican revisions are agreed in returning to the provisions of 1549, and of the Scottish line since 1637, in restoring the Lord's Prayer to this place immediately after the Consecration Prayer, instead of using it after the Communion, as was done from 1552 to 1892. They also agree in prefixing to it Cranmer's paraphrase of the brief Latin Prologue, 'Præceptis salutaribus moniti, et divina institutione formati, audemus dicere.' This original Anglican version of 1549, which is now unanimous except for our American variant, reads, 'As our Saviour Christ hath commanded and taught us, we are bold to say.' It would certainly seem that the burden of proof is on us, as to why we should not conform our usage to that of all other branches of the Anglican Communion.

The use of some form of this Prologue is as old as the employment of the Lord's Prayer itself in the Liturgy. In fact, much the earliest evidence for the use of the Lord's Prayer in the service comes from some undeniable echoes of this Prologue in the writings of St. Cyprian, who died in the year 258,[94] just ninety years before we find clear testimony in St. Cyril of Jerusalem[95] for its employment in the Liturgy.

Apostles used the Lord's Prayer as a prayer of eucharistic consecration, which appears even in Duchesne, is properly ignored by Eisenhofer: *Handbuch der katholischen Liturgik* (Freiburg: Herder, 1933), II. 197.

93. *The Scottish Communion Office*, ed. H. A. Wilson (Oxford Clarendon, 1922), 223.

94. *De oratione dominica*, c. 2: cf. Eisenhofer, *Handbuch der katholischen Liturgik* (Freiburg: Herder, 1933), II. 199.

95. *Catecheses* xxiii. 11–18.

Nothing has ever better illustrated the stubbornness of conservative resistance to unaccustomed language than the history of the Prologue in this country. The Revision Report of 1919 proposed it in Cranmer's text, but with the faltering ending 'let us say.' Even that encountered uncomprehending opposition, and in 1922 it was brought forward again, modified to 'And now, as our Saviour Christ hath taught us, let us say.' In this form it went through the processes of preliminary and final adoption by the General Conventions of 1922 and 1925. At this point liturgical scholars, especially those abroad, expressed in no uncertain terms what they thought of the American banality of 'let us say' — turning from the raising of solemn prayer to God in order to interpose a mere admonition to the people. The Revision Commission had to admit that it had been at fault in trying to compromise with ignorant conservatism, and had allowed the Church to accept a liturgical monstrosity which was also a piece of abject bathos. In its final Report in 1928, the Commission notified the Convention that it had exercised the grant of 'editorial' powers which had been made in 1925, in order that the whole process of revision might be wound up in the next triennium, by substituting th pan-Anglican 'we are bold to say.' With the acceptance of that report by the General Convention, the action became final.[96]

Since then, the use of the Prologue has been assimilated, and found to be of devotional value, by most members of the Church. There remains a minority who still resent it, simply because they do not understand it. They have a perfectly honest perplexity as to why they should have to profess themselves 'bold to say' a form which they have always been accustomed to take absolutely for granted.

That is just it. The Lord's Prayer should never be taken for granted. The 'Fatherhood of God' was considered to be a simple axiom of religion by the 'Liberalism' of the nineteen century. So far from being an axiom, it is a tremendous paradox. Without the assurance of explicit revelation, it would an incredible assumption, displaying enormous arrogance, for feeble man to claim the Creator of the illimitable universe his 'Father.' The ancient Jew, who thought almost as favorably of himself as a modern 'Liberal' or 'Humanist,' who exalted the preeminence of his own 'Chosen People' over others by asserting that God is 'a father to Israel' (Jer. 31:9), that 'Israel is my son, even my firstborn' (Ex. 4:22), and acclaimed David (Ps. 2:7, 89:19 f., 26 f.), and Solomon (2 Sam 7:14, 1 Chron. 17:13, 22:10, 28:6) as chosen 'sons' of God, never called upon God as Father. Even the heightened devotional language of the later poets and prophets never got nearer to the incredible truth than some sort of figure of speech: '*Like as* a father' (Ps. 103:13); or the adoptive relation of 'A father of the fatherless, and a judge of the widows, is God' (Ps. 68:5), and 'Doubtless thou are our father, though Abraham be ignorant of us, and Israel acknowledge us not' (Isa. 63:16); or as a metaphor of the Creator in 'But now, O Lord, thou art our father; we are the clay and thou our potter; and we are all the work of thy hand' (Isa. 64:8), and 'Have we not all one father? Hath not one God created us?' (Mal. 2:10).

---

96. Journal of General Convention, 1928, 473.

In the full light of the Christian revelation, we necessarily put far more into these expressions than their authors intended. Looking at them objectively, and weighing their limitations, we are in some position to understand the immense advance of thought in the teaching of our Lord. That the Fatherhood of God is a factual reality, constituting a personal paternal and filial relation between God and man, was revealed in Christ and by Christ. Indeed, it was the only original *theological* teaching which he gave.

The early Church recognized it for what it was, an enormous enlargement of spiritual horizons. So St. Paul avows, with a sense of wonder and awe, 'Because ye are sons, God hath sent the spirit of his Son into your hearts, crying, Abba — "Our Father"' (Gal. 4:6; cf. Rom. 8:15). So far from the Fatherhood of God being an axiom of 'natural religion,' it is only because 'our Saviour Christ hath commanded and taught us' that we can possibly be so 'bold' as 'to say' such stupendous words.

In the days of the Persecutions, the 'Discipline of the Secret' made this most sacred form from our Lord's own lips a matter of reserved teaching, imparted to candidates for Baptism only at the very end of their catechumenate, and carefully guarded from all alien ears. The Lord's Prayer was never said in full and aloud in the primitive Church, except in its 'reddition' at a Baptism, and at this place in the Liturgy. Here, with all non-communicants excluded from a church more sedulously 'tiled' than any lodge, the faithful, after the consummation of the Christian Sacrifice, might be 'bold to say' these tremendous words.

The restrictions of the *Disciplina arcani* have long passed away. The Church of Rome retains a remembrance of them in ordering a silent recitation of the Lord's Prayer, with nothing but the beginning and ending said aloud, at all ordinary office of the Church except Baptism and the Eucharist; but it did no hesitate to add the full form of the prayer to the special *Preces* which medieval times appended to Lauds and Vespers on the weekdays of the Lenten and Ember seasons. We have restore the Lord's Prayer to all our services, and regard no service complete without it, so that it is a constant element of all devotions, public and private. That is as it should be. The Prayer cannot be used too often; but it can, and sometimes is, used to lightly. The witness of the Prayer Book (apart from the eighteenth-century Family Prayers) indicates that there should always be some sort of devotional preparation leading up to the Lord's Prayer: even private devotions should not be begun with it. And this special setting in the Eucharistic Liturgy possesses great values, both for teaching and for devotion, in emphasizing the particularly sacred character of these words of our Lord himself.

It may, however, be admitted that even those who are fully cognizant of all these considerations, and fully appreciate the values of the historical tradition, are not quite happy as to the exact phrase adopted by Cranmer. The word 'bold,' to their minds, carries some overtones of what is known in the vernacular as 'brashness.' We are not sure that this is an objection. Not to feel that there is an immense presumption in hailing the Most High God as 'Our Father,' marks a residue of the self-complacencies of an outworn 'Liberalism.'

'We are bold' is an obvious reference to 'Let us come boldly unto the throne of grace' of Heb. 4:16, and 'In whom we have boldness and access with confidence by the faith of him' of Eph. 3:22. The word in both cases is *parrhesia*, which in the great majority of its occurrences in the New Testament is translated 'confidence': 'as that when he shall appear, we may have confidence,' in 1 John 2:28, then have we 'confidence toward God' (*ibid.* 3:21), and 'This is the confidence that we have in him' (*ibid.* 5:14). This is not the same thing as the Latin *audemus* ('we dare.') It is perhaps a better idea: we may note that the Greek introduction of the Lord's Prayer in the Antiochene, Byzantine, and Alexandrian rites alike employs *both* the words *parrhesia* and *tolmān* (Lat. *audere*). At one juncture we were in favor of trying to satisfy the unreconciled objectors by making the phrase 'we have confidence to say,' and actually certified it to the Committee on the Ministration to the Sick, so that it appears in that form in the Prayer Book Study on that subject. But it has been justly objected that the alteration spoils the cadence of the phrase, being intrinsically ugly and full of sibilants. It would not be in line with the Latin, and it would be a departure from the unanimous use of all the rest of the Anglican Communion. The universal Anglican formula has the considerable advantage that while it has ties with that great verse in Hebrews in the familiar Authorized Version, and can be sublimated to any desired degree with the 'confidence' meaning which is implicit there, it does not shrink from the warning which overweening humanity needs, that there is presumption in claiming the King of the Universe as 'Our Father,' and nothing less than the command and teaching of our Lord qualifies us to do so. Rightly understood, it has the virtues of both the Greek and Latin Prologues. And it may well be hoped that its continued use will bring to all the understanding of it which many have already attained.

The only changes that need be made are to drop the apologetic American 'And now,' and to return to Cranmer's full form, 'As our Saviour Christ hath commanded and taught us, we are bold to say,' as in all the current revisions throughout he Anglican Communion.

The Holy Communion

It seems desirable to give the above heading of the final major division of the service in full, rather than merely 'Communion' (Scotland, South Africa), 'The Communion' (Ceylon, India 1952), or even 'The Communion of Priest and People' (England). The title we propose expresses most simply and adequately the dignity and importance of this realization and completion of the whole eucharistic action. Incidentally, it marks the point of origin of the expression which a natural metonymy has made the most frequently employed name of the whole service in our Church. And it echoes and justifies balanced title which we have proposed for the Liturgy.

1. The Breaking of the Bread

Although we have seen reason to include the Lord's Prayer in the section entitled 'The Consecration,' after the pattern of all the current Anglican revisions, it does not seem advisable to go along with them in putting the ritual Breaking of the Bread and the *Pax Domini* in that division. In the Western rites, these ancient features follow the Lord's Prayer immediately. But as a matter of classification, they obviously do not belong with The Consecration: they are preparations for The Holy Communion.

After the Lord's Prayer, the Scottish Liturgy has the rubric, 'Here the Presbyter shall break the consecrated Bread; and silence may be kept for a brief space.' And at the same place, the English and the most recent Indian revisions permit, and the uses of Scotland and Ceylon require, the Priest to say, 'The peace of the Lord be alway with you,' the People answering, 'And with thy spirit,' as in the First Prayer Book.

Throughout the first millennium, the Universal Church both East and West used flat cakes of leavened bread — the Eastern rites still do. This bread has to be broken into portions for the Communion. Thus the original aim of this ceremony was purely practical: and so obvious a necessity that 'The Breaking of the Bread' is much the most common name for the Eucharist in the New Testament.

The ceremony is still necessary, if leavened bread is used as the English, Scottish, Indian, and South African rites expressly permit — or if one employs the scored sheets of unleavened bread which better preserve the original symbolism of participation in the One Oblation than do individual wafers — which from this point of view are as little desirable as the 'individual communion cups' of the Protestant Denominations: cf. St. Paul's 'For we being many are one bread, and one body: for we are all partakers of that one bread' (1 Cor. 10:17).

Even after the coming in of 'people's hosts' made the Fraction unnecessary for its original purpose, the Roman Church retained a vestige of this ceremony by a 'token' breaking of the 'priest's host' at this point. At least this much can be and should be retained, since in some cases it is all that is left of an action which was felt to be so significant in the early Church. And since we have proposed to remove an unhistorical and unorganic place for the ancient 'Breaking of the Bread' from the Narrative of the Institution, we should certainly provide for it the right place, which is here.

The Eastern rites have a Blessing of intending communicants between the Lord's Prayer and the Fraction. The Western survival of this is the *Pax Domini*, as is shown by the triple sign of the Cross at that point. The manner in which the ceremony of the Commixture arose, and assimilated to itself this triple crossing of the Bishop's Blessing of the people, is a most peculiar medieval development, too complicated to go into here.[97] The merits of our proposal to restore the significant articulation of the ancient liturgies here, in the form in which they appeared in the First Prayer Book and some of the current revisions, are not involved in the question of Roman ceremonial.

The manner in which this material has been put to use in Ceylon has been cited above on p. 220. Those provisions, and those of the Scottish liturgy, can be readily combined. The Scottish rubric quoted above should come first. It contains most intelligent use of the neglected expedient of 'ritual silence,' which elsewhere finds expression only on p. 543 of our Prayer Book, in the Ordination of Priests.[98] Then the *Pax* and its response: after which we propose, as in Ceylon and India 1952, the *Benedictus qui venit*.

We have discussed before the problems of the use of the *Benedictus* in the Liturgy, and noted the conclusion that this point seems to be the best available place for it, being exactly the setting where we first find it, in the text of the *Apostolic Constitutions*, and also, by a rather remarkable coincidence, at the nearest attainable analogue of the position at which it is actually sung at High Mass in the Latin rite. Of course it remains to be seen just how strong is the pressure from one side to restore the *Benedictus* to the place immediately after the *Sanctus*, which it occupied in the text of the Missal, where it is said at Low Mass, and in the First Prayer Book: and how strong is the reluctance of the other side to admit it there; and what may be the decision of the mind of the Church between those contending forces. But it may be pointed out that the location which India and Ceylon propose for it is a more meaningful context, without the dubious relevancy and the controverted rationale which it has after the *Sanctus*. In that location, it would furnish an entirely suitable choral response to the *Pax*, and it would impart a certain quality of movement to the service, looking forward to the coming experience of Holy Communion, marked by the close verbal connection of the words 'Blessed is he that cometh' and 'We do not presume to come . . . trusting in our own righteousness.'

2. The 'Humble Access' and the **Agnus Dei**

1. The Question of Order

The Roman order of parts is to put the singing of the *Agnus Dei* immediately after the *Pax*. The literary connection is excellent: 'The peace of the Lord . . .' being followed by '. . . grant us thy peace.' We have been repeatedly requested to restore this sequence.

---

97. Scudamore, *Notitia Eucharistica* (London: Rivingtons, 1876), II. 671–8.

98. Ed. Note: After the person to be ordained has made vows to the bishop and the bishop has concluded with a collect but before the *Veni, Creator Spiritus*, the following rubric appears: "¶ After this, the Congregation shall be desired, secretly in their Prayers, to make their humble supplications to God for all these things; for the which Prayers there shall be silence kept for a space."

So far as we can make out, this cannot be done. The immovable obstacle in the way is the Prayer of Humble Access. This closely corresponds to the prayers of preparation for his own communion which the Priest says in the Latin rite while the Choir is singing the *Agnus*. That device, of making the Humble Access a private prayer of the celebrant, occulted by the *Agnus*, is not open to us. Cranmer made an excellent move in bringing this matter out of its obscurity as a private supplication and sharing this preparation with the people, causing the Priest to 'saye in the name of all them that shall receyue the Communion, this prayer.' The demand today is precisely in the opposite direction, that the Humble Access be allowed for congregational recitation: which we propose to grant.

The Humble Access must come immediately before the communion of the clergy. And the organic function of the *Agnus* as now used is to be sung to cover the administration to them. It has never been sung for its own sake: although at first it was used to cover the Fraction, before that once lengthy feature was abbreviated and put back to the *Embolismus* of the Lord's Prayer.

But the existence of the Humble Access as a prayer to be said aloud, and perhaps by all present, confronts us with the dilemma that we can have the *Agnus* in its Roman sequence, or we can have it in its Roman function: but we cannot have it both ways. It can come after the *Pax*, as is done in the Indian draft of 1952 (after an interpolated *Benedictus*): but in that case it would be what it has never been, a canticle sung for its own sake, and accompanying no ritual action — a needless prolongation of the service. Or it can come after the Humble Access, where it would not be in its Roman context, but where it would fulfil its appointed Roman office of accompanying the communion of those in the sanctuary. We prefer the latter.

2. The Prayer of Humble Access

A number of complaints have been received as to the language of this prayer. The objections are to the passage, 'so to eat the flesh of thy dear Son Jesus Christ, and to drink his blood, that our sinful bodies may be made clean by his body, and our souls washed through his most precious blood.' The criticisms are twofold.

First, those who do not like these expressions speak, with some exaggeration, of 'cannibalistic language.' Perhaps not to much attention need be given to such strictures, in view of the like accusations which were hurled at the heads of the early Christians. The words complained of are certainly a direct quotation of John 6:53: 'Except ye eat the flesh of the Son of man, and drink his blood, ye have no life in you.' They have the merit of confronting apathetic minds with such an affirmation of the Real Presence as can hardly be evaded. They have stood unaltered in every revision of the Liturgy in every branch of the Anglican Communion since 1548. Any change whatever in them now would result in weakening their force. There are many in all parties of the Church who would regret that: and in sum, we feel we dare not propose deserting the unanimous Anglican consensus to please some people who resent the language of Holy Scripture.

The other criticism is that the passage concludes with a popular medieval conceit, expressing the fanciful idea that the Species of Bread is designed to nourish the body, and the Wine to animate the soul. The fact is that this poetic antithesis is so trivial, and, as it were, so fragile, that we pay no attention to it whatever in saying the words, and the only thing which registers upon our consciousness is the characteristic Anglica emphasis upon the benefits of the Holy Communion upon the whole man, body and soul alike — the Roman Mass speaks only of its effect upon the soul.

However, if the people are to be permitted to say this prayer along with the Priest, it is important that its language should be realistic and veridical. Therefore instead of 'that our sinful bodies may be made clean by his body, and our souls washed through his most precious blood,' we propose 'that our sinful souls and bodies may be made clean by his most precious Body and Blood.'

We also propose the word 'nature' in lieu of 'property,' to restore the original meaning of a word now obsolete in this sense; and desire to replace the phrase 'in these holy Mysteries,' which was in the First Prayer Book, and was deleted in the Second as not applicable to the changed position of the Prayer. As it has been brought back to its original location, the omitted phrase should be restored.

3. Agnus Dei

The Hymn *Agnus Dei* was introduced into the Roman Rite by Pope Sergius at the end of the seventh century, originally to cover the Breaking of the Bread. Its present use to take up the time consumed by the communion of the officiants is often very desirable, especially when there are several in the chancel. While it is being sung, all can be communicated with reverence and dignity, without imposing upon the patience of the waiting congregation. We have restored it for use immediately after the Humble Access, as in the Scottish 1929: Ceylon, like the First Prayer Book, requires it. So does the Indian Liturgy of 1933, but during the communion of the people, as did 1549: the Indian of 1952 permits it after the *Pax* and *Benedictus*, where it has no function.

The objection sometimes heard, that the *Agnus* is a prayer to Christ, while the rest of the Liturgy is addressed to God, does not seem to be important. This is a point of the service where every communicant is moved to render personal devotion to our Lord.

The *Agnus* is lawfully sung in our present service, under the rubric permitting 'a Hymn' after the Humble Access. The only difficulty of so doing is that it stands much too close to our present place for the *Gloria in Excelsis*, which incorporates its text. This was a cogent reason for removing it from the service in 1552, and has been an obstacle to its restoration in England, South Africa, etc. That difficulty would vanish if the *Gloria* were restored to the beginning of the Liturgy: which is what Ceylon does, and what we propose to do.

3. The Administration of the Holy Communion

1. *The Sentences, and the Bidding*

The compromise of the Elizabethan Prayer Book of 1559, which combined the 'Catholic' Sentences of Administration of the Sacrament from 1549, and the 'Protestant' ones from 1552, resulted in phrases far too long to be used for each communicant. Most clergy do not try to do so, but repeat the Sentences deliberately enough to be reverent and impressive, meanwhile communicating whatever number of persons their recitation happens to cover: as has been pithily expressed, they 'talk slow, and walk fast.' The trouble with that is that the priest is often out of hearing of the first of such a group before he comes to the end of his Sentence, if he is only reasonably expeditious in his ministration, and speaks in a tone designed to contribute to the devotion of the person then communicating, without disturbing that of others.

Some priests, however, manage to give a certain partisan accent to their administration, by using the entire formula once, and thereafter continuing, according to their own preferences in the matter, with one or the other half of it exclusively.

Sanction is actually given to this partisanship in the English revision of 1928, by proposing the optional use of a Sentence of Invitation which covers the content of the formulas for both kinds, and thereafter allowing the use of either half of the old double Sentences to each communicant. Or else, permission given to 'say the whole form of words to each row of communicants, or to a convenient number within each row, instead of saying them to each communicant severally.' Such half-measures simply call attention to the unsatisfactory nature of the present basic provisions, and emphasize the diversity of present practice.

What is needed is a formula brief enough to be employed for each communicant, sufficiently balanced to be acceptable to all parties, and comprehensive enough to be an adequate statement of the essential truth. Scotland and South Africa take the form of 1549, which falls short of the first of these objectives. India (1933) and Ceylon adopt the forms of the *Apostolic Constitutions*, 'The Body of Christ, the Bread of Life,' and 'The Blood of Christ, the Chalice of Life': which leave considerable to be desired as to the second requirement.

We propose as Sentences of Administration the first twelve words of Cranmer's formulas of 1549: 'The Body of our Lord Jesus Christ, which was given for thee,' and 'The Blood of our Lord Jesus Christ, which was shed for thee.' This is short enough for individual use. It is a statement of the basic reality, without homiletical additions of any sort. Moreover, it is a perfectly balanced form: it combines the Catholic 'Corpus Domini nostri Jesu Christi' of the Latin Mass, with the Protestant 'der für dich gegeben ist' and 'das für deine Sünde vergossen ist' of Hermann of Cologne. This individual emphasis is of great importance in Anglican thought, and the most 'Catholic-minded' member of the Church would feel his devotion impoverished if he were deprived of it. If each of us can realize the fact that the Body and Blood of Christ have been given for me, then any added phrases become superfluous — at least at this vital instant.

Yet we do not wish to lose the added 'homiletical' matter. The point is, that such supplemental expressions as we now have, in order to explain and apply the meaning of the Communion, can really be much better prefaced to the act in the form of a Bidding to Communion. Moreover, such a Bidding would be serviceable in its own right. There is sometimes an awkward pause at this point, caused by some uncertainty on the part of timid communicants as to just when to start for the altar-rail. This pause actually witnesses to a former ritual link which has dropped out of the service. The Eastern 'Elevation' at the *Sancta sanctis* was originally a bringing forth of the consecrated Elements with a word and gesture of invitation. And when this became overloaded with supplementary ceremonies, the Apostolic Constitutions renewed its purpose by adding significantly, 'Blessed is he that cometh.' Rome has an analogous feature in the form of holding up a communion-wafer, saying, 'Behold the Lamb of God.' Cranmer transformed this into an invitatory chant, 'Christ our Pascal Lambe' — though this was eliminated in the Second Prayer Book.

We therefore propose a Bidding to Communion, after the English form, slightly enlarged to take in all we desire to eliminate from the Sentences of Administration: 'The Body of our Lord Jesus Christ, which was given for you, and his Blood which was shed for you, preserve your bodies and souls unto everlasting life. Take this in remembrance that Christ died for you, and feed on him in your hearts by faith, with thanksgiving.'

2. Rubrics

In the attendant rubrics, we propose to retain the provision for a Hymn during the Communion-time, and to add to it the permission for an Anthem. This is a reversion to the First Prayer Book, which gave a page of what Cranmer called 'Post-Communion' anthems. They were popularly so called in his day because they came after the Priest's communion, in an age when the people almost never communicated at a High Mass. This restored feature will facilitate the use of the last one of the Proper Anthems, to which we have referred before.

The 'sufficient opportunity' rubric may also be preserved. The directions for a second Consecration have been removed to a place after the service, as most Anglican revisions have done.

South Africa permits, and India and Ceylon require, that the consumption of any of the consecrated Elements which remain unexpended at the conclusion of the general Communion shall take place forthwith at that time. This is, of course, the original place for that necessary action. The present rubric which directs that 'what remaineth' shall be covered with 'a fair linen cloth,' and the further rubric after the end of the service that such overplus be consumed 'immediately after the

Blessing,' have existed unchanged since 1662, when they were adopted from the Scottish provisions of 1637. The only reason for such a roundabout procedure is that by 1637 people had simply forgotten what had once been done in the service, and previous Prayer Books had failed to specify what Cranmer must have thought could safely be taken for granted.

The present custom is undesirable, since it much slows up the clear-cut termination of the rite. As things stand now, the celebrant is given a choice as to which of two rubrics he is to disobey: whether to 'let them depart with this Blessing,' or whether to wait until after that Blessing to consume the Elements. If he is really going to 'let them depart,' he must ignore that performance with the 'fair linen cloth,' and take the Ablutions in an unauthorized place. If he waits to do so until after the Blessing, he does not actually 'let them depart' at that point, since he knows and everybody knows that sheer reverence will hold them kneeling until the Sacrament has been disposed of; with perhaps the singing of the *Nunc Dimittis* to occupy their minds during the awkward delay. Churchmen of every party have become quite aware of the inconvenience and illogicality of our present rubrical provisions; and it is very common in all sorts of churches to see 'the Ablutions' performed while the last group of communicants are returning to their seats — or even during the singing of the *Gloria*.

The obvious thing to do is to wind up the action of the Communion-time in a definite way, by the consumption of any overplus of the consecrated Elements, and the cleansing and replacing of the Vessels. This latter is not now directed at all, except by the inference that until such cleansing is carried out, some of the sacramental species still 'remains.' It is still a matter of living memory that there was quite a struggle to get this inference universally accepted, and 'the Ablutions' performed in a seemly manner. The explicit provisions we propose would end a conflicting diversity of practice which does not involve any principles not generally accepted by all parties, and there fore not infringing the rights of any party; they will deliver all the clergy from the inescapable necessity of breaking a rubric, into which the retention of the incompatible rubrics of 1549 and 1662 has entrapped us all; and they will clear till whole service of an impending aftermath.

The terms in which our present rubric have always been put involve also another matter, namely the question of the Reservation of the Sacrament. Undoubtedly the historians are quite correct who maintain that the injunction that 'the consecrated Bread and Wine . . . shall not be carried out of the Church' was directed against the irreverence of some Puritans who took them for common use, and not against such a taking of them from the altar to the Communion to the Sick as the First Prayer Book specifically provided — and therefore that it has no bearing upon the subject of Reservation. But when the letter of a rubric does not represent the intention of those who enacted it, that rubric ought to be changed. We propose to protect those who have conscientious objections to the breaking of the letter of the law by specifically excepting 'any which may be required for the Communion of the Sick, or of others who, for weighty cause, could not be present at the Celebration of the Liturgy,' from the application of that mandatory language. This is in terms of the Scottish General Rubric since 1912. But it represents a continuing Scottish custom of reserving for the sick which finds expression in the Nonjurors' rite of 1718, in Torry's edition of the Scottish rite in 1849, and in Forbes' in 1862.[99]

4. The Postcommunion

1. The Thanksgiving

The concluding division of the Communion section may very well begin with the accustomed Salutation, as in the First Prayer Book, the Nonjurors' service of 1718, and the rites of India and Ceylon.

With or without this, all the recent Anglican revisions preface the Thanksgiving after Communion with some kind of Bidding. This seems particularly desirable if, as has often been requested of us, the people are to be permitted to say this Thanksgiving with the Priest. The congregational recitation of the General Thanksgiving at Morning and Evening Prayer since the adoption of our last revision in 1928 has been so generally accepted that it has established a desire to do the same thing at the Liturgy. There does not appear to be any reason against it. In fact, the inclusion of this final piece of 'self-activity' would give a satisfying conclusion to the service. It is especially to be desired since we design to return the *Gloria in Excelsis* to its original place at the beginning of the Liturgy.

The Postcommunion Thanksgiving might conceivably be condensed. It is much longer than its analogue in the old Latin service, the Postcommunion Collect, since Cranmer reshaped it from its Western form of a typical short 'Gallican variable' Collect to the pattern of the considerably more extensive fixed Thanksgiving which we find in all the Eastern rites. But we do not consider it too long to provide a dignified and adequate ending of the Liturgy. And its comprehensive character, and the ready flow of its ample style, make it particularly suitable for congregational use.

Instead of Cranmer's well-worn cliché of 'his saving Death and Passion,' we propose 'his saving Death and Resurrection,' as an effective echo of the comprehensive language of the 'Oblation' paragraph of the Consecration Prayer.

2. The Last Collect

The Scottish, English, and South African revisions have all gone off on a mistaken tack in providing a permission to add *another* 'Postcommunion' prayer at

---

99. Cf. p. 208 above. The whole question of the Communion of the Sick, will be discussed in a separate *Prayer Book Study*.

this point, at the discretion of the Priest. This is derived from inaccurate information, which is sometimes worse than none.

As we have just noted, the Roman Mass has a short variable Collect at this place, which is known as the 'Postcommunion.' It is always a prayer for grace by virtue of the Sacrament which has just been received. That definition is essential. No prayer can rightly be called a 'Postcommunion' which does not conform to it. Above all, no Collect becomes an actual 'Postcommunion' merely because it is said after the Communion.

The trouble about any talk of Anglican 'Postcommunion' is that there are no prayers of the requisite content in our Prayer Book. In the American Book, the only one capable of qualifying for the character and function of a Roman 'Post-communion' might be the Collect for Maundy Thursday.[100] Our own — and only — proper 'Postcommunion' is the fixed Thanksgiving which Cranmer, following the standards of the Greek rites, substituted for the Western Collect varying with the day. Even if we had the right sort of material available, it would be a needless duplication to add another Thanksgiving for the Sacrament received, or another prayer for the graces of a good Communion.

And this situation is no different in the British books, which have been mistakenly trying to provide something analogous to the third variable Collect of the Latin Mass. The Scottish and South African extend the list of Collects which Cranmer provided in 1549 to end the 'Ante-Communion' (which the American Prayer Book has transferred from a place after the Communion Service to p. 49, following the Occasional Prayers, and assigned for use after the Collect of the Day at the Offices and the Liturgy), and allow their insertion after the Collect, or before the Blessing. The only one of these which even approaches the ideas of a real 'Postcommunion' is the South African version of the fixed prayer *Placeat* at the end of the Latin Mass. In addition, the Scottish provides an elaborate apparatus of ten prayers for festivals and seasons, and two for other occasions, which it explicitly calls 'Postcommunion,' and permits 'immediately before the Blessing'; but only one of the lot is a true 'Postcommunion.' The English revision allows the insertion of any Collects in the Prayer Book after the Intercession, or before the Blessing: but this does not add any 'Postcommunion,' which are simply not there.

How did these books go astray? And if the added Collects are not 'Postcommunion,' what are they? The fact is that the whole idea of a 'Last Collect' in the English Liturgy derives from the circumstance that the three services of Ordination add a special prayer which the rubric directs to be said 'after the last Collect, and immediately before the Benediction.' Now in the Ordinal of 1550,

---

100. Ed. Note: ALMIGHTY Father, whose dear Son, on the night before he suffered, did institute the Sacrament of his Body and Blood; Mercifully grant that we may thankfully receive the same in remembrance of him, who in these holy mysteries giveth us a pledge of life eternal; the same thy Son Jesus Christ our Lord, who now liveth and reigneth with thee and the Holy Spirit ever, one God, world without end. *Amen.*

the Communion Service to which this reference was made was of course that of 1549. In the First Prayer Book, the 'last Collect,' which stood immediately before the 'Benediction,' was nothing more nor less than the Post-communion Thanksgiving. But as soon as the Second Prayer Book interpolated the *Gloria* between Thanksgiving and Blessing, the rubric, which has stood unaltered down to the present day, became not only inaccurate, but actively misleading. Not unnaturally, it gave rise to the interpretation that the normal rite might be expected, or at least permitted, to contain another 'last Collect,' analogous to these final prayers of the Ordinal services. The American service for the Consecration of Churches gives just such a prayer for use immediately before the 'final Blessing.' And a partial knowledge of the Roman provisions caused this inferential insertion to be called a 'Post-communion.'

However, the special prayers in the Ordinal are most definitely not 'Postcommunion.' They are in fact the survivals of a *fourth* variable Collect of the Latin Mass, which was called the '*Super populum.*' This again was a 'Gallican variable' Collect, and corresponded to a fixed Prayer of Benediction in all the Greek rites. We find it provided for nearly all Masses in the ancient Leonine Sacramentary, for most in the Gelasian and for many in the Gregorian. The present Roman Missal has now eliminated it from all services, except only those for the weekdays of Lent, which are distinctly conservative of a number of ancient features. This prayer 'Over the People' was the original Benediction of the Latin liturgy, as it still is in the Greek rites. Its gradual elimination from the 'Western' forms accompanied and resulted from the introduction of a sacerdotal Benediction at the end of the service. It may be called a 'Benedictory' or 'Commendatory' Collect. Its theme is always a petition for some enabling grace for perseverance in righteous living. It looks forward to the time to come, while the 'Post-communion' looks backward upon the Sacrament which has just been received in Holy Communion.

The British books failed to draw these vital historical distinctions. They leaped to the conclusion that if a special prayer was to follow the Communion, it must needs be a 'Postcommunion.' They did not realize that there was question here of two entirely different sorts of Collects, the true 'Postcommunio' and the quite distinct 'Super populum.' And, lacking any definition of the requisite content and function of the proper 'Postcommunion,' they did not even begin to ask themselves whether there were any need, or indeed any room, for such a feature in our service.

Though an actual 'Postcommunion' would be a completely superfluous duplication, there may be exceptional occasions when it might be desirable to have a 'Super populum' supplication, to gather up the message of the whole service, and to express it in a final devotional form to remain with the worshipers as they depart, as an enabling inspiration for their daily life. It was precisely for this reason that the services in the Ordinal added true 'Super populum' Collects as a final commendation and special benediction of the newly ordained Deacon, Priest, or

Bishop. And of course it is this, not a 'Post-communion,' for which the English, Scottish, and South African Prayer Books are feeling.

Some clergy are in the habit of appending to the Liturgy a 'Last Collect,' summing up the purpose of the Sermon. Such a custom is quite along the lines of ancient precedent for the use of this kind of a prayer. While it is hardly to be reprobated, we have concluded that it is better not to encourage it by a permissive rubric at this point. We conceive that it is of especial importance at present to shorten and simplify the conclusion of the service. A rubric which would invite further elaborations here does not seem to be desirable.

The fact is that such a feature is really superfluous on normal occasions, as the progressive Roman disuse of it shows. In our service, we not only have the sacerdotal Benediction which supplanted the 'Super populum' in the Roman rite, but Cranmer prefixed to it the beautiful words of Phil. 4:7: 'The peace of GOD (which passeth all vnderstanding) kepe your heartes and mindes in the knowledge and loue of GOD, and of his sonne Iesus Christ our lord.' This was presumably suggested by the Greek 'Let us go forth in *peace*,' to which Cranmer turned from the untranslatable 'Ite, missa est' of the Latin. And it completely fulfils the 'benedictory' or 'commendatory' content of the obsolete 'Super populum' Collect.

Appended Matter

1. The General Rubrics

1. The 'Ante-Communion.'

There is now very little use, and even perhaps little potential usefulness, of the peculiar Anglican device of employing the preliminary portions of the Liturgy (approximately what we propose calling 'The Ministry of the Word') under some circumstances, stopping short of the actual celebration of the Sacrament.

Cranmer's anxiety to promote the full use of the Liturgy, and to insure that the people should not merely be present at its celebration, but should actually receive the Sacrament, took the curious and (as it proved) self-defeating form of forbidding its celebration unless a certain minimum number had signified beforehand their intention to communicate. Upon any occasion when this 'quorum' of communicants was not in evidence, the Priest was required to terminate the service after the 'offertory' with one or more added Collects.

Cranmer may have hoped that the spectacle of a truncated service would make a successful appeal by the reproach of a lost spiritual opportunity. But it seems that his chief reason for insisting upon the performance of at least this 'Ministry of the Word' on Sundays and Holy Days was that his Lectionary for the offices of Morning and Evening Prayer was wholly based upon the secular Calendar of the dates of the twelve months, and had no reference or no appropriateness whatever to the seasons of the Christian Year. The Liturgy alone was the carrier of scriptural teaching for the Church's dramatization of its faith through the Christian Seasons.

We are no longer limited by Cranmer's restrictions upon the number of intending communicants. His hopes were frustrated, because his methods were directed in a negative direction. His objectives of frequent and general communions have been pretty well realized in our days simply by the clergy's announcing and holding frequent celebrations, in the confidence that if attendants come to these services, some of them will communicate.

Moreover, 'Ante-Communion' is no longer essential in order to keep in touch with the Christian Year, since the lessons for each Sunday at Morning and Evening Prayer in the Lectionary of 1943 have been carefully conformed to the teaching of the Epistles and Gospels for those occasions. In 1928, the former requirement of the 'Ante-Communion' on Sundays and Holy Days when the Sacrament was not celebrated was reduced to a mere permission. Morning Prayer, without the 'Ante-Communion,' is the provision of many parishes most of the time for their principal Sunday service.

There remains a universal need for the 'Ante-Communion' on Good Friday and the morning of Easter Even, where the Prayer Book supplies proper Epistles and Gospels, but when it is not the custom to celebrate the Eucharist. And there is some use for it during the time of every young minister's diaconate, since the American revision of 1928 permits the new procedure of a Deacon's taking the Liturgy through the Gospel — the point at which the American books have always terminated the 'Ante-Communion.'

We are now proposing to extend the curtailed American outline of this feature through the Sermon, including the Creed, and to permit the addition of an Offering, and the General Intercession, either in the form of the Prayer for the Church, a Litany, the Bidding Prayer, or suitable Collects; after which a priest shall conclude the service with the Benediction, or a Deacon with The Grace.

This would provide a reasonably balanced and complete service of public worship, whether it were used alone, or in combination with Morning Prayer either in full, or in its shortened form with only a First Lesson, and a transfer to the altar-service at the first Canticle. As it is now, strict conformity with the rubrics on the use of Morning Prayer in conjunction with the 'Ante-Communion' produces a four-lesson service, with a minimum of prayers of any kind, which is enough of a liturgical monstrosity so that there is little wonder that small use is made of the present permissions. On the other hand, anyone who has ever tried to construe the rubrics of Morning Prayer 'when the Holy Communion is immediately to follow' as applying equally to a combination with the 'Ante-Communion,' finds himself embarked on the liturgical impossibility of a service which contains no prayers at all!

2. The Order for a Second Consecration

The First Prayer Book gave no directions as to what should be done in case insufficient quantities of the Elements had been consecrated for the communion of all the people. In the days of the Puritans, some clergy simply took more bread or wine, and distributed them with no consecration whatever, in the belief that, as Peter Martyr said, 'the words belong rather to men than either to bread or wine.'[101] The XXIst Canon of 1604 took action against that abuse, saying, 'Furthermore, no Bread or Wine newly brought shalbe vsed: but first the words of institucion shalbe rehearsed when the said Bread and Wine bee present vpon the Communion Table.' This was a revival of the provisions of Cranmer's *Order of Communion* of 1548:

> Note, that if it doth so chaunce, that the wyne halowed and consecrate dooth not suffice or bee ynough for theim that dooe take the Communion, the priest after the firste Cup or chalice be emptied, may go again to ye aultare, and reuerentlie, and deuoutlie, prepare, and consecrate an other, and so the thirde, or more lykwise, begynning at these woordes, *Simili modo, postquam cenatum est*, and ending at these wordes, *qui pro uobis & pro multis effundetur in remissionem peccatorum*.

The Scottish of 1637 brought such requirements back into the Prayer Book:

> And to the end there may be little left, he that officiates is required to consecrate with the least, and then if there be want, the words of consecration may be repeated again, over more, either bread or wine: the Presbyter beginning at these words in the prayer of consecration (Our Saviour in the night that he was betrayed, took, &c.).

It is to be noted that the Words of Institution were at that time considered to be the 'Words of Consecration'; and that either 'species' alone might be consecrated by the use of them. The directions of 1662 further permitted the use of either half of the formula:

> If the consecrated Bread or Wine be all spent before all have communicated, the Priest is to consecrate more, according to the forme before prescribed: beginning at (Our Saviour Christ in the same night &c) for the blessing of the Bread; and at (likewise after Supper &c.) for the blessing of the Cup.

The Scottish Liturgy of 1764 however ordered that for a Second Consecration the Consecration Prayer be said entire, from 'All glory' through 'that they may become

---

101. Strype, *Cranmer*, App. lxi.

the body and blood of thy most dearly beloved Son' at the end of the Invocation proper. This required a reconsecration in both kinds; and it no longer regarded the repetition of the formula of the Institution as sufficient for that purpose. And these provisions have been in all the American books to the present day.

The English draft of 1928 went part way toward meeting the Scottish standards, printing the Institution and the Invocation paragraphs in an 'Order for a Second Consecration' after the service, but still allowing a 'Consecration in One Kind,' with the use of half the Institution narrative, but always with the Invocation. The Scottish Liturgy of 1929 in turn allows a Second Consecration with the use of the Institution and Invocation paragraphs only, but continues to insist upon a consecration in both kinds. South Africa allows the use of either the Scottish 1929 or the English 1662.

It is surely a pity to mutilate the Consecration Prayer by excising the Thanksgiving for the Redemption, the Oblation, and the Benefits of Communion and the Doxology. To do so, indeed, raises most serious questions as to the actual validity of the resulting form for the purposes of a Prayer of Consecration. Due consideration has been given to the Scottish compromise: but we found it impossible to recommend sanctioning it. On the contrary, we consider that with the shortening of the Consecration Prayer which we are advocating, there will be no appreciable hardship in requiring the repetition of the entire Prayer for a Second Consecration. And it seemed worth while to giving in the rubric the information which many people do not know, that the celebrant should himself receive again from the newly consecrated Elements before he proceeds with the Administration. A second Consecration is in fact a second Celebration. And from the time of the primitive *Agapé* down, the Church has always adhered to the principle that the priest must always first partake of the Sacrament which he has celebrated before he gives it to the people.

3. Intinction

The House of Bishops has signified approval for the administration of the Sacrament by the method known as 'Intinction,' with the Wafer dipped in the Chalice. The House of Deputies in 1952 ran into difficulties of detail, and wound up by rejecting the process of a 'piecemeal' revision of the Prayer Book. We are proposing it again as part of a systematic revision. We have reversed the order of the clauses of the rubric as presented in our special Report on this subject in 1952, so as to put first the normal form of the Administration, and the exception afterward; and conformed the combined Sentence of Administration to those proposed in the text of the service.

4. The 'Canonical Rubrics.'

The disciplinary rubrics covering repelling offenders from the Holy Communion cover matters which might perhaps be better treated in the Canons than in so inflexible a form as they hold in the Prayer Book. The Scottish Church does this, and then reprints the Canon (XXVI) in the Prayer Book. It is interesting to note that this Canon makes it clear that the right of excommunication is reserved to the Bishop, and the parish priest may do no more than refuse Communion in an emergency only until the Bishop can hear the case. This is implied in our present provisions, as revised in 1662, though it is by no means so lucidly stated.

The Irish Prayer Book of 1926 considerably condenses this matter:

> If the Minister shall have knowledge or reasonable ground to believe that any person who is living in open and notorious sin intends to come to the Holy Communion, so that scandal would thereby arise, he shall privately admonish him not to presume to come to the Lord's Table till the cause of offence shall have been removed; and in every such case the Minister shall have regard to the Canon relating thereto.

However, it is certainly of advantage that regulations for the discipline of the laity should be before their eyes in the Prayer Book which they all have, rather than shut up in a law-book which they do not see. We should be glad of the counsel of the Canonists of the Church as to the terms in which this matter should be set forth. In the meantime, therefore, we propose to include these 'Canonical Rubrics' in very much their present form. We correct the word 'Minister' to ' 'Priest,' in conformity with the other rubrics of the Liturgy. The present usage is distinctly inaccurate, since, in the nature of the case, powers of excommunication have never been exercised by a Deacon. And as in the Irish form above, we have substituted 'he shall admonish him' rather than 'advertise,' which now means something quite different.

2. The Exhortation

We propose to retain the first of the three 'Long Exhortations,' that on p. 85 f. of our present Prayer Book, with the rubric requiring its use on three occasions of the year, and permitting it at other times. Cranmer thought so well of this matter that he made it a required part of every celebration, except on weekdays. Experience has shown that this is not desirable, and successive Prayer Books have made it permissive, and removed it out of the normal text to this position after the service.

South Africa, India, and Ceylon eliminate it entirely. There is something to be said for this action. This Exhortation is in fact the clearest and most complete exposition of Cranmer's own doctrine of the Eucharist. It has a strong 'Zwinglian' color, with an undue emphasis upon the Commemoration of our Lord's sacrificial Death. This is counterbalanced in Cranmer's text, which survives in the English and Scottish versions, by a forceful expression of that idea of an 'Incorporation' into Christ which we have seen to be the redeeming feature of his doctrine, and which sublimates his presentation of the 'Memorial' to an assertion of the 'Real Presence' which actually goes considerably beyond anything the Roman Liturgy has to offer: 'For then we spiritually eate the fleshe of Christe, and drinke his bloude, then we dwell in Christ and Christ in vs, wee bee made one with Christ,

& Christ with vs.' But we have noted that this saving clause has been dropped from the American text, as twice expressed at the end of the Consecration Prayer, and in the Humble Access.[102]

We think that Cranmer's balance must be recovered. In the second paragraph (for, following the English revision of 1928, we have divided it into paragraphs for greater intelligibility when read or said), we propose to insert, 'who *took upon him our flesh, and* humbled himself even to the death upon the Cross,' in order to balance the Passion with the Incarnation, as in the first paragraph of the Consecration Prayer. And in the third paragraph, where there is a statement of the purpose of the Institution of the Sacrament, we insert a paraphrase of Cranmer's point, which we consider would be much more effective here than in its original parenthetical position: 'for a continual remembrance of his death, *and for a spiritual partaking of his life, that we may be one with him and he with us*, to our great and endless comfort.'

If something of this sort is done — *but only if it is done* — then this Exhortation is worth keeping. Though it does not perhaps provide any teaching not elsewhere contained or implied, it is a lucid summary of such teaching. It has sufficient value both for instruction and for devotion to continue to print it in the Prayer Book, to allow its use in the rite at discretion, and even to give point to certain occasions of the Church Year by prescribing its use then.

Two occurrences of the misleading word 'lively' have been corrected to 'living.'

We have appropriated the matter of the second Exhortation, now on p. 86 ff., to the new Office of Preparation.[103] The devotional values of this so-called 'Warning' or announcement of a coming celebration of the Liturgy are even greater than those of our first Exhortation. South Africa, which drops the third Exhortation entirely, requires the use of the second 'at the least before the Great Festivals.' Yet at the present time it goes almost utterly unused by us. We have endeavored to give the substance of this form a function which will enable it to be usefully employed, and a position which will at least insure that it will be read by the possessors of the Prayer Book.

But the third or 'scolding' Exhortation on p. 88 f., which is directed to be said by the Priest 'in case he shall see the People negligent to come to the Holy Communion,' may well be eliminated from the Prayer Book, as South Africa has done.

3. The Proper Prefaces

We have said before that we consider it advisable to remove the Proper Prefaces to this position after the service, in order to clear the text of the Liturgy of the

---

102. P. 166 above.
103. P. 240 f.

three pages now occupied by these seasonal variants, only one of which can be used on any occasion. This has been done by all the current Anglican revisions.

There seems to be a very general desire for the provision of more Proper Prefaces for the seasons and occasions of the Christian Year. We have received many suggestions that we conform to the other Anglican revisions in doing so.

A hopeful review of this material in the other Anglican books has brought us to the reluctant conclusion that none of those forms seem to be very good. They are nearly all distinctly prosaic and pedestrian unsuitable for insertion at a point of the service where devout emotion and its verbal expression are on a very high plane indeed. Such an occasional gleam of inspiration as some of them occasionally display turns out upon examination to be abstracted from some other prayer in the Prayer Book, after the incorrigible habit of making new devotional forms by a 'scissors-and-paste' adaptation of existing matter which is so often a weakness of Anglicans when they set about devising an expression for a new need. Moreover, most of these proposed Prefaces are so lacking in rhythm that they 'scan' badly when one attempts to apply to them the principles of the very ancient (indeed, pre-Christian) *Cantus Solemnis* which has always been the liturgical musical setting of the Preface. There is not one Proper Preface among all those found in the English, Scottish, South African, Indian, or Ceylon liturgies which the Commission feels it can recommend for adoption.

It may be said that nearly all the Proper Prefaces in the Sarum Missal which Cranmer did not accept for his First Prayer Book are so inferior to those which he did adopt as not to be worth having. And in just the same way, our Revision Commission in 1928 took all of this material then under consideration in the other Anglican Churches which was at all comparable with the Prefaces which we already had: namely successful adaptations of the Sarum Prefaces for the Epiphany, and for the Nativity (now used on three feasts of the Incarnation), and a new composition, drawn entirely from Holy Scriptures, for All Saints'.

We believe that the requests for a greater number of Proper Prefaces are quite legitimate, and that such provisions would be real enrichments of the rite, adding variety and judicious emphasis to the occasions of the Church Year. But we also think that inferior matter ought not to be admitted to the Prayer Book merely to fill the vacuum; that nothing should be adopted which is not comparable in quality with the Proper Prefaces which we now have.

We have given considerable thought to this problem, and are prepared to bring forward certain suggestions to meet it. But again we emphasize the fact that these proposals are submitted only for discussion. We very much hope that in the length and breadth of the Church there can be found such devotional and literary ability as will be able greatly to improve upon anything which we have been able to work out.

1. Advent

The Proper Preface for the season of Advent adopted by Scotland and Ceylon is as follows:

> Because thou hast given salvation unto mankind through the coming of thy well-beloved Son in great humility, and by him wilt make all things new when he shall come again in his glorious majesty to judge the world in righteousness.

That will not do at all. 'In great humility,' and 'come again in his glorious majesty to judge,' have been simply purloined from the Advent Collect, which is said every day throughout the season. We cannot consider appointing those phrases to be said over again in the Preface.

The only other version for Advent is in the Indian rite:

> Through Jesus Christ our Lord; who, at his first coming into the world in fashion as a man, did promise in the form of God to come again with glory, that he might receive his people into the place which he had prepared for them, that as kings they might reign with him for ever.

Here 'first coming' has been lifted from the Collect for Advent III, 'come again with glory' from the Nicene Creed, 'place . . . prepared for them,' and 'might reign with him,' from the Ascension Preface. 'In fashion as a man,' and 'in the form of God,' are from Phil. 2:6, 8, in the Epistle for Palm Sunday. This use of Scripture is legitimate enough in itself, though the inevitable mental cross-reference to a quite different occasion of the year is nearly enough to bar its use here.

And the employment of all these quotations, with their necessary distractions of thought toward their original contexts, prevents their being welded into a real continuum of their own. This form persists in being as disjointed in its effect as it is in its sources.

Dr. Massey H. Shepherd on p. 58 of his little book entitled *The Living Liturgy* advances two suggestions for an Advent Preface. One of them is based upon two verses of the *Benedictus*, from Luke 1:69, 79. It seems entirely acceptable, since its language expresses admirably the characteristic Advent themes, yet is familiar, closely integrated, and does not infringe any expressions now used in the Eucharistic Liturgy:

> Who hast raised up a mighty salvation for us in the Kingdom of thy Son, Jesus Christ our Lord; to give light to those that sit in darkness and in the shadow of death, and to guide our feet into the way of peace.

2. Lent

Scotland, India, and Ceylon have gone back to the Sarum rite in providing two Proper Prefaces for the season of Lent: one, treating the theme of spiritual discipline, for use up to Passion Sunday, and the other on the Passion of our Lord, for the rest of the season. Our present Prayer Book recognizes this division of the season, giving the separate heading 'Passiontide' to the last two weeks. Lent, in its original function of a preparation for the feast of the Resurrection, was at first three days, then one week, then two. The Roman veiling of cross and images in the church on Passion Sunday still marks this distinctive period. Everything before that was added on for the quite different purpose of a period of intensive preparation for the Easter Baptisms, and has a different quality of its own.

The Latin Preface for the first 4½ weeks stresses the subject of Fasting only; it is the slightest and perhaps the poorest of the Prefaces: Qui corporali jejunio vitia comprimis, mentem elevas, virtutem largiris et præmia ' — Who by bodily fasting dost suppress vices, elevate the mind, bestow virtue and rewards.'

Scotland and Ceylon enlarge this sole emphasis upon literal Fasting — which few people nowadays treat as of primary importance, and none whatever carry out with anything like the rigor of medieval requirements — to an expression of the general control over our lower natures:

> Because thou hast given us the spirit of discipline, that we may triumph over the flesh, and live not unto ourselves but unto him who died for us and rose again.

Here, though there is no plagiarism of words, the phrase that we may triumph over 'the flesh' is rather too obvious a paraphrase of 'that, our flesh being subdued to the Spirit' of the Collect for Lent I to be altogether acceptable. And the mention of the Resurrection seems irrelevant at this point in the early part of Lent, and in this connection.

The Indian Preface enlarges on the theme of Fasting, and couples with it the subject of Temptation, after the pattern of the Epistle and Gospel on Lent I:

> Through Jesus Christ our Lord; who for our sakes did as at this time fast forty days and forty nights, and was at all points tempted like as we are, yet without sin, to the intent that we, which are tempted, may, through him, come boldly unto the throne of grace, that we may obtain mercy and find grace to help in time of need.

The appropriation of 'didst fast forty days and forty nights' from the Collect of Lent I is undesirable. The quotation from Heb. 4:15 f. is excellent, although the interpolated expressions *to the intent that,* '*which* are tempted,' and 'through him' seem totally unnecessary, and also are deficient in form and cadence.

We think something can be made of this by dropping the allusion to the forty-day fast, as having only an inferential application, and being irrelevant in conjunction with the fine quotation from Hebrews, and by subsuming the whole question of self-discipline into the effective form of the resisting of temptation. Broadening the base of the proposed Preface by taking in elements of Heb. 4:14 also would give us something to this effect:

> Who hast sent thine only Son to be a great High Priest who is touched with the feeling of our infirmities, being at all points tempted like as we are, yet without sin; that we may come boldly unto the throne of grace, to obtain mercy, and to find grace to help in time of need.

3. Passiontide

The same three rites appoint the Passiontide Preface for use from Passion Sunday up to but not including Maundy Thursday. They make other provisions for Maundy Thursday, and regard Good Friday and Easter Even as 'aliturgical' days, inappropriate for the celebration of the Eucharist. The Roman rite uses its Passiontide Preface also upon Maundy Thursday. There is surely no incongruity in having it upon that occasion, so overshadowed by the coming Passion, and destined to show forth a perpetual memorial of the Lord's death till he come. As we see little utility in a Proper Preface assigned to a single day of the year, and consider the formula for Maundy Thursday adopted (with variations) by Scotland, England, South Africa, and Ceylon to be particularly prosaic, we propose to follow Sarum by extending the use of the Passiontide Preface to Maundy Thursday.

The Latin 'Preface of the Passion and the Cross' is not worth much, being a string of artificial conceits and stilted antitheses. Literally translated (since it would be labor lost to try to 'Cranmerize' it), it runs as follows:

> Who hast established the salvation of mankind upon the Wood of the Cross: that whence death sprang, thence life should arise; and that he who conquered upon the Wood, should be conquered also by the Wood; through Christ our Lord.

The Scottish version tries to enrich the underlying idea here with devotional matter from Holy Scripture:

Because thou didst give thine only Son, our Saviour Jesus Christ,	Christmas Preface.
to redeem mankind from the power of darkness;	Col. 1:13.
who, having finished the work thou gavest him to do,	John 17:4.
was lifted up upon the cross that he might draw all men unto himself,	John 12:32.

Because thou didst give thine only Son, our Saviour Jesus Christ,	Christmas Preface.
and, being made perfect through suffering,	Heb. 2:10.
might become the author of eternal salvation to all them that obey him.	Heb. 5:9.

India and Ceylon found this too wordy, and condensed it:

Through Jesus Christ our Lord; who, being found in fashion as a man, humbled himself and became obedient unto death, even the death of the Cross,	Phil. 2.8.
that being lifted up from the earth, he might draw all men unto him.	John 12:32.

The incorporation of the text from Philippians, found in the Epistle for Palm Sunday in the midst of the use of this Preface, is still less fortunate than its employment in the Indian Preface for Advent. Perhaps they felt, with some justification, that the Scottish use of John 17:4 was not altogether happy in this connection. As originally used in the High-Priestly Prayer,' its natural reference to our Lord's previous life and work is perfectly clear; but when it is imported into this context of the Passion, the reflection is bound to arise that it was not until the last moment upon the Cross that he said, 'It is finished.'

We should prefer something of this order:

> Because thou didst give thine only son, our Saviour Jesus Christ, to redeem mankind from the power of darkness; who was lifted up upon the Cross, to draw all men unto him; and was made perfect through suffering, that he might become the Author of eternal salvation to all that obey him.

4. Easter

In the Easter Preface, some exceptions have been taken to Cranmer's translation of the original expression, 'Qui mortem nostram moriendo destruxit et vitam resurgendo reparavit.' Literally, this is 'Who by dying hath destroyed our death, and by rising again hath renewed (our) life.' Cranmer had rather a penchant for saying 'eternal' or 'everlasting life,' where all that the text he was translating gave was simply 'life': notably the Collect for Peace in Morning Prayer,[104] where perhaps 'fulness of life' would be much nearer the idea of the original *vivere* than

---

104. Ed. Note: O GOD, who art the author of peace and lover of concord, in knowledge of whom standeth *our eternal life*, whose service is perfect freedom; Defend us thy humble servants in all assaults of our enemies; that we, surely trusting in thy defence, may not fear the power of any adversaries, through the might of Jesus Christ our Lord. Amen.

'eternal life.' However, the implication of Immortality is quite in order here, and represents what the Latin is trying to say. The difficulty is in the connotations of the word 'restored,' which suggests that an effect of the Resurrection was to recover for man the gift of Immortality which was bestowed upon Adam, and of which he was deprived as a penalty for sin. Without in any way disputing the import of St. Paul's saying, 'For as in Adam all die, even so in Christ shall all be made alive,' it simply is the case that physical immortality has not been reconferred, and that the idea of 'everlasting life' which our Easter Preface proposes has no dependence upon the story in Genesis. Since the idea of immortality has quite properly been brought forward here, we think that it would be well to make a frank departure from the Latin original, and say, 'hath *assured* to us everlasting life.' That says something worth saying, for it intimates that the immemorial hope and wish for personal immortality was made an assured fact in Christian belief through the Resurrection of our Lord.

It has been suggested that the Easter Preface might be permitted by rubric at a Requiem Eucharist. Such a use of it would be entirely appropriate. We are, however, suggesting a version of the new Latin Preface for such occasions. If something of that sort is adopted, there would be no need to use the Easter Preface for that purpose. But if it proves that the time is not ripe for such a move, then a rubric allowing the use of the Easter Preface might be helpful.

5. *All Saints*

Our present Preface for All Saints was adopted in 1928 from the Scottish Prayer Book of 1912. It differs from this form only in saying 'that' instead of 'to the end that' a somewhat stilted phrase which is apt to crop up in modern British collect-making, but which Cranmer did not employ except in the more formal style of rubrics and Exhortations. It first appeared in the Scottish Draft Liturgy of 1889 in this version:

> Who art glorified in all thy Saints, in whom, crowning their graces, thou crownest thine own gifts, and hast compassed us about with so great a cloud of witnesses that in their fellowship, and after their example, we may run with patience the race that is set before us, and together with them receive the crown of glory that fadeth not away.

This form is commendable for at least trying to express an idea of its own — such as it is — instead of falling back upon borrowings of devotional language already in use in other connections. Of course the employment of scriptural language is absolutely legitimate: the Holy Scriptures have always furnished the warp and woof out of which the Church's forms of worship have been woven.

But the triple reiteration of the word 'crown' was anything but satisfactory. And interpolating the words 'in their fellowship,' and 'after their example' into the passage from Heb. 12:1 was not at all judicious. It effectively broke up the fine figure of the original context. The 'great cloud of witnesses' there are all the prize-winners of former years, gathered in a vast Olympic arena, to see us run our race today. The interpolation of 1889, and perhaps even more the simplification of this to 'rejoicing in their fellowship ' in the present Scottish, American, and Indian forms, would rather bring up a picture of a pleasant pause to fraternize with the audience, than they would concentrate our attention upon the original idea of tensing every nerve to acquit ourselves manfully in their sight. This expression can be employed to very good effect in the Commemoration of the Saints in the General Intercession, as is done by England and Ceylon, and as we are proposing. It really does not belong here in the Preface.

The English version in 1928, which has been copied by Ceylon and somewhat abbreviated by South Africa, is this:

> Who in the righteousness of thy Saints hast given us an ensample of godly living, and in their blessedness a glorious pledge of the hope of our calling: That, being compassed about with so great a cloud of witnesses, we may run with patience the race that is set before us: And with them receive the crown of glory that fadeth not away.

Here 'the righteousness of thy Saints' is an echo of Rev. 19:8, and the idea of 'their blessedness' appears in the next verse. 'An ensample of godly living' is taken from the Collect for Easter II. Cranmer actually wrote 'example' in 1549, though the text of 1 Peter 2:21 in the Epistle for that Sunday said 'ensample.' The Elizabethan Book of 1559 made the Collect say 'ensample,' to conform to the Epistle: and in that form it has remained, although the Authorized Version of 1611, adopted in the Prayer Book of 1662, reads 'example.' The obsolete form 'ensample' certainly seems too affected for any new form. 'A glorious pledge' is original, having no scriptural or liturgical source. 'The hope of our calling' reflects Eph. 1:18 and 4:4. The quotation from the Collect for Easter II is not too obvious, especially as the 'example' there is that of our Lord, and our applying it to the following of his footsteps by the Saints is a perfectly legitimate inference, with something of the independent value of a new assertion. And if with South Africa we say 'example' instead of 'ensample,' it cannot be considered to be objectionable at all.

The balance of the two expressions in the exordium of this Preface supplies a distinctly noble statement of the inspiratiom for the tasks of life to be derived from the contemplation of those whose Christian course has been victorious, and provide: a far more adequate basis for the triumphant peroration in the words of Heb. 12:1 and 1 Pet. 5:4 than that undesirable interpolation of 'rejoicing in their fellowship.'

Perhaps from familiarity, we prefer to continue to say 'and together with them, may receive' etc. And in spite of familiarity, we think we ought to say 'may run with *endurance* the race that is set before us.' 'Patience' is a poor translation of the Greek word in the Authorized Version. The Revised Standard makes it 'perseverance' — but 'endurance' is obviously better in this context.

6. *Feasts of Apostles*

The Scottish and Indian liturgies are the only ones which provide a Proper Preface for the feasts of Apostles and Evangelists. (St. John on December 27 is excepted, since that day of course takes the Preface of the great Christmas Octave.) The other revisions are content to take care of these festivals by the extention of the use of the Preface for All Saints to which we have referred.[105]

The old Latin Preface of the Apostles throws important emphasis upon the Ministry of the Apostolic Succession in the Church:

> It is verily meet and just, right and salutary, that we should humbly implore thee, O Eternal Shepherd, not to desert thy flock, but to guard it with continual protection through thy blessed Apostles; that it may be governed by the same rulers, whom thou hast bestowed upon the same to be over it as the delegated Pastors of thy work.

This Preface is echoed by the Scottish and Indian Preface for Ordinations, which may also be used upon the Ember Days:

> Through Jesus Christ our Lord, the great Shepherd of the sheep; who, for the feeding and guidance of his flock, did appoint divers orders of ministers in his Church.

Here the phrase from Heb. 13:20 is excellent. But the expression 'did appoint divers orders of ministers in his Church' duplicates one of the Ember Collects, and appears in all three services of Ordination — a circumstance which of itself ought to disqualify it for use in a Proper Preface appointed for exactly those occasions.

But for Apostles or Evangelists, these rites offer this:

> Through Jesus Christ our Lord, who did vouchsafe to choose thy servant Saint N. (or thy servants Saint N. and St. N.) to be of the company of the Apostles (or to be an Evangelist), by whose ministry thine elect might be gathered from every nation, and thy Church instructed in the way that leadeth unto everlasting life.

The echo of the *Te Deum* in the 'company of the Apostles' may be considered to be just within bounds; but the barely concealed theft of 'the way that leadeth to eternal life' from the Collect of SS. Philip and James is not tolerable. And the scope

---

105. P. 297.

of this Preface is as strictly confined to the preaching and teaching function of the Apostolate, as the Roman is to the ruling powers of the Episcopate. Both ideas have their place; but neither alone covers what we mean when we speak of the Church as 'Apostolic' in the Creeds. The Apostolic Ministry is certainly a ministry of the Sacraments as well as of the Word, and holds the charter of the 'extension of the Incarnation' in the mystical Body of Christ. It would be ample justification for having a Proper Preface for the feasts of the Apostles if we had one giving sufficient expression to all these ideas. The following gives an idea of how such a Preface could be constructed out of unimpeachable language from the Holy Scriptures:

Through that great Shepherd of the sheep, Jesus Christ our Lord:	Heb. 13:20.
who sent forth his blessed Apostles to teach all nations,	Matt. 28:19.
to wash them from their sins in his own blood, and make them kings and priests,	Rev. 1:5f.
offering up spiritual sacrifices acceptable unto thee;	1 Pet. 2:5.
that unto the end of the world he might be alway with those who believe in him.	Matt. 28:20.

This covers the ground of both the above Scottish Prefaces, and could be used not only on Feasts of Apostles, but at all Ordinations, and upon Ember Days.

7. Other Sundays

The proposed extension of the use of the Christmas and Easter Prefaces, and the new provisions for Advent, Lent, and Passiontide, would supply Proper Prefaces for all Sundays except those in Pre-Lent, the Trinity Season, and after the Octave of the Epiphany. Many suggestions have been made to us for a kind of 'Common of Sundays,' for use upon any Sunday not otherwise provided for.

The English 1928 offers the following for that purpose:

> Through Jesus Christ our Lord; for he is the true High Priest, who hath washed us from our sins, and hath made us to be a kingdom and priests unto thee our God and Father.

What appropriateness this has to a Sunday does not appear. And we think we have made better use of these ideas on the Feasts of Apostles.

Ceylon is the only other rite making such a provision; as follows:

> Through Jesus Christ our Lord: Who on the first day of the week did rise from the dead, that we might live in him by the power of the Holy Ghost.

This makes the point that every Sunday is a 'weekly Easter.' It quite omits to mention that the Sending of the Holy Ghost was also 'on the first day of the week.' And it has something of the air of an attempt which was never properly finished off, to commemorate the Holy Trinity.

The present Roman rite assigns the Trinity Sunday Preface to all undesignated Sundays. We think it much too theological to be used on more than half the Sundays of the year. It has no special appositeness to Sundays as such, and must have been chosen for the purpose simply as the crown of the Church's doctrine.

It has been suggested that we might use Bishop White's alternative Preface for Trinity Sunday upon these 'common Sundays':

> For the precious death and merits of thy Son Jesus Christ our Lord, and for the sending to us of the Holy Ghost, the Comforter; who are one with thee in thy Eternal Godhead.

There is undue emphasis here on the 'death' of our Lord; and the attempt to balance it up with a mention of his 'merits' is hardly successful. Protestantism has at times used the 'merits' of the Saviour in just as unrealistic and unethical a way as Catholicism ever did the 'Merits of the Saints.' And the word 'Comforter' has the same defects of obsolete meaning as we have noted for 'comfort' in general. It is not an adequate rendering of the Greek *Parakletos* — in fact, there is no adequate translation of that term. We see no sufficient reason for retaining this alternative Preface.

A possible combination of this American form with that of Ceylon might be:

> For the precious benefits thou hast vouchsafed to all mankind upon the first day of the week, in the rising from the dead of our Lord Jesus Christ, and the sending upon thine Apostles of the mighty power of thy Holy Spirit; who are one with thee in thy Eternal Godhead.

However, when we reflected that such a Common Preface for Sundays would be used on more than half the Sundays of the year, we decided that it would be tolerable only if it were the best such composition in the Prayer Book. This the above labored synthesis certainly is not; and until a form of such manifest excellence appears, we are opposed to offering any Preface as a 'Common of Sundays.'

8. *Commemorations of the Departed*

The Roman Missal in 1919 introduced a Proper Preface at Requiems, which is as fine a piece of gnomic Latin as has ever appeared for such a use. Unfortunately, it defies successful translation into English to pretty much the same degree as does the Latin Preface for Trinity Sunday — which we have observed that we have never been able to adopt in full. Here is the original:

Per Christum Dominum nostrum; in quo spes beatæ; resurrectionis effulsit, ut quos contristat certa moriendi conditio, eosdem consoletur futuræ immortalitatis promissio. Tuis enim fidelibus, Domine, vita mutatur, non tollitur: et, dissoluta terrestris hujus incolatus domo, æterna in cælis habitatio comparatur.

The Indian rite assays a literal translation:

> Through Jesus Christ our Lord, in whom there hath shined forth on us the hope of a blessed resurrection, that we who are grieved with the certain knowledge of our mortality may by the firm assurance of immortality be comforted; seeing that in death thy faithful servants die not, though they be changed; for when the house of their earthly tabernacle is dissolved, there is prepared for them an habitation eternal in the heavens.

Perhaps the less said about this rendering, the better. It certainly suffers by comparison with the crystal clarity and the exquisite cadences of the Latin. It is very heavy in hand, and picks up a little lightness and motion only when it turns into the stretch of the peroration of the original from 2 Cor. 5:1.

South Africa and Ceylon share another version, which turns to Holy Scripture for the expression of some of these ideas:

Through Jesus Christ our Lord; who hath brought life and immortality to light,	2 Tim. 1:10.
that we, who are burdened	2 Cor. 5:4.
by the weight of sin and death,	Rom. 5:12, 21, 6:23; 1 Cor. 15:56.
may grieve not as those who have no hope;	1 Thess. 4:13.
because we know that when our earthly tabernacle is dissolved, we have a better habitation.	2 Cor. 5:1; Heb. 11:16

This is an improvement, certainly — although it funks completely the clause 'Tuis enim fidelibus, Domine, vita mutatur, non tollitur,' which in some ways is the most distinctive idea contributed by the Latin form.

A version which preserves all the essential thoughts of the original, and puts them as far as possible into scriptural language, might run as follows:

Through Jesus Christ our Lord; who hath brought to light,	2 Tim. 1:10.
the living hope of a blessed resurrection,	1 Pet. 1:3.
that we may grieve not	1 Thess. 4:13.
for that we are all appointed once to die,	Heb. 9:27

Through Jesus Christ our Lord; who hath brought to light,	2 Tim. 1:10.
but may rejoice in the assurance of immortal life to come:	2 Tim 1:10
seeing that whosoever believeth in thine Only begotten Son doth not perish, but	John 3:16
is changed into the likeness of his glory;	Phil 3:21
for when the earthly house of our sojourning is dissolved, there is prepared for us an habitation eternal in the heavens.	2 Cor. 5:1

No doubt this can be improved. But we think that something of this order might be of great comfort to the bereaved. Of course its use would be permissive, at the discretion of the Priest — as indeed the use of the Requiem Eucharist which might contain it is now.

The Holy Liturgy

The Office of Preparation for the Holy Communion

¶ *The following Service for the corporate Preparation for the receiving of the Holy Communion may be used on any day preceding a stated Celebration of the Liturgy, and especially before the great Festivals.*

¶ *When it is so used, the Priest may add an Address or Meditation after* THE EXHORTATION. *And instead of rehearsing* THE DECALOGUE *in its Litany-form, he may in his discretion propound questions based upon* THE TEN COMMANDMENTS *and* THE LAW OF LOVE, *for each person to answer to his own conscience, in true penitent recognition of his sins before God.*

¶ *This Service may be employed as the basis of a private self-examination.*

¶ *This Office, from* THE BIDDING *to* THE COLLECT *inclusive, may also be used in the Liturgy after* THE COLLECT FOR PURITY, *and in place of* THE LAW OF LOVE, KYRIE ELEISON, *and* GLORIA IN EXCELSIS, *upon Sundays in Lent, or at other times at the discretion of the Priest.*

The Exhortation

DEARLY beloved, on _____ day next I purpose, through God's assistance, to administer to all such as shall be religiously and devoutly disposed the life-giving Sacrament of the Body and Blood of Christ: to be received by them in remembrance of his saving Cross and Passion, whereby alone we obtain remission of our sins, and are made partakers of the Kingdom of heaven. Wherefore it is our duty to render most humble and hearty thanks to Almighty God, our heavenly Father, for that he hath given his Son our Saviour Jesus Christ, not only to die for us, but also to be our spiritual food and sustenance in that holy Sacrament.

But since this is so divine and life-giving a thing to those who receive it worthily, and so dangerous to those who will presume to receive it unworthily, my duty is to exhort you in the mean time to consider the dignity of that holy Mystery, and the great peril of the unworthy receiving thereof; and so to search and examine your own consciences, and that not lightly, and after the manner of dissemblers with God, but so that ye may come holy and clean to such a heavenly Feast, in the marriage-garment required by God in holy Scripture, and be received as worthy partakers of that holy Table.

And because it is requisite that no man should come to the Holy Communion, but with a full trust in God's mercy, and with a quiet conscience, every person who doth intend to receive that holy Sacrament should make due examination of his offences against God, and against his neighbour, that he may be reconciled unto both.

But if there be any, who by this means cannot quiet his own conscience herein, but requireth further comfort or counsel, let him go to some discreet and learned Priest, and open his grief: that by the Ministry of God's holy Word he may receive the benefit of Absolution, together with such godly counsel and advice, as may avail to the quieting of his conscience, and the removing of all scruple and doubtfulness.

The Bidding

YE who mind to come to the Holy Communion of the Body and Blood of our Saviour Christ, must examine your lives and conduct by the rule of God's Commandments, in order worthily to confess your sinfulness to Almighty God with full purpose of amendment of life: that so ye may be meet partakers of those holy Mysteries.

The Decalogue

¶ Then the Priest shall rehearse distinctly THE TEN COMMANDMENTS; and the People, kneeling, shall ask God's mercy for their transgressions of every duty therein for the time past, and grace to keep the Law of God for the time to come.

GOD spake these words, and said:

I. I am the Lord thy God: thou shalt have none other Gods but me.
Lord, have mercy upon us, and incline our hearts to keep this law.

II. Thou shalt not make to thyself any graven image, nor the likeness of any thing that is in heaven above, or in the earth beneath, or in the water under the earth; thou shall not bow down to them, nor worship them.
Lord, have mercy upon us, and incline our hearts to keep this law.

III. Thou shalt not take the Name of the Lord thy God in vain.
Lord, have mercy upon us, and incline our hearts to keep this law.

IV. Remember that thou keep holy the Sabbath-day.
Lord, have mercy upon us, and incline our hearts to keep this law.

V. Honour thy father and thy mother.
Lord, have mercy upon us, and incline our hearts to keep this law.

VI. Thou shalt do no murder.
Lord, have mercy upon us, and incline our hearts to keep this law.

VII. Thou shalt not commit adultery.
Lord, have mercy upon us, and incline our hearts to keep this law.

VIII. Thou shalt not steal.
Lord, have mercy upon us, and incline our hearts to keep this law.

IX. Thou shalt not bear false witness against thy neighbour.
Lord, have mercy upon us, and incline our hearts to keep this law.

X. Thou shalt not covet.
Lord, have mercy upon us, and write all these thy laws in our hearts, we beseech thee.

The Law of Love

¶ Then shall the Priest say,

Hear also what our Lord Jesus Christ saith:

THOU shalt love the Lord thy God with all thy heart, and with all thy soul, and with all thy mind. This is the first and great commandment. And the second is like unto it: Thou shalt love thy neighbour as thyself. On these two commandments hang all the Law and the Prophets.

The Collect

¶ Then he shall say,

O ALMIGHTY Lord, and everlasting God, vouchsafe, we beseech thee, to direct, sanctify, and govern, both our hearts and bodies, in the ways of thy laws, and in the works of thy commandments; that, through thy most mighty protection, both here and ever, we may be preserved in body and soul; through our Lord and Saviour Jesus Christ. Amen.

¶ *The Priest may then add* THE GENERAL CONFESSION, THE COMFORTABLE WORDS, *and* THE ABSOLUTION, *from the Liturgy, together with other suitable Prayers, concluding with a Blessing.*

The Liturgy for the Celebration of the Holy Eucharist and the Administration of Holy Communion

The Ministry of the Word

The Introit

¶ *Before the Holy Liturgy, a Hymn or Anthem may be sung for* THE INTROIT.

¶ *At the Communion-time, the Holy Table shall have upon it a fair white linen cloth. And the Priest, standing reverently before the Altar, shall say* THE COLLECT FOR PURITY, *the People kneeling.*

¶ *But if a* LITANY *hath been said immediately before, the Priest may pass at once to the* KYRIE ELEISON.

The Collect for Purity

Priest. The Lord be with you.
People. And with thy spirit.
Priest. Let us pray.

A LMIGHTY God, unto whom all hearts are open, all desires known, and from whom no secrets are hid; Cleanse the thoughts of our hearts by the inspiration of thy Holy Spirit, that we may perfectly love thee, and worthily magnify thy holy Name; through Christ our Lord. *Amen.*

The Law of Love

¶ *Then shall the Priest say,*

Hear what our Lord Jesus Christ saith:

THOU shalt love the Lord thy God with all thy heart, and with all thy soul, and with all thy wind. This is the first and great commandment. And the second it like unto it: Thou shalt love thy neighbour as thyself. On these two commandments hang all the Law and the Prophets.

Kyrie Eleison

¶ *Then shall be said or sung,*

LORD, have mercy upon us.	or Kyrie eleison.
Christ, have mercy upon us.	*Christe eleison.*
Lord, have mercy upon us.	Kyrie eleison.

¶ *Each clause may be repeated thrice.*

Gloria in Excelsis

¶ *Upon all Sundays (except in Advent, and from Septuagesima to Palm Sunday inclusive); upon all Festivals; upon days within appointed Octaves; and upon all days in the Festal Seasons from Christmas to Epiphany, and from Easter to Trinity Sunday inclusive: shall be said or sung the Hymn* GLORIA IN EXCELSIS, *all standing.*

GLORY be to God on high, and on earth peace to men of good will. We praise thee, we bless thee, we worship thee, we glorify thee, we give thanks to thee for thy great glory: O Lord God, heavenly King, God the Father Almighty.

O Lord, the only-begotten Son, Jesus Christ: O Lord God, Lamb of God, Son of the Father: That takest away the sins of the world, have mercy upon us. Thou that takest away the sins of the world, receive our prayer. Thou that sittest at the right hand of God the Father, have mercy upon us.

For thou only art holy; thou only art the Lord; thou only, O Christ, with the Holy Ghost, art most high in the glory of God the Father. Amen.

The Collect of the Day

Priest. The Lord be with you.
People. And with thy spirit.
Priest. Let us pray.

¶ *Then shall the Priest say* THE COLLECT OF THE DAY; *the People kneeling.*

The Epistle

¶ Then, the People being seated, the Minister appointed shall turn to the People, and read THE EPISTLE, *first saying,*

HEAR the (___) Epistle (of Saint _____) (to_____); or, Hear the Lesson from the Book of _____

¶ The Epistle ended, he shall say,

Here endeth the Epistle (or, the Lesson).

The Gradual

¶ Here may be sung a Hymn or an Anthem.

The Gospel

¶ Then, all the People standing, the Priest or Deacon appointed shall read THE GOSPEL, *first saying,*

HEAR the Holy Gospel according to Saint _____

¶ Here the People shall say,

Glory be to thee, O Lord.

¶ And after the Gospel the People shall say,

Praise be to thee, O Christ.

The Creed

¶ Then shall be said the CREED *commonly called* THE NICENE. *But the Creed may be omitted from the Liturgy upon any day not a Sunday or Holy Day.*

I BELIEVE in one God: the Father Almighty, Maker of heaven and earth, And of all things visible and invisible:
 And in one Lord Jesus Christ, the only-begotten Son of God; Begotten of the Father before all worlds; God, of God, Light, of Light, Very God, of very God; Begotten, not made; Being of one substance with the Father; Through whom all things were made: Who for us men and for our salvation came down from heaven, And was incarnate by the Holy Ghost of the Virgin Mary, And was made man: And was crucified also for us under Pontius Pilate; He suffered and was buried: And the third day he rose again according to the Scriptures: And ascended into

heaven, And sitteth at the right hand of the Father: And he shall come again, with glory, to judge both the quick and the dead; Whose kingdom shall have no end.

And I believe in the Holy Ghost, The Lord, The Giver of life, Who proceedeth from the Father and the Son; Who with the Father and the Son together is worshipped and glorified; Who spake by the Prophets. And I believe in One Holy Catholic and Apostolic Church: I acknowledge one Baptism for the remission of sins: and I look for the resurrection of the dead: And the life of the world to come. Amen.

The Sermon

¶ *Then shall be declared unto the People what Holy Days, or Fasting Days, are in the week following to be observed; and, if occasion be, shall Notice be given of the Celebration of the Holy Liturgy, and of the Banns of Matrimony, and of other matters to be published; and special intercessions may be made here.*

¶ *Here followeth the* SERMON.

The Offertory

¶ *Then shall the Priest turn to the People, and begin the Offertory by saying one or more of these* SENTENCES *following.*

¶ *And* NOTE, *That these* SENTENCES *may be used on any other occasion of Public Worship when the Offerings of the People are to be received.*

OFFER unto God the sacrifice of thanksgiving, and pay thy vows unto the Most High. *Psalm 50:14.*

Give unto the Lord the glory due unto his Name: bring an offering, and come into his courts. *Psalm 96:8.*

Walk in love, as Christ also hath loved us, and given himself for an offering and a sacrifice unto God. *Eph. 5:2.*

I beseech you therefore, brethren, by the mercies of God, that ye present your bodies a living sacrifice, holy, acceptable unto God, which is your reasonable service. *Rom. 12:1.*

Charitable Offerings

While we have time, let us do good unto all men; and especially unto those who are of the household of faith. *Gal. 6:10.*

God is not unrighteous, that he will forget your works, and labour that proceedeth of love; which love ye have showed for his Name's sake, who have ministered unto the Saints, and yet do minister. *Heb. 6:10.*

Whoso hath this world's good, and seeth his brother have need, and shutteth up his compassion from him, how dwelleth the love of God in him? *1 St. John 3:17.*

And the King shall answer and say unto them, Verily I say unto you, Inasmuch as ye have done it unto one of the least of these my brethren, ye have done it unto me. *St. Matthew 25:40.*

Missionary Offerings

How then shall they call on him in whom they have not believed? and how shall they believe in him of whom they have not heard? and how shall they hear without a preacher? and how shall they preach, except they be sent? *Rom. 10:4.*

Jesus saith unto them, The harvest truly is plenteous, but the labourers are few: pray ye therefore the Lord of the harvest, that he send forth labourers into his harvest. *St. Luke 10:2.*

¶ During the Offertory, there may be sung a Hymn or an Anthem.

¶ The Priest or Deacon shall prepare so much Bread, and Wine mixed with a little pure water, as he shall think sufficient for the communion.

¶ The Church Wardens, or other representatives of the Congregation, shall receive the Alms for the Poor, and other Offerings of the People, and shall reverently bring them in a decent Basin to the Priest, who shall humbly present and place them upon the Holy Table.

¶ And the Priest shall then offer, and shall place upon the Holy Table, the Bread and the Wine.

¶ At the Presentation of the Alms and Oblations, a suitable Hymn may be sung, or one of the following SENTENCES *shall be said:*

THINE, O Lord, is the greatness, and the power, and the glory, and the victory, and the majesty: for all that is in the heaven and in the earth is thine; thine is the kingdom, O Lord, and thou art exalted as head above all. *1 Chronicles 29:11.*

All things come of thee, O Lord, and of thine own have we given thee. *1 Chronicles 29:14.*

The General Intercession

¶ Here the Priest may say authorized Prayers, or may ask the secret intercessions of the Congregation, for any who have desired the prayers of the Church.

¶ *Then the Priest shall say the following Prayer; or else, a* LITANY, *or* THE BIDDING PRAYER, *may be said here; omitting* THE LORD'S PRAYER.

¶ *Upon Weekdays which are not Holy Days, or in case a* LITANY *hath been said before in the same Service, all but the first and the last sentences of this Prayer may be omitted.*

Let us pray for the whole state of Christ's Church.

MOST merciful Father, we humbly beseech thee to accept our *[alms and]* oblations, and to receive these our prayers for the Universal Church: that thou wilt confirm it in the truth of thy holy faith, inspire it with unity and concord, and extend and prosper it throughout the world.

We beseech thee also, so to direct those in authority in all nations to maintain justice and the welfare of all mankind, that thy Church may abide in thy peace.

Give grace, O heavenly Father, to all Bishops, Priests, and Deacons, that both by their life and doctrine they may set forth thy true and living Word, and faithfully administer thy holy Sacraments.

And to all thy People give thy heavenly grace; that, with willing heart and due reverence, they may hear and receive thy holy Word, truly serving thee in holiness and righteousness all the days of their life.

And we most humbly beseech thee, of thy goodness, O Lord, to support and strengthen all those who, in this transitory life, are in trouble, sorrow, need, sickness, or any other adversity.

We also commend unto thy mercy all thy servants departed this life in thy faith and fear: Grant them thy peace in the land of the living, where the light of thy countenance shineth upon them.

Finally, we give thee most high praise and hearty thanks for all thy Saints, who have been the chosen vessels of thy grace, and the lights of the world in their several generations; beseeching thee, that we, rejoicing in their fellowship, and following their good examples, may be partakers with them of thy heavenly kingdom.

Grant this, O Father, for Jesus Christ's sake, our only Mediator and Advocate. *Amen.*

The Invitation

¶ *Here the Priest Or the Deacon may read* THE EXHORTATION TO THE HOLY COMMUNION; *the People standing. And this Exhortation shall be read upon the First Sunday in Advent, the First Sunday in Lent, and Trinity Sunday,*

¶ *Then shall the Minister say this* INVITATION TO THE HOLY COMMUNION:

YE that do truly and earnestly repent you of your sins, and are in love and charity with your neighbours, and intend to lead a new life, following the commandments of God, and walking from henceforth in his holy ways; Draw near with faith, and take this holy Sacrament to sustain and strengthen you, and make your humble confession to Almighty God, devoutly kneeling.

The General Confession

¶ Here silence may be kept for a brief space. Then shall this GENERAL CONFESSION *be made by the Priest or Deacon and all those who are minded to receive the Holy Communion, humbly kneeling.*

ALMIGHTY God, Father of our Lord Jesus Christ, Maker of all things, Judge of all men; We acknowledge and confess our manifold sins, Which we have committed by thought, word, and deed, Against thy Divine Majesty. We do earnestly repent, And are heartily sorry for these our misdoings. Have mercy upon us, most merciful Father; For thy Son our Lord Jesus Christ's sake, Forgive us all that is past; And grant that we may ever hereafter Serve and please thee in newness of life, To the honour and glory of thy Name; through the same Jesus Christ our Lord. Amen.

The Comfortable Words

¶ Here the Minister, standing up and turning to the People, shall say,

Hear what comfortable words our Saviour Christ saith unto all that truly turn to him:

COME unto me, all ye that travail and are heavy laden, and I will refresh you. *St. Matthew 11:28.*

So God loved the world, that he gave his only-begotten Son, to the end that all that believe in him should not perish, but have everlasting life. *St. John 3: 16.*

Hear also what Saint Paul saith: This is a true saying, and worthy of all men to be received, That Christ Jesus came into the world to save sinners. *1 Timothy 1:15.*

Hear also what Saint John saith: If we confess our sins, God is faithful and just to forgive us our sins, and to cleanse us from all unrighteousness. *1 St. John 1:9.*

¶ THE COMFORTABLE WORDS *may be omitted, save at the principal Celebration of the Liturgy upon each Sunday.*

The Absolution

⁋ Then the Priest (the Bishop if he be present), standing, and facing the People, shall say,

THE Almighty God, our heavenly Father, who of his great mercy hath promised forgiveness of sins to all those who with hearty repentance and true faith turn unto him; Have mercy upon you; pardon and deliver you from all your sins; confirm and strengthen you in all goodness; and bring you to everlasting life; through Jesus Christ our Lord. *Amen.*

The Consecration

Sursum Corda

⁋ Then the Priest, facing the People, shall say,

THE Lord be with you.
People. And with thy spirit.
Priest. Lift up your hearts.
People. We lift them up unto the Lord.
Priest. Let us give thanks unto our Lord God.
People. It is meet and right so to do.

The Preface

⁋ Then shall the Priest turn to the Altar, and say,

IT is very meet, right, and our bounden duty, that we should at all times, and in all places, give thanks unto thee, O Lord, Holy Father, Almighty, Everlasting God:

⁋ Here shall follow the PROPER PREFACE, *according to the time, if there be any specially appointed;*

Proper Prefaces: [Advent] [Christmas] [Epiphany] [Incarnation] [Lent] [Passiontide] [Easter] [Ascension] [Whitsuntide] [Trinity] [All Saints] [Apostles] [Commemoration of the Departed]

or else immediately shall be said,

THEREFORE with Angels and Archangels, and with all the company of heaven, we laud and magnify thy glorious Name; evermore praising thee, and saying,

Sanctus

¶ Priest and People.

HOLY, HOLY, HOLY, Lord God of hosts: Heaven and earth are full of thy glory: Glory be to thee, O Lord Most High. Amen.

The Prayer of Consecration

¶ Then the Priest, standing before the Altar, shall say,

The Thanksgiving

ALL glory be to thee, Almighty God, our heavenly Father, for that thou, of thy tender mercy, didst give thine only Son Jesus Christ to take our nature upon him, and to suffer death upon the Cross, for our redemption; who made there, by his one oblation of himself once offered, a full, perfect, and sufficient sacrifice for the sins of the whole world; and did institute, and in his holy Gospel command us to continue, a perpetual memory of that his precious death and sacrifice, until his coming again.

The Institution

FOR in the night in which he was betrayed, he took Bread; [*Here the Priest is to take the Bread into his hands.*] and when he had given thanks, he brake it, and gave it to his disciples, saying, Take, eat: This is my Body, which is given for you. Do this in remembrance of me.

Likewise, after supper, he took the Cup; [*Here he is to take the Cup into his hands.*] and when he had given thanks, he gave it to them, saying, Drink ye all of this: for this is my Blood of the New Covenant, which is shed for you and for many for the remission of sins. Do this, as oft as ye shall drink it, in remembrance of me.

The Oblation

WHEREFORE, having in remembrance his blessed Passion and precious Death, his mighty Resurrection and glorious Ascension, we thy humble servants do celebrate and make here before thy Divine Majesty, with these thy holy gifts which we now offer unto thee, the memorial thy Son hath commanded us to make.

The Invocation

AND we most humbly beseech thee to accept upon thine altar on high this our sacrifice of praise and thanksgiving, our bounden duty and service; and vouchsafe to bless and sanctify with thy Holy Spirit these thy gifts and creatures of bread and wine, that they may be unto us the most blessed Body and Blood of thy dearly beloved Son Jesus Christ.

The Supplication

AND here we offer and present unto thee, O Lord, our selves, our souls and bodies, to be a reasonable, holy, and living sacrifice unto thee; humbly beseeching thee, that we, and all thy whole Church, may worthily receive the most precious Body and Blood of thy Son, that we may obtain remission of our sins, and all other benefits of his Passion, be filled with thy grace and heavenly benediction, and made one body with him, that he may dwell in us, and we in him:

Through the same Jesus Christ our Lord; By whom, and with whom, in the unity of the Holy Ghost, all honour and glory be unto thee, O Father Almighty, world without end.

¶ *And all the People shall answer, Amen.*

The Lord's Prayer

As our Saviour Christ hath commanded and taught us, we are bold to say,

¶ *Priest and People*

OUR Father, who art in heaven, Hallowed be thy Name. Thy kingdom come. Thy will be done, On earth as it is in heaven. Give us this day our daily bread. And forgive us our trespasses, As we forgive those who trespass against us. And lead us not into temptation, But deliver us from evil. For thine is the kingdom, and the power, and the glory, for ever and ever. Amen.

The Holy Communion

The Breaking of the Bread

¶ *Here the Priest shall break the consecrated Bread; and silence may be kept for a brief space.*

¶ *Then shall the Priest say,*

THE peace of the Lord be alway with you.
People. And with thy spirit.

Benedictus qui venit

¶ *Here may be said or sung,*

BLESSED is he that cometh in the Name of the Lord. Hosanna in the highest.

The Prayer of Humble Access

¶ *Then shall the Priest, kneeling humbly at the Altar, say this* PRAYER OF HUMBLE ACCESS TO THE HOLY COMMUNION. *And this Prayer may be said by the People with the Priest.*

WE do not presume to come to this thy Table, O merciful Father, trusting in our own righteousness, but in thy manifold and great mercies. We are not worthy so much as to gather up the crumbs under thy Table. But thou art the same Lord, whose nature is always to have mercy. Grant us therefore, gracious Lord, so to eat the Flesh of thy dear Son Jesus Christ, and to drink his Blood, in these holy Mysteries, that our sinful souls and bodies may be made clean by his most precious Body and Blood, and that we may evermore dwell in him, and he in us. Amen.

Agnus Dei

¶ *Here may be said or sung the following Hymn:*

O LAMB of God, that takest away the sins of the world,
 Have mercy upon us.
O Lamb of God, that takest away the sins of the world,
 Have mercy upon us.
O Lamb of God, that takest away the sins of the world,
 Grant us thy peace.

¶ *And the Priest shall first receive the Holy Communion in both kinds himself, and then proceed to deliver the same to the Bishops, Priests, Deacons, and any others then present in the Sanctuary.*

The Administration of the Holy Communion

¶ *Then shall the Priest or the Deacon turn to the People, and say,*

THE Body of our Lord Jesus Christ, which was given for you, and his Blood which was shed for you, preserve your bodies and souls unto everlasting life. Take this in remembrance that Christ died for you, and feed on him in your hearts by faith, with thanksgiving.

¶ *Then shall the Priest deliver the Holy Communion to the People also, into their hands, all devoutly kneeling. And sufficient opportunity shall be given to those present to communicate.*

¶ *And when he delivereth the Bread, he shall say,*

THE Body of our Lord Jesus Christ, which was given for thee. *Amen.*

¶ *And the Minister who delivereth the Cup shall say,*

THE Blood of our Lord Jesus Christ, which was shed for thee. *Amen.*

¶ *During the Communion-time there may be sung a Hymn or an Anthem.*

¶ *If any of the consecrated Bread or Wine remain, apart from any which may be required for the Communion of the Sick, or of others who, for weighty cause, could not be present at the celebration of the Liturgy, the Priest and other Communicants shall, immediately after the Communion of the People, reverently eat and drink the same; and the Priest shall then cleanse the sacred Vessels, and replace them as at the beginning of the Liturgy.*

The Thanksgiving after Communion

¶ *Then shall the Priest say,*

The Lord be with you.
And with thy spirit.

Let us bless the Lord.

¶ *Priest and People*

ALMIGHTY and everliving God, We most heartily thank thee, For that thou dost vouchsafe to feed us who have duly received these holy mysteries With the spiritual food of the most precious Body and Blood of thy Son our

Saviour Jesus Christ, Assuring us thereby of thy favour and goodness towards us, That we are very members incorporate in the Mystical Body of thy Son, The blessed company of all faithful people, And are also heirs, through hope, of thy everlasting kingdom, By the merits of his saving Death and Resurrection. And we humbly beseech thee, O heavenly Father, so to assist us with thy grace, That we may continue in that holy fellowship, And do all such good works as thou hast prepared for us to walk in; Through the same Jesus Christ our Lord, To whom, with thee and the Holy Ghost, be all honour and glory, world without end. Amen.

The Benediction

¶ Then the Priest (the Bishop if he be present) shall let them depart with this Blessing:

THE Peace of God, which passeth all understanding, keep your hearts and minds in the knowledge and love of God, and of his Son Jesus Christ our Lord: And the Blessing of God Almighty, the Father, the Son, and the Holy Ghost, be upon you, and remain with you always. *Amen.*

General Rubrics

The Ministry of the Word

¶ Upon Sundays or other Holy Days, the Priest, or, in his absence, a Deacon, may say all that is appointed in the Liturgy through THE GENERAL INTERCESSION. *He may substitute a* LITANY, THE BIDDING PRAYER, *or other suitable Prayers, for the Prayer for the Whole State of Christ's Church. Then a Priest shall conclude the service with* THE BENEDICTION, *or a Deacon with* THE GRACE.

The Order for a Second Consecration

¶ If the consecrated Bread or Wine be spent before all have communicated, the Priest is to consecrate more, in both kinds, with the foregoing Prayer of Consecration. Then the Priest shall first receive the Sacrament in both kinds himself, and then proceed with the distribution of the Holy Communion.

Intinction

¶ Opportunity shall always be given to every Communicant to receive the consecrated Bread and Wine separately in the accustomed manner. But any

Communicant who may so desire may receive the Sacrament in both kinds simultaneously by Intinction, in such manner as is authorized by the Ordinary.

¶ When the Sacrament is so administered, it shall suffice for the Minister who delivereth the Sacrament to say,

THE Body and Blood of our Lord Jesus Christ, which were given for thee. Amen.

Unworthy Communicants

¶ If among those who come to be partakers of the Holy Communion, the Priest shall know any to be an open and notorious evil liver, or to have done any wrong to his neighbours by word or deed, so that the Congregation be thereby offended: he shall admonish him, that he presume not to come to the Lord's Table, until he have openly declared himself to have truly repented and amended his former evil life, that the Congregation may thereby be satisfied; and that he hath recompensed the parties to whom he hath done wrong; or at least declared himself to be in full purpose so to do, as soon as he possibly can.

¶ The same order shall the Priest use with those, betwixt whom he perceiveth malice and hatred to reign: not suffering them to be partakers of the Lord's Table, until he know them to be reconciled. And if one of the parties, so at variance, be content to forgive from the bottom of his heart all that the other hath trespassed against him, and to make amends for that wherein he himself hath offended, and the other party will not be persuaded to a godly unity, but remain still in his frowardness and malice: the Priest in that case ought to admit the penitent person to the Holy Communion, and not him that is obstinate.

¶ PROVIDED, That every Priest so repelling any, as is herein specified, shall be obliged to give an account of the same to the Ordinary, within fourteen days after, at the farthest.

The Exhortation to the Holy Communion

¶ After THE GENERAL INTERCESSION, the Priest or Deacon may read the following EXHORTATION. And NOTE, That this Exhortation shall be read upon the First Sunday in Advent, the First Sunday in Lent, and Trinity Sunday.

DEARLY beloved in the Lord: ye who mind to come to the Holy Communion of the Body and Blood of our Saviour Christ, must consider how Saint

Paul exhorteth all persons diligently to test and examine themselves, before they presume to eat of that Bread, and drink of that Cup. For as the benefit is great if with a true penitent heart and living faith we receive that holy Sacrament, so is the danger great, if we receive the same unworthily. Judge therefore yourselves, brethren, that ye be not judged of the Lord; repent you truly for your sins past; have a living and stedfast faith in Christ our Saviour; amend your lives, and be in perfect charity with all men: so shall ye be meet partakers of those holy Mysteries.

And above all things, ye must give most humble and hearty thanks to God, the Father, the Son, and the Holy Ghost, for the redemption of the world by the Death and Passion of our Saviour Christ, both God and man: who took upon him our flesh, and humbled himself even to the death upon the Cross for us miserable sinners, who lay in darkness and the shadow of death, that he might make us the children of God, and exalt us to everlasting life.

And to the end that we should always remember the exceeding great love of our Master and only Saviour, Jesus Christ, thus dying for us, and the innumerable benefits which by his precious blood-shedding he hath obtained for us, he hath instituted and ordained holy Mysteries, as pledges of his love, for a continual remembrance of his death, and for a spiritual partaking of his life, that we may be one with him and he with us, to our great and endless comfort.

To him therefore, with the Father and the Holy Ghost, let us offer the continual thanksgiving which is our bounden duty and service; submitting ourselves wholly to his holy will and pleasure, and studying to serve him in true holiness and righteousness all the days of our life. *Amen.*

Proper Prefaces

ADVENT

¶ From the First Sunday in Advent until Christmas Eve, except upon Ember Days and Saints' Days.

WHO hast raised up a mighty salvation for us in the Kingdom of thy Son, Jesus Christ our Lord: to give light to those that sit in darkness and in the shadow of death, and to guide our feet into the way of peace:

CHRISTMAS

¶ From Christmas Day until the Epiphany.

BECAUSE thou didst give Jesus Christ, thine only Son, to be born as at this time for us; who, by the operation of the Holy Ghost, was made very man, of the substance of the Virgin Mary his mother; and that without spot of sin, to make us clean from all sin:

EPIPHANY

¶ *Upon the Epiphany, and seven days after.*

THROUGH Jesus Christ our Lord; who, in substance of our mortal flesh, manifested forth his glory; that he might bring us out of darkness into his own glorious light:

THE INCARNATION

¶ *Upon the Feasts of the Purification, Annunciation, and Transfiguration.*

BECAUSE in the Mystery of the Word made flesh, thou hast caused a new light to shine in our hearts, to give the knowledge of thy glory in the face of thy Son Jesus Christ our Lord:

LENT

¶ *From Ash Wednesday until Passion Sunday, except upon Ember Days and Saints' Days.*

WHO hast sent thy Son to be a great High Priest who is touched with the feeling of our infirmities, being at all points tempted like as we are, yet without sin; that we may come boldly unto the throne of grace, to obtain mercy, and to find grace to help in time of need:

PASSIONTIDE

¶ *From Passion Sunday until Maundy Thursday inclusive, except upon Saints' Days.*

BECAUSE thou didst give thy Son our Saviour Jesus Christ to redeem mankind from the power of darkness; who was lifted up upon the Cross to draw all men unto him; and was made perfect through suffering, that he might become the Author of eternal salvation to all that obey him:

EASTER

¶ *From Easter Day until the Ascension Day, except upon Saints' Days.*

BUT chiefly are we bound to praise thee for the glorious Resurrection of thy Son Jesus Christ our Lord: for he is the very Paschal Lamb, which was offered for us, and hath taken away the sin of the world; who by his death hath destroyed death, and by his rising to life again hath assured to us everlasting life:

ASCENSION

¶ From Ascension Day until Whitsunday, except upon Feasts of Apostles.

THROUGH thy most dearly beloved Son Jesus Christ our Lord; who, after his most glorious Resurrection, manifestly appeared to all his Apostles, and in their sight ascended up into heaven, to prepare a place for us; that where he is, thither we might also ascend, and reign with him in glory:

WHITSUNTIDE

¶ Upon Whitsunday, and six days after.

THROUGH Jesus Christ our Lord; according to whose most true promise, the Holy Ghost came down as at this time from heaven, lighting upon the Disciples, to teach them, and to lead them into all truth; giving them boldness with fervent zeal constantly to preach the Gospel unto all nations; whereby we have been brought out of darkness and error into the clear light and true knowledge of thee, and of thy Son Jesus Christ:

TRINITY SUNDAY

¶ Upon the Feast of the Holy Trinity only.

WHO, with thine Only-begotten Son, and the Holy Ghost, art one God, one Lord, in Trinity of Persons and in Unity of Substance. For that which we believe of thy glory, O Father, the same we believe of the Son, and of the Holy Ghost, without any difference of inequality:

ALL SAINTS

¶ Upon All Saints' Day, and seven days after; and upon other Saints' Days, except those of Apostles, and those in the Octaves of Christmas and Ascension.

WHO, in the righteousness of thy Saints, hast given us an example of godly living, and in their blessedness a glorious pledge of the hope of our calling: that we, being compassed about with so great a cloud of witnesses, may run with endurance the race that is set before us, and, together with them, may receive the crown of glory that fadeth not away:

APOSTLES

¶ *Upon Feasts of the Apostles (except St. John Evangelist); upon Ember Days, except in Whitsuntide; and at Ordinations, except on Principal Feasts and their Octaves.*

THROUGH that great Shepherd of the sheep, Jesus Christ our Lord: who sent forth his blessed Apostles to teach all nations, to wash them from their sins in his own blood, and to make them kings and priests, offering up spiritual sacrifices acceptable unto thee; that unto the end of the world he might be alway with those who believe in him:

AT COMMEMORATIONS OF THE DEPARTED

THROUGH Jesus Christ our Lord; who hath brought to light the living hope of a blessed resurrection: that we may grieve not for that we are all appointed once to die, but may rejoice in the assurance of immortal life to come; seeing that whosoever believeth in thine Only-begotten Son shall not perish, but shall be changed into the likeness of his glory; for when this earthly house of our sojourning is dissolved, there is prepared for us an habitation eternal in the heavens:

CONCLUSION

¶ *After any of these Proper Prefaces, the Priest shall conclude:*

THEREFORE with Angels and Archangels, and with all the company of heaven, we laud and magnify thy glorious Name; evermore praising thee, and saying,

¶ *Priest and People*

HOLY, HOLY, HOLY, Lord God of hosts: Heaven and earth are full of thy glory: Glory be to thee, O Lord Most High. Amen.

www.ingramcontent.com/pod-product-compliance
Lightning Source LLC
Chambersburg PA
CBHW061342300426
44116CB00011B/1959